TEACHER'S EDITION

UNITED STATES
HISTORY

Emma J. Lapsansky-Werner   Peter B. Levy   Randy Roberts   Alan Taylor

PEARSON

Boston, Massachusetts   Chandler, Arizona   Glenview, Illinois   New York, New York

Cover Image: Small American flags for sale in a Megastore. Juanmonino/Getty Images.

PEARSON

ISBN-13: 978-0-13-330707-8
ISBN-10:   0-13-330707-7

8   16

Authors, Consultants, Partners

[Authors]

Emma J. Lapsansky-Werner

Emma J. Lapsansky-Werner is Professor of History and Curator of the Quaker Collection at Haverford College. After receiving her doctorate from the University of Pennsylvania, she taught at Temple University for almost two decades. Dr. Lapsansky-Werner's recent publications include *Quaker Aesthetics,* coauthored with Ann Verplanck, *Back to Africa: Benjamin Coates and the Colonization Movement in America, 1848–1880,* coedited with Margaret Hope Bacon, as well as *Struggle For Freedom,* a textbook on African American history, coauthored with Gary B. Nash and Clayborne Carson.

Peter B. Levy

Peter B. Levy is a Full Professor in the Department of History at York College of Pennsylvania, where he teaches a wide variety of courses in American history. He received his B.A. from the University of California, Berkeley, and his Ph.D. from Columbia University. Dr. Levy is the author of eight books and many articles, including: *The New Left and Labor in the 1960s; Civil War on Race Street: The Civil Rights Movement in Cambridge, Maryland;* and *100 Key Documents in American Democracy.* He lives in Towson, Maryland.

Randy Roberts

Randy Roberts is Distinguished Professor of History at Purdue University. An award-winning author, his primary research areas are sports and popular culture, and he has written, co-written, and edited more than 30 books. He has also won numerous teaching awards, including the Carnegie Foundation for the Advancement of Teaching as Indiana Professor of the Year. Among his work are books on Oscar Robertson, Joe Louis, the Alamo, and Vietnam. His most recent books are *A Team for America: The Army-Navy Game That Rallied a Nation,* and *Rising Tide: Bear Bryant, Joe Namath, and Dixie's Last Quarter,* co-authored with Ed Krzemienski. Roberts has served a consultant and on-camera commentator for PBS, HBO, and History Channel. He lives in Lafayette, Indiana, with his wife Marjie.

Alan Taylor

Alan Taylor is the Thomas Jefferson Memorial Foundation Chair at the University of Virginia. He earned his Ph.D. in history from Brandeis University and did a postdoctoral fellowship at the Institute of Early American History and Culture in Williamsburg, Virginia. He teaches courses in early American history and the history of the American West. Dr. Taylor is the author of eight books, including *The Internal Enemy: Slavery and War in Virginia, 1772–1832,* which won the 2014 Pulitzer Prize for American history, and *American Colonies* and *William Cooper's Town,* which won the Bancroft and Beveridge prizes, as well as the 1996 Pulitzer Prize for American history.

[Program Consultant]

Dr. Kathy Swan is an associate professor of curriculum and instruction at the University of Kentucky. Her research focuses on standards-based technology integration, authentic intellectual work, and documentary-making in the social studies classroom. Swan has been a four-time recipient of the National Technology Leadership Award in Social Studies Education. She is also the advisor for the Social Studies Assessment, Curriculum, and Instruction Collaborative (SSACI) at CCSSO.

[Program Partners]

NBC Learn, the educational arm of NBC News, develops original stories for use in the classroom and makes archival NBC News stories, images, and primary source documents available on demand to teachers, students, and parents. NBC Learn partnered with Pearson to produce the myStory videos that support this program.

Constitutional Rights Foundation is a nonprofit, nonpartisan, community-based organization focused on educating students about the importance of civic participation in a democratic society. The Constitutional Rights Foundation is the lead contributor to the development of the Civic Discussion Topic Inquiries for this program.

Reviewers & Academic Consultants

Pearson United States History was developed especially for you and your students. The story of its creation began with a three-day Innovation Lab in which teachers, historians, students, and authors came together to imagine our ideal Social Studies teaching and learning experiences. We refined the plan with a series of teacher roundtables that shaped this new approach to ensure your students' mastery of content and skills. A dedicated team, made up of Pearson authors, content experts, and social studies teachers, worked to bring our collective vision into reality. Kathy Swan, Professor of Education and architect of the new College, Career, and Civic Life (C3) Framework, served as our expert advisor on curriculum and instruction.

Pearson would like to extend a special thank you to all of the teachers who helped guide the development of this program. We gratefully acknowledge your efforts to realize Next Generation Social Studies teaching and learning that will prepare American students for college, careers, and active citizenship.

[Program Advisors]

Campaign for the Civic Mission of Schools is a coalition of over 70 national civic learning, education, civic engagement, and business groups committed to improving the quality and quantity of civic learning in American schools. The Campaign served as an advisor on this program.

Buck Institute for Education is a nonprofit organization dedicated to helping teachers implement the effective use of Project-Based Learning in their classrooms. Buck Institute staff consulted on the Project-Based Learning Topic Inquiries for this program.

[Program Academic Consultants]

Barbara Brown
Director of Outreach
College of Arts and Sciences
African Studies Center
Boston University
Boston, Massachusetts

William Childs
Professor of History Emeritus
The Ohio State University
Columbus, Ohio

Jennifer Giglielmo
Associate Professor of History
Smith College
Northhampton, Massachusetts

Joanne Connor Green
Professor, Department Chair
Political Science
Texas Christian University
Fort Worth, Texas

Ramdas Lamb, Ph.D.
Associate Professor of Religion
University of Hawaii at Manoa
Honolulu, Hawaii

Huping Ling
Changjiang Scholar Chair Professor
Professor of History
Truman State University
Kirksville, Missouri

Jeffery Long, Ph.D.
Professor of Religion and Asian Studies
Elizabethtown College
Elizabethtown, Pennsylvania

Gordon Newby
Professor of Islamic, Jewish and Comparative
    Studies
Department of Middle Eastern and South
    Asian Studies
Emory University
Atlanta, Georgia

Mark Peterson
Associate Professor
Department of Asian and Near Eastern
    Languages
Brigham Young University
Provo, Utah

William Pitts
Professor, Department of Religion
Baylor University
Waco, Texas

Benjamin Ravid
Professor Emeritus of Jewish History
Department of Near Eastern and Judaic
    Studies
Brandeis University
Waltham, Massachusetts

Harpreet Singh
College Fellow
Department of South Asian Studies
Harvard University
Cambridge, Massachusetts

Christopher E. Smith, J.D., Ph.D.
Professor
Michigan State University
MSU School of Criminal Justice
East Lansing, Michigan

John Voll
Professor of Islamic History
Georgetown University
Washington, D.C.

Michael R. Wolf
Associate Professor
Department of Political Science
Indiana University-Purdue University Fort
    Wayne
Fort Wayne, Indiana

Reimagine Learning

Realize Results. Social studies is more than dots on a map or dates on a timeline. It's where we've been and where we're going. It's stories from the past and our stories today. And in today's fast-paced, interconnected world, it's essential.

Instruction Your Way!

Comprehensive teaching support is available in two different formats:

- **Teacher's Edition:** Designed like a "T.V. Guide," teaching suggestions are paired with preview images of digital resources.

- **Teaching Support Online:** Teaching suggestions, answer keys, blackline masters, and other resources are provided at point-of-use online in Realize.

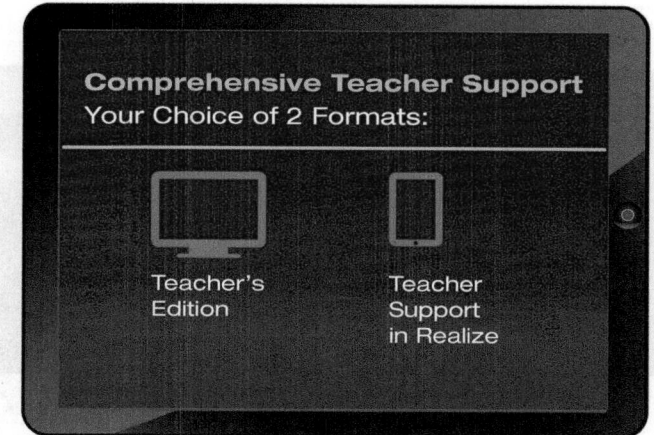

Comprehensive Teacher Support
Your Choice of 2 Formats:

Teacher's Edition

Teacher Support in Realize

Pearson Mastery System

This complete system for teaching and learning uses best practices, technology, and a four-part framework—Connect, Investigate, Synthesize, and Demonstrate—to prepare students to be college-and-career ready.

- Higher-level content that gives students support to access complex text, acquire skills and tackle rigorous questions.

- Inquiry-focused Projects, Civic Discussions, and Document-Based Questions that prepare students for real-world challenges;

- Digital content on Pearson Realize that is dynamic, flexible, and uses the power of technology to bring social studies to life.

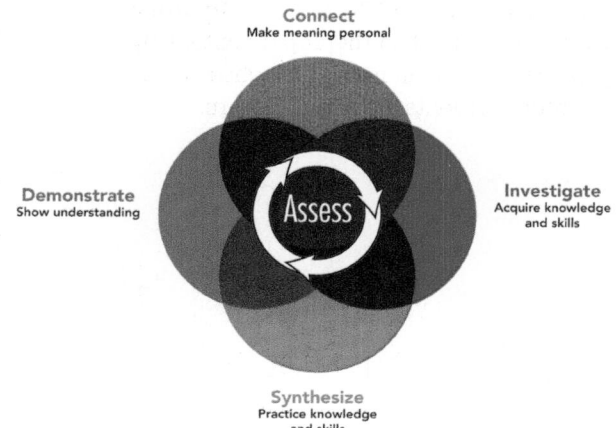

Connect
Make meaning personal

Assess

Demonstrate
Show understanding

Investigate
Acquire knowledge
and skills

Synthesize
Practice knowledge
and skills

Table of Contents for Today's Learners

Today's learners research new information by using a search engine and browsing by topic. Breaking out of a book metaphor of "chapters," this table of contents is organized by:

- **Topic:** As you decide what you want to teach, you search first for the topic.

- **Lesson:** Within each topic are several lessons where you will find a variety of diverse resources to support teaching and learning.

- **Text:** Each lesson contains chunked information called Texts. This is the same informational text that appears in the print Student Edition.

This organization saves time, improves pacing, and makes it easy to rearrange content.

» Go online to learn more and see the program overview video.

PEARSON
realize™

CONNECT! Begin the Pearson Mastery System by engaging in the topic story and connecting it to your own lives.

Preview—Each Topic opens with the Enduring Understandings section, allowing you to preview expected learning outcomes.

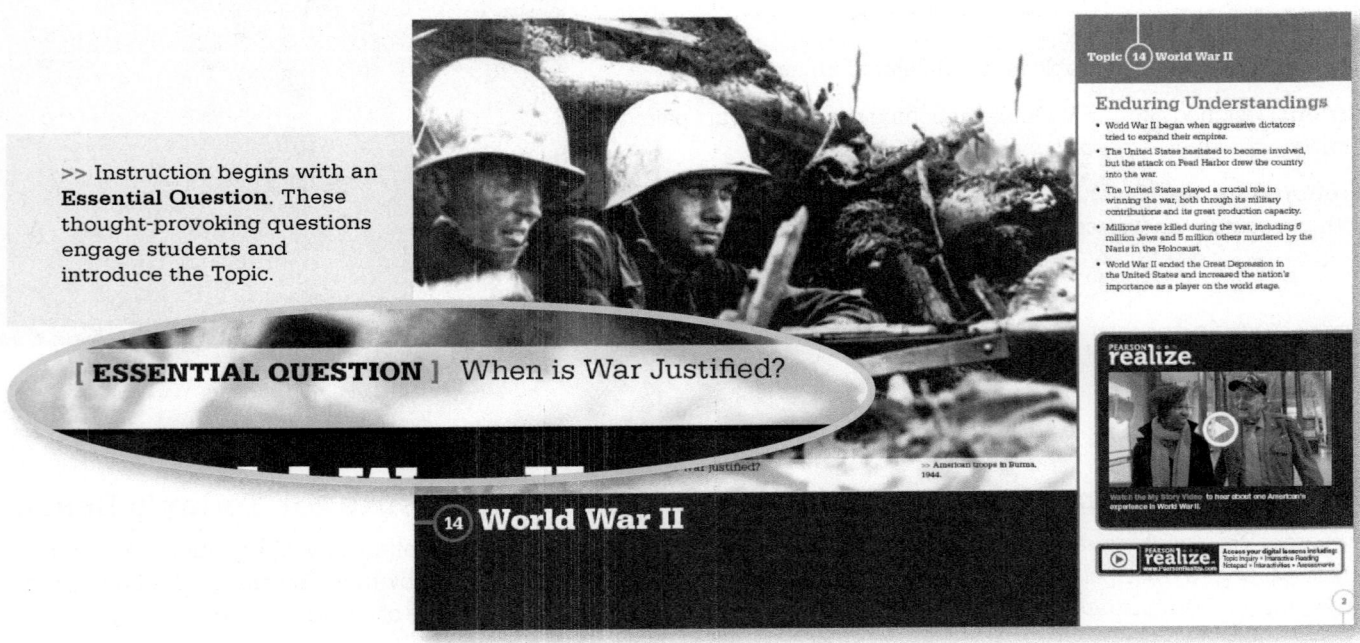

>> Instruction begins with an **Essential Question**. These thought-provoking questions engage students and introduce the Topic.

[ESSENTIAL QUESTION] When is War Justified?

14 World War II

Developed in partnership with NBCLearn, the **My Story** videos help students connect to the Topic content by hearing the personal story of an individual whose life is related to the content students are about to learn.

INVESTIGATE! Step two of the Mastery System allows you to investigate the topic story through a number of engaging features as you learn the content.

>> **Active Classroom Strategies** integrated in the daily lesson plans help to increase in-class participation, raise energy levels and attentiveness, all while engaging in the story. These 5-15 minute activities have you use what you have learned to draw, write, speak, and decide.

>> **Interactive Primary Source Galleries:** Use primary source image galleries throughout the lesson to see, analyze, and interact with images that tie to the topic story content.

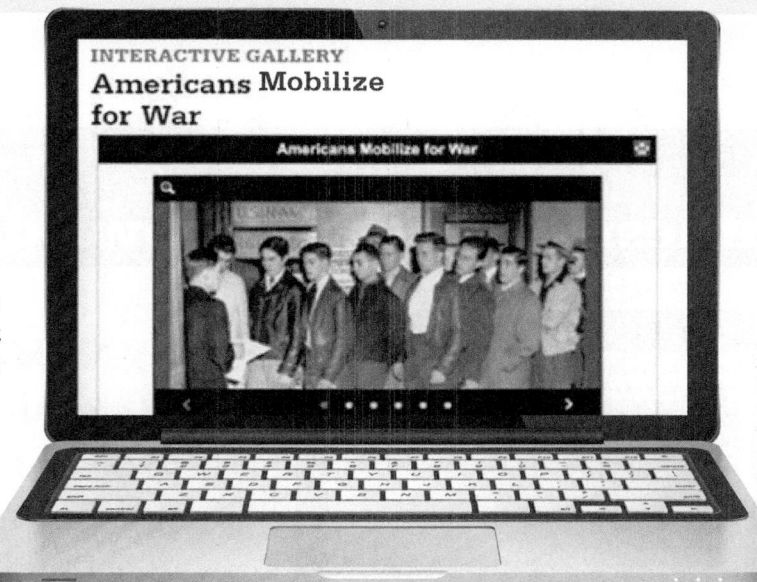

INTERACTIVE GALLERY
Americans Mobilize for War

Americans Mobilize for War

Investigate

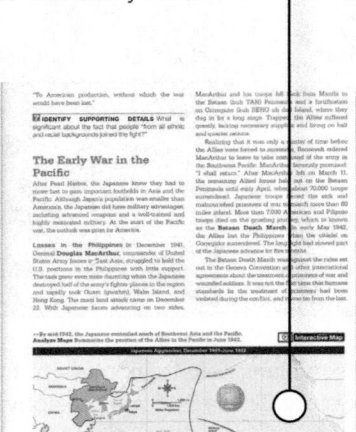

>> Feel like you are a part of the story with **interactive 3-D models**.

>> Continue to investigate the topic story through **dynamic interactive maps**. Build map skills while covering the essential standards.

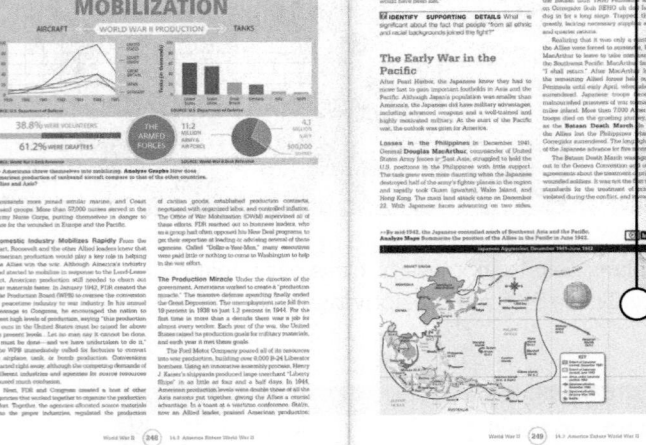

>> Learn content by reading narrative text online or in a printed Student Edition.

Synthesize: Practice Knowledge and Skills

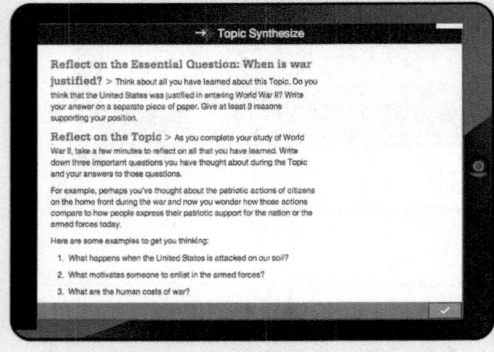

SYNTHESIZE!

In step three of the Mastery System, pause to reflect on what you learn and revisit an essential question.

Demonstrate: Show Understanding

DEMONSTRATE! The final step of the Mastery System is to demonstrate understanding of the text.

PEARSON realize™

>> **The digital course on Realize!** The program's digital course on Realize puts engaging content, embedded assessments, instant data, and flexible tools at your fingertips.

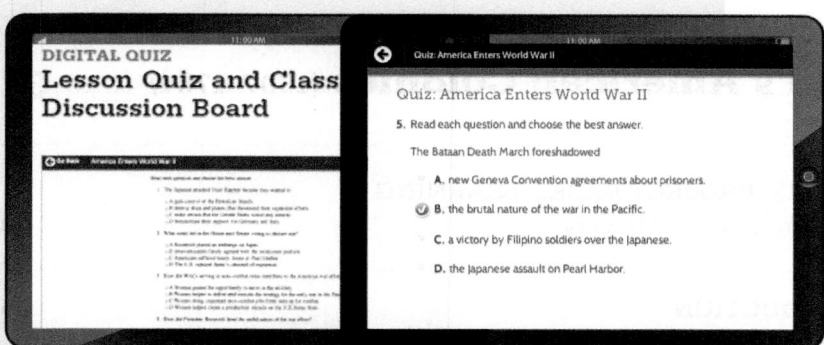

>> **Assessment**. At the end of each lesson and topic, demonstrate understanding through Lesson Quizzes, Topic Tests, and Topic Inquiry performance assessments. The System provides remediation and enrichment recommendations based on your individual performance towards mastery.

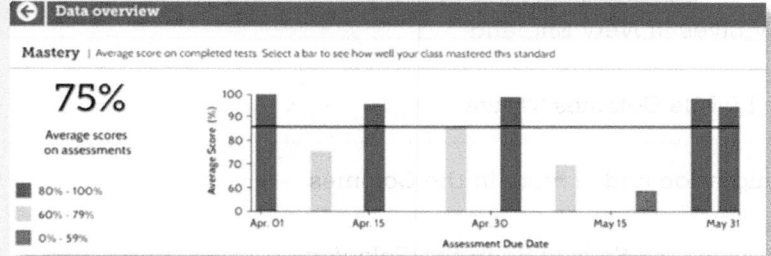

>> **Class and Data** features on Realize make it easy to see your mastery data.

Digital Course Content

Digital Course Content

Topic 7   Sectional Divisions and Civil War
(1846–1865)   **208**

Digital Course Content

Digital Course Content

Topic 14 World War II (1931–1945) — **478**

Digital Course Content

Digital Course Content

Digital Resources

Many types of digital resources help you investigate the topics in this course. You'll find biographies, primary sources, maps, and more. These resources will help bring the topics to life.

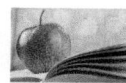 ## Core Concepts

 ### Culture

- What Is Culture?
- Families and Societies
- Language
- Religion
- The Arts
- Cultural Diffusion and Change
- Science and Technology

 ### Economics

- Economics Basics
- Economic Process
- Economic Systems
- Economic Development
- Trade
- Money Management

 ### Geography

- The Study of Earth
- Geography's Five Themes
- Ways to Show Earth's Surface
- Understanding Maps

- Earth in Space
- Time and Earth's Rotation
- Forces on Earth's Surface
- Forces Inside Earth
- Climate and Weather
- Temperature
- Water and Climate
- Air Circulation and Precipitation
- Types of Climate
- Ecosystems
- Environment and Resources
- Land Use
- People's Impact on the Environment
- Population
- Migration
- Urbanization

 ### Government and Civics

- Foundations of Government
- Political Systems
- Political Structures
- Conflict and Cooperation
- Citizenship

 ### History

- How Do Historians Study History?
- Measuring Time
- Historical Sources
- Archaeology and Other Sources
- Historical Maps

 ### Personal Finance

- Your Fiscal Fitness: An Introduction
- Budgeting
- Checking
- Investments
- Savings and Retirement
- Credit and Debt
- Risk Management
- Consumer Smarts
- After High School
- Taxes and Income

 ## Landmark Supreme Court Cases

- *Korematsu* v. *United States*
- *Marbury* v. *Madison*
- *McCulloch* v. *Maryland*
- *Gibbons* v. *Ogden*
- *Worcester* v. *Georgia*
- *Dred Scott* v. *Sandford*
- *Plessy* v. *Ferguson*
- *Schenck* v. *United States*
- *Brown* v. *Board of Education*
- *Engel* v. *Vitale*

- *Sweatt* v. *Painter*
- *Mapp* v. *Ohio*
- *Hernandez* v. *Texas*
- *Gideon* v. *Wainwright*
- *Wisconsin* v. *Yoder*
- *Miranda* v. *Arizona*
- *White* v. *Regester*
- *Tinker* v. *Des Moines School District*
- *Roe* v. *Wade*

- *Baker* v. *Carr*
- *Grutter* v. *Bollinger*
- *Edgewood* v. *Kirby*
- *Texas* v. *Johnson*
- *National Federation of Independent Businesses et al.* v. *Sebelius et al.*
- *Mendez* v. *Westminster* and *Delgado* v. *Bastrop*

Digital Resources

 **Interactive Primary Sources**

- Code of Hammurabi
- Psalm 23
- The Republic, Plato
- Politics, Aristotle
- Edicts, Asoka
- Analects, Confucius
- First Letter to the Corinthians, Paul
- The Quran
- The Magna Carta
- Travels, Ibn Battuta
- The Destruction of the Indies, Bartolomé de
    Las Casas
- Mayflower Compact
- English Petition of Right
- English Bill of Rights
- Two Treatises of Government, John Locke
- The Spirit of Laws, Baron de Montesquieu
- The Social Contract, Jean-Jacques Rousseau
- The Interesting Narrative of the Life of Olaudah
    Equiano
- "Give Me Liberty or Give Me Death," Patrick Henry
- "Remember the Ladies," Abigail Adams
- Common Sense, Thomas Paine
- Declaration of Independence
- Virginia Declaration of Rights
- Virginia Statute for Religious Freedom,
    Thomas Jefferson
- "To His Excellency, General Washington,"
    Phillis Wheatley
- Articles of Confederation
- Anti-Federalist Papers
- The Federalist No. 10, James Madison
- The Federalist No. 39, James Madison
- The Federalist No. 51
- The Federalist No. 78, Alexander Hamilton
- Northwest Ordinance
- Iroquois Constitution
- Declaration of the Rights of Man and the Citizen
- Farewell Address, George Washington
- Mexican Federal Constitution of 1824
- State Colonization Law of 1825

- Law of April 6, 1830
- Debate Over Nullification, Webster and Calhoun
- Turtle Bayou Resolutions
- Democracy in America, Alexis de Tocqueville
- 1836 Victory or Death Letter from the Alamo,
    Travis
- Texas Declaration of Independence
- Declaration of Sentiments and Resolutions
- "Ain't I a Woman?," Sojourner Truth
- Uncle Tom's Cabin, Harriet Beecher Stowe
- "A House Divided," Abraham Lincoln
- First Inaugural Address, Abraham Lincoln
- Declaration of Causes: February 2, 1861
- Emancipation Proclamation, Abraham Lincoln
- Gettysburg Address, Abraham Lincoln
- Second Inaugural Address, Abraham Lincoln
- "I Will Fight No More Forever," Chief Joseph
- How the Other Half Lives, Jacob Riis
- The Pledge of Allegiance
- Preamble to the Platform of the Populist Party
- Atlanta Exposition Address, Booker T. Washington
- The Jungle, Upton Sinclair
- Hind Swaraj, Mohandas Gandhi
- The Fourteen Points, Woodrow Wilson
- Two Poems, Langston Hughes
- Four Freedoms, Franklin D. Roosevelt
- Anne Frank: The Diary of a Young Girl, Anne Frank
- Charter of the United Nations
- Universal Declaration of Human Rights
- Autobiography, Kwame Nkrumah
- Inaugural Address, John F. Kennedy
- Silent Spring, Rachel Carson
- "I Have a Dream," Martin Luther King, Jr.
- "Letter From Birmingham Jail,"
    Martin Luther King, Jr.
- "Tear Down This Wall," Ronald Reagan
- "Freedom From Fear," Aung San Suu Kyi
- "Glory and Hope," Nelson Mandela

 # Biographies

- Abigail Adams
- John Adams
- John Quincy Adams
- Samuel Adams
- James Armistead
- Crispus Attucks
- Moses Austin
- Stephen F. Austin
- James A. Baker III
- William Blackstone
- Simón Bolívar
- Napoleon Bonaparte
- Chief Bowles
- Omar Bradley
- John C. Calhoun
- César Chávez
- Wentworth Cheswell
- George Childress
- Winston Churchill
- Henry Clay
- Bill Clinton
- Jefferson Davis
- Martin De León
- Green DeWitt
- Dwight Eisenhower
- James Fannin
- James L. Farmer, Jr.
- Benjamin Franklin
- Milton Friedman
- Betty Friedan
- Bernardo de Gálvez
- Hector P. Garcia
- John Nance Garner
- King George III
- Henry B. González
- Raul A. Gonzalez, Jr.
- Mikhail Gorbachev
- William Goyens

- Ulysses S. Grant
- José Gutiérrez de Lara
- Alexander Hamilton
- Hammurabi
- Warren Harding
- Friedrich Hayek
- Jack Coffee Hays
- Patrick Henry
- Adolf Hitler
- Oveta Culp Hobby
- James Hogg
- Sam Houston
- Kay Bailey Hutchison
- Andrew Jackson
- John Jay
- Thomas Jefferson
- Lyndon B. Johnson
- Anson Jones
- Barbara Jordan
- Justinian
- John F. Kennedy
- John Maynard Keynes
- Martin Luther King, Jr.
- Marquis de Lafayette
- Mirabeau B. Lamar
- Robert E. Lee
- Abraham Lincoln
- John Locke
- James Madison
- John Marshall
- George Marshall
- Karl Marx
- George Mason
- Mary Maverick
- Jane McCallum
- Joseph McCarthy
- James Monroe
- Charles de Montesquieu

- Edwin W. Moore
- Moses
- Benito Mussolini
- José Antonio Navarro
- Chester A. Nimitz
- Richard M. Nixon
- Barack Obama
- Sandra Day O'Connor
- Thomas Paine
- Quanah Parker
- Rosa Parks
- George Patton
- John J. Pershing
- John Paul II
- Sam Rayburn
- Ronald Reagan
- Hiram Rhodes Revels
- Franklin D. Roosevelt
- Theodore Roosevelt
- Lawrence Sullivan Ross
- Haym Soloman
- Antonio Lopez de Santa Anna
- Phyllis Schlafly
- Erasmo Seguín
- Juan N. Seguín
- Roger Sherman
- Adam Smith
- Joseph Stalin
- Raymond L. Telles
- Alexis de Tocqueville
- Hideki Tojo
- William B. Travis
- Harry Truman
- Lech Walesa
- Mercy Otis Warren
- George Washington
- Daniel Webster

- Lulu Belle Madison White
- William Wilberforce
- James Wilson
- Woodrow Wilson
- Lorenzo de Zavala
- Mao Zedong

21st Century Skills

- Identify Main Ideas and Details
- Set a Purpose for Reading
- Use Context Clues
- Analyze Cause and Effect
- Categorize
- Compare and Contrast
- Draw Conclusions
- Draw Inferences
- Generalize
- Make Decisions
- Make Predictions
- Sequence
- Solve Problems
- Summarize
- Analyze Media Content
- Analyze Primary and Secondary Sources
- Compare Viewpoints
- Distinguish Between Fact and Opinion
- Identify Bias
- Analyze Data and Models

- Analyze Images
- Analyze Political Cartoons
- Create Charts and Maps
- Create Databases
- Read Charts, Graphs, and Tables
- Read Physical Maps
- Read Political Maps
- Read Special-Purpose Maps
- Use Parts of a Map
- Ask Questions
- Avoid Plagiarism
- Create a Research Hypothesis
- Evaluate Web Sites
- Identify Evidence
- Identify Trends
- Interpret Sources
- Search for Information on the Internet
- Synthesize
- Take Effective Notes
- Develop a Clear Thesis
- Organize Your Ideas

- Support Ideas With Evidence
- Evaluate Existing Arguments
- Consider & Counter Opposing Arguments
- Give an Effective Presentation
- Participate in a Discussion or Debate
- Publish Your Work
- Write a Journal Entry
- Write an Essay
- Share Responsibility
- Compromise
- Develop Cultural Awareness
- Generate New Ideas
- Innovate
- Make a Difference
- Work in Teams
- Being an Informed Citizen
- Paying Taxes
- Political Participation
- Serving on a Jury
- Voting

Atlas

- United States: Political
- United States: Physical
- World Political
- World Physical
- World Climate
- World Ecosystems
- World Population Density
- World Land Use
- North Africa and Southwest Asia: Political
- North Africa and Southwest Asia: Physical
- Sub-Saharan Africa: Political
- Sub-Saharan Africa: Physical
- South Asia: Political
- South Asia: Physical
- East Asia: Political

- East Asia: Physical
- Southeast Asia: Political
- Southeast Asia: Physical
- Europe: Political
- Europe: Physical
- Russia, Central Asia, and the Caucasus: Political
- Russia, Central Asia, and the Caucasus: Physical
- North America: Political
- North America: Physical
- Central America and the Caribbean: Political
- Central America and the Caribbean: Physical
- South America: Political
- South America: Physical
- Australia and the Pacific: Political
- Australia and the Pacific: Physical

Creating an Active Classroom

This Social Studies program places a strong emphasis on

Inquiry in the form of

- Document-Based Questions
- Project-Based Learning
- Civic Discussions

Each inquiry strand requires students to formulate their own arguments based on evidence. To support this learning approach, the program integrates **Active Classroom strategies** throughout each lesson. These strategies encourage students to begin building their own arguments and collecting evidence about the past and present at even the earliest stages of a lesson.

You can use these strategies to help students participate in their own learning as you call upon them to

- draw
- write
- speak
- decide

You'll find a rich variety of these strategy suggestions throughout both the Teacher's Edition and online **Teacher Support** for each lesson.

Creating an Active Classroom

ACTIVE CLASSROOM STRATEGIES

ACTIVITY NAME	HOW TO ACTIVATE
Quickdraw	· Pair students and give them 30 seconds to share what they know about a concept or Key Term by creating a symbol or drawing.
Graffiti Concepts	· Ask students to reflect on the meaning of a concept or idea and create a visual image and/or written phrase that represents that concept. Allow approximately 3–5 minutes. · Next ask students to post their "graffiti" on the board or on chart paper and ask students to look at all the various responses. · Next discuss similarities and differences in the responses as a group.
Word Wall	· Ask students to chose one of the Key Terms for the lesson and create a visual image with a text definition. Allow approximately 3–5 minutes. · Ask students to post their words on the board or on chart paper and ask students to look at all the various responses. · Discuss similarities and differences in the responses as a group. · Pick a few favorites and post them on the cvlass "Word Wall" for the year.
Cartoon It	· Ask students to make a quick drawing of one compelling image from this lesson on a piece of paper. · Next ask students to turn their drawing into a political cartoon that illustrates a key concept or main idea from the lesson by adding a text caption or text "bubbles." · Ask students to share their cartoons with a partner or within small groups.
Wallpaper	· Ask students to review information they have learned in a topic and design a piece of "wallpaper" that encapsulates key learnings. · Then have students post their wallpaper and take a "gallery" walk noting what others have written and illustrated in their samples.
Quick Write	· Ask students to write what they know about a key idea or term in 30 seconds.
Make Headlines	· Have students write a headline that captures the key idea in a map, photo, timeline, or reading. · Ask students to share their headline with a partner.
Circle Write	· Break into groups and provide a writing prompt or key question. · Have students write as much as they can in response to the question or prompt for 1 minute. · Next have students give their response to the person on their right. That person should improve or elaborate on the response where the other person left off. · Continue to pass each response to the right until the original response comes back to the first person. · Each group then reviews all the responses and decides which is the best composition and shares that with the larger group.
Write 1-Get 3 (or Write 5-Get 4)	· Ask a question with multiple answers, such as: What are 4 key characteristics of _____ (a dictator)? What are the 5 key causes of _____? · Have students write down 1 response and then go around the room asking for 3 other responses. If they think a response is correct, ask them to write it down. · Have students keep asking and writing until they have 3 more responses on their page. · Have students share and discuss responses with the class.

ACTIVE CLASSROOM STRATEGIES

ACTIVITY NAME	HOW TO ACTIVATE
Sticky Notes	· Ask students to spend three minutes jotting down their response to a critical thinking question on a sticky note. · Ask students to work in pairs and share their responses. · Next ssk students to post their sticky notes on the board or on chart paper and read all the notes. · Discuss similarities and differences in the responses as a group.
Connect Two	· Select 10 to 12 words or phrases you think are important for students to know prior to reading a selection. · List the words on the board. · Ask students to "Connect Two" or choose two words they think might belong together, and state the reason. "I would connect _____ and _____ because _____." Consider posting their Connect Two statements on the board. · As students read the text they should look for evidence to support or refute their Connect Two statements.
Conversation With History	· Ask students to choose one of the people mentioned or pictured in the text and write down a question they would like to ask that person if they could. · Next ask students to write what they think that person would say in response and then what they would say in response to that.
Walking Tour	· Post passages from a reading around the room. · Ask small groups to tour the room and discuss each passage. · Summarize each passage as a class. · Alternatively, assign each small group to a passage and have them summarize that passage for the rest of the class.
Audio Tour	· Ask students to work in pairs. Have the first student give the second a verbal "tour" of a map or graph or infographic. · Have the second student give the first an explanation of what the graphic shows.
My Metaphor	· Post the following metaphor on the board: This (map, timeline, image, primary source) shows that _____ is like _____ because _____. · Ask students to fill in the metaphor prompt based on their understanding of the source.
Act It Out	· Choose an image in the lesson and ask students to think about one of the following questions as appropriate to the image: · What may have happened next in this image? · What may have happened just before this image? · What do you think the people in this image are thinking? · What do you think the people in this image are saying to each other?
If Photos/Images/Art Could Talk	· Ask the following questions about an image in the course: What do you think the person in this photo would say if they could talk? What's your evidence?

Creating an Active Classroom

ACTIVE CLASSROOM STRATEGIES

ACTIVITY NAME	HOW TO ACTIVATE
See-Think-Wonder	· Ask students to work in pairs. · Ask them to look at an image, map, or graph and answer these questions: · What do you see? · What does that make you think? · What are you wondering about now that you've seen this? · Have students share their answers with the class.
A Closer Look	· Project a map or image on the board and divide it into four numbered quadrants. · Have students count off from 1 to 4 into four small groups. Have each group look closely at the part of the image in their quadrant. · Have each small group report on what they observed and learned as a result of their focus on this part of the image.
Take a Stand	· Ask students to take a stand on a yes-or-no or agree/disagree critical thinking question. · Ask students to divide into two groups based on their answer and move to separate areas of the classroom. · Ask students to talk with each other to compare their reasons for answering yes or no. · Ask a representative from each side to present and defend the group's point of view. · Note: you can adapt this activity to have students take their place on a continuum line from 1 to 10 depending on how strongly they agree or disagree.
Rank It	· List a group of items/concepts/steps/causes/events on the board. · Ask students to rank the items/steps . . . according to X criteria (which is most important, which had the greatest impact . . . most influential, essential, changed, affected). · Ask students to provide a justification for the ranking decisions they made. · Then ask students to work in pairs to share their rankings and justifications. · Poll the class to see if there is agreement on the ranking. OR · Place stickies on the board with key events from the lesson or topic. · Break students into small groups and ask each group to go up and choose the sticky with what they think is the most significant event. · Ask the group to discuss among themselves why they think it is most significant. · Ask one person from each group to explain why the group chose that event.
Sequence It	· Place key events from a lesson or topic on sticky notes on the board. · Ask students to place the events in chronological order. · You could do this activity with multiple groups in different parts of the classroom.
PMI Plus/Minus/Interesting	· Place students in groups and give each group a 3-column organizer with headings Plus/Minus/Interesting for recording responses. · Ask students to analyze a text or examine an issue and then answer these three questions in their organizer: · What was positive about this text/issue? · What was negative about this text/issue? · What was interesting about this text/issue?

Celebrate Freedom

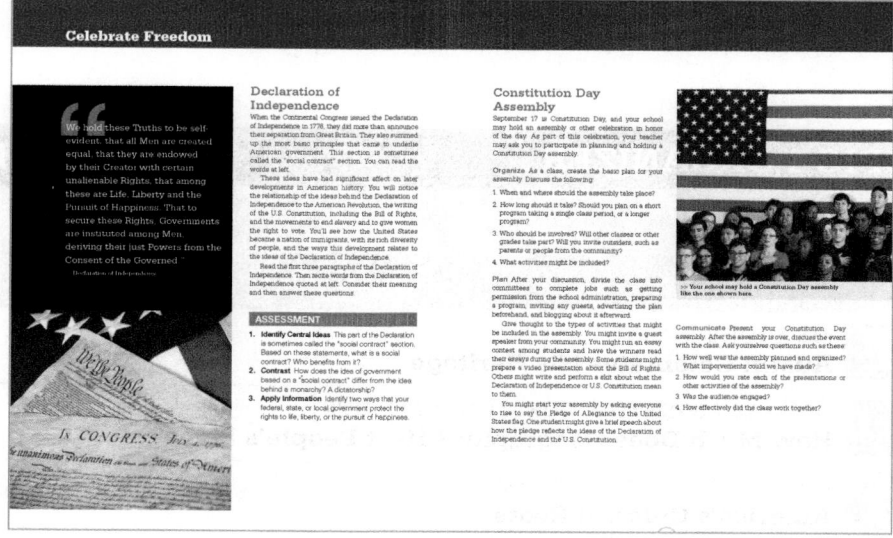

Objective 1: Analyze and evaluate the importance of the Declaration of Independence and the U.S. Constitution; **2:** Identify the full text of the first three paragraphs of the Declaration of Independence.

Quick Instruction

Using these materials, students can prepare for Celebrate Freedom Week by thinking about the importance of the Declaration of Independence and the U.S. Constitution. Have students read the first three paragraphs of the Declaration of Independence. Then ask them to recite the "social contract" section. The materials will help you make links between Celebrate Freedom Week and your course of study.

Aa Vocabulary Development: Before students recite the words of the Declaration of Independence, review key terms such as *self-evident, endowed, unalienable* and *consent*. Ask students to compose a sentence using each word. Then have students paraphrase the excerpt from the Declaration, putting the ideas into their own words.

Have students recite the Declaration to each other or as a whole class.

During the school year, remember to help students look back to the ideas expressed in the Declaration, especially if your course includes topics like: the American Revolution, writing of the U.S. Constitution, Abolitionist Movement, Emancipation Proclamation, Women's Suffrage Movement, and immigration and American diversity.

Identify Central Ideas *an agreement between the people and the government; the people benefit because they control the government, which is created by the people to ensure that they will have their rights protected.*

Contrast *In a monarchy, all rights come from the royal power; rights are not created or determined by the people. In a dictatorship, power is concentrated in the hands of one person; the people have few or any rights.*

Apply Information *Answers will vary, but might include ideas such as: local and state governments provide police protection to ensure everyone's safety. The federal government protects against discrimination based on characteristics like race, gender, national background, or disabilities.*

Further Instruction

Constitution Day Assembly Help students organize and carry out a Constitution Day assembly.

Organize Students may need help getting organized. Ask them to consider additional questions such as these:

1. What activities will keep students of different grade levels interested?
2. Should you hang posters around the school or get permission to make announcements about the assembly?
3. How can you make this year's Celebrate Freedom Week special?

Plan After the discussion, divide the class into committees that will work on various aspects of the assembly. Depending on how much time you have and the skills and

interests of your students, you might suggest committees such as these:

- Administrative Committee: prepares a proposal for the school administration, explaining the purpose of the assembly and what will be needed. The Administrative Committee also organizes the final assembly.
- Advertising Committee: publicizes the assembly in the school and community. This may include creating posters, using social media and other online resources, and contacting local media outlets.
- Activity Committees: plan and execute the individual parts of the program.

Communicate After the assembly, ask some students to publish photos taken during the assembly or to write a letter to the local newspaper about the assembly. If you invited guest speakers, others should send thank-you notes to the speakers. Have students write a thank-you note to the school administrator for allowing them to present the assembly.

■ **ADDITIONAL LESSON RESOURCES**

- Print student text
- Declaration of Independence
- United States Constitution
- Pledge of Allegiance to the U.S. Flag
- Celebrate Freedom resources

America's Cultural Roots

TOPIC 1 ORGANIZER	PACING: APPROX. 7 PERIODS, 3.5 BLOCKS
	PACING
Connect	1 period
MY STORY VIDEO **Austin Celebrates His Heritage**	10 min.
DIGITAL ESSENTIAL QUESTION ACTIVITY **How Much Does Geography Affect People's Lives?**	10 min.
DIGITAL OVERVIEW ACTIVITY **America's Cultural Roots**	10 min.
TOPIC INQUIRY: DOCUMENT-BASED QUESTION **Changing Perspectives on American Indians**	20 min.
Investigate	2–4 periods
TOPIC INQUIRY: DOCUMENT-BASED QUESTION **Changing Perspectives on American Indians**	Ongoing
LESSON 1 The Peoples of the Americas	30–40 min.
LESSON 2 The West Africans	30–40 min.
LESSON 3 Europeans Make Contact	30–40 min.
LESSON 4 Spain and France in the Americas	30–40 min.
Synthesize	1 period
DIGITAL ACTIVITY **America's Cultural Roots**	10 min.
TOPIC INQUIRY: DOCUMENT-BASED QUESTION **Changing Perspectives on American Indians**	20 min.
Demonstrate	1–2 periods
DIGITAL TOPIC REVIEW AND ASSESSMENT **Many Cultures Meet**	10 min.
TOPIC INQUIRY: DOCUMENT-BASED QUESTION **Changing Perspectives on American Indians**	20 min.

NOTES

Document-Based Inquiry
Changing Perspectives on American Indians

In this Topic Inquiry, students work independently to explore the changing ways that historians have viewed American Indian groups. Students will reflect on this information and then write an essay in which they answer the question: **How have conceptions of American Indians changed over time?**

STEP 1: CONNECT
Develop Questions and Plan the Investigation

Launch the Project
Before introducing Jacques Cartier's letter, encourage students to reflect on what they know of interactions between European explorers/colonists and American Indian populations. Suggest that students think about these encounters as they read Cartier's letter. Present Jacques Cartier's letter to the King of France and provide opportunities to discuss and answer questions students may have about the information in the letter.

Suggestion: Provide opportunities for multiple readings to help students gather as much background information as necessary.

Generate Questions
Present the excerpt from John Dryden's poem The Conquest of Granada and the image of Roger Williams with Narragansett Indians. Students may benefit from working with a partner to discuss the poem and the image. Encourage partners to answer the discussion questions and take notes that capture information from the poem and image. Suggest that students note any conflicting information or views they have and to briefly describe why their responses might be different.

Suggestion: Students may benefit from an oral reading of the Dryden poem, during which unfamiliar vocabulary and allusions can be clarified.

Resources
• Student Instructions

⏻ PROFESSIONAL DEVELOPMENT

America's Cultural Roots
Be sure to view the America's Cultural Roots Professional Development resources in the online course.

STEP 2: INVESTIGATE
Apply Disciplinary Concepts and Tools

Read and Analyze Documents
Students will work individually to read and analyze five sources that highlight varying perceptions of American Indians. The final source is written by a modern American Indian scholar who presents a counter perception. While students should examine each source in detail, they should not lose sight of their main goal of answering the question about how conceptions of American Indians have changed over time. Refer students to helpful resources within the core content of the Topic to help answer any lingering questions or to confirm changing views and information.

Suggestion: Consider briefly previewing the documents or viewing them as a class to clarify any vocabulary or content issues.

Check Student Understanding
Ensure students answer the multiple choice and short answer questions that accompany each document. When students have completed reading the documents and answering the associated questions, meet as a class to review students' responses. Point out to students that they might disagree with the viewpoints of the historians based on their own knowledge of the subject.

Suggestion: Consider pausing here to review students' answers before proceeding. Clarify any misunderstandings before students move on to the next step.

Resources
• **Document A:** Excerpt from In Defense of the Indians, by Bartolomé de Las Casas, 1550
• **Document B:** Painting of Pigeon's Egg Head (The Light) Going and Returning from Washington, by George Catlin 1837–39
• **Document C:** A History of the United States (1834–74), by George Bancroft, 1876
• **Document D:** Speech at Lake Mohonk, by Henry L. Dawes, 1883
• **Document E:** Excerpt from The Earth Shall Weep, by James Wilson, 1998
• **Document F:** Excerpt from Native Historians Write Back, by Susan A. Miller, 2009

STEP 3: SYNTHESIZE
Evaluate Sources and Use Evidence to Formulate Conclusions

Synthesize the Information in the Documents

Now have students record notes that describe the similarities and differences among the historians' viewpoints, how the viewpoints have changed over time and why these differences may have developed. For students who are having trouble, encourage them to think about the factors that might influence a historian's perspective about American Indians, such as the historian's gender, ethnicity, life and work experience, and the era in which he or she lived.

Suggest students think about the following questions:

- How might information about the author, including his or her background, language, and point of view, shape the content of the source?
- What information in the sources can you identify as biased?
- How might you evaluate the validity of a source based on corroboration with other sources you have read?

Write the Essay

Students should now write their essays. Review the essay criteria and clarify any questions students may have. They may benefit from peer reviews of one another's writing. Remind students to offer detailed, constructive criticism of one another's work.

Suggestion: Present the Rubric for Document-Based Assessment Essay so students can better understand what is expected.

Resources

- Rubric for Document-Based Assessment Essay

STEP 4: DEMONSTRATE
Communicate Conclusions and Take Informed Action

Publish the Writing Projects

When students have completed their writing projects, hold a class discussion about the question, How have conceptions of American Indians changed over time? See if the class can reach a consensus on one or more reasons why. Record these reasons for the class to view.

Then, ask the class to turn these conclusions into informed action. Review the question, Why is it important to study the misconceptions of earlier historians? Challenge them to describe the positive and negative effects on our understanding historical eras by reevaluating the works of earlier historians.

Suggestion: Extend the activity by having students conduct library and Internet research to locate additional examples of changing perceptions of American Indians or other topics they learned about in the Lessons.

America's Cultural Roots

Driven by curiosity and new ideas about the human experience, Europeans embarked on an age of exploration in the 1400s that would eventually engage cultures from Europe, Africa, and the Americas. Christopher Columbus's accidental "discovery" of the Americas in 1492 began a chain of events that would bring death and devastation to some and wealth and success to others. How would the interaction among cultures after 1492 affect the Americas and the world?

▮ CONNECT

MY STORY VIDEO

Austin Celebrates His Heritage

Watch a video about a brother and sister as they learn more about their ancestry.

Check Understanding What musical instrument is essential to Native American culture? *(drum)*

Determine Point of View What words best describe Austin's perspective about his heritage? *(pride, eagerness to find out more, desire to set a good example)*

DIGITAL ESSENTIAL QUESTION ACTIVITY

How Much Does Geography Affect People's Lives?

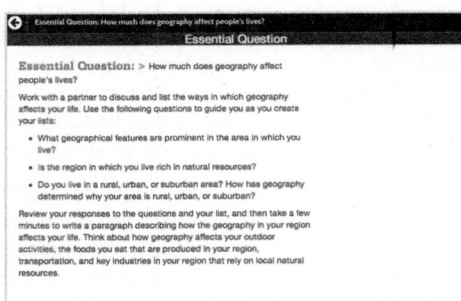

Ask students to think about the Essential Question for this topic: How much does geography affect people's lives? If students have not already done so, ask them to complete their lists and to try to categorize each one. Then discuss students' lists as a class. When students have finished writing their paragraphs, invite volunteers to share them with the class.

Identify Patterns Compare students' lists. Did most students describe the same geographical effects on their lives? If so, why was that the case?

Determine Relevance Are certain geographic features more valued than others? *(Yes. Areas that contain useful water sources are of high value, as are those that provide natural resources that support communities.)*

Generate Explanations How might lack of access to valued geographic resources affect the interaction between people or cultures? *(Those who have access to valued geographic resources are more likely to be protective of the resources; those who do not have access are more likely to seek out those resources, creating competition and perhaps conflict.)*

DIGITAL OVERVIEW ACTIVITY

America's Cultural Roots

Display the image of the grasslands and the Great Colorado Sand Dunes. During this topic students will learn about the race to control the vast territories and natural resources of the North and South American continents. This photo captures just a small part of the vast expanse of open lands that Europeans battled to control.

Check Understanding Based on your knowledge of geography, in what region of North America might this photograph have been taken? *(The mountains and grasslands are similar to the American West.)*

Analyze Photographs What does the photograph tell you about the availability of beneficial natural resources in this area of North America? *(The area in the photo looks rather desolate and not very hospitable. I can imagine that the mountainous areas in the background might provide mineral resources to be used, but the area does not look as if it could support a great many people.)*

Topic Inquiry

Launch the Topic Inquiry with students after introducing the topic.

PEARSON
realize™

www.PearsonRealize.com
Access your Digital Lesson

The Peoples of the Americas

Supporting English Language Learners

Use with the reading, **Early Inhabitants of the Americas.**

Explain to students that they will use their prior knowledge and experience to help them understand the effects climate change had on early Paleo-Indian development.

Beginning Use simple spoken language to summarize the section titled *Climate Change Encourage Adaptation.* Ask students to use their prior knowledge about climate change to answer the following simple questions: Do oceans rise as polar ice melts? Do skilled hunters kill lots of animals? If there are fewer animals, what can people eat?

Intermediate Silently reread the section titled *Climate Change Encourages Adaptation.* Think about what you know about climate change and how it affects us today. Use your prior knowledge when you talk to a partner about how climate change affected early Paleo-Indians. When polar ice caps melted, the oceans _____. Skilled hunters killed _____ animals. When there are fewer animals, people can eat more _____. Populations _____ when there is more food.

Advanced Silently reread the section titled *Climate Change Encourages Adaptation.* Think about what you know about climate change. Talk with a partner about how climate change affects us today. Then partners can use this knowledge to talk about how climate change affected the early Paleo-Indians.

Advanced High Silently reread the section titled *Agriculture Emerges.* Talk with a partner about the relation between food supply and population growth. Use what you know about small villages growing into cities to support your ideas.

Use with the reading, **Early Cultures in North America.**

Explain to students that they will demonstrate listening comprehension by retelling or summarizing spoken information.

Beginning Use simple language to explain the shared characteristics of the different American Indian groups. Have students demonstrate their comprehension by completing the following sentence frames: Most American Indian groups believed there were _____ in plants, animals, and bodies of water. American Indians _____ own private property. _____ hunted and fought wars. _____ took care of the children and the meals. Then have partners take turns retelling the characteristics shared by different American Indian groups.

Intermediate Use simple spoken language to summarize the shared characteristics of the different American Indian groups. Then have pairs of students demonstrate listening comprehension by retelling the shared characteristics to each other.

Advanced Use spoken language to summarize the section titled *Shared Characteristics Across Cultures.* Have students demonstrate listening comprehension by writing three or four short sentences about the shared characteristics. Then ask students to get partners and discuss their summaries.

Advanced High Use spoken language to summarize the section titled *Shared Characteristics Across Cultures.* Have partners demonstrate listening comprehension by retelling the information about the belief in spirits and the role of the shaman in the different American Indian groups.

▣ Differentiate Instruction

Use the Differentiated Instruction notes throughout the lesson plan to support the varied skill sets, levels of readiness, and interests in the mixed-ability classroom.

Challenge These notes include suggestions for expanding the activity for advanced students.

On-Level These notes include suggestions for modifying the activity to address different interests or learning styles.

Extra Support These notes include ideas for providing more scaffolding or reading support.

Special Needs These notes provide ideas for adapting instruction to support the needs of various special needs students.

■ NOTES

Topic ① Lesson 1

The Peoples of the Americas

Objectives

Objective 1: Explain how American Indians may have come to North America.

Objective 2: Describe the process by which different American Indian groups and cultures developed.

Objective 3: Describe the major culture areas prior to the arrival of Europeans in North America.

LESSON 1 ORGANIZER	PACING: APPROX. 1 PERIOD, .5 BLOCKS			
			RESOURCES	
	OBJECTIVES	**PACING**	**Online**	**Print**
Connect				
DIGITAL START UP ACTIVITY **The Peoples of the Americas**		5 min.	●	
Investigate				
DIGITAL TEXT 1 **Early Inhabitants of the Americas**	Objective 1	10 min.	●	●
DIGITAL TEXT 2 **Early Cultures in North America**		10 min.	●	●
INTERACTIVE TIMELINE **American Indian Cultures**	Objectives 2, 3	10 min.	●	
INTERACTIVE MAP **Native American Culture Regions of North America**		10 min.	●	
Synthesize				
DIGITAL ACTIVITY **Cultural Adaptation and Geography**		5 min.	●	
Demonstrate				
DIGITAL QUIZ **Lesson Quiz and Class Discussion Board**		10 min.	●	

PEARSON realize ™
www.PearsonRealize.com

Go online to access additional resources including:
Primary Sources • Biographies • Supreme Court cases •
21st Century Skill Tutorials • Maps • Graphic Organizers.

■ CONNECT

DIGITAL START UP ACTIVITY
The Peoples of the Americas

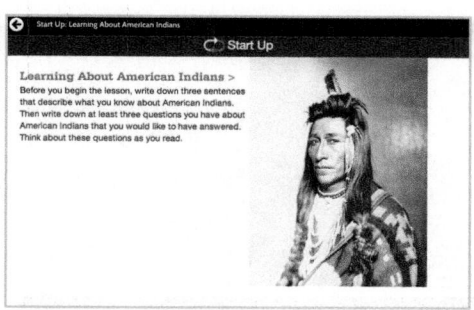

Project the Start Up Activity Ask students to write down their descriptions as they enter and get settled. Then have them share their ideas with another student, either in class or through a chat or blog space.

Discuss Take a moment to reflect on how students have learned about American Indians. Ask students what information or sources have shaped their perspective on American Indians?

Tell students that in this lesson they will be exploring the questions that experts still have about how humans first came to populate North America and the factors that shaped the rise of early American Indian cultures.

Aa Vocabulary Development: Use the Interactive Reading Notepad to preview the Key Terms and Academic Vocabulary in this lesson with students.

⇅ FLIP IT!
Assign the Flipped Video for this lesson.

■ STUDENT EDITION PRINT PAGES 4–9

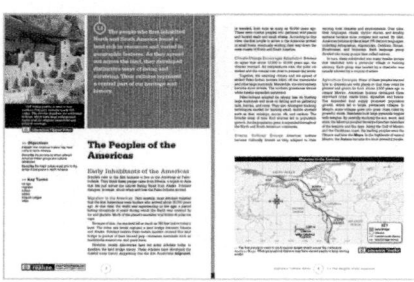

■ INVESTIGATE

DIGITAL TEXT 1
Early Inhabitants of the Americas

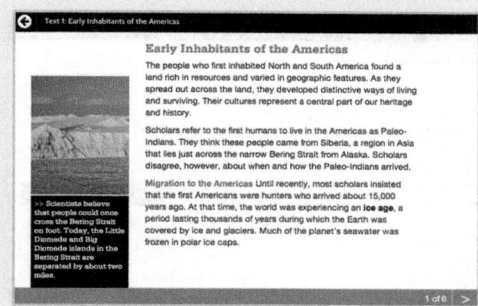

Objective 1: Explain how American Indians may have come to North America.

Quick Instruction
Digital Map: Migration to the Americas
Project the map and encourage students to trace the migration routes experts theorize that Paleo-Indians used to migrate to the Americas. Ask students to discuss what geographical features may have encouraged southward migration. *(Glaciers in the northern part of North America probably forced people to move south.)*

Draw Conclusions What does the map tell you about our current understanding of how the Americas were first populated? *(The map presents two distinct theories about how humans first arrived in the Americas. This tells me that experts are still not sure how the first peoples migrated to the Americas.)*

ELL Use the ELL activity described in the ELL chart.

Further Instruction
Summarize Challenge students to use information from the map and the reading to describe the sequence of events that led to the migration of people throughout the continents of North and South America. *(Scholars think that an ice age period forced people to start moving south away from polar*

ice caps. Paleo-Indian hunters crossed a land bridge connecting Asia with North America in pursuit of prey. About 12,000 to 10,000 years ago, the climate warmed. The warming climate and the spread of skilled Paleo-Indian hunters killed off large prey and the environment became more diverse. This led to greater abundance of food, which in turn encouraged population growth. As the population grew, it expanded throughout the North and South American continents.)

Continue the discussion by asking volunteers to suggest how different climates and environments might have encouraged the development of different cultures. *(Different climates and environments would affect how people lived—what foods they ate, the homes in which they lived.)* Be sure students understand that over time, their languages, rituals, mythic stories, and kinship systems became more complex and varied.

Identify Cause and Effect Why were larger populations able to live together in permanent villages? *(The emergence of agriculture and several important crops led to population increases and permanent settlements because people no longer had to follow herds of animals to hunt.)*

The Peoples of the Americas

DIGITAL TEXT 2
Early Cultures in North America

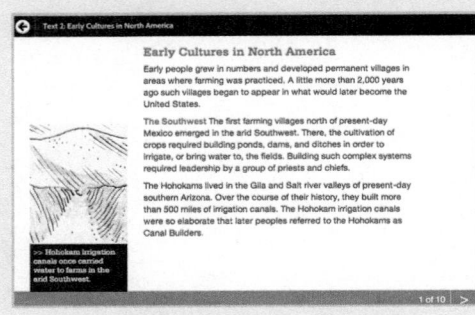

INTERACTIVE TIMELINE
American Indian Cultures

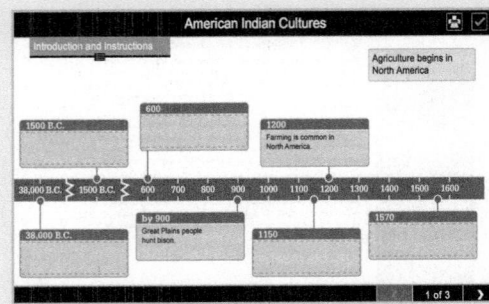

INTERACTIVE MAP
Native American Culture Regions of North America

Objectives 2: **Describe the process by which different American Indian groups and cultures developed; 3: Describe the major culture areas prior to the arrival of Europeans in North America.**

Quick Instruction

Interactive Timeline: American Indian Cultures Project the Interactive Timeline and invite volunteers to discuss what they have learned about the information on each tile. After you have worked your way through all the tiles, challenge students to complete the interactivity by placing the tiles in the correct order on the timeline.

Interactive Map: Native American Culture Regions of North America Project the Interactive Map and click through the hotspots. Introduce the activity by explaining geography played a significant role in the cultural development of different North American culture regions.

Digital Image: Cliff Palace Pueblo Direct students attention to the image of the Anasazi Cliff Palace Pueblo. Use it as a springboard for a class discussion about the environmental challenges some American Indian groups faced. Ask: What problems did the Indians living in what is now the American Southwest encounter? *(The region has a very dry climate and water is often very scarce.)* How did they adapt to their environments? *(Some groups like the Hohokam built ponds, dams, and ditches in order to irrigate, or bring water to,*

the crop fields. The canyon lands in which the Anasazi lived forced them to build elaborate and complicated structures into the sides of cliffs for relief from the heat and for protection.)

ACTIVE CLASSROOM

Have students Make Headlines for each event depicted in the Interactive Timeline. Ask: If you were to write a headline for each event that captured its most important aspect, what would that headline be? Emphasize to students that their headlines should capture why the event is significant, such as how it might affect migration on the continent. Allow them to use subheadings if they would like. Have students pass their headlines to a partner for them to review.

ACTIVE CLASSROOM

Ask students to use the *Write 1-Get 3* strategy to describe four defining cultural attributes influenced by geography. *(Attributes include food, clothing, shelter, settlement patterns, artwork, and religious ceremonies.)*

D **Differentiate: Challenge/Gifted** Ask students to do additional research on one of the events described on the tiles and present their findings.

ELL Use the ELL activity described in the ELL chart.

Further Instruction

Start a discussion distinguishing between American Indian groups living in the Southwest and those living farther north. *(The Indians living farther north lived in regions that had temperate climates and greater rainfall. Forests, lakes, rivers, and coastal areas were all much more common than in the Southwest. The northern regions also contain a greater number of animals that could be hunted for food and other uses. These features provided greater sources of food for these groups.)*

Make Generalizations What factors may have contributed to the rapid population growth in the Northeast? *(This region featured vast forests and water that provided good farming and plenty of food sources.)*

Make Predictions American Indian groups did not have centralized nations like those in Europe. Instead, political power was spread among many local chiefs with limited authority. How might this fact impact future relations with Europeans in North America? *(Sample answer: I think it will lead to disorganization and a lack of power in future contact with Europeans.)*

SYNTHESIZE

DIGITAL ACTIVITY

Cultural Adaptation and Geography

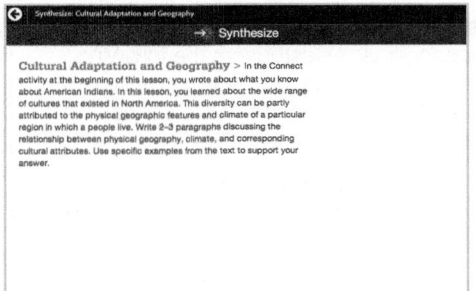

Before students write their paragraphs, have partners think about the following questions: Do you think it is possible for humans to adapt to any kind of climates or environments? Why or why not? Based on what you have learned in the Lesson, what is the most interesting way Paleo-Indians adapted to survive? Have pairs share their answers with the class.

Discuss Ask students to think about the questions they wrote down about American Indians at the beginning of the lesson. Invite volunteers to share their questions and the answers to their questions. Encourage students who have unresolved questions to do additional research to find answers.

DEMONSTRATE

DIGITAL QUIZ

Lesson Quiz and Class Discussion Board

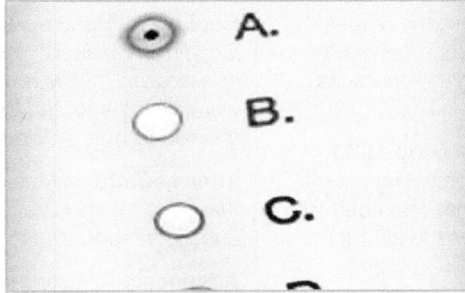

Assign the online Lesson Quiz for this lesson if you haven't already done so. Students will be offered automatic remediation or enrichment based on their score.

Pose these questions to the class on the Discussion Board: In *American Indians* you read about how humans first populated the Americas and how American Indians developed cultures well adapted to local climate, landscapes, and ecosystems.

Draw Conclusions What impact did climate change that occurred twelve to ten thousand years ago have on the populating of the Americas?

Identify Patterns What historical developments that you read about in this lesson are still evident in American life today?

Topic Inquiry

Have students continue their investigations for the Topic Inquiry.

The West Africans

Supporting English Language Learners

Use with the reading, **The Kingdoms of West Africa.**

Tell students that they will talk about the kingdoms of West Africa using language ranging from simple key words and expressions to more abstract and content-based vocabulary. Read the text as a class, pausing to explain any difficult vocabulary or concepts.

Beginning Have students work with a partner to jot down the names of the three kingdoms in West Africa that grew in importance between A.D. 300 and 1500 Then have partners take turns naming the countries and the dates in which they rose to importance.

Intermediate Ask students to draw a timeline from A.D. 300 to 1500 showing the rise of each of the three West African kingdoms. Have them jot down the name of the ruler beneath the kingdom name. Then partners can refer to their timelines as they take turns talking about the kingdoms and their rulers using content-based vocabulary.

Advanced Divide students into groups of three and assign one kingdom to each group. Give groups a few minutes to prepare information about their kingdom, its ruler, when it was in power, and what it was known for. One group begins by sharing its information with the other two. Then the other two follow.

Advanced High Ask partners to take turns sharing what they learned about trade and the growing role of Islam in each of the three kingdoms of West Africa between A.D. 300 and 1500.

Use with the reading, **Characteristics of West African Societies.**

Explain to students that they will demonstrate reading comprehension by responding to a series of questions. Give students a few minutes to read the text silently. As they read, provide support by answering students' questions about vocabulary or concepts.

Beginning Read aloud the section titled *The West African Slave Trade.* Explain any difficult vocabulary or concepts. Ask students the following questions: What was traded along with gold, salt, and ivory? In Africa, were slaves adopted by the families that owned them? Were slaves allowed to marry? Did the children of slaves become slaves?

Intermediate Ask students to reread the section titled *The West African Slave Trade.* Then have partners take turns asking and answering simple questions about the text.

Advanced Ask students to reread the section titled *The West African Slave Trade.* Then have partners answer the following questions: Who was sold into slavery? How was African slavery different from slavery in America

Advanced High Ask students to reread the section titled *The West African Slave Trade.* Then have partners ask and answer questions about slave armies and slave officials.

D Differentiate Instruction

Use the Differentiated Instruction notes throughout the lesson plan to support the varied skill sets, levels of readiness, and interests in the mixed-ability classroom.

Challenge These notes include suggestions for expanding the activity for advanced students.

On-Level These notes include suggestions for modifying the activity to address different interests or learning styles.

Extra Support These notes include ideas for providing more scaffolding or reading support.

Special Needs These notes provide ideas for adapting instruction to support the needs of various special needs students.

■ NOTES

PEARSON
realize.™
www.PearsonRealize.com

Go online to access additional resources including:
Primary Sources • Biographies • Supreme Court cases •
21st Century Skill Tutorials • Maps • Graphic Organizers.

Objectives

Objective 1: Describe the development and cultural characteristics of West Africa in the fifteenth century.

Objective 2: Summarize West African religions, culture, and society.

Objective 3: Explore the roots of the system of slavery practiced in the Americas.

LESSON 2 ORGANIZER		PACING: APPROX. 1 PERIOD, .5 BLOCKS			
				RESOURCES	
		OBJECTIVES	**PACING**	**Online**	**Print**
Connect					
DIGITAL START UP ACTIVITY **Salt and Gold**			5 min.	●	
Investigate					
DIGITAL TEXT 1 **The Kingdoms of West Africa**		Objective 1	10 min.	●	●
DIGITAL TEXT 2 **Characteristics of West African Societies**		Objectives 2, 3	10 min.	●	●
INTERACTIVE GALLERY **Artifacts of West African Kingdoms**			10 min.	●	
Synthesize					
INTERACTIVE CHART **West African Kingdoms**			5 min.	●	
Demonstrate					
DIGITAL QUIZ **Lesson Quiz and Class Discussion Board**			10 min.	●	

The West Africans

▐ CONNECT

DIGITAL START UP ACTIVITY
Salt and Gold

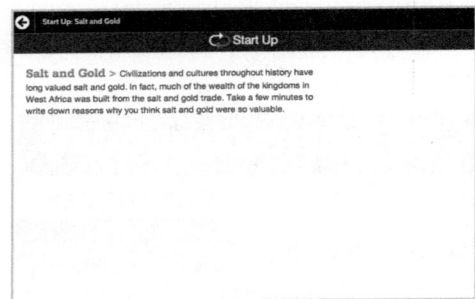

Project the Start Up Activity Ask students to consider the activity as they enter and get settled. Have students write their responses and share their ideas with another student, either in class or through a chat or blog space.

Discuss Take a moment to reflect on why cultures around the world value certain things. Challenge students to identify sources of wealth in today's world. *(Possible answers include money, or capital, oil, or energy resources, technology, abundant food sources)*

Tell students that in this lesson they will be learning about how valuable natural resources fueled the development of powerful and complex West African kingdoms between the 400s and the 1400s.

Aa Vocabulary Development: Use the Interactive Reading Notepad to preview the Key Terms and Academic Vocabulary in this lesson with students.

⇵ FLIP IT!
Assign the Flipped Video for this lesson.

▐ STUDENT EDITION PRINT PAGES 10–14

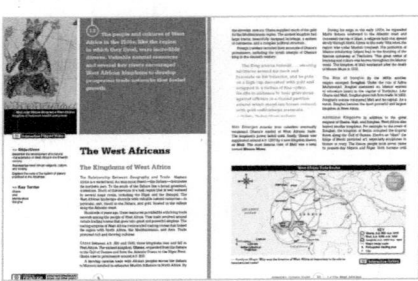

▐ INVESTIGATE

DIGITAL TEXT 1
The Kingdoms of West Africa

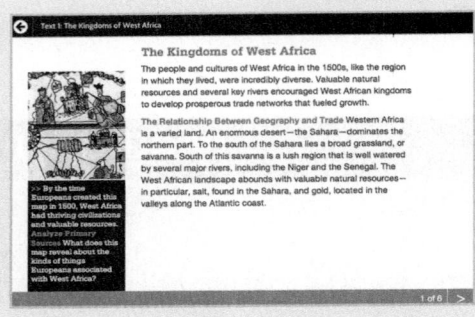

Objective 1: Describe the development and cultural characteristics of West Africa in the fifteenth century.

Quick Instruction
Digital Map: West African Trade Routes
Invite a student to identify the main idea of the map. *(to show the strategic location of West African to international trade routes)* Ask students to identify the locations of the Ghana, Mali, and Songhai empires. Be sure students understand how the presence of resources such as gold and salt helped lead to the development of powerful kingdoms in West Africa. *(Gold and salt, which were abundant in West Africa, were valued by people throughout Africa, Europe, and Asia. Consequently, as traders and merchants sought out these resources, the West African empires built and controlled trading routes that linked these regions, bringing wealth and thriving cultures.)*

ELL Use the ELL activity described in the ELL chart.

Further Instruction
Go through the Interactive Reading Notepad questions and use them to extend the discussion of the dominant empires of West Africa. Be sure students understand the role trade played in the emergence of these kingdoms.

Determine Relevance What was the impact of Mali's trade networks with regions in North Africa? *(Trade and contact with the people of North Africa led to the emergence and increasing importance of Islam.)*

Contrast How did the smaller empires south of the three great West African kingdoms differ in the their trade practices? *(These smaller empires lacked the vast resources of gold and salt. Instead, they relied on artistic abilities and cloth making to expand their trade networks.)*

DIGITAL TEXT 2

Characteristics of West African Societies

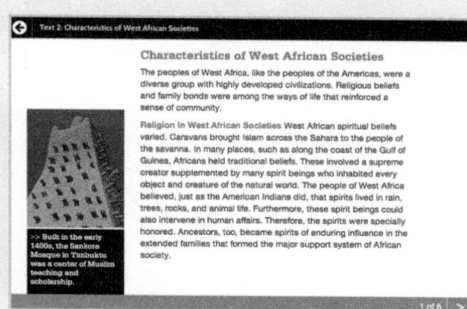

INTERACTIVE GALLERY

Artifacts of West African Kingdoms

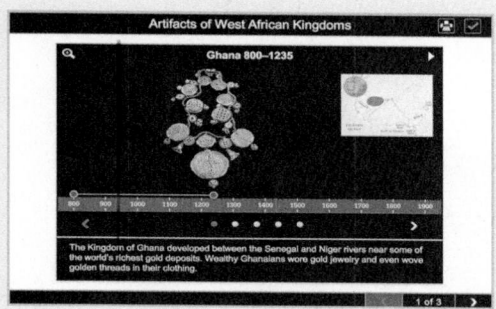

Objectives 2: Summarize West African religions, culture, and society; 3: Explore the roots of the system of slavery practiced in the Americas.

Quick Instruction

Guide students to understand that the economic development of West African kingdoms was influenced by natural resources in the region and resultant trade networks. In addition, traditional African religious beliefs and elements of Islam encouraged cultural developments in education, the arts, and commerce.

Interactive Gallery: Artifacts of West African Kingdoms Project the Interactive Gallery. Look at each image individually and then the collection of images as a whole. What does the image of the Songhai manuscript suggest about that empire? *(The image tells me that education and the pursuit of knowledge were important elements in the Songhai kingdom.)*

ACTIVE CLASSROOM

Have students write a headline that captures the action in one of the images in the Interactive Gallery. Ask: If you were to write a headline that captured the most important aspect of an image, what would that headline be? Pass your headline to a partner for them to review—they can keep yours or ask for theirs back.

D Differentiate: Extra Support Pair students to review the text and write down key characteristics of each West African kingdom that they find. Have pairs go revisit and complete the interactivity.

ELL Use the ELL activity described in the ELL chart.

Further Instruction

Make sure students understand that slavery was common in West Africa and that it was an important part of West Africa's economy. Point out that slavery was a common fate for people throughout the world who were conquered or captured during warfare.

Infer Why might an enslaved person in West Africa have been in a relatively better position than an enslaved person in the Americas? *(Although brutal, slavery in West Africa offered enslaved people more freedom and opportunities to escape bondage.)*

Summarize the role the Portuguese played in expanding the slave trade. *(When the Portuguese came into contact with the kingdoms of West Africa, they became involved in the African slave trade. They established trading forts in West Africa, including some that became major trading centers for enslaved people. Portuguese and other Europeans began shipping enslaved people to Europe; eventually large numbers of slaves were sent across the Atlantic to new plantations in the Americas.)*

The West Africans

INTERACTIVE CHART
West African Kingdoms

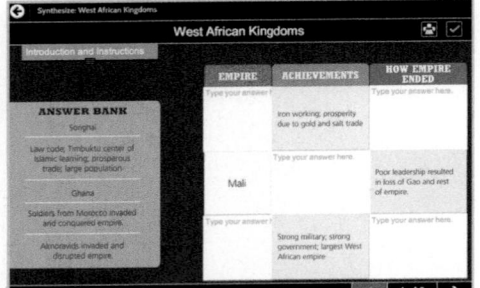

Project the Interactive Chart and have students fill in the graphic organizer to check their understanding of the cultural characteristics of the West African kingdoms.

Discuss Pair students and ask them to think about and discuss what life would have been like in West Africa before the arrival of Europeans.

■ ACTIVE CLASSROOM

Imagine that you are having a conversation with a citizen from one of the West African kingdoms described in this lesson. Write down a question you'd like to ask, then what that person would say to you, and what you would say in response.

DIGITAL QUIZ
Lesson Quiz and Class Discussion Board

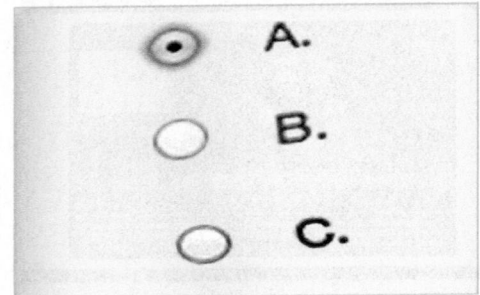

Assign the online Lesson Quiz for this lesson if you haven't already done so. Students will be offered automatic remediation or enrichment based on their score.

Pose these questions to the class on the Discussion Board:

In *The West Africans* you read about diverse civilizations in West Africa with advanced trade networks and complex political structures.

Summarize What were the key reasons that West African kingdoms emerged as powerful societies?

Make Predictions How will the growing presence of Europeans in West Africa affect the kingdoms in the region?

Topic Inquiry
Have students continue their investigations for the Topic Inquiry.

Europeans Make Contact

Supporting English Language Learners

Use with the reading, **Change Sweeps Through Europe in the 1400s.**

Tell students that they can use learning strategies, such as comparing and contrasting, to help them develop grade-level vocabulary and concepts.

Beginning Use simple spoken language to summarize the section titled *A Divided Society.* Ask partners to use the following sentence frames to compare the two extremes of European society: Five percent of the population controlled most of the land; they were _____ and the great _____. Three fifths of Western Europeans were _____, or working poor.

Intermediate Use simple spoken language to summarize the section titled *A Divided Society.* Ask partners to compare the ruling elite with the working poor and the relation each had with the land.

Advanced Ask students to silently reread the section titled *A Divided Society.* Then have them work with a partner to compare and contrast wealth and poverty in European society in the fifteenth century.

Advanced High Ask students to silently reread the section titled *A Divided Society.* Have partners compare the life of the commoners in good years and bad years. Encourage them to compare the most prosperous commoners with the less prosperous ones.

Use with the reading, **Christopher Columbus Explores the Americas.**

Read aloud the sections titled *Columbus Sails West* and *The Impact of Columbus's Voyage.* Tell students that you would like them to look at the map of the four voyages of Columbus while you reread some or all of the text.

Beginning Use simple spoken language to retell the information in the first paragraph. Show students the map key to help them determine which line represents the first voyage. Then ask students to run their finger along the route of the first voyage from Spain to the Bahamas.

Intermediate Use simple spoken language to summarize the information about Columbus's first voyage. Ask students to run their finger along the route of the first voyage from Spain to the Bahamas. Have them move their finger south to the other set of islands. Ask: What are these islands called?

Advanced Use spoken language to summarize the information about Columbus's first voyage while students trace the path on the map. Then have one partner look at the map and use it to help him or her describe the second voyage. The other partner listens to the description and uses his or her finger to trace the second voyage on the map.

Advanced High Read aloud the section titled *The Impact of Columbus's Voyage.* Ask one partner to use the map to describe the third voyage while the other partner traces it on the map. Then partners change roles and repeat the activity with the fourth voyage.

⬀ Differentiate Instruction

Use the Differentiated Instruction notes throughout the lesson plan to support the varied skill sets, levels of readiness, and interests in the mixed-ability classroom.

Challenge These notes include suggestions for expanding the activity for advanced students.

On-Level These notes include suggestions for modifying the activity to address different interests or learning styles.

Extra Support These notes include ideas for providing more scaffolding or reading support.

Special Needs These notes provide ideas for adapting instruction to support the needs of various special needs students.

■ NOTES

Europeans Make Contact

Objectives

Objective 1: Describe the conditions in Europe in the fifteenth century.

Objective 2: Analyze how the changes taking place in Europe shaped Europeans' worldview and economic expansion.

Objective 3: Describe the major developments on the Iberian Peninsula at the end of the Middle Ages and the start of the Renaissance.

Objective 4: Explain the goals of Christopher Columbus and the consequences of his explorations.

Objective 5: Analyze how contact with Europeans affected the people of the Americas.

LESSON 3 ORGANIZER		OBJECTIVES	PACING	RESOURCES Online	Print
Connect					
DIGITAL START UP ACTIVITY **Prince Henry the Navigator**			5 min.	●	
Investigate					
DIGITAL TEXT 1 **Change Sweeps Through Europe in the 1400s**		Objective 1	10 min.	●	●
DIGITAL TEXT 2 **Europe Expands Its Influence**		Objective 2	10 min.	●	●
INTERACTIVE GALLERY **The Renaissance**			10 min.	●	
DIGITAL TEXT 3 **The Portuguese and Spanish Explore New Routes**		Objective 3	10 min.	●	●
DIGITAL TEXT 4 **Christopher Columbus Explores the Americas**		Objective 4	10 min.	●	●
3-D MODEL **Seafaring Technologies**			10 min.	●	
DIGITAL TEXT 5 **The Spanish Build an American Empire**			10 min.	●	●
DIGITAL TEXT 6 **The Columbian Exchange**		Objective 5	10 min.	●	●
BEFORE AND AFTER **The Columbian Exchange**			10 min.	●	
Synthesize					
DIGITAL ACTIVITY **Cultures Collide**			5 min.	●	
Demonstrate					
DIGITAL QUIZ **Lesson Quiz and Class Discussion Board**			10 min.	●	

PACING: APPROX. 1 PERIOD, .5 BLOCKS

Go online to access additional resources including:
Primary Sources • Biographies • Supreme Court cases •
21st Century Skill Tutorials • Maps • Graphic Organizers.

PEARSON
realize™
www.PearsonRealize.com

■ CONNECT

DIGITAL START UP ACTIVITY
Prince Henry the Navigator

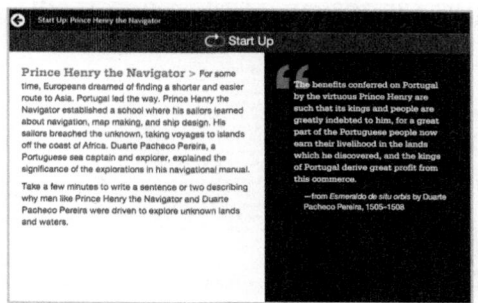

Project the Start Up Activity As students enter and get settled, direct their attention to the information in the activity and to the quote from Duarte Pacheco Pereira. Let students reflect on the question and share their ideas with a partner before writing their answers.

Discuss Ask students to discuss what personal characteristics they would expect to see in the great explorers *(Possible answers: brave, ambitious, intelligent, self-sufficient, resourceful, leadership ability, resilient)*

Tell students that in this lesson they will be learning how Europeans in the 1400s experienced a cultural, technological, and economic transformation that lifted the continent out of the Middle Ages.

Aa Vocabulary Development: Use the Interactive Reading Notepad to preview the Key Terms and Academic Vocabulary in this lesson with students.

⟲ FLIP IT!
Assign the Flipped Video for this lesson.

■ STUDENT EDITION PRINT PAGES 15–24

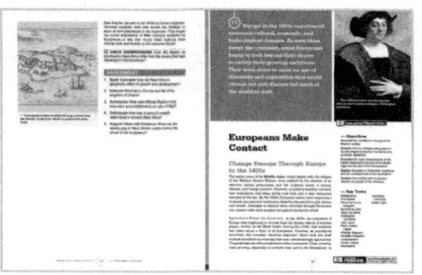

■ INVESTIGATE

DIGITAL TEXT 1
Change Sweeps Through Europe in the 1400s

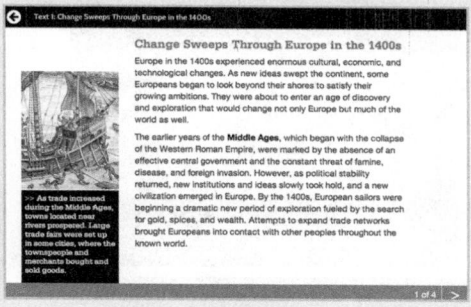

Objective 1: Describe the conditions in Europe in the fifteenth century.

Quick Instruction

Digital Image: Medieval Peasants Project the image of the peasant farmers. Use the image as a springboard to discuss what life was like for Europeans in the 1400s. Ask students to find descriptions of life in Europe at the time. *(People and economies were dependent on agriculture to survive, and most people lived in the countryside. Cities, however, were growing; inequities of wealth and poverty divided European society; a small percentage of the population controlled almost all of the land.)*

Support Ideas with Examples How were extremes of wealth and social inequality perpetuated in fifteenth century Europe? *(Wealth and power were inherited, so most commoners could never rise above the class into which they were born. Small farmers and peasants relied on landowners and were often at the mercy of factors that were out of their control, like bad farming conditions or diseases.)*

ELL Use the ELL activity described in the ELL chart.

Further Instruction
Briefly discuss with students the political structures and issues that characterized Europe in the 1400s. Ensure student understanding of how monarchs ruled with the help of the elite class, who in turn needed the support of common citizens.

Support Ideas with Examples What examples in the text indicate that European economies were becoming more diverse in the 1400s? *(Cities were growing and small-scale manufacturing of cloth, tools, weapons, and ceramics was becoming more important. In addition, European sailors began searching for gold, spices, and wealth beyond Europe. Building new trade networks brought Europeans into contact with other peoples throughout the known world, placing more economic importance on commerce and trade.)*

Hypothesize In your opinion, why were the kingdoms of Europe in 1400s in a state of constant war? *(Europe was made up of many kingdoms, each looking to expand its power and territories. There seemed to be little political stability, and new discoveries and trade routes probably heightened competition among kingdoms.)*

Europeans Make Contact

DIGITAL TEXT 2

Europe Expands Its Influence

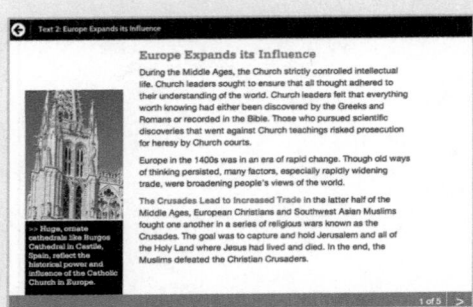

INTERACTIVE GALLERY

The Renaissance

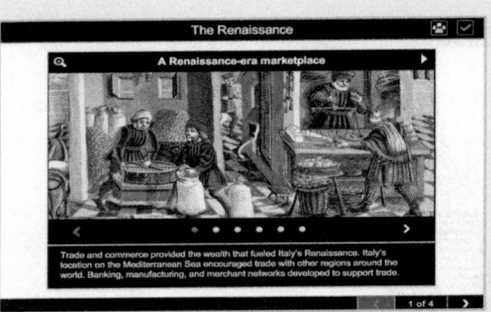

DIGITAL TEXT 3

The Portuguese and Spanish Explore New Routes

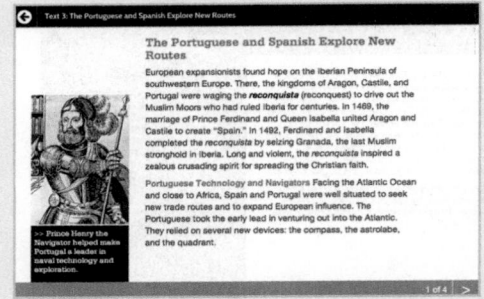

Objective 2: **Analyze how the changes taking place in Europe shaped Europeans' worldview and economic expansion.**

Quick Instruction

Interactive Gallery: The Renaissance
Project the gallery on the whiteboard and click the images to explore how the Renaissance changed political and economic trends and sparked new ideas in art, literature, architecture, philosophy. Discuss some of the causes that ignited the Renaissance. *(Greater knowledge of the world and different cultures; a spirit of curiosity and the desire to know more about the natural world)* Explain that the Renaissance marked the transition from medieval times to the early modern world.

Analyze Images How does the Agnese atlas express Renaissance ideals? *(It shows the Renaissance ideal of wide-ranging curiosity and the desire to learn about the world beyond Europe.)*

👥 ACTIVE CLASSROOM

Use the Rank It Strategy. Ask students to rank the images shown in the Interactive Gallery based on which one best represented the renewed interest in learning characterized by Renaissance art and science. Ask students to provide a justification for the ranking decisions they made. Then ask students to share their rankings and discuss the rationale for their choices.

D **Differentiate:** **Extra Support** Explain that the word Renaissance means *rebirth*. Point out that Renaissance thinkers felt that their era was a time of rebirth after what they saw as the disorder and disunity of the medieval world.

Further Instruction

Discuss how Europe in the 1400s was in an era of rapid change. Review the Interactive Reading Notepad questions to extend the discussion about how European views of the world were broadening.

Express Problems Clearly What risks did Renaissance thinkers face? *(Renaissance thinkers who pursued scientific discoveries that went against Church teachings risked prosecution for heresy by Church courts.)*

Summarize How did the Crusades help to expand Europe's horizons? *(Because of the Crusades, Europeans learned about distant lands and different ways of life. Trade was encouraged, which increased demand for new products. European traders expanded their businesses to Asia.)*

Use Context Clues Besides controlling more territory, how did the Islamic world threaten Europeans? *(The Muslim empires were wealthier, more powerful, and more technologically advanced. They also controlled vast trade networks that limited European commerce.)*

Objective 3: **Describe the major developments on the Iberian Peninsula at the end of the Middle Ages and the start of the Renaissance.**

Quick Instruction

Project the image of Prince Henry the Navigator on the whiteboard. Explain that Prince Henry was a Portuguese nobleman who established a school for Portuguese mariners where they learned about navigation, map making, and ship design.

Draw Conclusions What impact did Prince Henry's school have on the Portuguese empire? *(The school helped make Portugal a leader in naval technology and exploration, greatly increasing the country's power and wealth.)*

Cite Evidence How did technology aid the Portuguese in expanding their explorations? *(New navigation instruments, such as the compass, and ship-related technologies, such as lateen sails, made longer voyages quicker and safer.)*

Further Instruction

Connect What relationship exists between the *reconquista* and Spain's interest in exploration? *(The reconquista probably gave the Spanish a great boost in confidence and a desire to expand the kingdom and increase their wealth and power. It also inspired Spain to spread the Christian faith in distant lands.)*

DIGITAL TEXT 4
Christopher Columbus Explores the Americas

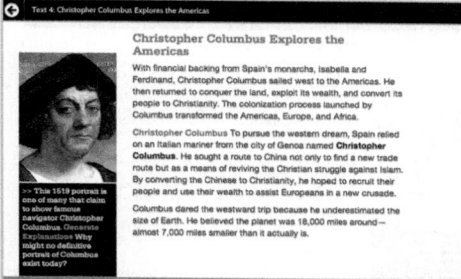

3-D MODEL
Seafaring Technologies

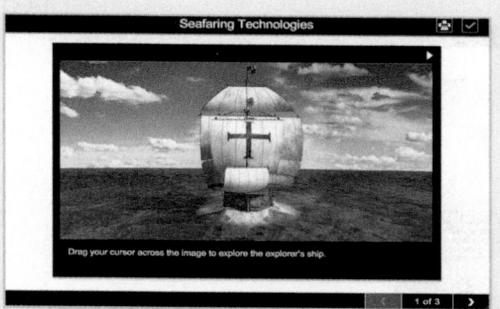

Evaluate Impact Who was Bartolomeu Dias? What role did he play in the age of exploration? *(Dias was a Portuguese mariner who learned how to use the counterclockwise winds and currents of the South Atlantic to get around southern Africa. That discovery eventually opened up sea routes to India, opening an immensely profitable trade route.)*

Objective 4: Explain the goals of Christopher Columbus and the consequences of his explorations.

Quick Instruction

3-D Model: Seafaring Technologies Project the 3-D Model, and click through the red circles with students. Explain that innovations in navigation transformed European exploration. New ships used rudders to steer and lateen sails to turn into the wind. As ships were able to travel further, new tools helped explorers find their way through uncharted waters great distances away.

Apply Concepts The cross staff and the back staff improved navigation. These instruments allowed mariners to calculate their north-south position on the planet. As Europeans sailed west into the Atlantic, what limitations might these instruments have? *(Sailors could not use these instruments to calculate their east-west position, or longitude, on Earth.)*

📖 ACTIVE CLASSROOM

Have students Make Headlines for each seafaring innovation depicted in the 3-D Model. Ask: If you were to write a headline for each innovation that captured the most important aspect that should be remembered, what would that headline be? Emphasize to students that their headlines should not just say what the innovation does but also capture why it is significant, how it will affect exploration, and so on. Allow them to use subheadings if they would like. Have students pass their headlines to a partner for them to review.

ELL Use the ELL activity described in the ELL chart.

Further Instruction

Go through the Interactive Reading Notepad questions and use the discussion as a springboard to explore the impact of Christopher Columbus's voyages to the Americas.

Identify Central Issues Why was Christopher Columbus eager to find a new route across the Atlantic? *(He sought a route to China to find a new trade route).*

Draw Conclusions How did Columbus's voyages affect the struggle between European Christians and Muslim kingdoms? *(The lands that Columbus and other European Christians claimed provided a source of riches that enabled European Christendom to grow more powerful and wealthy than the Muslim world.)*

Evaluate Arguments Christopher Columbus believed that as a Christian he had the right and duty to dominate the people he came across. What do you think of Columbus's belief? *(Sample answer: In today's world, some would consider Columbus's beliefs to be immoral, and dehumanizing. However, Columbus lived in a different time with different attitudes.)*

Europeans Make Contact

DIGITAL TEXT 5

The Spanish Build an American Empire

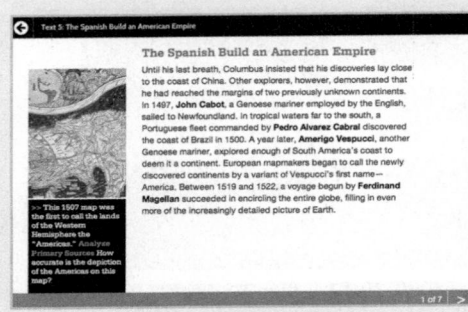

DIGITAL TEXT 6

The Columbian Exchange

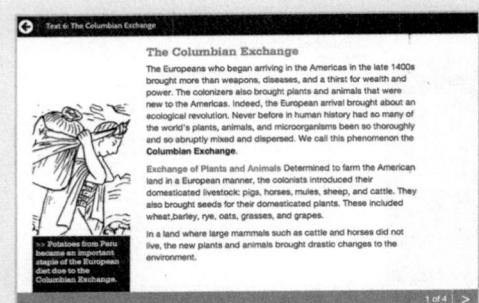

BEFORE AND AFTER

The Columbian Exchange

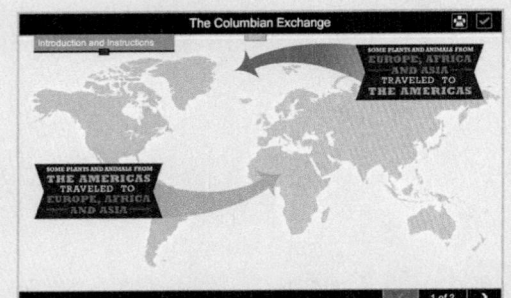

Objective 5: Analyze how contact with Europeans affected the people of the Americas.

Quick Instruction

Before and After: The Columbian Exchange Project the interactive map on the whiteboard and move the slider to reveal the plants and animals that were exchanged in the Columbian Exchange. Encourage students to discuss the plants and animals that have become vital parts of the cultures on both sides of the Atlantic. Invite volunteers to discuss aspects of the exchange that surprised them or that they find interesting.

Infer How do you think the Columbian Exchange affected the environment in the Americas? *(The environment in the Americas would have changed greatly. Introducing new plants, crops, and animals would have had a profound effect on the environment. In addition, silver and gold mining operations changed the America's environment as well.)*

Connect Is there still a global exchange among the continents? Explain. *(Yes. In many ways the global exchange is even greater now. Modern transportation allows people to travel easily from continent to continent, exchanging ideas as well as other products. Communication technologies also contribute to a global exchange. People using computers and telephones can speak with others around the world, which exchanges ideas and elements of cultures.)*

👥 ACTIVE CLASSROOM

Conduct a Graffiti Concepts activity. Ask students to reflect on the plants and animals involved in the Columbian Exchange and create a visual image and/or phrase that highlights the significance of a particular example. (Allow approximately 3-5 minutes.) Then ask students to post their "graffiti" on the board or on chart paper and ask students to look at all the various examples then discuss them as a group.

Further Instruction

Begin a discussion about how the arrival of Europeans in the Americas affected the peoples of the Americas. Be sure students understand that although European exploration and colonization of the Americas brought about significant benefits, it also came at great cost to many American Indians. Assign the Primary Source: Bartolomé de Las Casas, Destruction of the Indies to extend the discussion.

Summarize What role did disease play in the defeat of the native populations of the Americas? *(Disease and the successive epidemics reduced the native populations, making it very difficult, and in some cases impossible, for the American Indian groups to fight back.)*

Draw Conclusions Do the positive benefits of European exploration outweigh the negative aspects for the people of the Americas? Explain. *(Yes. Although European exploration undoubtedly led to many deaths and had great negative consequences for many cultures, connecting the Americas to the rest of the world had greater benefits for more people around the world.)*

■ SYNTHESIZE

DIGITAL ACTIVITY
Cultures Collide

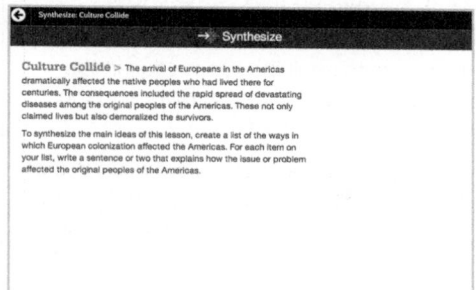

Ask students to recall the Topic Essential Question, "How much does geography affect people's lives?" Have them use the Think Pair Share strategy to discuss how geography and environments shaped the lives of the peoples of the Americas before Europeans arrived. Encourage students to reflect on their discussions as they create their lists and write their sentences.

Discuss Ask students to think about the effects of irreparable cultural and environmental change. Invite students to discuss how a person, community, or culture might overcome these challenges.

■ DEMONSTRATE

DIGITAL QUIZ
Lesson Quiz and Class Discussion Board

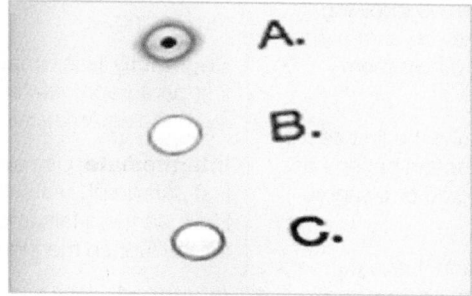

Assign the online Lesson Quiz for this lesson if you haven't already done so. Students will be offered automatic remediation or enrichment based on their score.

Pose these questions to the class on the Discussion Board:

In *Europeans Make Contact* you read about the forces that led to European exploration in the 1400s and the eventual arrival in the Americas. European exploration and initial colonization of the Americas had a profound impact on people throughout the world.

Draw Conclusions Europeans embarked on exploring the world for many reasons— the search for wealth and power, territorial conquest, curiosity about the world, and religious faith. Which, in your opinion, was the primary motivation for the age of exploration in the 1400s? Explain.

Make Predictions Will the world see another era like the Renaissance, in which creative minds reevaluate knowledge and seek out new understandings of the world? Explain.

Topic Inquiry
Have students continue their investigations for the Topic Inquiry.

Spain and France in the Americas

Supporting English Language Learners

Use with the reading, **European Rivalries Spread to the Americas.**

Tell students that you will ask them to express their opinions about the conflicts among various European nations that spread to the Americas.

Beginning Use simple spoken language to summarize the first section of *European Rivalries Spread to the Americas.* Introduce the following statements: I agree with _____. I disagree with _____. As you summarize, pause to allow students to use these sentence frames to help them express their opinions about the growing rivalries.

Intermediate Use simple spoken language to summarize the first section of the text. Ask partners to talk about how different European nations dealt with land conflicts. Then have them say whether they agree or disagree with the measures taken.

Advanced Ask students to silently reread the first section. Have partners name two distinct issues that caused conflict. Then each partner can choose one of the issues and share their opinion about it with the other partner.

Advanced High Ask students to silently reread the second section. Have partners talk about the religious divisions between the European nations and how they dealt with them in the Americas. Ask them to express their opinions about the Spanish monarch's effort to suppress Protestantism in the Americas.

Use with the reading, **The French Settle in North America.**

Before reading the text, have students study the map of the new French territories. Ask them to locate the Great Lakes, the St. Lawrence River, and Quebec. Explain that they can use the information on the map to help develop background knowledge that will support their comprehension of the reading.

Beginning Use simple spoken language to retell the information in the first paragraph. Ask students to point to the St. Lawrence River and the surrounding American Indian settlements on the map.

Intermediate Use simple spoken language to retell the information in the first paragraph. Ask students to locate the St. Lawrence River on the map. Have partners talk about why the St. Lawrence River was a good location for the French mariners.

Advanced Have students read the section titled *France Establishes New France* silently. Ask them to locate Quebec on the map. Ask: Where is Quebec located? Why is this a good place for a French trading post?

Advanced High Read the section titled *France Establishes New France* silently. Ask partners to identify the locations of the French forts and the American Indian settlements on the map. Have them talk about what the proximity of the forts to the settlements shows about French-Indian relations.

▣ Differentiate Instruction

Use the Differentiated Instruction notes throughout the lesson plan to support the varied skill sets, levels of readiness, and interests in the mixed-ability classroom.

Challenge These notes include suggestions for expanding the activity for advanced students.

On-Level These notes include suggestions for modifying the activity to address different interests or learning styles.

Extra Support These notes include ideas for providing more scaffolding or reading support.

Special Needs These notes provide ideas for adapting instruction to support the needs of various special needs students.

■ NOTES

Objectives

Objective 1: Explain the religious rivalry among European Nations.

Objective 2: Describe Spanish society in New Spain and Peru.

Objective 3: Evaluate the causes and effects of Spanish imperial policies in the American Southwest.

Objective 4: Explain how the fur trade affected the French and the Indians in North America.

Objective 5: Describe the French expansion into Louisiana.

LESSON 4 ORGANIZER		PACING: APPROX. 1 PERIOD, .5 BLOCKS			
		OBJECTIVES	PACING	**RESOURCES**	
				Online	Print
Connect					
	DIGITAL START UP ACTIVITY **Contrasting Two Empires**		5 min.	●	
Investigate					
	DIGITAL TEXT 1 **European Rivalries Spread to the Americas**	Objective 1	10 min.	●	●
	DIGITAL TEXT 2 **Governing the Spanish American Empire**	Objective 2	10 min.	●	●
	DIGITAL TEXT 3 **Spanish Explorers Seek Wealth in the North**		10 min.	●	●
	DIGITAL TEXT 4 **Colonization and Conflict in New Mexico**	Objective 3	10 min.	●	●
	INTERACTIVE GALLERY **Effects of American Silver and Gold on Spanish Economy**		10 min.	●	
	DIGITAL TEXT 5 **The French Settle in North America**	Objective 4	10 min.	●	●
	DIGITAL TEXT 6 **Living in New France**		10 min.	●	●
	INTERACTIVE CHART **Spanish and French Exploration and Colonization of North America**	Objective 5	10 min.	●	
Synthesize					
	DIGITAL ACTIVITY **Establishing New Colonies**		5 min.	●	
Demonstrate					
	DIGITAL QUIZ **Lesson Quiz and Class Discussion Board**		10 min.	●	

Spain and France in the Americas

■ CONNECT

DIGITAL START UP ACTIVITY
Contrasting Two Empires

> Start Up: Contrasting Two Empires

IT'S COMING!

Project the Start Up Activity Ask students to read the quotes as they enter and get settled. Encourage students to reflect on what they learned about the Spanish conquest of the Aztecs and the Inca as they formulate their responses to the questions.

Discuss Based on their answers to the activity questions, encourage students to predict whether relations between the American Indians and the European colonists will remain the same or change. Invite volunteers to support the changes they predict with specific ideas or examples.

Tell students that in this lesson they will be exploring the early Spanish and French colonies in North America and the effects they had on American Indian populations.

Aa Vocabulary Development: Use the Interactive Reading Notepad to preview the Key Terms and Academic Vocabulary in this lesson with students.

⇅ FLIP IT!
Assign the Flipped Video for this lesson.

■ STUDENT EDITION PRINT PAGES 25–33

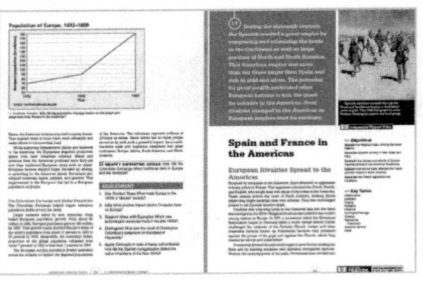

■ INVESTIGATE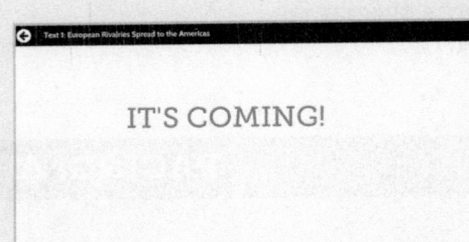

DIGITAL TEXT 1
European Rivalries Spread to the Americas

> Text 1: European Rivalries Spread to the Americas

IT'S COMING!

Objective 1: Explain the religious rivalry among European nations.

Quick Instruction
Digital Map: Protestant and Catholic Division, mid-Sixteenth Century Project the map and invite students to identify the areas under Protestant and Catholic influence. Ensure student understanding of the Protestant Reformation and Martin Luther's role. Explain that Luther and other dissenters became known as Protestants because they protested against the power of the pope and the Church, which they viewed as corrupt and materialistic. Connect religious rivalry to the broader conflict between European nations.

Infer What factors led to the Protestant movement's spread throughout many northern European countries in the 1500s? *(Unlike the Catholic Church, which was unified under the power of the pope, the Protestant movement lacked a central power. Protestants soon divided into many different denominations, including Lutherans, Calvinists, Baptists, Anglicans, and Quakers.)*

Predict Consequences What will be the result of the Catholic-Protestant conflict as it moves from Europe to North America? *(The struggle between the Catholic and Protestant countries will intensify and sharply divide the new world colonies.)*

ELL Use the ELL activity described in the ELL chart.

Further Instruction
Review the issues that divided the nations of Europe during the 1500s. *(With the wealth Spain gained from the Americas, it financed an aggressive military policy in Europe. This led to the European empires fighting for territory. In addition, Protestants challenged the power of the Catholic Church, which divided European nations and even people within nations.)*

Summarize How did the European powers respond to Spain's successes in the Americas? *(Spain's new-found wealth in the Americas motivated other European nations to join the quest for colonies and riches in the Americas. The Dutch, French, and English explored the coast of North America, seeking places where they might establish their own colonies. They also encouraged pirates to rob Spanish treasure ships.)*

Hypothesize Why do you think European nations encouraged pirates and the attacking of Spanish treasure ships? *(Attacking the Spanish ships was much easier and cheaper than establishing colonies in the Americas and acquiring riches through mining and other means.)*

DIGITAL TEXT 2
Governing the Spanish American Empire

Text 2: Governing the Spanish American Empire

IT'S COMING!

DIGITAL TEXT 3
Spanish Explorers Seek Wealth in the North

Text 3: Spanish Explorers Seek Wealth in the North

IT'S COMING!

Objective 2: Describe Spanish society in New Spain and Peru.

Quick Instruction

Digital Image: Spanish Slaves Direct students' attention to the historical illustration and discuss what specific aspects of the illustration suggest about the conquistador's view of the indigenous population. *(Possible responses: Groups of local people carrying supplies for the conquistadors, who rode on horseback, indicate that the conquistadors viewed the inhabitants of the Americas as slaves and inferior.)*

Infer Why did the Spanish think it necessary to construct presidios near the missions? *(The Spanish had to rely on force to control the indigenous populations. They also probably feared uprisings.)*

Use Context Clues How did Spanish friars view American Indian religions? *(The friars obviously did not respect these religions. They forced native populations to surrender their traditions in favor of Christian beliefs. The friars also destroyed temples and sacred images.)*

Further Instruction

Use the Interactive Reading Notepad questions as a springboard to begin a discussion about the political and social structures of New Spain and Peru.

Summarize How did the Spanish maintain control over their American colonies? *(Colonial officials developed a complex system of racial hierarchy known as the castas. Spanish monarchs did not permit elected assemblies in their colonies in order to maintain control over the leadership in New Spain and Peru. To control the viceroys, the Spanish Crown forced them to share power with a Crown-appointed council and an archbishop.)*

Predict Consequences The majority of Spanish colonists were men who generally married Indian women. What effects might this have on preserving the castas system? *(Sample answer: I think the population in New Spain and Peru eventually would become dominated by the mestizos, who would one day overthrow the system to make it more fair.)*

Generate Explanations Why did the Spanish develop carefully planned towns with town halls and churches arranged around a central plaza, and streets set up in grid systems? *(All these features were probably how urban centers were in Spain. This would help introduce and maintain Spanish culture in the Americas.)*

Objective 3: Evaluate the causes and effects of Spanish imperial policies in the American Southwest.

Quick Instruction

Interactive Gallery: Effects of American Silver and Gold on Spanish Economy Project the Interactive Gallery and click on the images to reveal information about the impact of gold and silver on the Spanish economy. Introduce the activity by asking students to identify why cultures value gold and silver. Explain that European economies used coins made from gold and silver as a way to conduct commerce. Point out that the silver and gold mines in the Americas increased Spain's economic strength in the short term but in the long term led to inflation and a weakening of the economy. Ask: what does the golden llama suggest about gold's value? *(It suggests that gold was valued by many diverse cultures because of its physical beauty and properties. But it also shows that cultures valued gold not only for economic reasons but for spiritual reasons as well.)*

Spain and France in the Americas

DIGITAL TEXT 4
Colonization and Conflict in New Mexico

IT'S COMING!

INTERACTIVE GALLERY
Effects of American Silver and Gold on Spanish Economy

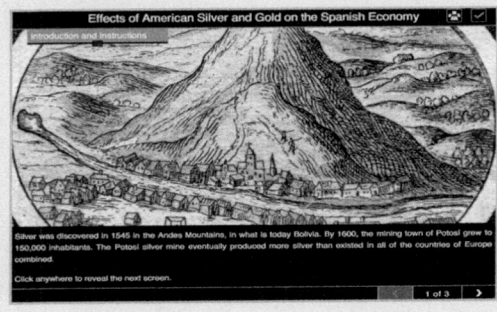

DIGITAL TEXT 5
The French Settle in North America

IT'S COMING!

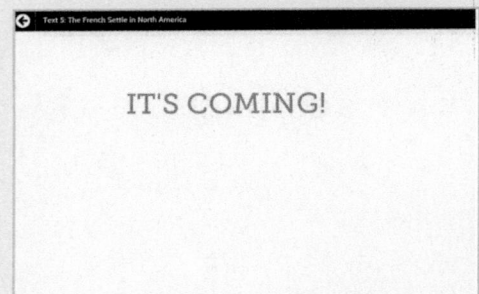

ACTIVE CLASSROOM

Organize students to create a Circle Write. Break students into groups and provide this question as a writing prompt: What role did the search for gold and silver play in the Spanish exploration of the Americas? Have students write as much as they can for one minute then switch with the person on their right. The next person tries to improve or elaborate the response where the other person left off. Continue to switch until the paper comes back to the first person. The group then shares their collective response with the class as a whole.

D Differentiate: Challenge Encourage students to research current uses of gold and silver in today's world, not only for economic purposes but also in technological applications. Have students share their findings with the class.

Further Instruction

Use the Interactive Reading Notepad questions to begin a discussion about the Spanish push north into Florida and New Mexico. Discuss the reasons Hernando de Soto and Francisco Vásquez de Coronado led expeditions into the lands north of Mexico. *(They both were seeking lands rich with gold.)* Ask students to describe the results of these expeditions *(De Soto's search found no gold and the conquistadors massacred American Indian villages, ravaged fields, emptied storehouses, and burned towns. The Spanish also left behind deadly new diseases. Coronado did not find gold after being fooled by the Pueblos. Coronado took revenge on the Pueblos.)*

Infer Why do you think the Spanish attack on the French in Florida was so brutal? *(The Spanish were particularly offended by the presence of French Protestants encroaching on their territories. The Spanish consider the French Protestants as heretics and a threat to their Catholic religion.)*

Draw Conclusions How did the Pueblo Revolt of 1680 affect Spanish-Indian relations? *(Ironically, the revolt somewhat improved relations between the Spanish and the Pueblos. Both groups realized that they had to compromise. The Pueblos accepted Spanish authority, while the Spanish colonists practiced greater restraint. Both groups needed one another for mutual protection against the Apaches.)*

Objective 4: Explain how the fur trade affected the French and the Indians in North America.

Quick Instruction

Infer What do the voyages and goals of explorers working for France in the 1500s tell you about France's opinion of North America? *(France was not convinced that great wealth could be obtained in North America. Many of the French explorers were more interested in finding a Northwest Passage—a water route to Asia.)*

Cite Evidence How did the French and European demand for beaver pelts create hostilities in New France? *(American Indian groups had become dependent on trading with the French and competition among these groups grew significantly. American Indians began hunting in rival groups' lands. This provoked wars between groups. In addition, French traders were pushed to use force as they competed to gain new hunting grounds and to protect what they already had.)*

ELL Use the ELL activity described in the ELL chart.

Further Instruction

Distinguish How did the French conquest of North America differ from that of the Spanish? *(Although the French were obviously keen on exploiting the natural resources in New France, they were not interesting in seizing and taking over lands from the American Indians.)*

DIGITAL TEXT 6

Living in New France

INTERACTIVE CHART

Spanish and French Exploration and Colonization of North America

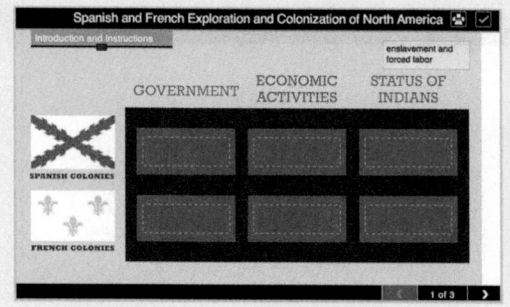

Evaluate Impact How did Samuel de Champlain affect the French relationship with American Indian groups in New France? *(Champlain forged mutually beneficial trade agreements with the Montagnais, Algonquin, and Huron Indians. In return, the Indians expected Champlain to aid them in their wars with their enemies. Champlain's victory over the Iroquois resulted in heightened conflicts with the Iroquois.)*

Generate Explanations What reasons explain why the French Jesuits were not as successful as the Spanish friars in establishing Christianity among the American Indians? *(The French Jesuits did not develop a mission system like the Spanish friars. They also did not use as much force to convert the Indian populations. The Jesuits did not have structured military support like the friars had with the presidios.)*

Objective 5: Describe the French expansion into Louisiana.

Quick Instruction

Interactive Chart: Spanish and French Exploration and Colonization of North America Project the Interactive Chart, and invite students to place the tiles in the correct locations on the chart. As students complete the interactivity, invite them to share their reasons behind their tile selection. Invite volunteers to briefly summarize the descriptions of everyday life in the Spanish and French colonies in North America.

Compare How were the family structures of many French colonists similar to those of Spanish colonists in New Spain? *(Many French colonists, called coureurs de bois, married Indian women. The children of these marriages become known as the metis. These intermarriages created a class of people who were of both French and American Indian descent.)*

🎥 ACTIVE CLASSROOM

Direct students to have a Conversation with History. Ask students to imagine that they are having a conversation with a metis or mestizo. Students should write down a question they would like to ask, then what that person would say to them, and what they would say in response.

Further Instruction

Begin a discussion about the founding of Louisiana. Be sure students understand the role of Robert de La Salle. Invite volunteers to describe de La Salle's purpose in exploring the Mississippi River and the significance of his journey. *(De La Salle was hoping to find a Northwest Passage to the Pacific. Instead, he found the Gulf of Mexico. La Salle claimed the territory around the Mississippi River basin for France, naming it Louisiana, in honor of King Louis XIV.)*

Infer What strategic challenges might the French encounter by maintaining two colonies in North America, one in the north and the other far south on the Gulf of Mexico? *(The colonies were so far apart that defending them and coordinating governance would be difficult.)*

Hypothesize Which country, Spain or France, has the best chance of sustaining the colonies in the Americas? Use specific evidence to support your answer. *(Sample answer: I think the French colonies will be more successful. The geography and natural resources of New France can better support the colony in the long run. In addition, the French built better relationships with the Indian populations.)*

Spain and France in the Americas

■ SYNTHESIZE

DIGITAL ACTIVITY
Establishing New Colonies

IT'S COMING!

Discuss Before students begin their lists and descriptions, lead the class in a brief review of the chronology of Spanish and French colonization of North America. When students have completed the activity, ask if they think Spanish and French leaders would reconsider the actions they took, and if so, what would they have done differently to prevent the issues or problems from developing.

■ DEMONSTRATE

DIGITAL QUIZ
Lesson Quiz and Class Discussion Board

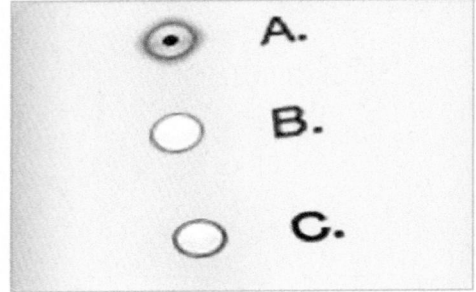

Assign the online Lesson Quiz for this lesson if you haven't already done so. Students will be offered automatic remediation or enrichment based on their score.

Pose these questions to the class on the Discussion Board:

In *Spain and France in the Americas,* you read about how Spain's successful explorations in the Americas motivated other European nations, including France, to join the quest for colonies in the Americas. The political, social, and religious rivalries raging in Europe emerged in the Americas as European empires vied for territory in the new world.

Generate Explanations Why do you think so many Spanish and French citizens were willing to leave behind their lives in Europe to start new lives in the colonies of North America?

Draw Conclusions How did the Spanish and French colonies in North America affect the American Indian populations and cultures?

Topic Inquiry
Have students continue their investigations for the Topic Inquiry.

America's Cultural Roots

■ SYNTHESIZE

DIGITAL ACTIVITY
America's Cultural Roots

Ask students to reflect on the Essential Question for the topic: How much does geography affect people's lives? Remind students of the discussions and ideas they considered at the beginning of the topic.

Ask students if what they wrote down in the Essential Question activity is comparable to what they learned in the lessons. Ask, "How do the ways geography affects your lives differ from the ways geography affected the lives of the peoples of the Americas, Africans, and early European colonists? How were they the same?" Post students' responses on the Class Discussion Board.

Next ask students to reflect on the topic as a whole. Before students create their graphic organizers, have them jot down 1-3 questions they've thought about during the topic. Share these examples if students need help getting started:

- How did the original peoples of the Americas use natural resources to their benefit?
- How did the geography of South America, Mexico, and the American Southwest help and hinder Spain's colonization plans?
- How did European colonists adapt to varied geographic regions?

You may ask students to share their questions and answers on the Class Discussion Board.

Topic Inquiry
Have students complete Step 3 of the Topic Inquiry.

■ DEMONSTRATE

DIGITAL TOPIC REVIEW AND ASSESSMENT
America's Cultural Roots

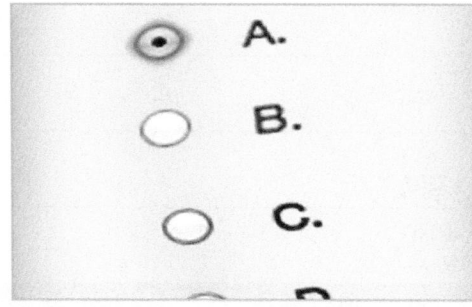

Students can prepare for the Topic Test by answering the questions in the Topic Review and Assessment online. They can also prepare by reviewing their answers to the Interactive Reading Notepad questions or reviewing their notes in the Reading and Notetaking Study Guide.

DIGITAL TOPIC TEST
America's Cultural Roots

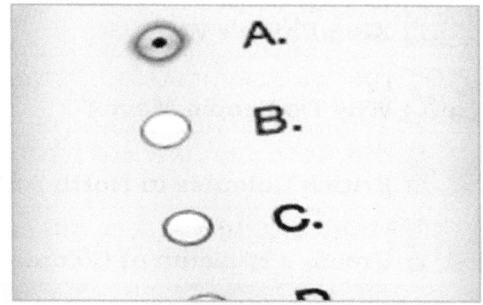

TOPIC TEST
Assign the Topic Test to assess students' understanding of topic content.

BENCHMARK TESTS
Assign these benchmark tests as you complete the relevant topics to monitor student progress toward mastering the course content and as preparation for the End-of-Course Test.

Benchmark Test 1: Topics 1–3
Benchmark Test 2: Topics 4–6
Benchmark Test 3: Topics 7–9
Benchmark Test 4: Topics 10–12
Benchmark Test 5: Topics 13–15
Benchmark Test 6: Topics 16–18
Benchmark Test 7: Topics 19–20

England's American Colonies

TOPIC 2 ORGANIZER	PACING: APPROX. 9 PERIODS, 4.5 BLOCKS
	PACING
Connect	1 period
MY STORY VIDEO **King Philip's War**	10 min.
DIGITAL ESSENTIAL QUESTION ACTIVITY **Why Do People Move?**	10 min.
DIGITAL OVERVIEW ACTIVITY **British Colonies in North America, 1750**	10 min.
TOPIC INQUIRY: PROJECT-BASED LEARNING **Create a Museum of Colonial History**	20 min.
Investigate	3–6 periods
TOPIC INQUIRY: PROJECT-BASED LEARNING **Create a Museum of Colonial History**	Ongoing
LESSON 1 The Southern Colonies Take Root	30–40 min.
LESSON 2 New Lives in New England	30–40 min.
LESSON 3 The Middle Colonies Thrive	30–40 min.
LESSON 4 Immigration and Slavery in the Colonies	30–40 min.
LESSON 5 Economic and Social Life in the Colonies	30–40 min.
LESSON 6 Creating an American Identity	30–40 min.
Synthesize	1 period
DIGITAL ACTIVITY **Reflect on the Essential Question and Topic**	10 min.
TOPIC INQUIRY: PROJECT-BASED LEARNING **Create a Museum of Colonial History**	20 min.
Demonstrate	1–2 periods
DIGITAL TOPIC REVIEW AND ASSESSMENT **England's American Colonies**	10 min.
TOPIC INQUIRY: PROJECT-BASED LEARNING **Create a Museum of Colonial History**	20 min.

TOPIC INQUIRY: PROJECT-BASED LEARNING

Create a Museum of Colonial History

In this Topic Inquiry, students create a media presentation of select images with captions to introduce a new Museum of Colonial History to the public. Students will explore the three regions of the colonial era to deepen their understanding of how people lived in and adapted to their environments in early colonial history. Students will then choose artifacts to represent aspects of life and society in each colonial region and write captions explaining the social significance of each artifact.

STEP 1: CONNECT
Develop Questions and Plan the Investigation

Launch the Project and Generate Questions

Display the letter from Zebulon Rolfe of the Museum of Colonial History. Tell students that for their project, each team will research colonial life in each region and then create a media presentation from images of artifacts or illustrations. Each image will have a caption that describes not only how the object represents some aspect of colonial life in that region but also how it was used to help the colonists adapt to their environment. Share the questions with students and ask them to think about which artifacts might represent colonial life.

Suggestion: To provide extra support, have students restate the goal of the project in their own words. Brainstorm specific examples of artifacts used in colonial America to prompt student thinking.

Plan the Investigation

Organize the class into teams and assign each team a region. Have students sign the Project Contract. Have students prepare by beginning the Need-to-Know Questions while keeping the Guiding Question—How do people live in and adapt to new places?—in mind.

Discuss Review the questions that guide students in breaking down the Guiding Question: How do people live in and adapt to new places? Point out that this process of breaking down a question into smaller ones will be useful for them as they complete this project but is a skill that will help them throughout their academic and professional careers.

Resources
- Project Launch
- Project Contract
- Student Instructions
- Information Organizer
- Project Tracker

STEP 2: INVESTIGATE
Apply Disciplinary Concepts and Tools

Research Your Colonial Region

Students will now commence their research. Begin by directing students to review the relevant Skills Tutorials. Remind students to keep track of their work in the Project Tracker as they continue to use the Need-to-Know Questions to guide their work. Discuss as a class or meet with groups individually to review the characteristics of each colonial region. Ensure that groups are familiarized with the colonies included in their regions.

Discuss Before having groups begin their research, explain that they should locate more information than they will need to complete their project. That way, they will be able to choose the artifacts that are most compelling, complementary, and suitable for presenting through a variety of visual means.

Suggestion: Review applicable Internet use rules before students commence their research.

Resources
- Rubric for Presenting the Museum of Colonial History

⏻ PROFESSIONAL DEVELOPMENT

Project-Based Learning
Be sure to view the Project-Based Learning Professional Development resources in the online course.

Create a Museum of Colonial History *(continued)*

STEP 3: SYNTHESIZE
Evaluate Sources and Use Evidence to Formulate Conclusions

Write Your Captions

Having acquired a variety of artifacts and information about the economic, social, and political significance of the colonial artifacts, students must now decide how best to present the information. Remind students that each caption must explain the social, political, or economic significance of each artifact. Review the following criteria:

- Answers the Guiding Question
- Explains at least two significant social, political, or economic aspects of life related to the creation of the object or its use

Groups should now write their captions. Clarify any questions students may have.

Create Your Presentation

In this step, groups must decide how best to present their artifacts and captions. The Student Instructions suggestions include a digital portfolio or a simple trifold with printed images or illustrations and typed captions. Emphasize to groups that if they choose to create a trifold they need to ensure that the organization of information on it is clear and legible.

Suggestion: Preview and explore the Prezi (www.prezi.com) digital tool as a resource for students to create a digital portfolio.

Encourage students to engage in peer reviews of one another's writing. Remind students to offer detailed, constructive criticism of one another's work.

STEP 4: DEMONSTRATE
Communicate Conclusions and Take Informed Action

Present Your Artifacts

Have students present their portfolios to the class or an invited audience. To help students structure their presentations, give them a time limit and have them use a clock to monitor their delivery.

Suggestion: Give groups time in class to practice their presentations and solicit feedback about how to improve their deliveries.

Reflect on the Project

Conclude by reviewing the project and eliciting students' answers to these questions: What went well? What could be improved upon? What are three lessons you have learned from this project?

Resources
- Team/Peer Assessment

INTRODUCTION

England's American Colonies

England successfully established permanent colonies in North America starting in the first few decades of the 1600s. Differences in geography and patterns of settlement between the colonies encouraged regional social and economic differences to develop. Geography, economic activities, and culture interacted to create distinct regional identities. A multitude of ethnic and racial groups arrived, establishing a diversity of religious practices, social customs, and cultural traditions. In the 1700s, an American identity was emerging, shaped by new philosophical discussions about the right of individuals that would affect religion and politics throughout the colonies.

CONNECT

MY STORY VIDEO
King Philip's War

Watch a video about King Philip's war.

Check Understanding Why did the Wampanoag people start King Philip's War? *(They resented the encroachments on their land by English settlers.)*

Hypothesize Given the outcome of the war, should the Wampanoag have chosen some other way to voice their frustrations? If so, what? *(Students may offer suggestions about calling for conferences with the English settlers. Some, however, may decide that the Wampanoag had no other options than to fight.)*

DIGITAL ESSENTIAL QUESTION ACTIVITY
Why Do People Move?

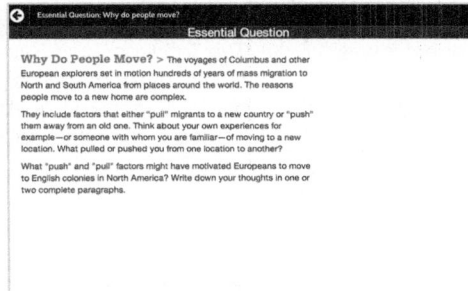

Ask students to think about the Essential Question for this Topic: Why do people move? Complex issues "pushed" many Europeans away from their homelands in search of more fulfilling lives. Other factors "pulled" some Europeans toward new places.

Identify Central Issues What types of push factors force people to move places today? *(famine, war, government unrest, lack of jobs or opportunities, weather or geographic disasters)* What types of pull factors draw people to new places today? *(employment opportunities, families, money, land)*

Identify Cause and Effect How does moving to a new place change people? *(People often have to adopt new customs, languages, and lifestyles.)* How do they change the locations to which they move? *(Many people who move bring elements of their cultures with them, which creates a mixture of cultures. Sometimes migrating people affect populations and the environment.)*

DIGITAL OVERVIEW ACTIVITY
British Colonies in North America, 1750

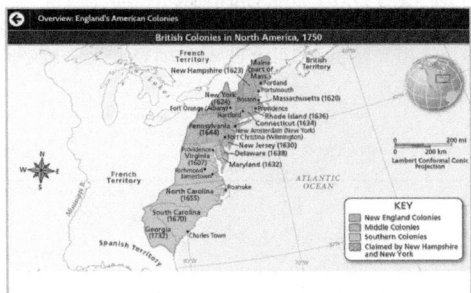

Display the map showing the borders of English colonies in North America in 1750. Explain that in this topic students will examine the geographic, social, and economic factors that shaped England's North American colonies. The topic will also explore the early peoples who made the colonies home and the ways in which they adapted to the conditions in each region.

D Differentiate: Extra Support Highlight key settlements in each colony. Invite volunteers to identify regions and cities on the map with which they are familiar.

Analyze Maps Based on what you know of climate and weather patterns in North America, what challenges might people in New England face to establish a thriving colony? *(New England is farther north than most other colonies. People will have to deal with a colder climate, which will affect what crops can be grown and what industries can develop.)*

Topic Inquiry
Launch the Topic Inquiry with students after introducing the Topic.

The Southern Colonies Take Root

Supporting English Language Learners

Use with the reading, **England Establishes Colonies in North America.**

Use simple spoken language to summarize the first four paragraphs of the text, placing emphasis on the following new expressions: stagnant economy, generate new wealth, obtain a charter.

Beginning Use simple language to explain the meaning of each of these expressions. Then ask students to use the words to complete the following sentence frames: When we get a certificate of permission, we _____. A _____ is an economy that is not growing. Workers raising plantation crops would _____.

Intermediate Pause after each of the new expressions to explain its meaning. In groups of three, assign one expression to each student. Have them take turns using the expression in a sentence about the English colonies.

Advanced Ask partners to talk about the meaning of the new expressions. Give students a few minutes to prepare a short speech using all three expressions. Then partners take turns presenting their speeches.

Advanced High Ask partners to talk about the meaning of the new expressions. Have partners talk about the charter obtained from the king and what it allowed the British to do. Talk about whether or not it was successful.

Use with the reading, **Early Challenges in Jamestown.**

Explain to students they will use their own experiences to help them understand the motivation of colonists to work their own land.

Beginning Use simple spoken language to summarize the section titled *The Tobacco Crop Saves Jamestown.* Point out that the Virginia Company let the colonists own the land they worked. Ask: Do you work harder when you gain something from the work you do? Do you think that because the colonists owned the land, they would work harder to grow the crops?

Intermediate Use simple spoken language to summarize the section titled *The Tobacco Crop Saves Jamestown.* Ask students to think about what makes them work harder. Ask: Do you think that the colonists worked harder because they owned the land? Why?

Advanced Use spoken language to summarize the section titled *The Tobacco Crop Saves Jamestown.* Ask partners to talk about what the Virginia Company did to save the colony. Prompt students to discuss their own experiences with work to help them understand the colonists' motivation.

Advanced High Use spoken language to summarize the section titled *The Tobacco Crop Saves Jamestown.* Ask partners to think about their own experiences to help them understand the owners' motivation to work hard. Have them talk about why this motivation was not enough for the company to make a profit.

◘ Differentiate Instruction

Use the Differentiated Instruction notes throughout the lesson plan to support the varied skill sets, levels of readiness, and interests in the mixed-ability classroom.

Challenge These notes include suggestions for expanding the activity for advanced students.

On-Level These notes include suggestions for modifying the activity to address different interests or learning styles.

Extra Support These notes include ideas for providing more scaffolding or reading support.

Special Needs These notes provide ideas for adapting instruction to support the needs of various special needs students.

■ NOTES

Objectives

Objective 1: Explain why England wanted colonies and how they were planned.

Objective 2: Describe how Jamestown was settled, why the colony struggled, and how it survived.

Objective 3: Explain the relationship between American Indians and settlers in the Southern Colonies.

Objective 4: Discuss how Maryland, the Carolinas, and Georgia were settled.

LESSON 1 ORGANIZER		PACING: APPROX. 1 PERIOD, .5 BLOCKS			
				RESOURCES	
		OBJECTIVES	**PACING**	**Online**	**Print**
Connect					
DIGITAL START UP ACTIVITY **Analyze Maps**			5 min.	●	
Investigate					
DIGITAL TEXT 1 **England Establishes Colonies in North America**		Objective 1	10 min.	●	●
DIGITAL TEXT 2 **Early Challenges in Jamestown**		Objective 2	10 min.	●	●
INTERACTIVE GALLERY **Problems Faced by Jamestown**			10 min.	●	
DIGITAL TEXT 3 **Expansion in Virginia Creates Conflict**		Objective 3	10 min.	●	●
DIGITAL TEXT 4 **England Expands Its Southern Colonies**		Objective 4	10 min.	●	●
INTERACTIVE GALLERY **James Oglethorpe and the Founding of Georgia**			10 min.	●	
Synthesize					
DIGITAL ACTIVITY **Sequence Key Events**			5 min.	●	
Demonstrate					
DIGITAL QUIZ **Lesson Quiz and Class Discussion Board**			10 min.	●	

The Southern Colonies Take Root

■ CONNECT

DIGITAL START UP ACTIVITY
Analyze Maps

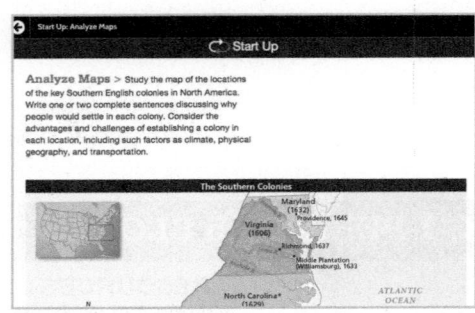

Project the Start Up Activity Have students complete the activity as they enter. Call on volunteers to share their ideas with the class. Be sure to draw attention to bodies of water and point out the lines of latitude on the map and explain that many English colonies were located within latitudes associated with temperate climate patterns that support crops.

Discuss Why might colonists have settled near the Atlantic coast? What advantage did other bodies of water, especially rivers, offer colonists?

Tell students that they will learn about the first English colonies established in North America. They will explore the reasons why colonists left Europe and settled certain areas. They will also take a closer look at how colonists interacted with American Indians.

Aa Vocabulary Development: Use the Interactive Reading Notepad to preview the Key Terms and Academic Vocabulary in this lesson with students.

↡ FLIP IT!
Assign the Flipped Video for this lesson.

■ STUDENT EDITION PRINT PAGES: 38–43

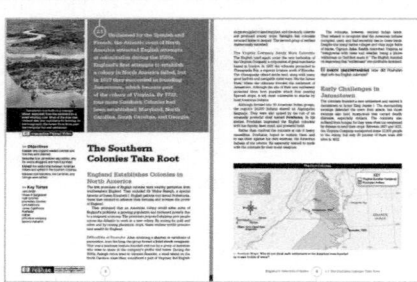

■ INVESTIGATE

DIGITAL TEXT 1
England Establishes Colonies in North America

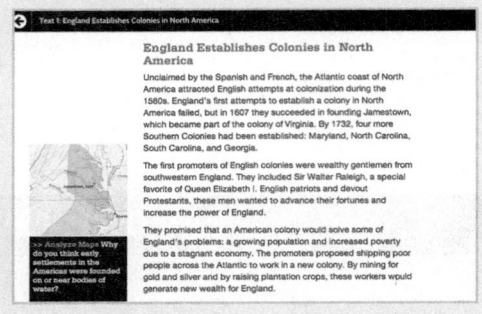

Objective 1: Explain why England wanted colonies and how they were planned.

Quick Instruction

Check Understanding Why did England want to start colonies in North America? *(to alleviate England's problems of overpopulation and poverty, to increase trade and wealth, to expand English power, to gain more resources)*

Make Inferences What benefit did potential colonists stand to gain from plans to send them to North America to farm and mine? *(They were leaving behind impoverished conditions in England for the potential of greater economic opportunity in North American colonies.)*

D Differentiate: Extra Support Add the key words *charter* and *joint-stock company* on the class Word Wall. Point out that the root word of *charter* comes from the Old French, meaning "letter, document, or agreement." The word *stock* refers to a sum of money, or an investment. Have students write and share definitions for the two terms. Then, challenge them to write a sentence in which they use both words to show meaning and relationship.

ELL Use the ELL activity described in the ELL chart.

Further Instruction
Have students work in small groups to complete the Interactive Reading Notepad questions. Review their answers as a class. Be sure students understand that the motivation behind establishment of Roanoke and Jamestown was largely economic.

Draw Conclusions Why would investors contribute money to joint-stock companies to found colonies? *(They contributed only a part of the money so they were not risking all of their wealth. Also, they were promised a share of the wealth that the colonies produced. Spanish and French colonies had generated great wealth so it probably seemed like a good risk likely to return more than it cost.)*

Identify Central Issues What key point of conflict existed between English colonists and American Indians? *(English colonists considered undeveloped land to be wilderness open to farming and production. American Indians considered these lands theirs. They had ancestral ties to the lands and used the lands for hunting and other needs.)*

www.PearsonRealize.com
Access your Digital Lesson

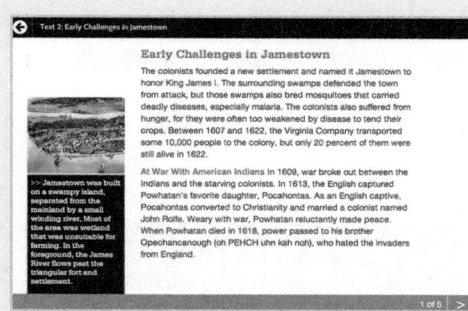

DIGITAL TEXT 2

Early Challenges in Jamestown

DIGITAL TEXT 3

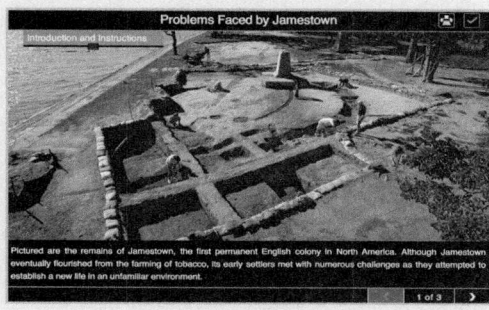

INTERACTIVE GALLERY

Problems Faced by Jamestown

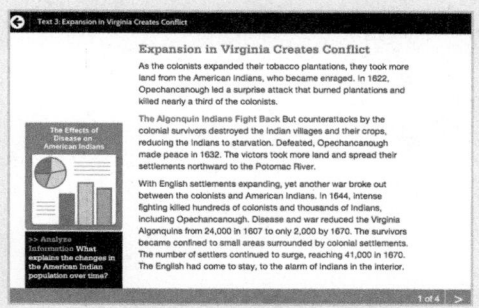

Expansion in Virginia Creates Conflict

Objective 2: Describe how Jamestown was settled, why the colony struggled, and how it survived.

Quick Instruction

Interactive Gallery: Problems Faced by Jamestown To begin, ask students to predict what challenges colonists might have faced in establishing the colony at Jamestown. Call on volunteers to share their ideas. Project the Interactive Gallery and click through the images. How did the geography of Jamestown both help and hurt colonists? *(The location on the river made it easy to come and go, and provided some protection against attack. However, the wetlands also encouraged the spread of disease, and it proved more difficult to farm than the colonists had anticipated.)*

ACTIVE CLASSROOM

Organize students into small groups and project the image of the fort at Jamestown in the Interactive Gallery. Have students use A Closer Look strategy to investigate the image. Use a whiteboard tool to divide the image into four numbered quadrants. Tell each student in a group to examine one quadrant. Instruct them to write down answers to the following questions: 1. What does this part of the image tell you about life in Jamestown? 2. What does this make you wonder about Jamestown? 3. How might you find out an answer to your questions? If time allows, invite each group to share some of their responses with the class, or post them on the class blog.

D Differentiate: **Challenge** Assign student groups to investigate the structure and processes of government in the Jamestown colony. Have them research the workings of the House of Burgesses. Instruct them to use what they learned to prepare a slideshow or an infographic display in which they illustrate and describe how the House worked and what it did.

ELL Use the ELL activity described in the ELL chart.

Further Instruction

Analyze Information Why might the English crown have decided to take over the Virginia colony in 1624? *(By then, the colony was well established, and the colonists were having success raising and trading tobacco. The colony was becoming prosperous. The crown might have thought it advantageous to take control of the colony in order to reap more reward from its productivity.)*

Draw Conclusions What does the success of tobacco farming and the distribution of free land suggest about the economy of the Virginia colony? *(The colony was largely agrarian, or dependent on agriculture and the trade in agricultural goods.)*

Apply Concepts What precedent did the House of Burgesses establish in the English colonies? *(The House of Burgesses established a precedent for local self-rule and representative government.)*

Objective 3: Explain the relationship between American Indians and settlers in the Southern Colonies.

Quick Instruction

Read aloud the statement by Governor William Berkeley: "I thank God, there are no free schools nor printing [in Virginia], and I hope we shall not have these [for a] hundred years; for learning has brought disobedience and heresy . . . into the world, and printing has divulged [spread] them, and libels [untruths] against the best government. God keep us from both!" Ask students to consider the statement. Have them Think-Pair-Share what the statement means. You may want to encourage them to break up the statement into parts and paraphrase those meanings. Discuss their responses.

Analyze Primary Sources In the statement above, what does William Berkeley really fear? *(public education and the spread of ideas through a free press)*

Evaluate Information Was Governor Berkeley justified in trying to prevent Bacon's Rebellion? Why or why not? *(Answers will vary. Students may argue that Berkeley was justified in trying to prevent greater violence and conflict with American Indians in order to save lives and protect the colony.)*

The Southern Colonies Take Root

DIGITAL TEXT 4
England Expands Its Southern Colonies

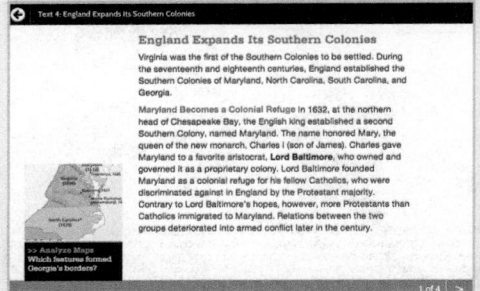

INTERACTIVE GALLERY
James Oglethorpe and the Founding of Georgia

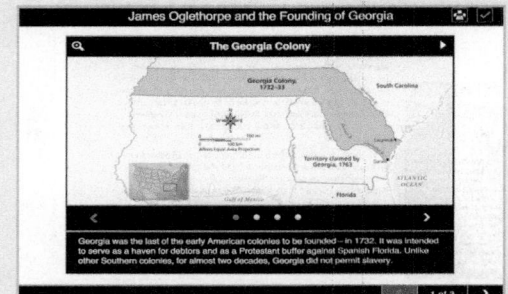

Further Instruction

Compare Study the chart about the effects of disease on American Indians. How is the fate of these American Indians similar to the fate of early colonists in Jamestown? *(Early colonists died from illness and disease spread in the wetlands of the Jamestown colony. Their bodies were not prepared to fight off these illnesses. Likewise, American Indians were not prepared for the diseases carried by colonists from Europe. Once infected, many died.)*

Objective 4: Discuss how Maryland, the Carolinas, and Georgia were settled.

Quick Instruction

Interactive Gallery: James Oglethorpe and the Founding of Georgia Project the Interactive Gallery and click through the images. Call attention to the Landing at Savannah. Ask students to write three to five sentences in which they describe the settlement. Ask: How does the Landing at Savannah show the allotment of land and homes to colonists? *The land and home allotments appear to be the same in size and relatively uniform. Each house looks about the same and sits on a long tract of land.)* What does this suggest about the society and economy of the colony? *(This suggests that the colony was fairly equitable in its land distribution and that the colonists likely farmed their plots of land.)* Based on this image, what does Savannah have in common with Jamestown? *(It was settled on a river and is surrounded by forested land.)*

Contrast In what ways did each Southern Colony have a distinct identity? *(Each colony was settled by different groups of people for different purposes. The Virginia Colony began as a commercial farming venture. Maryland began as a refuge for Catholics, though many Protestants settled there. The Carolinas also began as commercial colonies for farming and trade. George started out as a colony for English debtors as well as other poor workers and artisans and religious refugees. The leader of the Georgia colony, James Oglethorpe, envisioned an egalitarian society and enacted strict laws.)*

📷 ACTIVE CLASSROOM

Tell students to use the Take a Stand strategy to write a statement by James Oglethorpe. Assign some students to write a statement to the English king to persuade him to permit Oglethorpe to found the colony of Georgia. Assign other students to write a statement to English citizens to encourage them to join the colony. In each statement, Oglethorpe should argue his position and cite reasons to support his case. Have students present their statements to the class or post them on the class discussion board.

Further Instruction

Hypothesize Why do you think Carolinians rejected rule by the proprietors in favor of rule by the Crown? *(Most of the colonists were probably farmers and workers. They likely lacked the great wealth of the proprietors. They probably resented having their lives controlled by a wealthy minority and may have hoped for fairer treatment by the crown and royal governors, especially as they had elected assemblies, similar to Virginia.)*

Synthesize Why do you think Lord Baltimore and James Oglethorpe both failed to achieve their colonial visions? *(Their visions were narrow, and their colonies were changing at a rate beyond their control. Many people came to the colonies, and Baltimore and Oglethorpe could not hope to impose their ideas on all of the people that settled in their lands, at least not long term without greater authority than they appear to have possessed.)*

■ SYNTHESIZE

DIGITAL ACTIVITY

Sequence Key Events

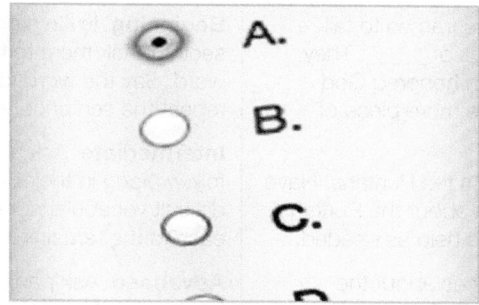

Project the Digital Activity Instruct students to work in pairs to brainstorm events and to list them in a sequence graphic organizer. Then, combine pairs into small groups to share and discuss their work. Encourage students to make revisions to their graphic organizers. Call on each group to share one of their charts with the class, and display completed charts in the classroom.

Discuss If the Jamestown colony had failed, as Roanoke had, do you think the English would have tried again to establish colonies? Why or why not?

■ DEMONSTRATE

DIGITAL QUIZ

Lesson Quiz and Class Discussion Board

Assign the online Lesson Quiz for this lesson if you haven't already done so. Students will be offered automatic remediation or enrichment based on their score.

Pose these questions to the class on the Discussion Board:

In *The Southern Colonies Take Root,* you learned about the first English colonies in the land that would become the United States. You explored how the Southern Colonies, in particular, were settled and examined the relationship between colonists and American Indians.

Analyze Information What economic benefits did the colonies offer to England and the crown?

Summarize For what reasons did people settle in the Southern Colonies?

Topic Inquiry

Have students continue their investigations for the Topic Inquiry.

New Lives in New England

Supporting English Language Learners

Use with the reading, **Disagreement with the Church of England.**

Read aloud the section titled *Puritan Beliefs and Values*. Read slowly so students can follow along in their books. Pause to explain difficult vocabulary or concepts.

Beginning Ask partners to use the following sentence frames to talk about the Puritans: The Puritans followed the teachings of _____. They valued _____, diligence, and _____. They believed men honored God by _____. Challenge them to work together to add one more piece of information about the Puritans.

Intermediate Ask small groups of students to discuss the Puritans. Have each student in the group take a turn to share an idea about the Puritans' beliefs and lifestyle. Other group members can provide help as needed.

Advanced Ask students to write two or three sentences about the Puritans and their beliefs. Then have partners take turns sharing the information. Finally, have partners work together to add any additional information that was not included in their sentences.

Advanced High Ask students to read the section silently and take notes about the Puritans. Encourage them to prepare a short presentation about the Puritans and their beliefs. Then have students form a group and take turns presenting their ideas to others in the group. Group members should ask questions to clarify information and add any information they think is needed.

Use with the reading, **English Relationships with American Indians.**

Read aloud the section titled *The Pequot War*. Ask students to follow along in their book. Tell students that this pre-reading will help prepare them to read the section again independently.

Beginning Invite students to take turns reading sentences from the section. Ask them to raise their hand when they come across an unfamiliar word. Say the word for them and clarify the meaning. Then have them repeat the sentence and continue reading.

Intermediate Ask a student to read aloud the first paragraph while others follow along in their book. Then answer any questions students have about difficult vocabulary or concepts. Repeat this with different students reading each of the remaining paragraphs.

Advanced Ask partners to take turns reading the section aloud. Encourage them to ask each other questions about pronunciation, word meaning, and content during and after the reading. Have them ask you any questions that they are not able to answer themselves.

Advanced High Ask students to read the section silently and jot down any questions they have about pronunciation, word meaning, and content. Then students can work with a partner to help answer the questions. Encourage students to use a dictionary to look up any words or pronunciations that are unfamiliar.

▶ Differentiate Instruction

Use the Differentiated Instruction notes throughout the lesson plan to support the varied skill sets, levels of readiness, and interests in the mixed-ability classroom.

Challenge These notes include suggestions for expanding the activity for advanced students.

On-Level These notes include suggestions for modifying the activity to address different interests or learning styles.

Extra Support These notes include ideas for providing more scaffolding or reading support.

Special Needs These notes provide ideas for adapting instruction to support the needs of various special needs students.

■ NOTES

PEARSON ●●●
realize ™
www.PearsonRealize.com

Go online to access additional resources including:
Primary Sources • Biographies • Supreme Court cases •
21st Century Skill Tutorials • Maps • Graphic Organizers.

Objectives

Objective 1: Explain why some Puritans left England.

Objective 2: Describe the Puritan colony in Massachusetts and explain why Rhode Island, Connecticut, and New Hampshire were founded.

Objective 3: Analyze the relationship between New Englanders and American Indians.

LESSON 2 ORGANIZER	PACING: APPROX. 1 PERIOD, .5 BLOCKS			
			RESOURCES	
	OBJECTIVES	PACING	Online	Print
Connect				
DIGITAL START UP ACTIVITY **The Pilgrims Contemplate Self-Government**		5 min.	●	
Investigate				
DIGITAL TEXT 1 **Disagreement With the Church of England**	Objective 1	10 min.	●	●
INTERACTIVE GALLERY **Puritan Values and Society**		10 min.	●	
DIGITAL TEXT 2 **Puritans Arrive in North America**	Objective 2	10 min.	●	●
3-D MODEL **Plymouth Plantation**		10 min.	●	
DIGITAL TEXT 3 **English Relationships With American Indians**	Objective 3	10 min.	●	●
INTERACTIVE CHART **Colonial Conflicts in New England**		10 min.	●	
Synthesize				
DIGITAL ACTIVITY **The Decision to Move to New England**		5 min.	●	
Demonstrate				
DIGITAL QUIZ **Lesson Quiz and Class Discussion Board**		10 min.	●	

Topic ② Lesson 2

New Lives in New England

■ CONNECT

DIGITAL START UP ACTIVITY
The Pilgrims Contemplate Self-Government

Project the Start Up Activity Instruct students to read the quotation and answer the questions as they enter and get settled.

Discuss What purpose did Robinson think government should fulfill? *(promote the common good)* What does he think the Pilgrims should do to accomplish that purpose? *(select leaders who will promote the common good, show them honor and obedience according to the law)* How does his suggestion reflect the idea of representative government? *(encourages them to select leaders and to choose the leaders who will run government on their behalf)*

Tell students that they will learn why some Puritans left England and about the colonies they founded. They will also examine the relationship between these colonists and American Indians.

Aa Vocabulary Development: Use the Interactive Reading Notepad to preview the Key Terms and Academic Vocabulary in this lesson with students.

⇅ FLIP IT!
Assign the Flipped Video for this lesson.

■ STUDENT EDITION PRINT PAGES: 44–49

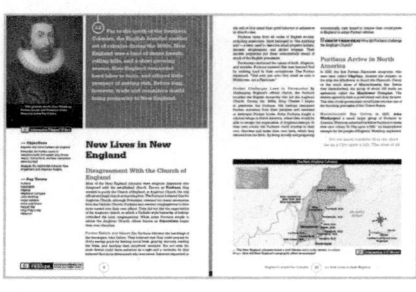

■ INVESTIGATE

DIGITAL TEXT 1
Disagreement With the Church of England

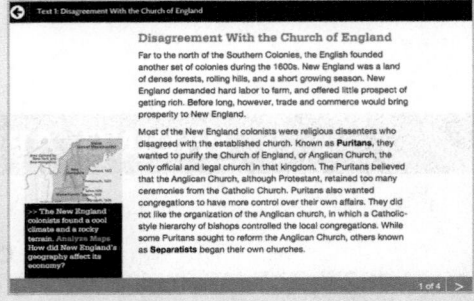

INTERACTIVE GALLERY
Puritan Values and Society

Objective 1: Explain why some Puritans left England.

Quick Instruction
Interactive Gallery: Puritan Values and Society Project the Interactive Gallery and click through the slides. Prompt students to consider what values they can infer from the images. Ask: How did Puritan values likely shape their colony? *(Puritan values emphasized hard work, order, community, and education. These values probably encouraged Puritans to work hard at their trades and to work together for one another's benefit. They probably encouraged Puritans to focus on order in society, fairness, and schooling.)*

Infer How might Puritan values have contributed to a sense of community in the New England colonies? *(These values probably would have helped keep Puritan colonies together. They would have strengthened a sense of responsibility for oneself and others, and encouraged individual hard work for the greater good of the colony.)*

👥 ACTIVE CLASSROOM
Organize students into small groups and assign each group one of the images that depicts Puritan activity in the Interactive Gallery. Tell students to use the If Images Could Talk strategy to analyze the image and write two or three sentences in which they imagine what a central person in their image is saying. Students should support their sentences with specific evidence from the text.

D Differentiate: Extra Support Display a series of sentences to help students distinguish between Puritans, Separatists, and Anglicans, as shown below. Have students work with a partner to identify specific evidence from the text that correctly completes each sentence.

- Separatists are *like* Puritans because _____.
- Separatists are *unlike* Puritans because _____.
- Puritans are *like* Anglicans because _____.
- Puritans are *unlike* Anglicans because _____.

ELL Use the ELL activity described in the ELL chart.

Further Instruction
Explain that the word *pilgrim* means "one who journeys in foreign lands." It comes from a Latin word meaning "foreigner." The Separatists chose to call themselves pilgrims based on a bible verse that reads, in part, "[T]hey were strangers and pilgrims on the earth." Prompt students to discuss why the Pilgrims adopted that name for themselves. Emphasize that Pilgrims were Separatist Puritans. You may wish to add the three terms—Puritan, Separatist, and Anglican—to the Word Wall.

Explain How did starting a colony in New England benefit the Puritans and the Separatists? *(They could escape the persecution of the Anglican Church. They could worship in their own churches and make their own laws according to their beliefs.)*

Draw Conclusions Why would the English crown permit the Puritans and Separatists to settle colonies? *(Sending religious dissenters to the colonies removed them from England without resorting to further acts of persecution and violence. It removed agitators and dissenters without provoking more domestic trouble.)*

DIGITAL TEXT 2

Puritans Arrive in North America

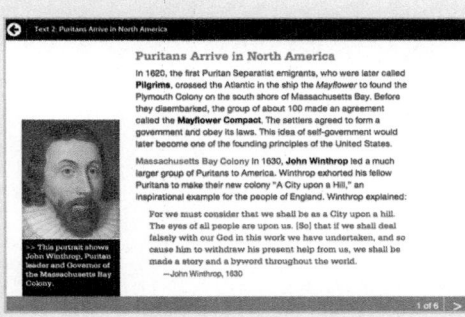

3-D MODEL

Plymouth Plantation

DIGITAL TEXT 3

English Relationships With American Indians

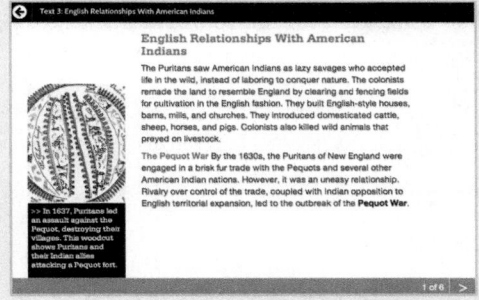

Objective 2: Describe the Puritans' colony in Massachusetts and explain why Rhode Island, Connecticut, and New Hampshire were founded.

Quick Instruction

Read aloud the quote from John Winthrop: "For we must consider that we shall be as a City upon a hill. The eyes of all people are upon us. [So] that if we shall deal falsely with our God in this work we have undertaken, and so cause him to withdraw his present help from us, we shall be made a story and a byword throughout the world." What does this statement tell you about the purpose and the culture of the Massachusetts Bay Colony? *(The Puritans established their colony as a religious haven only for their own people and believers. It indicates that they felt that they had a divine mandate, and they meant to shape their colony according to their religious beliefs, mores, and tenets. It implies a sense of distinction between the Massachusetts Bay Colony and other communities.)*

Determine Relevance What significant political precedent did Massachusetts establish? *(Massachusetts settlers established a republic in which Puritan men elected not only their assembly members but also their governor and deputy governor.)*

ACTIVE CLASSROOM

Conduct a My Metaphor activity. Give students the following prompt so they can create a metaphor based on the content of a key asset in the 3-D model. Rotate the 3-D model for students to view from different perspectives: This image shows that _____ is like _____ because _____.

Further Instruction

Direct student pairs to read the text and answer the Interactive Reading Notepad questions. Then, call on students to share their responses. If time allows, organize students into groups to complete Primary Sources: Mayflower Compact. Be sure that students understand that the Separatists, or Pilgrims, who founded Plymouth Colony and the Puritans who founded Massachusetts Bay Colony were two distinct groups.

Identify Central Issues What social and political precedent did Rhode Island set? *(Rhode Island set a precedence for religious liberty and toleration. Its colonial government established a precedent for the separation of church and state.)*

Make Inferences What does the Puritans' treatment of Anne Hutchinson suggest about the status of women in New England society? *(Women were not treated as equals and had little to no role in government.)*

Objective 3: Analyze the relationship between New Englanders and American Indians.

Quick Instruction

Begin by displaying the image of the Puritan assault on the Pequot. Ask students to predict what they will learn about in this text. Then, ask them to predict what circumstances led to conflict among New England colonists and American Indians. Have them share their ideas.

Interactive Chart: Colonial Conflicts in New England Project the Interactive Chart and work through the causes and effects of conflict with American Indians. Why did the colonists feel entitled to claim land already inhabited by American Indians? *(New England colonists, especially the Puritans, felt an inherent superiority over the American Indians. They did not think that the American Indians were civilized or that they were using the land to its proper potential.)*

Draw Conclusions Why might American Indians have resisted conversion to Christianity and settlement in prayer towns? *(American Indians had an established history rooted in the land, with their own beliefs, languages, ways of life, and customs. Many probably resented the colonists' conversion efforts in light of the conflict between the two groups.)*

New Lives in New England

INTERACTIVE CHART

Colonial Conflicts in New England

	Colonial Conflicts in New England		
Introduction and Instructions			
	CAUSES	SHORT-TERM EFFECTS	LONG-TERM EFFECTS
PEQUOT WAR 1636			
KING PHILIPS' WAR 1675			
About 3,000 American Indians killed			
	Check Answers		1 of 3 ❯

💬 ACTIVE CLASSROOM

Organize students into small groups. Have them use the Circle Write strategy to answer the following question: How did the circumstances and outcomes of the Pequot War and King Philip's War shape future relations between American Indians and English colonists? When student groups have completed their responses, have them select part of their response to share with the class. Post completed writings on the class blog or discussion board.

ELL Use the ELL activity described in the ELL chart.

Further Instruction

Write the following words and phrases on the board: *Puritans, land, trade, farming, Pequots,* and *King Philip's War*. Tell students to watch for the these words and their significance as they read the text. Then, have students work through the text and answer the Interactive Reading Notepad questions with a partner.

Identify Main Idea and Details Using the words written on the board, summarize the main idea of the text and explain it with supporting details. *(The Puritans and American Indians, such as the Pequots, had very different ways of life and expectations of their relations with each other. These differences led to conflict over land and trade, and eventually, to war. The colonists wanted to settle more and more land for economic activity such as* farming. American Indians did not want to give up more of their ancestral lands. This led first to the Pequot War and then to King Philip's War. After these wars, the colonists seized most American Indian lands in New England.)

Make Inferences Why did Puritans think missionary work among American Indians was worthwhile? *(Many Puritans thought that they were teaching the American Indians a better way of life and saving their souls as well. The Puritans probably thought that they were demonstrating kindness by showing the American Indians what they considered correct religious beliefs and way to live.)*

■ SYNTHESIZE

DIGITAL ACTIVITY
The Decision to Move to New England

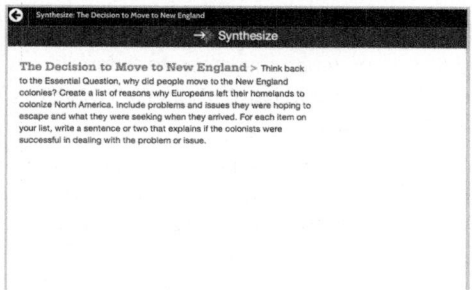

Project the digital activity Instruct students to work individually to brainstorm lists of reasons why Europeans came to colonize North America. Then, tell students to share their reasons with a partner. Have student pairs write a sentence in response to each item on their lists. Call on pairs to share one or two of their ideas.

Discuss Do you think that most colonists made a good decision in going to North America? Why or why not?

■ DEMONSTRATE

DIGITAL QUIZ
Lesson Quiz and Class Discussion Board

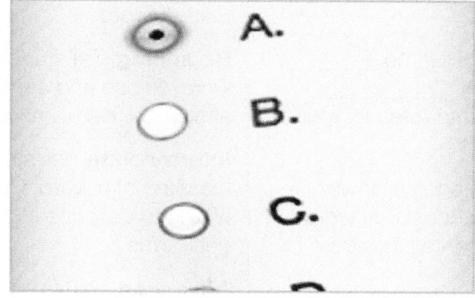

Assign the online Lesson Quiz for this lesson if you haven't already done so. Students will be offered automatic remediation or enrichment based on their score.

Pose these questions to the class on the Discussion Board:

In *New Lives in New England,* you explored the causes and effects of English colonization of the New England colonies. You examined reasons that colonists established the colonies as well as the challenges that they faced. You also explored colonists' relations with American Indians.

Compare and Contrast What similarities and differences existed between the motivations of the Separatists, Puritans, and Anglicans to colonize North America?

Integrate Information If you were a New England colonist, how might you have advised others to deal with American Indians?

Topic Inquiry
Have students continue their investigations for the Topic Inquiry.

The Middle Colonies Thrive

Supporting English Language Learners

Use with the reading, **New Netherland and Its Neighbors.**

Use simple spoken language to summarize the section titled *Diversity in New Netherland Thrives*. Tell students that they will demonstrate listening comprehension of your summary by taking notes. Pause often to give students time to jot down notes.

Beginning Write the following cloze notes as a bulleted list: no _____ assembly; tolerated various _____ groups; colonists from _____, _____, and _____ ; most colonists _____ or _____. Have students listen to your summary and use what they hear to complete the notes.

Intermediate Ask students to listen to the information and jot down notes about the most important information. Notes can consist of words or short phrases. When you have finished, choose students at random to read their notes aloud.

Advanced Ask students to listen to the information and jot down notes about the most important information. Notes can consist of short and long phrases. If needed, ask students to raise their hand to ask you to pause longer so they can write their notes. Then choose volunteers to read their notes aloud.

Advanced High Ask students to listen to the information and jot down notes about the most important information. When you have finished summarizing, ask students to partner. Have partners take turns using their notes to retell the information in the text.

Use with the reading, **Religious Toleration in Pennsylvania.**

Read aloud the section titled *Quaker Beliefs and Values*. Explain to students that they can request assistance, use non-verbal cues, and convey ideas by defining or describing when they do not know the exact English word.

Beginning Tell students to raise their hand when they hear an unfamiliar word. Pause and say the word slowly and clearly. Have students repeat it after you. Then continue reading the passage.

Intermediate Tell students to raise their hand when they do not know the meaning of a word. Pause and provide a simple definition or use simple words to describe it. Ask: Did the Quakers allow other faiths? Did Quakers bear arms?

Advanced Pause after reading the sentence *the Quakers sought an 'Inner Light' to understand the Bible.* Ask partners to discuss what they think the phrase *Inner Light* means. Have them use other words to define or describe what the expression means.

Advanced High Ask students to take turns retelling the information in the section to less proficient classmates. Encourage them to use simple language in place of words like *tolerated, pacifists,* and *Inner Light.*

▣ Differentiate Instruction

Use the Differentiated Instruction notes throughout the lesson plan to support the varied skill sets, levels of readiness, and interests in the mixed-ability classroom.

Challenge These notes include suggestions for expanding the activity for advanced students.

On-Level These notes include suggestions for modifying the activity to address different interests or learning styles.

Extra Support These notes include ideas for providing more scaffolding or reading support.

Special Needs These notes provide ideas for adapting instruction to support the needs of various special needs students.

■ NOTES

PEARSON
realize™
www.PearsonRealize.com

Go online to access additional resources including:
Primary Sources • Biographies • Supreme Court cases •
21st Century Skill Tutorials • Maps • Graphic Organizers.

Objectives

Objective 1: Explain how Dutch New Netherland became English New York.

Objective 2: Describe William Penn's relationship with the American Indians in Pennsylvania.

Objective 3: Compare and contrast the Pennsylvania Colony with other colonies.

Objective 4: Analyze the importance of religious and ethnic diversity in the Middle Colonies.

LESSON 3 ORGANIZER		PACING: APPROX. 1 PERIOD, .5 BLOCKS			
				RESOURCES	
		OBJECTIVES	**PACING**	**Online**	**Print**
Connect					
DIGITAL START UP ACTIVITY **The Purchase of Manhattan**			5 min.	●	
Investigate					
DIGITAL TEXT 1 **New Netherland and Its Neighbors**		Objective 1	10 min.	●	●
DIGITAL TEXT 2 **Religious Toleration in Pennsylvania**		Objective 2	10 min.	●	●
INTERACTIVE GALLERY **The Middle Colonies**			10 min.	●	
Synthesize					
DIGITAL ACTIVITY **Compare and Contrast the Southern, Middle, and New England Colonies**			5 min.	●	
Demonstrate					
DIGITAL QUIZ **Lesson Quiz and Class Discussion Board**			10 min.	●	

The Middle Colonies Thrive

■ CONNECT

DIGITAL START UP ACTIVITY
The Purchase of Manhattan

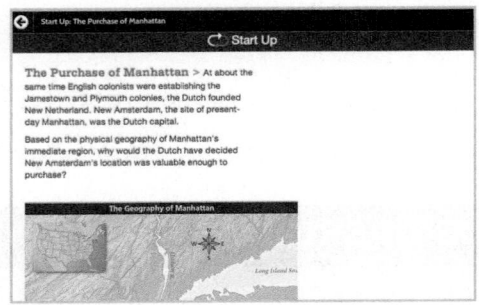

Project the Start Up Activity Have students study the map and answer the question as they enter and get settled. Ask students to share their responses with the class.

Discuss Why would the Dutch want to establish colonies in North America located so close to the English colonies? *Like other nations, they hoped to profit from land, resources, and trade in North America. They might have found this to be a promising location because of its geographic advantages.)*

Tell students that they will explain how the Dutch and Swedes established colonies in North America. They will also examine the relations of colonists with American Indians and will take a closer look at the politics, religion, and economic activity of the region.

Aa Vocabulary Development: Use the Interactive Reading Notepad to preview the Key Terms and Academic Vocabulary in this lesson with students.

ℕ FLIP IT!
Assign the Flipped Video for this lesson.

■ STUDENT EDITION PRINT PAGES: 50–54

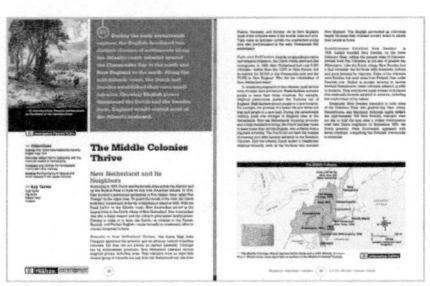

■ INVESTIGATE

DIGITAL TEXT 1
New Netherland and Its Neighbors

Objective 1: Explain how Dutch New Netherland became English New York.

Quick Instruction
Display a T-chart on the board labeled "push factors" and "pull factors." Discuss the factors that motivated the English to establish colonies in North America.

Contrast How did the colonizers of New Netherland and New Sweden differ from the English colonists to the north and south? *(The Dutch and the Swedes were fewer in number. They generally did not have the same motivations to leave their homelands as many English did. The Dutch and the Swedes were mostly interested in commercial enterprises. They wanted to farm and trade with American Indians for furs. They did not establish representative governments, but they did extend religious tolerance to colonists.)*

ELL Use the ELL activity described in the ELL chart.

Further Instruction
Work through the text and the Interactive Reading Notepad with students, as a class. Be sure that students understand that New Amsterdam, on Manhattan Island, became New York City and New Netherland became New York. Today, Manhattan Island remains a part of New York City. Be sure that they understand, too, that most of New Sweden became Delaware.

Draw Conclusions Why did England benefit from control of the Atlantic Coast? *(England could largely control shipping to and from North America and could dominate trade. It better enabled them to protect and expand their colonies in North America.)*

Hypothesize For what reasons did the Dutch not go to greater lengths to hold onto New Netherland? *(The Dutch might have lacked the naval and other military resources of the English. They might not have had the money or weapons to defend the colony or fight a war. They also might have lacked the will to go to war to retain the colony, as most of the Dutch people did not seem motivated to settle in the colony.)*

DIGITAL TEXT 2
Religious Toleration in Pennsylvania

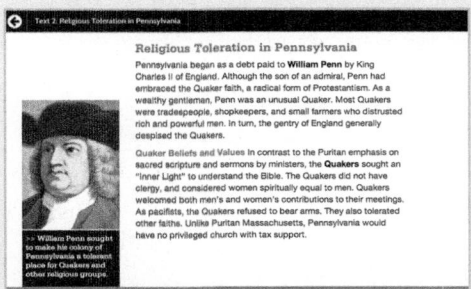

INTERACTIVE GALLERY
The Middle Colonies

Objective 2: Describe William Penn's relationship with the American Indians in Pennsylvania.

Quick Instruction

Interactive Gallery: The Middle Colonies
Project the Interactive Gallery and click through the images. What characteristics distinguished the Middle Colonies from other colonial regions? *(mostly middle class settlers in a colony with no dominant religious or ethnic group and a great degree of religious toleration, as well as a low level of conflict with American Indians)*

📷 ACTIVE CLASSROOM

Pose the question: What was life like in the Middle Colonies? Then, have students take a sheet of paper and fold it into quarters. Tell them to use the Write-1-Get-3 Strategy to answer the question and solicit their classmates' responses. When students have finished the exercises, discuss what they have learned.

ELL Use the ELL activity described in the ELL chart.

Further Instruction

Interpret In what ways was the "City of Brotherly Love" an appropriate name for Philadelphia? *(The name reflected the religious and ethnic diversity of the colony and the welcome it extended to a variety of people of different backgrounds to come and join the colony. It also reflected the pacifist nature of the Quakers and the inclination of colonists in Pennsylvania to avoid conflict with American Indians.)*

Determine Relevance What impact did the Middle Colonies have on the culture and politics of the English colonies as a whole? *(The Middle Colonies set a standard for tolerance, diversity, and peaceful relations that over time would influence people in other colonies. In particular, the Middle Colonies' pluralism would influence later principles regarding religious freedom and cultural diversity.)*

The Middle Colonies Thrive

▌ SYNTHESIZE

DIGITAL ACTIVITY
Compare and Contrast the Southern, Middle, and New England Colonies

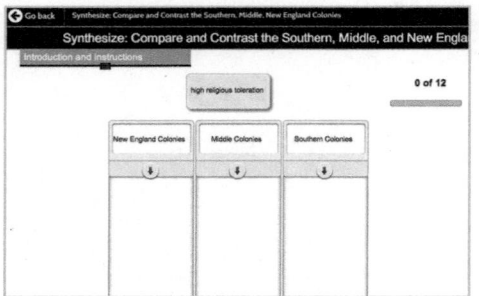

Project the Interactive Chart Have students work in small groups to complete the activity. Then, call on each group to share their ideas with the class.

💬 ACTIVE CLASSROOM

Conduct a Circle Write activity. Break students into small groups to focus on this writing prompt: How did physical geography affect the economy of each region? Have students write as much as they can for one minute then switch with the person on their right. The next person tries to improve or elaborate the response where the other person left off. Continue to switch until the paper comes back to the first person. Ask groups to share their responses with the rest of the class.

Discuss What advantages did each set of colonies have? How did each set of colonies contribute to the success of the whole?

▌ DEMONSTRATE

DIGITAL QUIZ
Lesson Quiz and Class Discussion Board

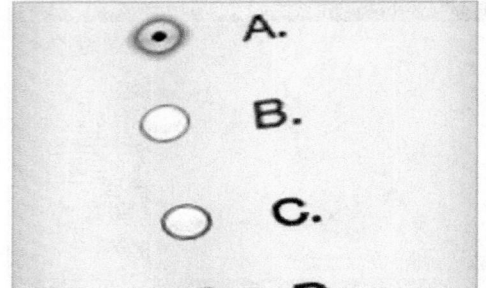

Assign the online Lesson Quiz for this lesson if you haven't already done so. Students will be offered automatic remediation or enrichment based on their score.

Pose these questions to the class on the Discussion Board:

In *The Middle Colonies Thrive,* you learned about the establishment of New Netherland and New Sweden, and you read about how these colonies came to be ruled by England. You also examined the founding of Pennsylvania and other Middle Colonies and identified characteristics that distinguished the Middle Colonies from other English colonies.

Support Ideas with Evidence What evidence supports the idea that religious and ethnic diversity thrived in the Middle Colonies?

Connect What relationship exists between the Middle Colonies' economy and the physical geography of the region?

Topic Inquiry
Have students continue their investigations for the Topic Inquiry.

Immigration and Slavery in the Colonies

Supporting English Language Learners

Use with the reading, **Immigrants Populate the Colonies.**

Read aloud the section titled *Immigrants from England*. Tell students to write down any unfamiliar words they hear as you read.

Beginning Select difficult words from the text, such as *indentured servants.* Teach the meanings using images, dramatization, and other visual methods. Then reread the text and ask students to recall the meanings of these and other words as you read them.

Intermediate Have students read the text with a partner. Tell students to use a print or online dictionary to look up the meanings of any unfamiliar words.

Advanced Ask partners to share the lists of unfamiliar words that they wrote as you read the section aloud. Provide students with one- or two-word definitions or have them use a thesaurus to look up any words they cannot define.

Advanced High Ask partners to share the lists of unfamiliar words they wrote. Encourage them to work together to define all of the words. Have them ask you for assistance as needed.

Use with the reading, **Africans in the American Colonies.**

Read aloud the section titled *Slavery Varies*. As students listen, ask them to look at the picture of the African slaves in the Southern Colonies working in the fields to see how it supports the information in the text.

Beginning Ask partners to use what they learned from listening to the text and looking at the picture to help them summarize the information: In the Southern Colonies, enslaved Africans worked _____. They raised _____, _____, _____, and _____. A white _____ supervised the enslaved Africans and _____ those who resisted.

Intermediate Ask students to use what they learned from listening to the text and looking at the picture to respond to the following simple questions about slavery in the Southern Colonies: What work did the enslaved Africans in the Southern Colonies do? Who supervised their work? What happened if the enslaved Africans resisted?

Advanced Ask partners to use what they learned from listening to the text and looking at the picture to take turns retelling basic information about the life and work of enslaved Africans in the Southern Colonies.

Advanced High Ask partners to look carefully at the image of the enslaved Africans working in the field. Encourage them to use the details in the image to talk about the work enslaved Africans did in the fields and how they were treated.

ⓓ Differentiate Instruction

Use the Differentiated Instruction notes throughout the lesson plan to support the varied skill sets, levels of readiness, and interests in the mixed-ability classroom.

Challenge These notes include suggestions for expanding the activity for advanced students.

On-Level These notes include suggestions for modifying the activity to address different interests or learning styles.

Extra Support These notes include ideas for providing more scaffolding or reading support.

Special Needs These notes provide ideas for adapting instruction to support the needs of various special needs students.

◼ NOTES

Immigration and Slavery in the Colonies

Objectives

Objective 1: Explain how European immigration to the colonies changed between the late 1600s and 1700s.

Objective 2: Analyze the development of slavery in the colonies.

Objective 3: Describe the experience of enslaved Africans in the colonies.

LESSON 4 ORGANIZER	PACING: APPROX. 1 PERIOD, .5 BLOCKS				
				RESOURCES	
		OBJECTIVES	PACING	Online	Print
Connect					
DIGITAL START UP ACTIVITY **Indentured Servants**			5 min.	●	
Investigate					
DIGITAL TEXT 1 **Immigrants Populate the Colonies**		Objective 1	10 min.	●	●
INTERACTIVE MAP **Diversity of the 13 Colonies**			10 min.	●	
DIGITAL TEXT 2 **Enslaved Africans Provide Labor**		Objective 2	10 min.	●	●
DIGITAL TEXT 3 **Africans in the American Colonies**		Objective 3	10 min.	●	●
INTERACTIVE GALLERY **Africans Become African Americans**			10 min.	●	
Synthesize					
DIGITAL ACTIVITY **Diversity in the Colonies**			5 min.	●	
Demonstrate					
DIGITAL QUIZ **Lesson Quiz and Class Discussion Board**			10 min.	●	

PEARSON
realize™
www.PearsonRealize.com

Go online to access additional resources including:
Primary Sources • Biographies • Supreme Court cases •
21st Century Skill Tutorials • Maps • Graphic Organizers.

CONNECT

DIGITAL START UP ACTIVITY
Indentured Servants

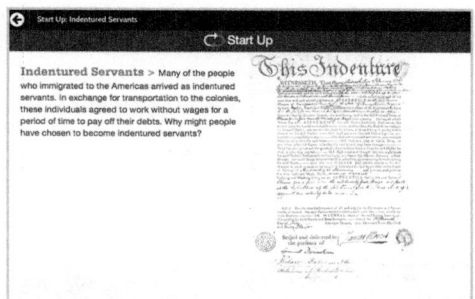

Project the Start Up Activity Have students answer the question as they enter and get settled.

Discuss What does the existence of indentured servitude in the colonies suggest about conditions in Europe at the time? *(Indentured servitude suggests that economic and social conditions in Europe were poor. People must have had strong motivation to leave Europe and emigrate to the colonies under the terms of indentured servitude.)*

Tell students that in this lesson they will investigate the way in which European immigration to the colonies changed between the late 1600s and 1700s. They will also learn how enslaved Africans came to the colonies.

Aa Vocabulary Development: Use the Interactive Reading Notepad to preview the Key Terms and Academic Vocabulary in this lesson with students.

↺ FLIP IT!
Assign the Flipped Video for this lesson.

STUDENT EDITION PRINT PAGES: 55–59

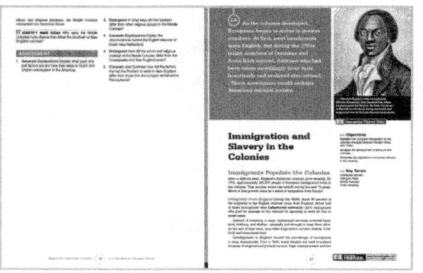

INVESTIGATE

DIGITAL TEXT 1
Immigrants Populate the Colonies

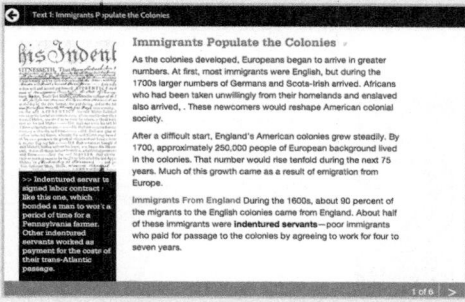

INTERACTIVE MAP
Diversity of the 13 Colonies

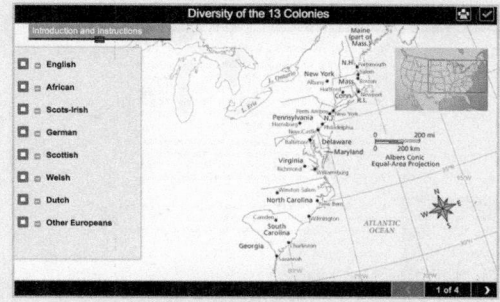

Objective 1: **Explain how European immigration to the colonies changed between the late 1600s and 1700s.**

Quick Instruction

Interactive Map: Diversity of the 13 Colonies Project the Interactive Map and click through the layers one at a time. Then, display all of the layers at once and call on volunteers to answer the questions. Ask: Why are the areas labeled *African,* largely in the South? *(Because southern plantations had the greatest need for the labor of enslaved Africans.)*

📖 ACTIVE CLASSROOM

Organize students into pairs. Have the first student give the second a verbal "tour" of the Interactive Map in which he or she explains what it *shows.* Have the second student give the first an explanation of what it *means.*

D Differentiate: Extra Support Highlight numerical figures in the text. Point out that by 1700, 250,000 Europeans lived in the colonies. Then, point out that 250,000 Scots-Irish came to the colonies during the 1700s. Prompt students to understand that the population more than doubled because the Scots-Irish were not the only people to emigrate to the colonies in the 1700s. Many more people, of English, German, African and other heritages, came, too.

ELL Use the ELL activity described in the ELL chart.

Further Instruction

To help students navigate the text and the Interactive Map, draw a chart with columns labeled "English," "Scots-Irish," "Germans," "Welsh," "Africans," "Dutch," and "Swedes and French." As they move through the text and the map, have students record details about why each group of people came to the colonies, where they settled, and what they did there. Encourage students to share their completed charts. You may wish to let partners provide feedback to revise their charts.

Connect How did the union of England, Scotland, and Wales as Great Britain affect the colonies? *(It changed the demographics of the people moving to the colonies. After the formation of Great Britain, more Scottish immigrants came to the colonies.)*

Hypothesize How might you expect the new groups of colonists to interact with the old, and why? *(The Middle Colonies were known for greater tolerance, so they would have been more welcoming to the new groups of Scots-Irish, Welsh, and Germans. New England would have been relatively less welcoming. Different groups of colonists likely would have lived together because of cultural, religious, and language differences.)*

Immigration and Slavery in the Colonies

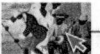

DIGITAL TEXT 2

Enslaved Africans Provide Labor

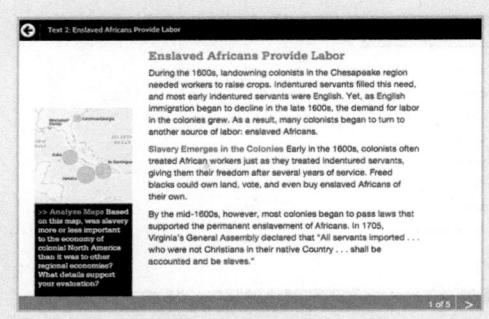

DIGITAL TEXT 3

Africans in the American Colonies

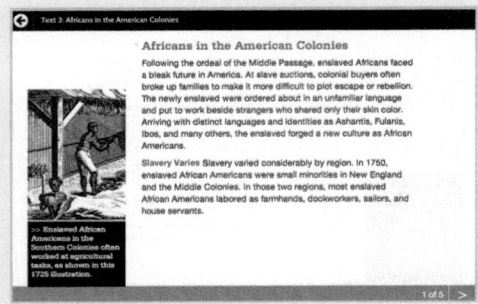

INTERACTIVE GALLERY

Africans Become African Americans

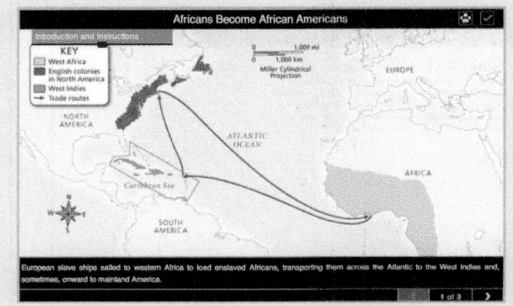

Objective 2: Analyze the development of slavery in the colonies.

Quick Instruction

Read aloud the statement from the Virginia General Assembly: "All servants imported . . . who were not Christians in their native Country . . . shall be accounted and be slaves." Prompt students to paraphrase this statement in their own words and discuss its meaning.

Make Inferences What does the deck plan of a slave ship suggest about how enslaved Africans were treated? *(It suggests that enslaved Africans were treated as little more than trade goods.)* How does the General Assembly statement reinforce this inference? *(It shows that English colonists did not consider enslaved Africans to be people equal to the colonists because they were not considered civilized.)*

Further Instruction

Explain Use the key words *Middle Passage* and *triangular trade* to explain the expansion of the slave trade. *(The enslavement of Africans contributed to the development of triangular trade, which in turn encouraged the expansion of the slave trade and the transport of enslaved Africans on the Middle Passage across the Atlantic Ocean.)*

Analyze Primary Sources Reread the quotation by Alexander Falconbridge. What does this statement suggest about the enslaved Africans' response toward enslavement and the Middle Passage? *(It suggests that at least some enslaved Africans would rather have died from lack of nourishment than have suffered slavery and endured the Middle Passage.)*

Objective 3: Describe the experience of enslaved Africans in the colonies.

Quick Instruction

Interactive Gallery: Africans Become African Americans Project the Interactive Gallery and click on the images.

Analyze Primary Sources Reread the quote by Mary Prince. What does this statement tell you about the life of many enslaved persons on a plantation? *(It shows that enslaved persons faced great hardship. Their life was defined by work, and the work was difficult, long, and dangerous. They suffered from injury and illness, had little time to themselves, had little food, and spent the bulk of their days in the fields.)* What does it reveal about the ways in which colonial masters viewed enslaved Africans? *(White colonial masters viewed enslaved Africans as little more than animals harnessed for their labor. They worked their slaves tirelessly, showed them little consideration, and appear to have made little to no effort to protect them against illness and injury.)*

Draw Conclusions What impact did the use of enslaved Africans have on the Southern Colonies' economy? *(Enslaved Africans did most of the labor on southern farms, especially large plantations. They were the driving force behind the production of cash crops, such as tobacco, sugar, rice, and indigo. Plantation owners spent money to purchase enslaved Africans but spent little to house and feed them. Much of the Southern Colonies' economic success was probably due to enslaved Africans' work.)*

🖳 ACTIVE CLASSROOM

Have students reflect on the images in the Interactive Gallery as they use the Quick Write strategy to respond to this prompt: Describe the experience of enslaved Africans in the colonies. Then, ask them to share their work with a partner. Have partners provide feedback and instruct students to make revisions as needed. Finally, post students' writings on the class blog.

ELL Use the ELL activity described in the ELL chart.

Further Instruction

To extend the lesson, have students read Primary Sources: *Olaudah Equiano, The Interesting Narrative of the Life of Olaudah Equiano,* and prompt students to connect the story to the larger context of the lesson.

Support Ideas with Examples What examples from the text indicate that enslaved African Americans created a unique culture in North America? *(Enslaved African Americans carried their own cultures and traditions with them to North America. A unique culture developed when they adopted elements of European culture. For example, some blended African religious traditions with the Christianity practiced by their masters.)*

Explain How did feigning ignorance and working slowly amount to a subtle form of rebellion? *(Slaves had few choices and little power. Slow work slowed the productivity of the plantations and lessened profits, however little. Withholding some of their skill and intelligence and labor was a form of defiance that likely gave them some sense of power in a largely powerless situation.)*

SYNTHESIZE

DIGITAL ACTIVITY

Diversity in the Colonies

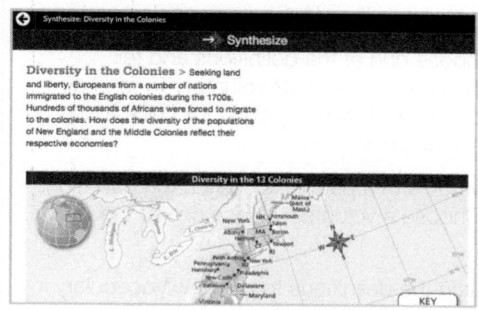

Project the Digital Activity Tell students to work in pairs to brainstorm and answer the question. Then, combine pairs into groups and have them discuss and revise their responses. Call on each group to share one response.

Discuss How did African slavery bolster the economy of the Middle and Southern Colonies?

DEMONSTRATE

DIGITAL QUIZ

Lesson Quiz and Class Discussion Board

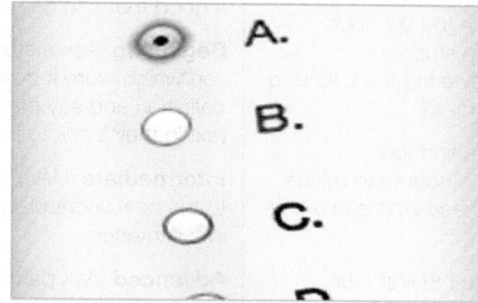

Assign the online Lesson Quiz for this lesson if you haven't already done so. Students will be offered automatic remediation or enrichment based on their score.

Pose these questions to the class on the Discussion Board:

In *Immigration and Slavery in the Colonies,* you investigated the changing demographics of immigrants to the English colonies and examined the introduction of African slavery to North America.

Analyze Information What cultural impact did immigration and the importation of enslaved Africans have on the English colonies in North America?

Hypothesize How might the United States be different today without the acceptance of diversity that was established in colonial times?

Topic Inquiry

Have students continue their investigations for the Topic Inquiry.

Economic and Social Life in the Colonies

Supporting English Language Learners

Use with the reading, **England and Its Colonial Economy.**

Explain to students that you will speak to them about mercantilism and the British Economy. Begin by discussing the meaning of the word *mercantilism*.

Beginning Use simple spoken language to summarize the first four paragraphs of *England and Its Colonial Economy*. Have students demonstrate comprehension of the information by answering the following question: What benefits did England gain from its colonies?

Intermediate Use spoken language to summarize the first four paragraphs of *England and Its Colonial Economy*. Ask students to define the words *monarchs* and *rivals*. Then have them use these words in a few sentences to talk about the policy of mercantilism.

Advanced Use more complex language to summarize the first four paragraphs of *England and Its Colonial Economy*. Ask partners to talk about the policy of mercantilism and how the empire could build wealth in the form of silver or gold.

Advanced High Read aloud the first four paragraphs of *England and Its Colonial Economy*. Ask students to write a few sentences describing mercantilism and why it was so successful in the colonial economy.

Use with the reading, **Regional Economic Differences.**

Read aloud the text, pausing after the following words: commodities, lumber, stagnated, staple crop. Use a few simple words to define or describe each of these difficult words. Write these definitions on the board: a good that can be sold, wood, stopped growing, crops people need.

Beginning Ask a student to choose one of the definitions and tell you which word it describes. Then choose another volunteer to read a definition and say the new word. Tell students they can look back at the text in their book to help them find the new word.

Intermediate Have students work with a partner to match the definitions to the new vocabulary words. Choose a volunteer to use one of the words in a sentence.

Advanced Ask partners to match the definitions to the new vocabulary words. Challenge them to use each of the words in a sentence. The context of the sentences should come from the text.

Advanced High Ask students to work individually to match the definitions to the new vocabulary words. Challenge them to use each word in a sentence. Encourage them to use the words in a context other than the one in the text.

◱ Differentiate Instruction

Use the Differentiated Instruction notes throughout the lesson plan to support the varied skill sets, levels of readiness, and interests in the mixed-ability classroom.

Challenge These notes include suggestions for expanding the activity for advanced students.

On-Level These notes include suggestions for modifying the activity to address different interests or learning styles.

Extra Support These notes include ideas for providing more scaffolding or reading support.

Special Needs These notes provide ideas for adapting instruction to support the needs of various special needs students.

■ NOTES

PEARSON
realize™
www.PearsonRealize.com

Go online to access additional resources including:
Primary Sources • Biographies • Supreme Court cases •
21st Century Skill Tutorials • Maps • Graphic Organizers.

Objectives

Objective 1: Analyze the economic relationship between England and its colonies.

Objective 2: Explain the impact of geography on the economies of the New England, Middle, and Southern colonies.

Objective 3: Compare and contrast differences in the social structure of the three major colonial regions.

LESSON 5 ORGANIZER		PACING: APPROX. 1 PERIOD, .5 BLOCKS		
	OBJECTIVES	PACING	RESOURCES Online	Print
Connect				
DIGITAL START UP ACTIVITY **Paul Revere, Silversmith**		5 min.	●	
Investigate				
DIGITAL TEXT 1 **England and Its Colonial Economy**	Objective 1	10 min.	●	●
DIGITAL TEXT 2 **Regional Economic Differences**	Objective 2	10 min.	●	●
INTERACTIVE MAP **Comparing the English Colonies**		10 min.	●	
DIGITAL TEXT 3 **Regional Social Differences**	Objective 3	10 min.	●	●
INTERACTIVE GALLERY **A New Kind of Society**		10 min.	●	
Synthesize				
DIGITAL ACTIVITY **Comparing Regional Cultures**		5 min.	●	
Demonstrate				
DIGITAL QUIZ **Lesson Quiz and Class Discussion Board**		10 min.	●	

Economic and Social Life in the Colonies

■ CONNECT

DIGITAL START UP ACTIVITY
Paul Revere, Silversmith

Project the Start-Up Activity Ask students to answer the questions as they enter and get settled.

Discuss Invite volunteers to discuss what new information they learned about Paul Revere. Ask: What information surprised or impressed you? Why?

Tell students that in this lesson they will be learning about the economic relationship between England its colonies, the economic impact of physical geography on the colonies, and the similarities and differences in social structure between the three regions developing in North America.

Aa Vocabulary Development: Use the Interactive Reading Notepad to preview the Key Terms and Academic Vocabulary in this lesson with students.

⇅ FLIP IT!

Assign the Flipped Video for this lesson.

■ STUDENT EDITION PRINT PAGES: 60–66

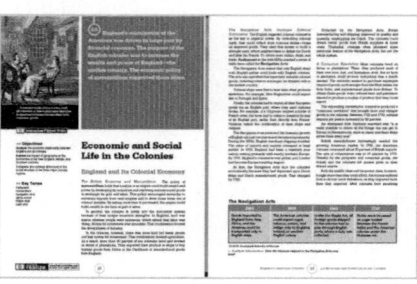

■ INVESTIGATE

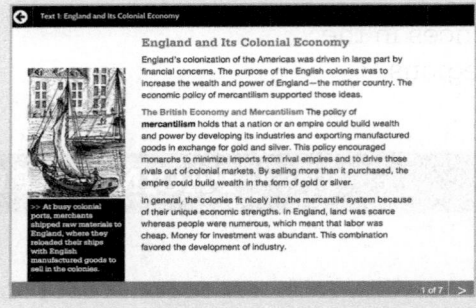

DIGITAL TEXT 1
England and Its Colonial Economy

Objective 1: Analyze the economic relationship between England and its colonies.

Quick Instruction
Direct students' attention to the image of the colonial port. Invite volunteers to explain what the image might suggest about the colonial economy in the 1600s. *(increasing populations leading to urbanization and large bustling cities; dependence on sea-going trade.)* Ask: What might this tell you about England's view of the colonies? *(The colonies were becoming increasingly important to England's economy and its strength as a world empire.)*

Generate Explanations How did England's mercantilism policies affect the industrialization of England? *(In England, land was scarce but people were numerous, which meant that labor was cheap and money for investment was abundant. English colonies in North America were expected to provide the raw materials that England lacked and then purchase its manufactured goods in return. This combination favored the development of industry in England.)*

ELL Use the ELL activity described in the ELL chart.

Further Instruction
Draw Conclusions What benefits did the Navigation Acts provide to Britain? *(The acts promoted the dramatic growth of English colonial commerce and the nation's prosperity. During the 1600s, English merchant shipping increased and the value of imports and exports increased. By 1700, England's commerce was global, and London*

had become Europe's leading seaport.) How did the acts affect the colonies? *(At first, the Navigation Acts hurt the colonists economically because they had depended upon Dutch ships and Dutch manufactured goods. By 1700, however, the colonists were able to obtain better goods from British suppliers at lower costs.)*

Summarize the economic and political effects of the colonial trade imbalance on the colonists. *(The trade imbalance led to many colonists accruing debts. This led to a growing sense of uneasiness and discontentment among the colonists with their relationship with England.)*

Predict Consequences What economic and cultural impact will the triangular trade system have on the colonies? *(The triangular trade system will probably help the economies in the Southern colonies where slavery was needed for agricultural production. However, the trade would also lead to a dependence on slavery that will continue to grow significantly.)*

PEARSON realize.™ www.PearsonRealize.com
Access your Digital Lesson

DIGITAL TEXT 2
Regional Economic Differences

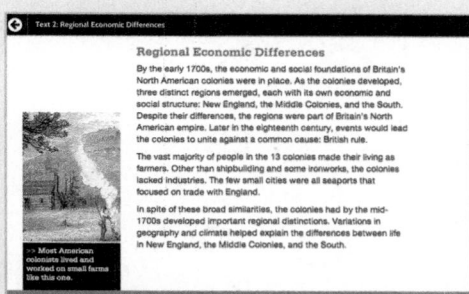

INTERACTIVE MAP
Comparing the English Colonies

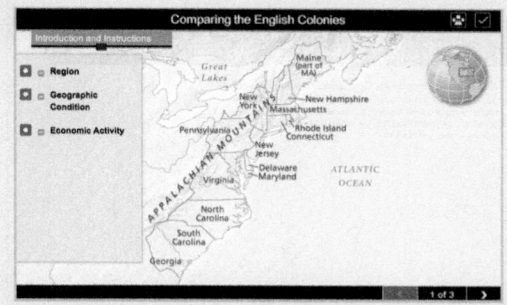

DIGITAL TEXT 3
Regional Social Differences

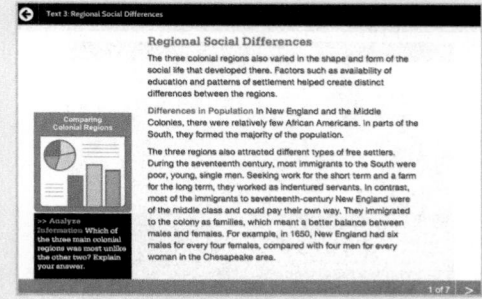

Objective 2: Explain the impact of geography on the economies of the New England, Middle, and Southern colonies.

Quick Instruction
Interactive Map: Comparing the English Colonies Introduce the map activity by asking students to think about how geography affects their town and region. Project the map on the whiteboard and select the squares to explore the three regions of the English colonies.

Analyze Information How did geography affect the economy in each of the three regions? (*The rocky terrain in the north did not lend itself to large crop production. This forced the northern colonists to turn to other industries, like lumber or shipbuilding. In the Middle Colonies, the geography had a mixed landscape with some fertile soils. The Middle Colonies, however, had access to ideal harbors for shipping centers. The Southern Colonies included mountains, some fertile valleys, and a coastal plain also suited for growing crops. Crops grown for trade were crucial to the economy of the Southern Colonies.*)

ACTIVE CLASSROOM
Conduct a Take a Stand activity. Have students take a stand on which of the three regions they think will be the most prosperous. Have students physically move to the part of the room associated with their preferred region and group with other like-minded students. Ask each group to create a justification for their choice and have one person present the group's opinion to the class.

ELL Use the ELL activity described in the ELL chart.

Further Instruction
Encourage students to discuss other factors that might influence the development of the three colonies. (*Possible responses might include climate and weather; importance of educational opportunities; relationships with local American Indian groups*)

Make Generalizations How did agriculture affect the populations of the three colonial regions? (*Agriculture was not as lucrative in New England, so only small family farms developed. Instead, coastal towns grew from shipping fish and lumber. Successful crop production in the Middle Colonies led to export trade and the growth of seaports; cash crops characterized the Southern colonies.*)

Draw Conclusions How did the development of cash crops in the Southern colonies encourage the trade in enslaved people? (*As cash crops became more important to the Southern economy, larger plantations emerged. The large plantations needed more workers—enslaved people.*)

Objective 3: Compare and contrast differences in the social structure of the three major colonial regions.

Quick Instruction
Interactive Gallery: A New Kind of Society Project the Interactive Gallery and click on each image. For each, prompt students to describe how it shows the similarities and differences between life in England and the colonies.

Analyze Images What does the fourth image in the gallery, the congested London street, suggest about the living conditions in England and why many might have chosen to emigrate to the North American colonies? (*The image portrays a troubling scene and what appears to be a conflict in the streets, with soldiers and a large number of people milling about. Overcrowded conditions and uncertain economic times probably pushed many English people to seek better living conditions in colonies.*)

ACTIVE CLASSROOM
Conduct a Quick Write activity. Direct students to write for thirty seconds and share what they know about the factors that encouraged English citizens to move to the North American colonies.

D Differentiate: Challenge Encourage interested students to research the Virginia House of Burgesses and compare it to the English political system at the time.

Economic and Social Life in the Colonies

INTERACTIVE GALLERY
A New Kind of Society

Further Instruction

Express Ideas Clearly How might the cultural diversity in the Middle Colonies have led to more economic opportunities for immigrants? *(Without dominant ethnic or religious groups in the middle colonies, immigrants could easily assimilate into colonial life. They could practice their trades or run businesses without facing discrimination.)*

Cite Evidence What evidence in the text shows that women were denied essential social and political rights in the colonies? *(Women could not own property, could not vote, could not hold political office, and could not serve on a jury.)*

Analyze Information How do colonial educational goals and opportunities compare to educational goals and opportunities today? *(Education in the colonies (apart from New England) was less valued than today because it was not as crucial to providing the skills most colonists needed to earn a productive living. Consequently, schools were not as widely available outside of the North. Schools beyond elementary level were even rarer.)*

▮ SYNTHESIZE

DIGITAL ACTIVITY
Comparing Regional Cultures

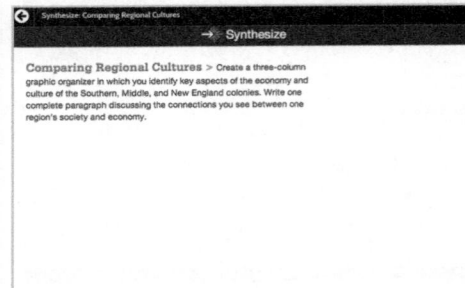

Discuss Remind students to use pre-writing techniques before they begin writing. For this writing response, they should create a three-column graphic organizer identifying the most important aspects of the economies and cultures of the three colonial regions. Emphasize that students should focus on identifying and understanding how economic and cultural characteristics were intertwined to create the individual regional societies.

▮ DEMONSTRATE

DIGITAL QUIZ
Lesson Quiz and Class Discussion Board

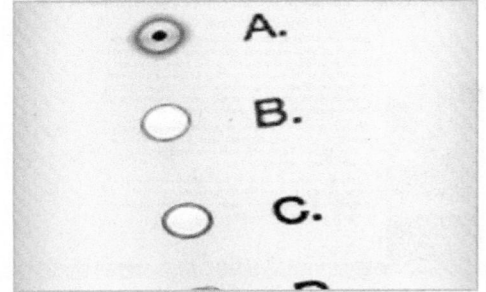

Assign the online Lesson Quiz for this lesson if you haven't already done so. Students will be offered automatic remediation or enrichment based on their score.

In *Economic and Social Life in the Colonies*, you read about how different groups of people brought unique skills to America's new society. In addition, unique geographic factors, economic activities, and cultures combined to shape distinct regional identities.

Pose these questions to the class on the Discussion Board:

Predict Consequences What are the potential consequences of the three colonial regions continuing to develop distinct economies and societies?

Connect What distinct aspects of the three colonial regions you learned about in the 1600s and 1700s are still evident today? Explain.

Topic Inquiry
Have students continue their investigations for the Topic Inquiry.

Creating an American Identity

Supporting English Language Learners

Use with the reading, **Early Government in the Colonies.**

Remind students that we often need support from teachers and peers to develop background knowledge that will help us understand the new information we read.

Beginning Read aloud the section titled *Foundations of English Government.* Point out that the Magna Carta was a document signed in 1215 limiting the king's ability to tax the nobles. Ask partners to look over the text and find out what the king had to do before placing a tax on the nobles.

Intermediate Ask partners to read the section titled *Foundations of English Government* and identify information about the Magna Carta. Ask them to write two or three sentences summarizing the role of the nobles in English government after the Magna Carta.

Advanced Ask partners to silently read the section titled *Foundations of English Government.* Ask one student to state information about the role of the nobles after the Magna Carta. Ask the other partner to use this information to talk about how the nobles gained more power and became part of Parliament.

Advanced High Ask partners to silently read the section titled *Foundations of English Government.* Have them write a short paragraph about the role of the nobles in the foundations of English government. Encourage them to ask classmates or the teacher for additional information to help them complete their paragraph.

Use with the reading, **New Ideas Empower Individuals.**

Read aloud the first two sections, pausing to explain vocabulary and concepts as needed. Ask students to listen carefully for information about the Enlightenment. Then have partners explain what intellectuals believed. Encourage more proficient students to use more specificity and detail in their explanations.

Beginning Ask partners to use the following sentence frames to help them talk about the Enlightenment: The Enlightenment was an _____ movement. People believed problems could be solved by using _____.

Intermediate Ask partners the following questions to guide them in a discussion about the Enlightenment: What was the Enlightenment? What did the thinkers believe?

Advanced Ask partners to share their ideas about the Enlightenment. Tell them to include details about what thinkers believed and what influenced these beliefs.

Advanced High Ask students to read the section titled *New Ideas About the Physical World.* Ask partners to choose one of the Enlightenment thinkers and talk about his beliefs. Encourage them to include details, such as what areas the thinker focused on and how these ideas influenced others.

▣ Differentiate Instruction

Use the Differentiated Instruction notes throughout the lesson plan to support the varied skill sets, levels of readiness, and interests in the mixed-ability classroom.

Challenge These notes include suggestions for expanding the activity for advanced students.

On-Level These notes include suggestions for modifying the activity to address different interests or learning styles.

Extra Support These notes include ideas for providing more scaffolding or reading support.

Special Needs These notes provide ideas for adapting instruction to support the needs of various special needs students.

■ NOTES

Creating an American Identity

Objectives

Objective 1: Explore how English traditions influenced the development of colonial governments.

Objective 2: Explain how the ideas of the Enlightenment shaped the colonists' worldview.

Objective 3: Describe how the Great Awakening affected colonial society.

LESSON 6 ORGANIZER	PACING: APPROX. 1 PERIOD, .5 BLOCKS			RESOURCES	
		OBJECTIVES	PACING	Online	Print
Connect					
DIGITAL START UP ACTIVITY **An Illegal Trade**			5 min.	●	
Investigate					
DIGITAL TEXT 1 **Early Government in the Colonies**			10 min.	●	●
INTERACTIVE GALLERY **Roots of Democracy**		Objective 1	10 min.	●	
INTERACTIVE GALLERY **Freedom of the Press**			10 min.	●	
DIGITAL TEXT 2 **New Ideas Empower Individuals**		Objective 2	10 min.	●	●
DIGITAL TEXT 3 **The Great Awakening**		Objective 3	10 min.	●	●
Synthesize					
DIGITAL ACTIVITY **Creating an American Identity**			5 min.	●	
Demonstrate					
DIGITAL QUIZ **Lesson Quiz and Class Discussion Board**			10 min.	●	

PEARSON
realize™
www.PearsonRealize.com

Go online to access additional resources including:
Primary Sources • Biographies • Supreme Court cases •
21st Century Skill Tutorials • Maps • Graphic Organizers.

■ CONNECT

DIGITAL START UP ACTIVITY
An Illegal Trade

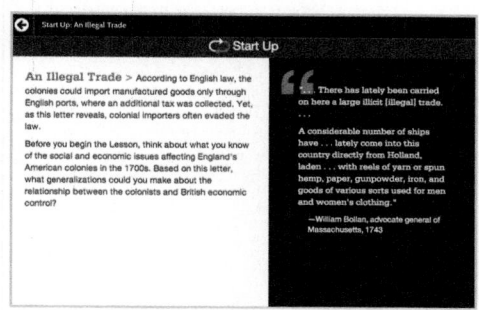

Project the Start Up Activity Ask students to answer the questions as they enter and get settled. Then have them share their ideas with another student.

Discuss Ask students: What predictions might you make about England's ability to effectively govern its American colonies? *(The colonists will become increasingly independent and will strongly disagree with England's control of what they see is their economy. Eventually England will lose its grip on the colonies.)*

Tell students that they learn how English traditions affected the development of colonial governments and the effect of both Enlightenment ideas the Great Awakening in the colonies.

Aa Vocabulary Development: Use the Interactive Reading Notepad to preview the Key Terms and Academic Vocabulary in this lesson with students.

⇅ FLIP IT!
Assign the Flipped Video for this lesson.

■ STUDENT EDITION PRINT
PAGES: 67–72

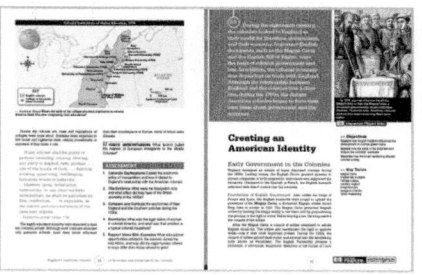

■ INVESTIGATE

DIGITAL TEXT 1
Early Government in the Colonies

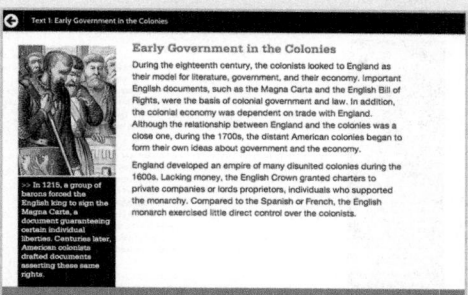

Objective 1: Explore how English traditions influenced the development of colonial governments.

Quick Instruction

Roots of Democracy: Interactive Gallery Before projecting the Interactive Gallery, encourage students to discuss what they consider to be the foundations of American democracy. *(Possible responses include "life, liberty, and the pursuit of happiness," freedom of speech and religion, freedom to own property)* Project the Interactive Gallery and select the images to learn more about the ideas that shaped the emerging American democracy in the 1600s and 1700s. Discuss how the ideas described in the gallery connect to students' view of American democracy.

Freedom of the Press: Interactive Gallery Project the Interactive Gallery. Click each image to display information about freedom of the press in the United States from the colonial era to the present. As students view the interactivity, encourage them to reflect on the role of the press in a democracy like the United States. Point out that the "press" also includes television, radio, and the Internet.

Draw Conclusions Why is the John Peter Zenger trial significant? *(In 1734, Zenger was accused of libel for publishing an article critical of an English governor, but was found not guilty in trial. The case established a legal basis for freedom of the press in the American colonies.)*

INTERACTIVE GALLERY
Roots of Democracy

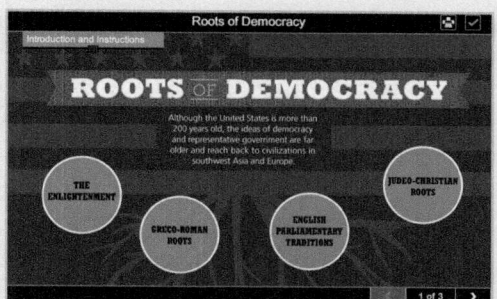

▶ ACTIVE CLASSROOM

Conduct a Circle Write activity. Break into groups and provide this question as a writing prompt: "What are the key roots of American democracy?" Have students write as much as they can for one minute then switch with the person on their right. The next person tries to improve or elaborate the response where the other person left off. Continue to switch until the paper comes back to the first person. Have the groups share their responses as the basis for a larger class discussion.

▶ ACTIVE CLASSROOM

Have students Make Headlines for one of the freedom of the press cases described in the interactivity. Ask: If you were to write a headline that captured the most important aspect that should be remembered, what would that headline be? Allow students to use subheadings to communicate more information. Have students pass their headlines to a partner for review.

D Differentiate: Extra Support Students having difficulty articulating key foundations of American democracy may benefit from a quick reading of the Preamble and Declaration of Natural Rights sections of the Declaration of Independence.

ELL Use the ELL activity described in the ELL chart.

Creating an American Identity

INTERACTIVE GALLERY

Freedom of the Press

Trial of John Peter Zenger (1735)

John Peter Zenger published newspaper articles criticizing the government of New York. He was imprisoned for libel—publishing a false statement to damage a person's reputation—but was acquitted by a jury.

DIGITAL TEXT 2

New Ideas Empower Individuals

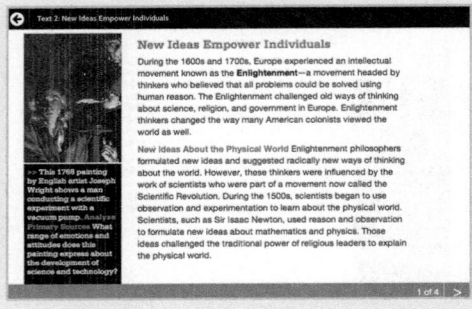

New Ideas Empower Individuals

During the 1600s and 1700s, Europe experienced an intellectual movement known as the **Enlightenment**—a movement headed by thinkers who believed that all problems could be solved using human reason. The Enlightenment challenged old ways of thinking about science, religion, and government in Europe. Enlightenment thinkers changed the way many American colonists viewed the world as well.

New Ideas About the Physical World Enlightenment philosophers formulated new ideas and suggested radically new ways of thinking about the world. However, these thinkers were influenced by the work of scientists who were part of a movement now called the Scientific Revolution. During the 1500s, scientists began to use observation and experimentation to learn about the physical world. Scientists, such as Sir Isaac Newton, used reason and observation to formulate new ideas about mathematics and physics. Those ideas challenged the traditional power of religious leaders to explain the physical world.

Further Instruction

Begin a brief discussion in which students share what they know about the English government. Students should be aware of the role of the monarchy and the emergence of Parliament. To extend the discussion, assign Primary Sources: The Magna Carta and Government and Civics Core Concepts: Political Systems.

Generate Explanations In your opinion, what were the primary effects of the Magna Carta and the English Bill of Rights? *(Both documents changed the relationship between government and its people, and increased the political rights of people ruled under a monarchy.)*

Infer How do you think England's policy of salutary neglect toward the 13 colonies would affect the colonies' future political and economic development? *(Allowing the colonists self-rule will encourage political independence from England. The colonies will initially benefit from the economic relationship with England, but eventually the colonies will disagree with the restrictions on free trade.)*

Express Ideas Clearly In your opinion, what role does freedom of the press play in a democracy? *(The freedom of the press to report on government is very important because it prevents government officials and agencies from acting in secrecy. Freedom of the press is like another check on the power of government.)*

Objective 2: Explain how the ideas of the Enlightenment shaped the colonists' worldview.

Quick Instruction

Direct students' attention to the 1768 painting by Joseph Wright. Ask students to describe what they see and to answer the caption question. Ask: Why might the experiment with the vacuum pump depicted in the painting impress observers? *(Most of the people were probably unfamiliar with vacuum pumps and the scientific concepts the experiment displayed.)* Encourage students to think about how new scientific ideas about the natural world and natural laws promoted by Enlightenment thinkers would be received by American colonists.

Infer Why might many rural colonists have been hesitant to embrace Enlightenment ideals, particularly in regard to religion? *(Religion and community churches played especially significant parts in rural areas. Churches were social gathering places that served not only religious purposes, but political and community ones as well. Any idea that would potentially change the relationship between government and the role of churches would probably not have been well received.)*

ELL Use the ELL activity described in the ELL chart.

Further Instruction

Assign the Primary Sources: English Bill of Rights and John Locke, *Two Treatises of Government* to extend the discussion of how Enlightenment ideas shaped the views of American colonists.

Connect What influence did John Locke's conception of natural rights have on political thought and how did this idea influence the American colonists' relationship with the English monarch? *(Locke believed that people had natural rights that came from their creator, and not from monarchs. In turn, increasing acceptance of this idea encouraged people, including American colonists, to question the obligations of a monarch toward his subjects.)*

Use Context Clues What can you conclude about Benjamin Franklin's standing in the colonies based on information in the reading? *(Franklin was wealthy, which allowed him to build this life around the pursuit of knowledge. He was also a printer, writer, and inventor, so Franklin was probably considered one of the influential intellectuals of the era.)*

DIGITAL TEXT 3

The Great Awakening

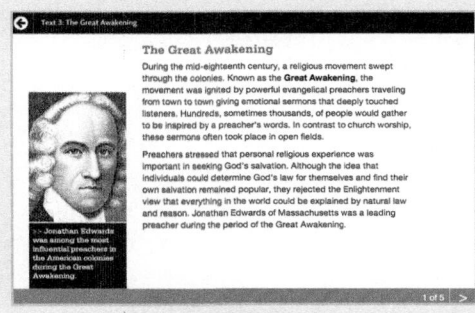

Text 3: The Great Awakening

The Great Awakening

During the mid-eighteenth century, a religious movement swept through the colonies. Known as the **Great Awakening**, the movement was ignited by powerful evangelical preachers traveling from town to town giving emotional sermons that deeply touched listeners. Hundreds, sometimes thousands, of people would gather to be inspired by a preacher's words. In contrast to church worship, these sermons often took place in open fields.

Preachers stressed that personal religious experience was important in seeking God's salvation. Although the idea that individuals could determine God's law for themselves and find their own salvation remained popular, they rejected the Enlightenment view that everything in the world could be explained by natural law and reason. Jonathan Edwards of Massachusetts was a leading preacher during the period of the Great Awakening.

>> Jonathan Edwards was among the most influential preachers in the American colonies during the Great Awakening.

1 of 5 >

Objective 3: Describe how the Great Awakening affected colonial society.

Quick Instruction

Project the image of Jonathon Edwards on the whiteboard. Explain that Edwards was among the most influential preachers in the American colonies during the Great Awakening. Invite a volunteer to read the excerpt from Edwards's sermon *Sinners in the Hands of an Angry God.* Encourage students to share their thoughts and feelings about the imagery and ideas in the passage.

Summarize the impact of the Great Awakening on the colonies. *By challenging traditional religious beliefs and practices, the Great Awakening intensified colonists' sense of themselves as individuals, helped spread ideas of equality, and challenged ideas of hierarchy in religious organization. The movement also encouraged the spread of democratic practices in the colonies, preparing the ground for further political transformation.)*

Further Instruction

Identify Cause and Effect Why did the Great Awakening cause division in established churches? *Some evangelical preachers such as George Whitefield urged listeners to forsake ministers who favored a more subdued and rational style. Preaching that individuals could find their own salvation, the Great Awakening challenged the authority of existing churches and led to the formation of new churches in the colonies. Many established congregations were split between those who followed the preachers of the Great Awakening and those who did not.)*

Determine Relevance What relationship did the ideas of the Enlightenment have with the Great Awakening? *(The idea that individuals were empowered to determine God's laws for themselves was popular; however, many colonists probably disagreed with the Enlightenment idea that everything in the world could be explained by natural law and reason. Many people may have felt that their religious views were being discarded and felt the need to reclaim what they thought was the importance of religion in society.)*

Creating an American Identity

■ SYNTHESIZE

■ DEMONSTRATE

DIGITAL ACTIVITY
Creating an American Identity

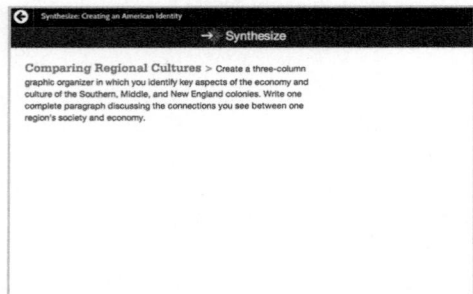

DIGITAL QUIZ
Lesson Quiz and Class Discussion Board

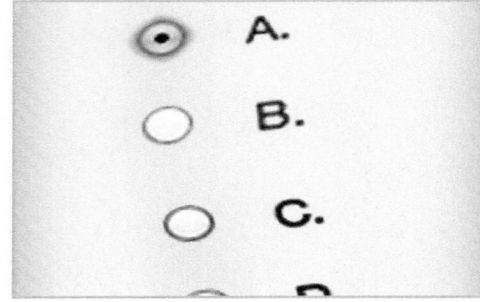

Discuss Before students begin their paragraphs, lead the class in a brief review of the essential ideas of the Enlightenment and the Great Awakening discussed in the lesson.

Assign the online Lesson Quiz for this lesson if you haven't already done so. Students will be offered automatic remediation or enrichment based on their score.

Remind students that in *Creating an American Identity* they read about how British legal and political traditions influenced colonial governments. They also explored the impact of cultural movements such as the Enlightenment and the Great Awakening.

Pose these questions to the class on the Discussion Board:

Synthesize How did the idea of natural law impact the Great Awakening and help prepare the ground for a political transformation in the colonies?

Make Predictions How might the Enlightenment idea that everything in the world can be explained by natural law and reason affect the role of religion in American public life?

Topic Inquiry
Have students continue their investigations for the Topic Inquiry.

England's American Colonies

■ SYNTHESIZE

DIGITAL ACTIVITY
Reflect on the Essential Question and Topic

First ask students to reconsider the Essential Question for the Topic: Why do people move? Tell them to review their responses to the Essential Question Activity. Have them revise any parts of the responses as needed.

Organize students into small groups. Direct each group to answer the three questions about political, economic, and social factors. Call on each group to share their ideas with the class or post their responses in the class discussion board.

Next, have students reflect on the Topic as a whole. Display the questions from the Topic Synthesize Activity. Instruct students to jot down notes in response to the three questions. Then, ask students to write a paragraph in which they describe what they think was the primary motivation that brought people to England's North American colonies. Tell them to be sure to cite evidence from each lesson in the Topic.

Direct students to exchange their paragraphs with a partner. They should read and provide feedback on each other's work. Then, have students revise their paragraphs to submit to the class blog or other common classroom resource.

Topic Inquiry
Have students complete Step 3 of the Topic Inquiry.

■ DEMONSTRATE

DIGITAL TOPIC REVIEW AND ASSESSMENT
England's American Colonies

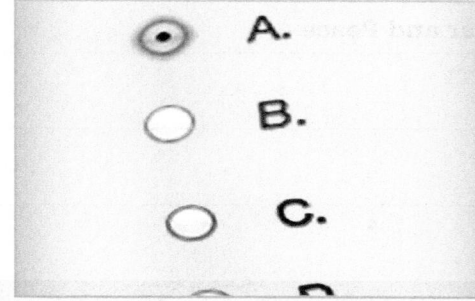

Students can prepare for the Topic Test by answering the questions in the Topic Review and Assessment online. They can also prepare by reviewing their answers to the Interactive Reading Notepad questions or reviewing their notes in the Reading and Notetaking Study Guide.

DIGITAL TOPIC TEST
England's American Colonies

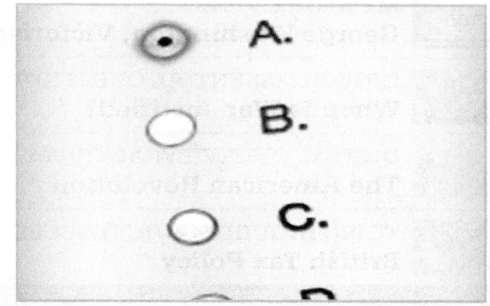

TOPIC TEST
Assign the Topic Test to assess students' understanding of topic content.

BENCHMARK TESTS
Assign these benchmark tests as you complete the relevant topics to monitor student progress toward mastering the course content and as preparation for the End-of-Course Test.

Benchmark Test 1: Topics 1–3
Benchmark Test 2: Topics 4–6
Benchmark Test 3: Topics 7–9
Benchmark Test 4: Topics 10–12
Benchmark Test 5: Topics 13–15
Benchmark Test 6: Topics 16–18
Benchmark Test 7: Topics 19–20

Topic (3)

The American Revolution

TOPIC 3 ORGANIZER	PACING: APPROX. 7 PERIODS, 3.5 BLOCKS
	PACING
Connect	1 period
MY STORY VIDEO **George Washington, Victories in War and Peace**	10 min.
DIGITAL ESSENTIAL QUESTION ACTIVITY **When Is War Justified?**	10 min.
DIGITAL OVERVIEW ACTIVITY **The American Revolution**	10 min.
TOPIC INQUIRY: CIVIC DISCUSSION **British Tax Policy**	20 min.
Investigate	2–4 periods
TOPIC INQUIRY: CIVIC DISCUSSION **British Tax Policy**	Ongoing
LESSON 1 The French and Indian War	30–40 min.
LESSON 2 Causes of the Revolution	30–40 min.
LESSON 3 The Colonists Declare Independence	30–40 min.
LESSON 4 Americans Win the Revolution	30–40 min.
Synthesize	1 period
DIGITAL ESSENTIAL QUESTION ACTIVITY **Reflect on the Essential Question and Topic**	10 min.
TOPIC INQUIRY: CIVIC DISCUSSION **British Tax Policy**	20 min.
Demonstrate	1–2 periods
DIGITAL TOPIC REVIEW AND ASSESSMENT **The American Revolution**	10 min.
TOPIC INQUIRY: CIVIC DISCUSSION **British Tax Policy**	20 min.

British Tax Policy

In this Topic Inquiry, students work in teams to examine different perspectives on this issue by analyzing several sources, arguing both sides of a Yes/No question, then developing and discussing their own point of view on the question: **Was British tax policy in America justified after the French and Indian War?**

STEP 1: CONNECT
Develop Questions and Plan the Investigation

Launch the Civic Discussion

Divide the class into groups of four students. Students can access the materials they'll need in the online course or you can distribute copies to each student. Read the main question and introduction with the students.

Have students complete Step 1 by reading the Discussion Launch and filling in Step 1 of the Information Organizer. The Discussion Launch provides YES and NO arguments on the main question. Students should extract and paraphrase the arguments from the reading in Step 1 of their Information Organizers.

Next, students share within their groups the arguments and evidence they found to support the YES and NO positions. The group needs to agree on the major YES and NO points and each student should note those points in their Information Organizer.

Resources
- Student Instructions
- Information Organizer
- Discussion Launch

STEP 2: INVESTIGATE
Apply Disciplinary Concepts and Tools

Examine Sources and Perspectives

Students will examine sources with the goal of extracting information and perspectives on the main question. They analyze each source and describe the author's perspective on the main question and key evidence the author provides to support that viewpoint in Information Organizer Step 2.

Ask students to keep in mind:

- **Author/Creator:** Who created the source? An individual? Group? Government agency?
- **Audience:** For whom was the source created?
- **Date/Place:** Is there any information that reveals where and when the source was created?
- **Purpose:** Why was the source created? Discuss with students the importance of this question in identifying bias.
- **Relevance:** How does the source support one argument or another?

Suggestion: Reading the source documents and filling in Step 2 of the Information Organizer could be assigned as homework.

Resources
- Student Instructions
- Information Organizer
- Source documents

 TOPIC INQUIRY: CIVIC DISCUSSION

British Tax Policy *(continued)*

<table>
<tr><td colspan="2">

STEP 3: SYNTHESIZE
Use Evidence to Formulate Conclusions

</td></tr>
</table>

Formulate Compelling Arguments with Evidence

Now students will apply perspectives and evidence they extracted from the sources to think more deeply about the main question by first arguing one side of the issue, then the other. In this way students become more prepared to formulate an evidence-based conclusion on their own.

Within each student group, assign half of the students to take the position of YES on the main question and the others to take the position of NO. Students will work with their partners to identify the strongest arguments and evidence to support their assigned YES or NO position.

Present Yes/No Positions

Within each group, those assigned the YES position share arguments and evidence first. As the YES students speak, those assigned NO should listen carefully, take notes to fill in the rest of the Compelling Arguments Chart (Step 3 in Information Organizer) and ask clarifying questions.

When the YES side is finished, students assigned the NO position present while those assigned YES should listen, take notes, and ask clarifying questions. Examples of clarifyin questions are:

- I think you just said [x]. Am I understanding you correctly?
- Can you tell me more about [x]?
- Can you repeat [x]? I am not sure I understand, yet.

Suggestion: You may want to set a 5 minute time limit for each side to present. Provide a two-minute warning so that students make their most compelling arguments within the time frame.

Switch Sides

The students will switch sides to argue the opposite point of view. To prepare to present the other position, partners who first argued YES will use the notes they took during the NO side's presentation, plus add any additional arguments and evidence from the reading and sources. The same for students who first argued the NO position.

STEP 4: DEMONSTRATE
Communicate Conclusions and Take Informed Action

Individual Points of View

Now the students will have the opportunity to discuss the main question from their own points of view. To help students prepare for this discussion, have them reflect on the YES/NO discussions they have participated in thus far and fill in Step 4 of their Information Organizers.

After all of the students have shared their points of view, each group should list points of agreement, filling the last portion of Step 4 on their Information Organizers.

Reflect on the Discussion

Ask students to reflect on the civic discussion thinking about:

- The value of having to argue both the YES and NO positions.
- If their individual views changed over the course of the discussion and why.
- What they learned from participating in the discussion.

Resources

- Student Instructions
- Information Organizer

INTRODUCTION

The American Revolution

Britain and France each claimed large areas of land in North America. In 1754, their competition ignited the French and Indian War. Though Britain emerged the victor, it also inherited new problems. Britain's American colonies wanted to expand westward, but Britain wanted to keep the peace with American Indians. Meanwhile, Britain had incurred large war debts, for which it chose to tax the colonies. A series of laws meant to restrict colonial settlement and raise taxes increased tensions between the British government and the American colonists. In 1775, fighting broke out between British troops and the colonists, and the American Revolution had begun. It would prove to be a war of independence.

CONNECT

MY STORY VIDEO

George Washington, Victories in War and Peace

Watch a video about George Washington's leadership during the American Revolution.

Check Understanding What event in American history in 1776 is celebrated every year on December 25? (Georgia Washington's crossing of the Delaware River, leading to victory at the Battle of Trenton)

Identify Central Issues What risk did Washington take on December 25? (Washington knew that he needed a convincing victory at this time, or that he might lose the struggle against Britain. He took a big risk by going on the offensive and attacking the Hessians at Trenton, and with his victory, the Revolution was saved.)

DIGITAL ESSENTIAL QUESTION ACTIVITY

When Is War Justified?

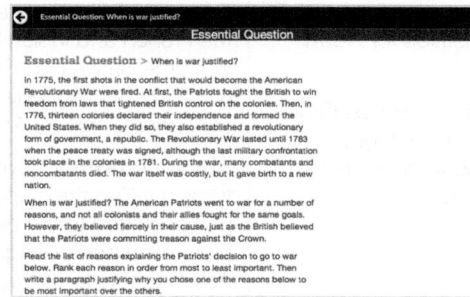

Project the Digital Essential Question Activity. Have students read through the activity. Then, ask them to work in pairs to rank the list of reasons for going to war. Remind students to write a paragraph to explain their rankings. Call on student pairs to share their rankings and explanations.

Make Predictions What reasons do you think Patriots will give to justify going to war against Britain? (They will cite reasons such as the defense of their political ideas, the right to protect their property and way of life, and the right to reject a government that they feel has failed to provide representation.) What reasons might colonists opposed to the revolution offer to explain why the war was not justified? (They might say that the colonists were all British citizens who had benefited from the protection, trade, and governance of Britain and that they owed Britain their loyalty. They might state that the problems between Britain and the colonies could be resolved through negotiations and compromise.)

DIGITAL OVERVIEW ACTIVITY

The American Revolution

Begin by projecting the painting of Washington at Valley Forge. Call on students to describe what they see in the image. You may wish to draw attention to details, such as General Washington or the wintery weather conditions.

Explain to students that during the winter of 1777 to 1778, more than 12,000 colonial soldiers camped at Valley Forge, just twenty miles northwest of Philadelphia, which had been lost to the British. Although the soldiers suffered from cold, sickness, and food shortages, they emerged from Valley Forge as a well-trained, more organized fighting force.

Discuss Why would several months of encampment have helped the Continental Army become a more professional, better prepared force? (Months of encampment provided time for training and learning how to work together. It may also have helped unite colonists who had otherwise not forged ties. It may have helped increase the prestige of commanders, including Washington.)

Topic Inquiry

Launch the Topic Inquiry with students after introducing the topic.

The French and Indian War

Supporting English Language Learners

Use with the reading, **Competition for North American Colonies**.

Listening
Before reading aloud the section titled, *Europeans Compete for American Indian Allies*, review the meanings of the following academic words: advantage, dominated, rival.

Beginning Use simple spoken language to summarize the first four paragraphs, placing emphasis on the new academic vocabulary. Ask students to use the words *advantage*, *dominated*, and *rival* to complete the following sentence frames: France and England were _____. France had an _____ over Britain; they controlled more territory. The American Indians _____ the frontier areas.

Intermediate Use simple spoken language to summarize the first four paragraphs, including use of the academic words *advantage*, *dominated*, and *rival*. Ask: Which countries were rivals? What advantage did the British have over the French? What did the American Indians dominate?

Advanced Use spoken language to summarize the first four paragraphs, including use of the academic words *advantage*, *dominated*, and *rival*. Ask partners to write one or two sentences about the competition for North American colonies.

Advanced High Read aloud the section titled *The British Colonies Grow Stronger*. Ask partners to use the new academic words *advantage*, *dominated*, and *rival* to write two to three sentences about the relations between the French, the British, and the American Indians.

Use with the reading, **An Important British Victory**.

Speaking
Explain to students that monitoring themselves as they speak and using self-correcting techniques will help improve their oral language skills.

Beginning Use simple language to explain the steps that led to the French and Indian War. Have students demonstrate their comprehension by completing the following sentence frames: George Washington led _____ troops against the _____. Washington's troops _____ the French. Then the French _____. Washington _____. This defeat sparked the _____. Then have partners practice telling each other the steps. Encourage them to employ self-corrective techniques to improve their fluency and pronunciation.

Intermediate Use simple spoken language to summarize the steps that led to the French and Indian War. Students can take notes as they listen. Then ask partners to take turns telling each other the steps. Encourage them to monitor their own spoken language and self-correct as needed.

Advanced Use spoken language to summarize the steps that led to the French and Indian War. Ask partners to take turns telling each other what the British and French troops did. Encourage them to monitor their own spoken language, focusing on correct word use and subject/verb agreement. Ask students to self-correct any errors they identify.

Advanced High Have students read the text silently. Ask partners to take turns retelling the steps that led to the French and Indian War, and how the power shifted to the British in 1758 and 1759. Encourage them to monitor their own spoken language, focusing on correct word use and grammar. Ask students to self-correct any errors they or their partner identify.

▣ Differentiate Instruction

Use the Differentiated Instruction notes throughout the lesson plan to support the varied skill sets, levels of readiness, and interests in the mixed-ability classroom.

Challenge These notes include suggestions for expanding the activity for advanced students.

On-Level These notes include suggestions for modifying the activity to address different interests or learning styles.

Extra Support These notes include ideas for providing more scaffolding or reading spuport.

Special Needs These notes provide ideas for adapting instruction to support the needs of various special needs students.

■ NOTES

PEARSON
realize ™
www.PearsonRealize.com

Go online to access additional resources including:
Primary Sources • Biographies • Supreme Court cases •
21st Century Skill Tutorials • Maps • Graphic Organizers.

Objectives

Objective 1: Explain the relationship among the British colonists, the French, and the American Indians in the mid-eighteenth century.

Objective 2: Describe the causes and major events of the French and Indian War.

Objective 3: Analyze the causes and effects of Pontiac's Rebellion.

Objective 4: Summarize how the wars and their outcomes changed the relationship between Britain and the colonies.

LESSON 1 ORGANIZER		PACING: APPROX. 1 PERIOD, .5 BLOCKS			
				RESOURCES	
		OBJECTIVES	PACING	Online	Print
Connect					
DIGITAL START UP ACTIVITY **European Settlers Move West**			5 min.	●	
Investigate					
DIGITAL TEXT 1 **Competition for North American Colonies**		Objective 1	10 min.	●	●
DIGITAL TEXT 2 **An Important British Victory**		Objective 2	10 min.	●	●
INTERACTIVE MAP **Battles of the French and Indian War**			10 min.	●	
DIGITAL TEXT 3 **Pontiac's Rebellion**		Objectives 3, 4	10 min.	●	●
Synthesize					
DIGITAL ACTIVITY **Effects of the French and Indian War**			5 min.	●	
Demonstrate					
LESSON QUIZ **Lesson Quiz and Class Discussion Board**			10 min.	●	

The French and Indian War

■ CONNECT

DIGITAL START UP ACTIVITY
European Settlers Move West

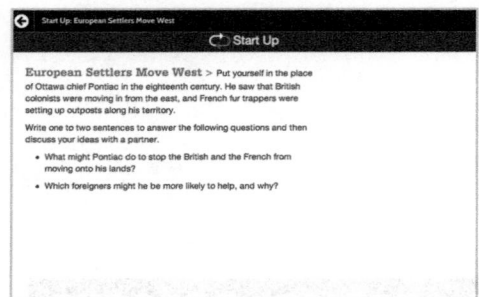

Project the Start Up Activity Ask students to answer the questions as they enter and get settled. Then have them share their ideas with another student.

Discuss Why did the British and French start colonies in North America? *(The British wanted land and resources. The French wanted to conduct trade, largely in furs.)* Why might Pontiac have considered allying with either the French or the British? *(He might have gained weapons to prevent encroachment on native lands.)*

Tell students that in this lesson they will explore the causes and effects of the French and Indian War.

Aa Vocabulary Development: Use the Interactive Reading Notepad to preview the Key Terms and Academic Vocabulary in this lesson with students.

⮌ FLIP IT!

Assign the Flipped Video for this lesson.

■ STUDENT EDITION PRINT PAGES: 78–83

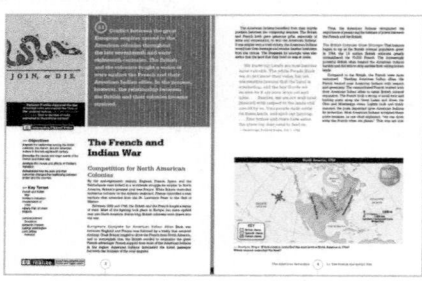

■ INVESTIGATE

DIGITAL TEXT 1
Competition for North American Colonies

Objective 1: Explain the relationship among the British colonists, the French, and the American Indians in the mid-eighteenth century.

Quick Instruction

Project the map of North America in 1754. Call on students to identify which lands were held by which European powers. Then, ask students to identify which European power held the most land. Finally, draw attention to the areas in which French and British claims touched. Invite students to identify these areas and to describe the strategic importance of associated geographic features.

Analyze Maps Along what physical features did the French establish their forts? *(lakes and rivers)* In what directions did the British most likely need to push in order to expand their territory in North America? *(west from the Thirteen Colonies and south from its northern colonies)* Why would the French want to stop British expansion in this direction? *(The French claimed lands in this area in order to control the fur trade and made use of the rivers and lakes to conduct trade. British expansion south and west would have disrupted French activities.)*

D Differentiate: Extra Support Point out the fact that lakes and rivers oftentimes define political borders between regions. Point out that the French relied on these rivers and lakes to conduct trade. Discuss the strategic importance of rivers in North America in the eighteenth century, as they were used to transport goods, and if necessary in time of war, military supplies.

ELL Use the ELL activity described in the ELL chart.

Further Instruction

Go through the Interactive Reading Notepad questions for Competition for North American Colonies. Discuss the answers with the class. Be sure students understand how conflicts over land contributed to the mounting tension between Britain and France. Point out that each European power relied on its North American colonies to generate wealth. France and Britain both needed the land, trade goods, resources, and markets of North America to expand their power.

Contrast How did British and French territories and purposes for colonization in North America differ? *(Britain and France both claimed large areas of land in North America. Most of Britain's claims lie to the north, in Canada, and along the Atlantic seaboard. Its territory was split by French claims, which comprised much of the interior of North America around the Great Lakes and the Mississippi, Missouri, and Ohio river systems. Britain established colonies to farm and conduct trade. French largely established military forts and trade outposts to conduct trade.)*

Identify Central Issues Why did American Indians want to maintain a balance of power between the British and the French in North America? *(American Indians feared one European power becoming more powerful than the other. Then, that power would not need the support of the American Indians and might deal with the American Indians more harshly. Balancing the interests of the British and the French kept the American Indians in an important role, which encouraged colonists from both nations to deal more fairly with the American Indians.)*

DIGITAL TEXT 2

An Important British Victory

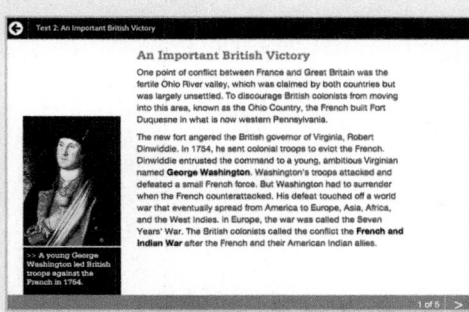

INTERACTIVE MAP

Battles of the French and Indian War

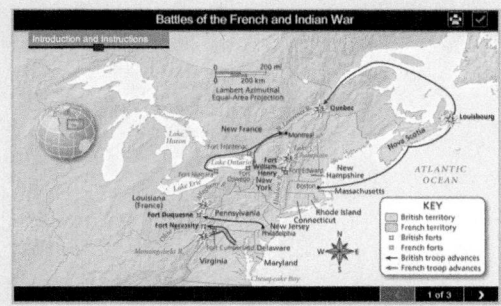

Objective 2: Describe the causes and major events of the French and Indian War.

Quick Instruction

Interactive Map: Battles of the French and Indian War Project the Interactive Map, and click through the battles. Point out the Ohio River valley. What geographic and strategic importance might the Ohio River valley have had for the French and for the British? Why might conflict have broken out in this area? *(The Ohio River valley lay on the borderlands between French and British territory. If the British pushed westward, they would need to push into the Ohio River valley and beyond. The French relied on the Ohio River and other river systems of this area to support their trade, so they would not want to give up lands in this area.)*

Sequence Events Summarize the sequence of events that set off the French and Indian War. *(The British wanted to move west into the Ohio River valley. To discourage British settlement, the French built a new fort, Fort Duquesne, in what is now western Pennsylvania. This new fort angered the British governor of Virginia. Governor Dinwiddie sent troops to push the French out of the fort. The colonial forces, under George Washington, attacked and won, but the French counterattacked, and defeated Washington. These battles helped ignite the war.)*

🎥 ACTIVE CLASSROOM

Conduct a Quick Write activity. Have students answer the following question: Why was it so important to Britain to defeat France in North America? You may wish to ask students to share their responses on a classroom blog or discussion board. If time allows, challenge each student to read and respond to one classmate's quick write.

ELL Use the ELL activity described in the ELL chart.

Further Instruction

Go through the Interactive Reading Notepad questions for an Important British Victory with the class.

Make sure that students understand that the French and Indian War was part of a greater conflict between the two European powers. This conflict also played out in Europe as well as among the two nations' other colonies in Asia and Africa. Guide students to understand that the central point of contention in North America was land. Britain wanted more land, and France's holdings were in the way. France did not want to give up its claims. Neither side was willing to compromise.

Explain Why did the American Indians first help the French and then the British during the war? *(At the outset of the war, most American Indians sided with the French. They perceived France as less of a threat since its colonies were primarily trading outposts. The French had fewer people and built smaller settlements. American Indian military support and geographic knowledge was a boon to the French. Then, Britain cut off French supplies, and many American Indians changed sides. They supported the British because the British now had better supplies. This tipped the war in Britain's favor.)*

Draw Conclusions What could the French or the British have done to avoid war? Why did they choose not to avoid war? *(The French could have permitted British expansion into French territories or agreed to sell or trade land claims, but France wanted its lands to support trade. The British could have negotiated for land from the French or slowed colonization efforts, but the British colonies had grown too populated, and Britain needed more land for more agricultural and other economic activities. Neither Britain nor France was willing to yield what it considered an advantage to the other nation. They each relied on their colonies to support their wealth and power.)*

The French and Indian War

DIGITAL TEXT 3
Pontiac's Rebellion

Objectives 3: **Analyze the causes and effects of Pontiac's Rebellion; 4: Summarize how the wars and their outcomes changed the relationship between Britain and the colonies.**

Quick Instruction

Display the political cartoon *Join, or Die*. Point out that Benjamin Franklin drew the cartoon in 1754, at the outset of the French and Indian War. He wanted the colonies to unite, under British rule, to better defend themselves against the French and their American Indian allies.

Infer What benefit does Franklin's cartoon suggest lies in colonial union? *(United colonies would be better able to protect themselves.)* Why might Britain support such a union during the French and Indian War? *(Britain needed its colonies to be strong and act together under its command to win the war.)* What hazards might such a colonial union pose for Britain after the war? *(Once the colonies had united and learned to act together for one purpose, they might be more difficult for Britain to control.)*

Summarize Why did Pontiac rally American Indians to fight the British, and why did the rebellion fail? *(Pontiac wanted to prevent British colonists from pushing west into the Ohio River valley and taking more American Indian lands and hunting grounds. The rebellion failed because the American Indians ran short on supplies and did not manage to capture key British forts.)*

Further Instruction

Have students work in pairs to complete the Interactive Reading Notepad questions for Pontiac's Rebellion. Then, review students' responses as a class.

Remind students that American Indians had hoped to balance British and French interests against each other. With the end of the French and Indian War, the French presence in the Ohio River valley and other frontier areas had been removed. Britain's colonists were now unchecked, save by their own government. Point out that Britain's colonies had been relatively autonomous prior to the French and Indian War. The American colonists expected to be able to settle and farm Britain's newly acquired lands. They also expected to continue governing themselves, without much interference from the British monarch or Parliament.

Evaluate Sources Read the primary source from the Proclamation of 1763. Why did the British monarch issue this proclamation? What part of the proclamation likely angered American colonists, and why? *(The British monarch issued the proclamation to appease American Indians and prevent further fighting with native peoples. The American colonists likely would have been angry at the statement reserving lands to the American Indians and prohibiting disruption of American Indian territories. American colonists wanted to settle these lands.)*

Compare Points of View For what reasons might American colonists have felt justified in settling the Ohio River valley? *(The American colonists had fought for the British in the French and Indian War so they felt entitled to settle the lands that Britain claimed from France during the war.)* How would many American Indians have felt about continued settlement? *(American Indians might not have considered British or French claims to their lands valid. They likely would have pointed out that France mainly built trade and military outposts, not large settlements with farming communities. They would have argued that they had not agreed to give up their lands to large scale colonization and settlement.)*

SYNTHESIZE

DIGITAL ACTIVITY
Effects of the French and Indian War

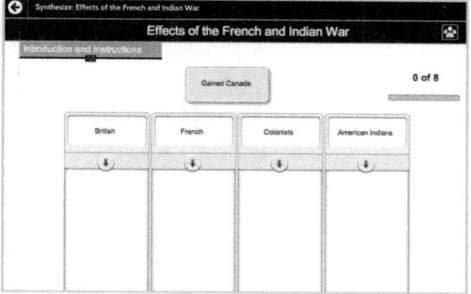

DEMONSTRATE

LESSON QUIZ
Lesson Quiz and Class Discussion Board

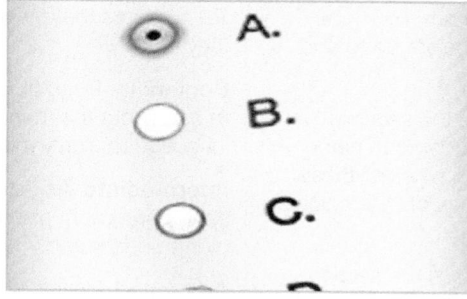

ACTIVE CLASSROOM

Conduct a Think Pair Share activity. Ask students to identify the effects of the French and Indian War on American colonists, American Indians, the British, and the French. Allow students to work alone or in groups to complete the tile sort. Instruct them to write down and discuss their answers with the class.

Discuss Tell students to consider the impact of Britain's victory in the French and Indian War on its American colonies. What predictions can they make about how Britain's relationship with its colonies might change? Have students cite evidence from the lesson to support their claims.

Assign the online Lesson Quiz for this lesson if you haven't already done so. Students will be offered automatic remediation or enrichment based on their score.

Pose these questions to the class on the Discussion Board:

In *The French and Indian War*, you read about the causes and effects of the French and Indian War. You learned how geography influenced events leading up to, during, and following the war. You also explored the impact of the war and its outcomes on Britain's relations with its colonies.

Identify Main Ideas What role did geography play in the outbreak of war? *(The war broke out over control of land in North America. Britain and France each had large territories in North America, and their colonial lands bordered each other. When Britain wanted to push west, France was in the way. France wanted to maintain its lands because of the geographic advantages offered by major rivers and lakes. France relied on these waterways to support trade from the interior.)*

Support Ideas with Evidence Which group was most responsible for the onset of the French and Indian War: the British, the French, the British American colonists, the French fur traders, or the American Indians? Support your ideas with evidence from the lesson. *(Students should state a clear position and support that position with evidence. For example, students may argue that the British American colonists were responsible because they first fired on the French Fort Duquesne.)*

Topic Inquiry
Have students continue their investigations for the Topic Inquiry.

Causes of the Revolution

Supporting English Language Learners

Use with the reading, **The Foundations of Colonial Government**.

Speaking
Have students use grade-level content area vocabulary to talk about the three branches of British government that North American colonies used as a basis for their own government. Encourage them to include information about who executive and legislative power belonged to and what the colonists' judicial rights were.

Beginning Use simple spoken language to paraphrase the section titled *British Government Serves as an Example*. Ask students to name the three branches of British government. Have them tell whether these branches were the same as or different from the branches of U.S. colonial government.

Intermediate Use simple spoken language to paraphrase the section titled *British Government Serves as an Example*. Ask partners to name the three branches of British government and to talk about to whom executive and legislative power belonged.

Advanced Ask students to read silently the section titled *British Government Serves as an Example*. With a partner, have students talk about the example set by the British. They should use the words executive, legislative, and judicial in their speech. Encourage them to talk about how the British government was the same as and different from the colonial U.S. government.

Advanced High Ask students to read silently the first three paragraphs of *The Foundations of Colonial Government*. Have partners talk about British liberty and the rights of citizens. Challenge them to say what the colonists liked best about colonial rule.

Use with the reading, **Protests Lead to Violence**.

Reading
Introduce the section titled *The Boston Massacre* by paraphrasing what caused it, how the protest developed, and what its final outcome was. Tell students that previewing a text will help them better understand what they read.

Beginning Read aloud the first paragraph, pausing often for students to ask about the meanings of unfamiliar words and phrases. Use simpler language to clarify meaning.

Intermediate Ask students to take turns reading aloud a paragraph. After each paragraph, give students an opportunity to ask about anything they didn't understand. Then ask them questions to confirm comprehension.

Advanced Have pairs of students take turns reading the section aloud. Encourage them to pause as needed to address any questions they or their partner may have. Provide help as needed.

Advanced High Have students read the section independently, jotting down any unfamiliar language or concepts. Then have partners ask and answer the questions. If partners are not able to clear up a query, have them ask you for help.

▣ Differentiate Instruction

Use the Differentiated Instruction notes throughout the lesson plan to support the varied skill sets, levels of readiness, and interests in the mixed-ability classroom.

Challenge These notes include suggestions for expanding the activity for advanced students.

On-Level These notes include suggestions for modifying the activity to address different interests or learning styles.

Extra Support These notes include ideas for providing more scaffolding or reading spuport.

Special Needs These notes provide ideas for adapting instruction to support the needs of various special needs students.

■ NOTES

PEARSON
realize™
www.PearsonRealize.com

Go online to access additional resources including:
Primary Sources • Biographies • Supreme Court cases •
21st Century Skill Tutorials • Maps • Graphic Organizers.

Objectives

Objective 1: Describe the colonists' political heritage.

Objective 2: Explain the colonists' reaction to new taxes.

Objective 3: Describe the methods the colonists used to protest British taxes.

Objective 4: Summarize how the colonists reacted to the Townshend Acts.

Objective 5: Understand the significance of the First Continental Congress in 1774.

LESSON 2 ORGANIZER		PACING: APPROX. 1 PERIOD, .5 BLOCKS			
				RESOURCES	
		OBJECTIVES	PACING	Online	Print
Connect					
	DIGITAL START UP ACTIVITY **What Is Revolution?**		5 min.	●	
Investigate					
	DIGITAL TEXT 1 **The Foundations of Colonial Government**	Objective 1	10 min.	●	●
	DIGITAL TEXT 2 **New Taxes Create Conflict**	Objective 2	10 min.	●	●
	DIGITAL TEXT 3 **Opposition to Taxes Strengthens**	Objective 3	10 min.	●	●
	INTERACTIVE GALLERY **Important People of the American Revolution**		10 min.	●	
	DIGITAL TEXT 4 **Protests Lead to Violence**	Objective 4	10 min.	●	●
	DIGITAL TEXT 5 **The First Continental Congress**	Objective 5	10 min.	●	●
	INTERACTIVE CARTOON **Analyzing Political Cartoons**		10 min.	●	
Synthesize					
	DIGITAL ACTIVITY **Ideas Inform a Revolution**		5 min.	●	
Demonstrate					
	LESSON QUIZ **Lesson Quiz and Class Discussion Board**		10 min.	●	

Causes of the Revolution

■ CONNECT

DIGITAL START UP ACTIVITY
What Is Revolution?

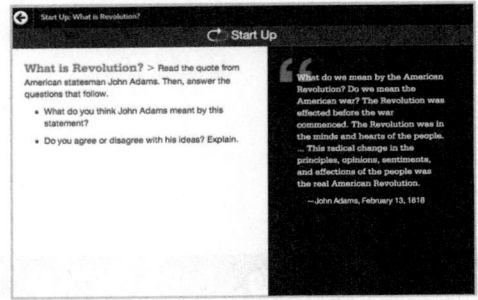

Begin by projecting the Digital Start Up Activity. Ask students to answer the questions as they enter and get settled. You may wish to have them share their ideas with each other or on a class blog or discussion board.

Discuss What does the term *revolution* mean? *(A revolution means a sudden or complete change. This can be a change in government, a change in a way of life, or a change in ideas.)* When does a political revolution begin? *(A political revolution begins when people have new expectations of government or when they decide that they want a change in leadership. It begins when people take action to radically change government.)*

Aa **Vocabulary Development:** Use the Interactive Reading Notepad to preview the Key Terms and Academic Vocabulary in this lesson with students.

↕ FLIP IT!
Assign the Flipped Video for this lesson.

■ STUDENT EDITION PRINT PAGES: 84–91

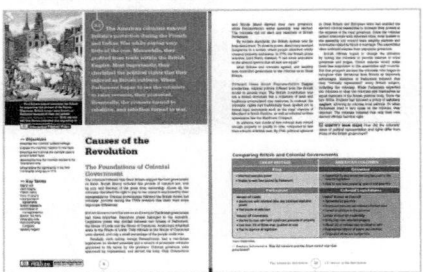

■ INVESTIGATE

DIGITAL TEXT 1
The Foundations of Colonial Government

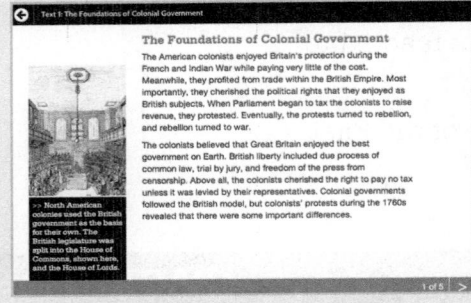

Objective 1: Describe the colonists' political heritage.

Quick Instruction
Begin by projecting the following terms: *royal charter, Mayflower Compact, colonial assembly,* and *salutary neglect*. Organize students into small groups, and assign each group a term for which to write a definition. Have groups share their definitions and post completed definitions on the class blog or Word Wall.

Determine Relevance For each term above, ask students how each contributed to growing tensions between the American colonists and the British. *(Governments in several colonies were based on royal charters, giving them a sense of independence from Britain. The first colonists in Massachusetts had established their colony based on an agreement known as the Mayflower Compact. This agreement gave colonists a tradition of popular rule that differed from hierarchical government in Britain. Many colonists had established colonial assemblies to which they reelected their own members to create and enforce laws in the colonies. They felt that their own assemblies superseded the power of British Parliament. Salutary neglect was a tradition by which the colonies had largely come to govern themselves, without minimal British oversight, a way of life to which colonists grew accustomed.)*

ELL Use the ELL activity described in the ELL chart.

Further Instruction
Project the chart *Comparing British and Colonial Governments*. Call on students to identify significant differences between British government and colonial government. Instruct students to write a few sentences in which they predict how those differences might lead to conflict. You may wish to post their predictions to the class blog or discussion board.

Compare What similarities existed among British and colonial governments? *(Colonial governments were modeled after British governments. They shared similar structures and ideas. For example, the British government had three branches, including a two-house legislature. Colonists largely followed British common law and adopted policies like trial by jury, due process, and the right to pay no tax that had not been levied by their representatives. In the colonies, as in Britain, wealthier men held most political power.)*

Contrast How did colonial political ideas and government structure differ from Britain's? *(Colonies had no representation in Parliament. In the colonies, more men also held the right to vote, making their assemblies more representative. Colonists believed that only their elected representatives, not British Parliament, had the right to tax them.)*

Solve Problems What solution could Britain offer the colonists to avoid conflict? Why do you think Britain does not do this? *(Britain could offer the colonists representation in Parliament. However, Britain does not want to extend that much power to the colonists or acknowledge that colonists have that right. If so, other colonists and British citizens might make similar demands.)*

DIGITAL TEXT 2
New Taxes Create Conflict

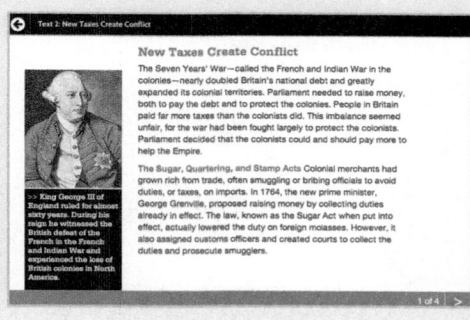

New Taxes Create Conflict

The Seven Years' War—called the French and Indian War in the colonies—nearly doubled Britain's national debt and greatly expanded its colonial territories. Parliament needed to raise money, both to pay the debt and to protect the colonies. People in Britain paid far more taxes than the colonists did. This imbalance seemed unfair, for the war had been fought largely to protect the colonists. Parliament decided that the colonists could and should pay more to help the Empire.

The Sugar, Quartering, and Stamp Acts Colonial merchants had grown rich from trade, often smuggling or bribing officials to avoid duties, or taxes, on imports. In 1764, the new prime minister, George Grenville, proposed raising money by collecting duties already in effect. The law, known as the Sugar Act when put into effect, actually lowered the duty on foreign molasses. However, it also assigned customs officers and created courts to collect the duties and prosecute smugglers.

>> King George III of England ruled for almost sixty years. During his reign he witnessed the British defeat of the French in the French and Indian War and experienced the loss of British colonies in North America.

1 of 4

DIGITAL TEXT 3
Opposition to Taxes Strengthens

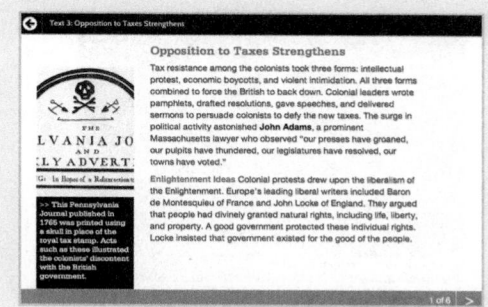

Opposition to Taxes Strengthens

Tax resistance among the colonists took three forms: intellectual protest, economic boycotts, and violent intimidation. All three forms combined to force the British to back down. Colonial leaders wrote pamphlets, drafted resolutions, gave speeches, and delivered sermons to persuade colonists to defy the new taxes. The surge in political activity astonished **John Adams**, a prominent Massachusetts lawyer who observed "our presses have groaned, our pulpits have thundered, our legislatures have resolved, our towns have voted."

Enlightenment Ideas Colonial protests drew upon the liberalism of the Enlightenment. Europe's leading liberal writers included Baron de Montesquieu of France and John Locke of England. They argued that people had divinely granted natural rights, including life, liberty, and property. A good government protected these individual rights. Locke insisted that government existed for the good of the people.

>> This Pennsylvania Journal published in 1765 was printed using a skull in place of the royal tax stamp. Acts such as these illustrated the colonists' discontent with the British government.

1 of 6

Objective 2: Explain the colonists' reaction to new taxes.

Quick Instruction

Project the chart titled *New Revenues for Britain*. Challenge students to predict how the colonists would respond to these acts. Have students write and share their predictions.

Analyze Information Why did the Stamp Act anger the colonists more than the Sugar and Quartering Acts had? (*The Sugar Act largely provided for enforcement of existing taxes on sugar, molasses, and similar goods. Colonists did not like the Quartering Act but were more willing to accept the argument that it was necessary for their defense and the regulation of trade. The Stamp Act aroused more anger because it was a new tax and affected goods that many colonists used. In short, the Stamp Act tax affected many more colonists.*)

D Differentiate: Challenge Assign students one of the following acts: Sugar Act, Quartering Act, and Stamp Act. Have students work individually, in pairs, or in small groups to write a short piece of flash fiction, a storyboard, or a script to illustrate the impact of their assigned law. Tell students to make sure that their creative work reflects the specific provisions of the act. For example, students working with the Sugar and Stamp Acts will want to show how these acts increased the costs of goods.

Further Instruction

Go through the Interactive Reading Notepad questions for New Taxes Create Conflict and discuss the answers with the class. Be sure that students explain how American colonists responded to each of the new acts of Parliament.

Support Ideas with Evidence What evidence supports the idea that Parliament was entitled to directly tax the colonists? (*Parliament made laws for Britain and the British empire. By tradition, the members of Parliament represented all British citizens, including its colonists. The British empire needed money to pay its debts, and since Parliament made laws for the empire, it was empowered to levy taxes on anyone in the empire.*)

Support Ideas with Evidence What evidence supports the idea that Parliament did not have the power to tax colonists? (*The idea of representation suggests that citizens entitled to vote should be permitted to vote for officials to represent their interests. Colonists were not permitted to vote for representatives to speak for them in Parliament. Rather, those colonists who could vote did so in colonial elections for members of colonial assemblies. As a result, they believed that members of the assemblies were their elected representatives, and only those representatives could tax them.*)

Objective 3: Describe the methods the colonists used to protest British taxes.

Quick Instruction

Interactive Gallery: Important People of the American Revolution Project the Interactive Gallery and click through the images. What ideas motivated some significant individuals who participated in events leading up the revolution? (*Some leaders were motivated by a desire for more democratic processes and self rule. Some sought greater equality through expanded representation. Some desired more political power for themselves or worried that British laws would hinder their economic activities and hurt them economically. Others wanted the ability to acquire more land and expand settlements.*)

Draw Conclusions Why did economic boycotts work to roll back British laws at first? (*The boycotts hurt Britain economically, costing the empire more rather than gaining it the taxes for which it had hoped. Parliament repealed the Stamp Act in order to restore trade and keep money flowing.*)

Causes of the Revolution

INTERACTIVE GALLERY

Important People of the American Revolution

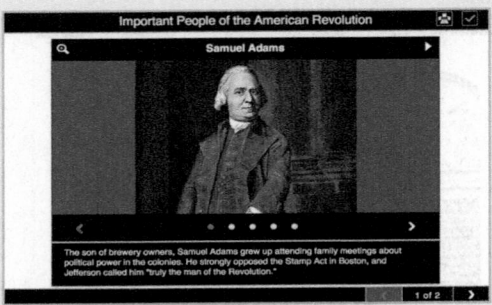

DIGITAL TEXT 4

Protests Lead to Violence

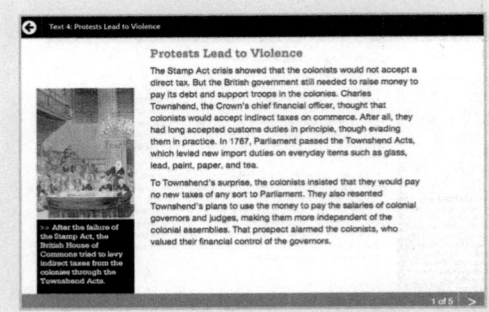

📺 ACTIVE CLASSROOM

Challenge students to write an interview question for each individual in the gallery. Then, organize students into groups and have them share and discuss their questions. Assign each group one of the individuals. Tell them to use the Conversation With History strategy to script an interview with their assigned person about his or her role in the revolution. If time allows, ask each group to act out its script. Otherwise, share their scripts in the class library or on the class blog.

Further Instruction

Have students work in small groups to complete the Interactive Reading Notepad questions for Opposition to Taxes Strengthens. Then, jigsaw the groups to have them compare their responses.

Apply Concepts How did Enlightenment principles support the case of the American colonists against taxation? *(Enlightenment principles, such as liberalism, suggested that people had divinely granted natural rights. Government existed to protect these rights. According to the social contract, government derived its power from the people. When government failed to protect the people's rights, they had a right to protest and even abolish that government to end the contract. Regarding taxation, colonists argued that Parliament was acting unlawfully and not protecting colonists' rights. For this reason, colonists had the right to resist taxation.)*

Evaluate Sources Read the primary source quote from Patrick Henry. What does Patrick Henry accuse the British government of doing? *(Colonists believed that British Parliament was exceeding its power in taxing them to pay for Britain's debt when no colonists served on or elected members to Parliament. They asserted that their elected representatives served in colonial government and so only those colonial governments could tax them.)*

Objective 4: Summarize how the colonists reacted to the Townshend Acts.

Quick Instruction

Being by projecting the following phrases: *Boston Incident, Boston Uprising, Boston Brawl,* and *Boston Massacre.* Prompt students to consider that each phrase could be used to describe the same event depending on perspective. Tell them to consider their responses from the perspective of an American colonist in Boston.

Analyze Information How do the different phrases seem to define the event differently depending on perspective? *(Boston Incident does not really assign fault and downplays events. Boston Brawl suggests that both sides of the event might have been to blame, making it an equal fight among colonists and soldiers. Boston Uprising implies that the colonists were to blame because they revolted and incited a response. Boston Massacre suggests that the British soldiers were responsible by acting without provocation and in excess.)*

ELL Use the ELL activity described in the ELL chart.

Further Instruction

Have students work individually to answer the Interactive Reading Notepad questions for *Protests Lead to Violence.* Then, ask them to share and revise their answers with a partner. If time allows, review their responses as a class. Be sure that students can summarize colonists' responses to the Townshend Acts.

DIGITAL TEXT 5

The First Continental Congress

INTERACTIVE CARTOON

The Horse "America" Throwing His Master"

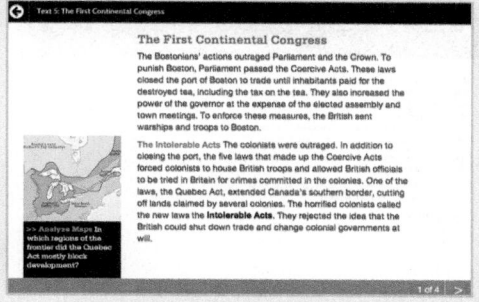

Explain Why did the Townshend Acts upset colonists? *(The Townshend Acts levied indirect taxes by placing import duties, or taxes, on goods imported to the colonies. The taxes raised prices on everyday goods, including glass, paint, paper, and tea. The Townshend Acts also gave Parliament the power to pay colonial governors, which reduced the power of the elected colonial assemblies over the appointed governors.)*

Make Generalizations Why were committees of correspondence a threat to British rule? *(They signalled a willingness among colonies to work together. They represented not only improved means of communications within and among colonies but also unity among the colonies against British rule. The committees were one more step closer to independence.)*

Make Predictions How might the British respond to the Boston Tea Party? *(The British might respond with more laws or perhaps even with troops and greater restrictions on colonial freedoms.)*

Objective 5: Understand the significance of the First Continental Congress in 1774.

Quick Instruction

Interactive Cartoon: The Horse "America" Throwing His Master" Project the Interactive Cartoon and explain that political cartoons often use metaphors to represent ideas, events, or people. Ask students to work through the activity in small groups, then review their findings as a class.

Analyze Political Cartoons Why did the artist choose to depict the American colonies and the British king as a horse and its rider? *(The imagery implies that the king is an unskilled rider trying to control the colonies and whip them into submission. It suggests that the colonies are more powerful than the rider and are capable of throwing off the rider in order to escape to freedom.)*

Interpret What made the Coercive Acts so intolerable? *(The Coercive Acts comprised a number of measures that colonists considered to be an abuse of British power: closing the Boston port to trade, increasing the power of the royal governor, sending warships and troops to Boston, forcing colonists to house troops, permitting British officers to be tried in Britain for crimes against colonists, and extending the boundary of Canada into lands claimed by colonists. These acts were considered such a breach of colonists' rights that they considered them intolerable.)*

Further Instruction

As a class, review and answer the questions in the Interactive Reading Notepad for the First Continental Congress. Point out that the First Continental Congress represented a fulfillment of Benjamin Franklin's earlier call for a colonial congress in his Albany Plan of Union. Be sure that students understand that the Continental Congress was a significant political and symbolic step, because the colonies were willing to overlook their individual interests in order to unite around a common goal.

Analyze Context Read Patrick Henry's quote from the First Continental Congress. What is the significance of his statement? How does it reflect the broader political shift within the colonies? *(Henry states that he is not a Virginian but an American. This statement signifies that the colonists are part of a bigger entity than just their individual colonies. They have shared interests and loyalties to one another, across colonial boundaries. It reflects a broader shift in which the colonies have begun to think of themselves as united in some fashion. It also shows that they have begun to think of themselves as Americans, distinct from the British.)*

Causes of the Revolution

SYNTHESIZE

DEMONSTRATE

DIGITAL ACTIVITY
Ideas Inform a Revolution

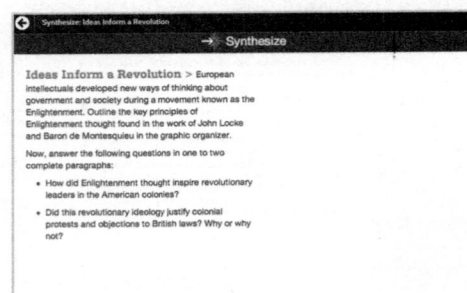

LESSON QUIZ
Lesson Quiz and Class Discussion Board

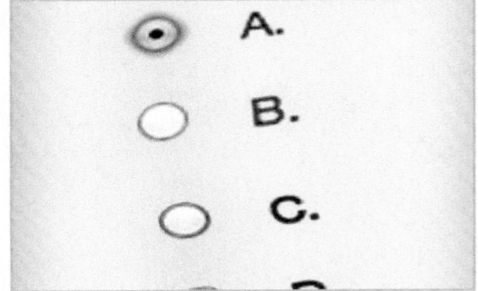

Cite Evidence What evidence would Britain have cited to justify passage of the Coercive Acts? *(In addition to claiming that Parliament had the authority to make laws for all citizens of the empire, including those in the colonies, Britain would have argued that the colonists had behaved unlawfully in seizing and destroying large amounts of British tea. They would have justified the acts as necessary to maintain order, secure trade, and recover payment for the lost tea.)*

Have students complete the graphic organizer by describing key principles of the Enlightenment. Then, tell students to Think-Pair-Share responses to the questions. Post students' completed paragraphs to the class blog or discussion board.

Discuss Have students think about the following question: What were the colonists' political, economic, and social grievances against Britain, and why did these grievances lead to conflict? Ask students to support their answers with examples from the text.

Assign the online Lesson Quiz for this lesson if you haven't already done so. Students will be offered automatic remediation or enrichment based on their score.

Pose these questions to the class on the Discussion Board:

In *Causes of the American Revolution*, you read about events leading up to the outbreak of war. You also explored Enlightenment ideals and political and economic motivations for colonial revolution.

Evaluate Arguments At this point, which side has the stronger case, Britain or the American colonists? Cite evidence from the lesson to support your position.

Make Predictions Given events such as the Boston Massacre, the Boston Tea Party, and the Coercive Acts, has war between Britain and the colonists become unavoidable? Explain.

Topic Inquiry
Have students continue their investigations for the Topic Inquiry.

The Colonists Declare Independence

Supporting English Language Learners

Use with the reading, **Colonists Disagree Over British Rule**.

Learning
Explain that the colonists were divided between two groups: Loyalists and Patriots. Tell students that they are going to create a concept map to help them organize the information they read about these two groups in *Colonists Disagree Over British Rule*.

Beginning Use simple spoken language to summarize the text. Ask students to name the two opposing groups of colonists. Write the names on a concept map on the board. Ask: Which group wanted to collect taxes? Add this information to the map. Ask: Which group wanted more free speech? Add this information to the map. Continue with other information.

Intermediate Use simple spoken language to summarize the text. Ask partners to draw a concept map with the names of the two opposing groups in separate circles in the center. Write the following concepts on the board and have partners write them on a spoke around the correct group: *collect taxes, more free speech, oaths of allegiance, Parliament and the Crown, militia drafts*. Tell students they can refer back to the text as needed.

Advanced Ask students to reread the text with a partner. Then have them work together to create a concept map to show what each of the opposing groups believed.

Advanced High Have students reread the text individually. Ask them to each create their own concept map to show what each of the opposing groups believed. Then have students get partners and compare their maps.

Use with the reading, **The Decision to Declare Independence**.

Listening
Explain to students that they will demonstrate listening comprehension by responding correctly to questions and requests.

Beginning Use simple spoken language to paraphrase the first two paragraphs of *The Decision to Declare Independence*. Ask the following questions to check listening comprehension: Did the book *Common Sense* make people want independence? Who wrote *Common Sense*? Did it propose independence from Britain?

Intermediate Use simple spoken language to paraphrase the first two paragraphs of *The Decision to Declare Independence*. Ask the following questions to check listening comprehension: What book made people want independence? Who wrote it? Did the book propose a union of new states?

Advanced Use spoken language to paraphrase the first two paragraphs of *The Decision to Declare Independence*. Ask students to talk about the book *Common Sense* and how it affected people.

Advanced High Use spoken language to paraphrase the first two paragraphs of *The Decision to Declare Independence*. Ask partners to talk about the book *Common Sense* and what it proposed. Ask: What type of language did it use?

▣ Differentiate Instruction

Use the Differentiated Instruction notes throughout the lesson plan to support the varied skill sets, levels of readiness, and interests in the mixed-ability classroom.

Challenge These notes include suggestions for expanding the activity for advanced students.

On-Level These notes include suggestions for modifying the activity to address different interests or learning styles.

Extra Support These notes include ideas for providing more scaffolding or reading spuport.

Special Needs These notes provide ideas for adapting instruction to support the needs of various special needs students.

■ NOTES

The Colonists Declare Independence

Objectives

Objective 1: Explain why fighting broke out to begin the American Revolution and the response of the Second Continental Congress.

Objective 2: Describe the Loyalists' view of the Patriots.

Objective 3: Analyze the impact of Thomas Paine's *Common Sense*.

Objective 4: Assess why Congress declared independence and the ideas underlying the Declaration of Independence.

LESSON 3 ORGANIZER		PACING: APPROX. 1 PERIOD, .5 BLOCKS			
				RESOURCES	
		OBJECTIVES	PACING	Online	Print
Connect					
DIGITAL START UP ACTIVITY **Debating Independence From a King**			5 min.	●	
Investigate					
DIGITAL TEXT 1 **The First Shots Are Fired**		Objective 1	10 min.	●	●
DIGITAL TEXT 2 **Colonists Disagree Over British Rule**		Objective 2	10 min.	●	●
DIGITAL TEXT 3 **The Decision to Declare Independence**		Objectives 3, 4	10 min.	●	●
INTERACTIVE GALLERY **Thomas Paine and *Common Sense***			10 min.	●	
Synthesize					
DIGITAL ACTIVITY **The Meaning of *Common Sense***			5 min.	●	
Demonstrate					
LESSON QUIZ **Lesson Quiz and Class Discussion Board**			10 min.	●	

PEARSON realize.™
www.PearsonRealize.com

Go online to access additional resources including: Primary Sources • Biographies • Supreme Court cases • 21st Century Skill Tutorials • Maps • Graphic Organizers.

CONNECT

DIGITAL START UP ACTIVITY

Debating Independence From a King

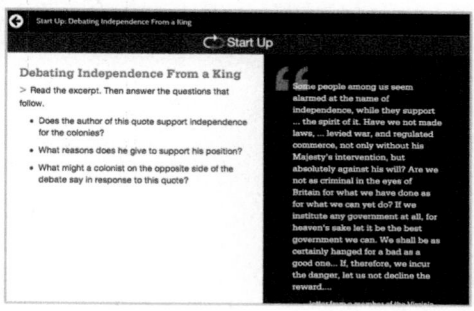

Project the Digital Start Up Activity Have students work in pairs to read and respond to the primary source quote as they enter and get settled. Then, call on pairs to share one or more of their responses.

Discuss What do American colonies stand to gain and lose from independence? *(The colonies could gain the right to establish their own governments and win control over their own affairs, including trade. They would lose the structure and protection of the British government, including its military.)*

Tell students that in this lesson they will explore the ideas and events that led the colonies toward independence.

Aa Vocabulary Development: Use the Interactive Reading Notepad to preview the Key Terms and Academic Vocabulary in this lesson with students.

⇅ FLIP IT!

Assign the Flipped Video for this lesson.

STUDENT EDITION PRINT PAGES: 92–96

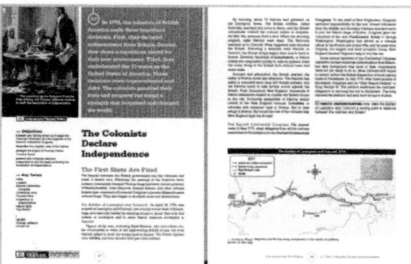

INVESTIGATE

DIGITAL TEXT 1

The First Shots Are Fired

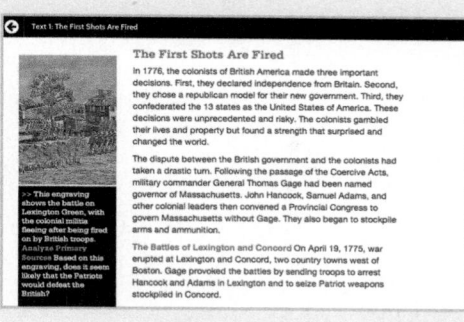

Objective 1: Explain why fighting broke out to begin the American Revolution and the response of the Second Continental Congress.

Quick Instruction

Point out the significance of the Second Continental Congress's decision to support Massachusetts. The soldiers and supplies from other colonies were an important symbol of political unity against the British, even if many colonists remained hesitant to declare independence.

Explain Why did war break out at Lexington and Concord? *(British General Thomas Gage sent British troops to arrest Patriot leaders John Hancock and Samuel Adams as well as to seize weapons that colonists had stockpiled in Concord. Paul Revere rode into the countryside to warn of the British advance. The colonial militia rallied to resist the British, and shots were fired.)*

Further Instruction

Have students work with a partner to complete the questions from the Interactive Reading Notepad. Then, review students' responses as a class. To extend the lesson, assign the students to complete Biography: George Washington.

Make Predictions Why might the war in the colonies prove more difficult for the British than they expected? *(If the British did not win a quick defeat, the British military would have to fight a prolonged war on unfamiliar territory and send troops and supplies across* the Atlantic Ocean. Communications and transportation would be slow. The colonists would be motivated to defend their lives, families, and property.)

Determine Relevance What was significant about King George III's response to the Olive Branch Petition? *(King George III rejected the petition and sent more troops to Boston. This action negated the colonists' last attempt at negotiation or compromise, and made further battle almost inevitable. It reinforced the colonists' decision to organize the Continental Army.)*

The Colonists Declare Independence

DIGITAL TEXT 2

Colonists Disagree Over British Rule

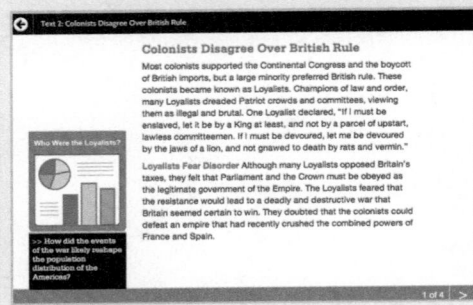

Objective 2: Describe the Loyalists' view of the Patriots.

Quick Instruction

Project the following quote made by a Loyalist: "If I must be enslaved, let it be by a King at least, and not by a parcel of upstart, lawless committeemen. If I must be devoured, let me be devoured by the jaws of a lion, and not gnawed to death by rats and vermin." Ask students to paraphrase the meaning of this statement, including the meaning of the metaphors, and have them share their responses. Guide students to conclude that not all colonists agreed with the goals of the American Revolution.

Summarize Why did some colonists oppose the Patriots and the American Revolution? *(Some colonists believed that they must remain loyal to Britain. They felt that the revolution was unlawful. Some also felt certain that the colonies could not hope to win, or they disagreed with the goals of the Patriots. Still others disliked Patriot methods, such as taxes, oaths of allegiance, and militia drafts. They became angry when Patriots shut down Loyalist newspapers and attacked Loyalists for opposing them.)*

D Differentiate: On Level Have students split into Patriot and Loyalist groups. Tell the Patriot group to list the reasons for going to war. Tell the Loyalist group to list the reasons to oppose the war. Then, have the groups share their lists.

ELL Use the ELL activity described in the ELL chart.

Further Instruction

Instruct student groups to work together to complete the Interactive Reading Notepad questions. Then, jigsaw the groups, and have students compare and revise their responses. Finally, review the answers to the questions as a class. Be sure to point out that not all Patriots were farmers and artisans and not all Loyalists were wealthy merchants and business leaders. Help students understand that many different people in the colonies supported opposite sides of the revolution.

Analyze Political Cartoons How does the political cartoon portray the Patriots? What cause does the cartoon seem to support, and how? *(The cartoon portrays the Patriots as forceful and repressive. It shows them as intolerant, compelling the Loyalists to their way of thinking. The cartoon seems to support the Loyalist cause by casting the Patriots in a negative light.)*

Hypothesize How might the Patriots have tried to persuade the Loyalists to support the revolution? *(Although the Patriots likely could not have swayed all Loyalists, they might have appealed to more Loyalists by showing them greater tolerance and appealing to them more through discussion and diplomacy rather than through force and intimidation. The Patriots could have organized a more focused campaign by which their leaders met with Loyalists and laid out their case for revolution.)*

Determine Relevance Why is it significant that many American Indians and African Americans opposed the revolution? *(American Indians and African Americans largely opposed the revolution because they worried about colonial rule. African Americans thought that they were more likely to win liberty under the British. American Indians wanted to stop colonial expansion. Their support helped the British and made the war more difficult for the colonists.)*

DIGITAL TEXT 3

The Decision to Declare Independence

INTERACTIVE GALLERY

Thomas Paine and *Common Sense*

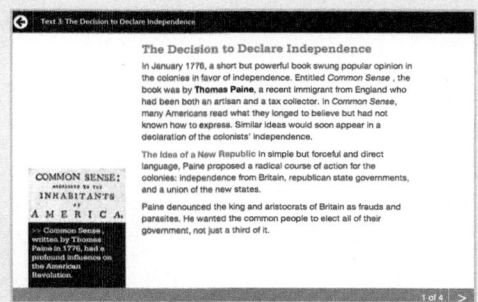

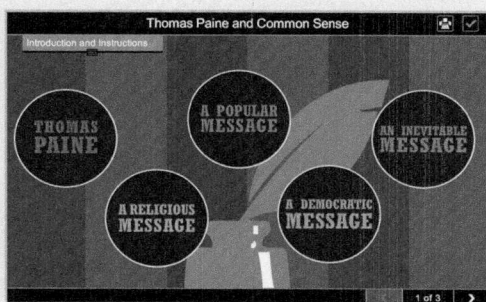

Objectives 3: Analyze the impact of Thomas Paine's *Common Sense*; 4: Assess why Congress declared independence and the ideas underlying the Declaration of Independence.

Quick Instruction

Interactive Gallery: Thomas Paine and *Common Sense* Project the interactive gallery. Click through the slides, and call on students to read aloud the captions and quotes. Ask individual students to identify what they consider the most powerful or persuasive statement from the selections. Have them record the statement, explain what it means, and explain why they consider it so important. Tell students to share their selections and ideas in groups. Then, call on each group to share one or two of their responses, if time allows.

Draw Conclusions How effective do you think the words of Thomas Paine were in rallying colonists to the cause of revolution? Explain. *(Possible answer: Thomas Paine's words likely reinforced the ideas of many colonists already committed to revolution. However, his powerful arguments might have persuaded many who were uncertain that the cause was just and that the war was winnable. I think his words were very effective in the way that they recorded the central ideas, driving principles, and goals of the revolutionary movement. They gave Patriots words and ideas to get behind and to use to motivate one another as well as to use to respond to Loyalists.)*

ACTIVE CLASSROOM

Organize students into groups. Tell each group to use the Cartoon It strategy to brainstorm ideas for political cartoons based on Thomas Paine's writings. Then, instruct each student to draw a political cartoon using one of the ideas brainstormed in the group. Display completed cartoons in the classroom.

ELL Use the ELL activity described in the ELL chart.

Further Instruction

Be sure that students understand that the American Revolution did not begin with a Declaration of Independence. The declaration did not come until more than a year into the fighting. Many colonists who fought in the revolution did so to defend their homes and property. They did not set out to build a new nation.

Draw Conclusions Why might Paine have focused much of his criticism on the class structure and aristocracy of Britain? *(Most American colonists were not aristocrats. Many had little wealth. They were artisans, farmers, laborers, and merchants. Focusing on the class structure helped draw clear lines between the British and the colonists and made the conflict about giving colonists the opportunity to shape their own lives and achieve greater economic success unburdened by the demands of royals and wealthy elites.)*

Synthesize How did the Declaration of Independence change the goals and the nature of the American Revolution? *(The Declaration gave the revolution a new purpose and spirit. The war was no longer just about resisting taxes, protesting laws, demanding representation, and protecting life and property. The war was now motivated in part by republican ideals of liberty and rights. The Declaration gave the Patriots added purpose in their fight, as well as powerful principles around which to rally.)*

The Colonists Declare Independence

▮ SYNTHESIZE

▮ DEMONSTRATE

DIGITAL ACTIVITY
The Meaning of *Common Sense*

LESSON QUIZ
Lesson Quiz and Class Discussion Board

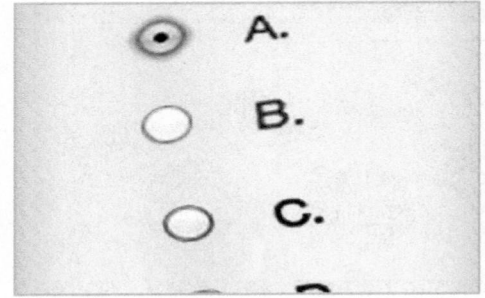

Have students read the excerpt from *Common Sense* and write their speeches. Then, tell students to share and revise their speeches in pairs. If time allows, call on students to present their speeches to the class. If not, post speeches to the class blog or discussion board.

Instruct students to consider the following question: Were Thomas Paine's ideas an accurate reflection of all or most American colonists at the time? Ask students to cite evidence from the text.

Assign the online Lesson Quiz for this lesson if you haven't already done so. Students will be offered automatic remediation or enrichment based on their score.

Pose these questions to the class on the Discussion Board:

In *The Colonists Declare Independence*, you read about the outbreak of war between Britain and the colonies. You also learned how colonists held differing views on the war and independence, and you explored what events and ideas led the colonies to declare independence from Britain.

Hypothesize How might the course of American history have been different had King George III accepted the "Olive Branch Petition"? Why do you think the king rejected the petition?

Evaluate Arguments To what degree do you think the Patriot leaders believed in the ideals espoused in the Declaration of Independence? Cite evidence from the text to support your position.

Topic Inquiry
Have students continue their investigations for the Topic Inquiry.

Americans Win the Revolution

Supporting English Language Learners

Use with the reading, **The War Begins**.

Learning
Tell students to study the chart about soldiers of the Revolutionary War. Encourage them to look at how many soldiers were in each army, what kind of training each had, and the number of casualties among soldiers. Explain that previewing the chart can help students better understand the text.

Beginning Ask students to look at the chart. Ask: What information tells you which army will be stronger? Does knowing this help you understand the text that says, *the Patriots had to win a hard and bloody war against the world's most powerful empire*?

Intermediate Ask: Why do you think the Continental soldiers suffered from hunger and cold? Tell students to use the information in the chart to discuss the casualties of Continental soldiers.

Advanced Tell students to use what they learned from the chart to explain what is meant by the text, *the odds seemed slight that the Patriots could win*.

Advanced High Tell students to look at the chart to help them understand Howe's statement, *. . . trained troops are invincible against any numbers or any position of untrained rabble*. Provide help with difficult language, as needed.

Use with the reading, **The War in the Middle States and Frontier**.

Speaking
Tell students that they will express their ideas about why France entered the war with partners or in small groups. Read the text as a class, pausing to explain any difficult vocabulary or concepts.

Beginning Ask partners to talk about why the French entered the war. Have them use these sentence frames to help them express their ideas: France and Britain were _____. France sent secret shipments of _____ and _____ to the Patriots. They also provided _____. After Saratoga, _____ fought with the _____ against the British.

Intermediate Divide students into small groups and ask them to talk about how the French helped the Patriots against the British. Encourage students in the group to take turns sharing their ideas about why France entered the war.

Advanced Ask partners to talk about why France risked an open alliance with the United States and what led to this alliance. Have them share their ideas about how this alliance helped the Patriots win the war.

Advanced High Have partners talk about Spain's motives and fears about entering the war. Ask them to share their ideas about what Spain stood to lose as a result of their alliance with the French.

▷ Differentiate Instruction

Use the Differentiated Instruction notes throughout the lesson plan to support the varied skill sets, levels of readiness, and interests in the mixed-ability classroom.

Challenge These notes include suggestions for expanding the activity for advanced students.

On-Level These notes include suggestions for modifying the activity to address different interests or learning styles.

Extra Support These notes include ideas for providing more scaffolding or reading spuport.

Special Needs These notes provide ideas for adapting instruction to support the needs of various special needs students.

■ NOTES

Americans Win the Revolution

Objectives

Objective 1: Explain the advantages the British held at the start of the war and the mistakes they made by underestimating the Patriots.

Objective 2: Describe the war in the Middle States and Frontier.

Objective 3: Assess why the British failed to win the war in the South.

Objective 4: Describe how the British were finally defeated and the terms of the Peace Treaty.

Objective 5: Analyze how the Revolution affected Americans and people worldwide.

LESSON 4 ORGANIZER		OBJECTIVES	PACING	RESOURCES	
				Online	Print
Connect					
	DIGITAL START UP ACTIVITY **Paine's Argument for a Military Advantage**		5 min.	●	
Investigate					
	DIGITAL TEXT 1 **The War Begins**	Objective 1	10 min.	●	●
	INTERACTIVE CHART **Advantages and Disadvantages of British and Colonists**		10 min.	●	
	DIGITAL TEXT 2 **The War in the Middle States and Frontier**	Objective 2	10 min.	●	●
	DIGITAL TEXT 3 **The War in the South**	Objective 3	10 min.	●	●
	DIGITAL TEXT 4 **The War Comes to a Conclusion**	Objective 4	10 min.	●	●
	INTERACTIVE TIMELINE **Turning Points of the American Revolution**		10 min.	●	
	DIGITAL TEXT 5 **The Impact of the Revolution**	Objective 5	10 min.	●	●
	INTERACTIVE MAP **North America, 1775–1783**		10 min.	●	
Synthesize					
	DIGITAL ACTIVITY **The Legacy of the Revolution's Ideas**		5 min.	●	
Demonstrate					
	LESSON QUIZ **Lesson Quiz and Class Discussion Board**		10 min.	●	

PACING: APPROX. 1 PERIOD, .5 BLOCKS

PEARSON realize™
www.PearsonRealize.com

Go online to access additional resources including:
Primary Sources • Biographies • Supreme Court cases •
21st Century Skill Tutorials • Maps • Graphic Organizers.

CONNECT

DIGITAL START UP ACTIVITY
Paine's Argument for a Military Advantage

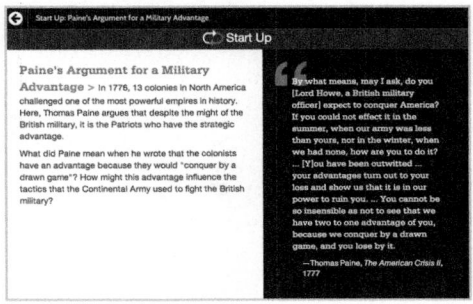

Have students read and respond to the quote from Thomas Paine as they enter and get settled. Be sure that students understand that a drawn game, as in chess, is one in which neither side can win a clear victory.

Discuss What geographic factors make a drawn game a victory for the colonies? *(The distance between Britain and her colonies makes the drawn game a victory for the colonies. To keep up the war, Britain must continually send troops and supplies across the ocean. The argument is that eventually Britain will become unable to maintain the transatlantic assault.)*

Tell students that in this lesson they will learn about significant events during the American Revolution, as well as analyze the immediate effects of the war.

Aa Vocabulary Development: Use the Interactive Reading Notepad to preview the Key Terms and Academic Vocabulary in this lesson with students.

⇅ FLIP IT!
Assign the Flipped Video for this lesson.

■ STUDENT EDITION PRINT PAGES: 97–105

INVESTIGATE

DIGITAL TEXT 1
The War Begins

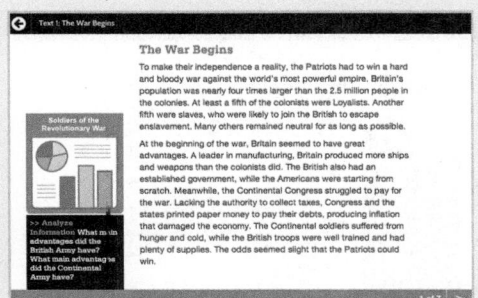

Objective 1: Explain the advantages the British held at the start of the war and the mistakes they made by underestimating the Patriots.

Quick Instruction
Interactive Chart: Advantages and Disadvantages of British and Colonists
Project the Interactive Chart. Have students take turns entering answers into the chart. Be sure to point out that the British took for granted that they had superior force of arms and numbers. However, several key advantages made all the difference for the colonists. Call attention to the resources that the British had, and point out that the Britain expected to win the war quickly because of its superior forces, arms, experience, and wealth.

Compare What advantages did the British have? *(powerful navy, highly trained soldiers and officers, Loyalist support, military weapons and supplies, including uniforms and boots)* What advantages did the colonies have? *(knowledge of the terrain, defense of family and property, leadership of George Washington, access to and knowledge of rifles and arms)*

▐▶ ACTIVE CLASSROOM
Organize students into pairs or small groups. Assign each group a role as either Patriots or Loyalists. Instruct the groups to use the Take a Stand strategy to write a short persuasive speech in which they try to persuade the other side why they cannot hope to win the war. Have students present their speeches in class.

INTERACTIVE CHART
Advantages and Disadvantages of British and Colonists

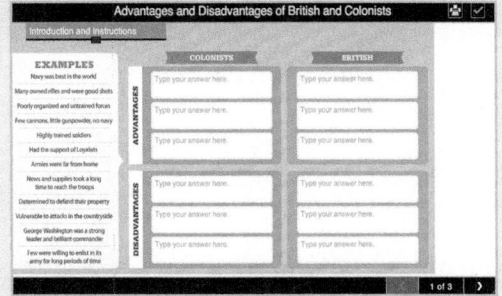

D Differentiate: Extra Support Project or display a world map. Have students locate Britain and the United States. Guide students to use the map scale to calculate the distance between Britain and its colonies in what would become the United States. *(Answers will vary but should be about 3,000 miles.)* Point out the logistical challenges of maintaining steady supplies for British forces given the time needed to cross the ocean. You may also wish to project a physical map of the eastern coast of the United States. Invite students to identify other geographic features that might have helped or hindered the British. *(The Appalachian Mountains would have posed a challenge. Rivers, if not well guarded, would have helped move British forces and supplies.)*

ELL Use the ELL activity described in the ELL chart.

Further Instruction
Have students work with a partner to complete the questions from the Interactive Reading Notepad. Then, review students' responses as a class. Be sure that students understand that the British expected to win the American Revolution quickly. British casualties and American victories came as a surprise. The British did not anticipate that they would be fighting a non-traditional war in which the colonial militias made use of the geography to strike British forces and supplies.

Make Predictions What advantages may tip the war in the colonists' favor, and why? *(The distance between Britain and North America will make it challenging for the British to maintain steady supplies for its military. The British military would also be unfamiliar with much of the territory in North America.)*

Americans Win the Revolution

DIGITAL TEXT 2

The War in the Middle States and Frontier

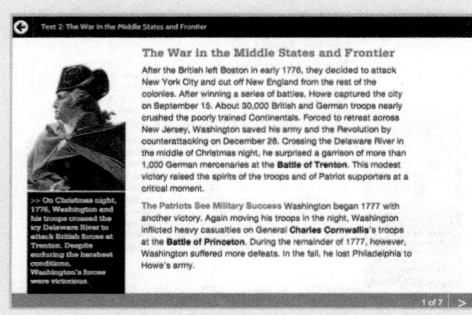

Infer Why did Lord William Howe put his forces in an exposed position at Bunker Hill? *(Howe thought that the British had superior numbers, skill, and arms to overcome the Patriots despite the vulnerable position. He did not think the Patriots had enough men or enough skill and weaponry to defeat the British no matter the fighting conditions.)*

Analyze Information Why did the colonists keep fighting despite hunger, illness, bad weather, poor supplies, inflation, lack of experience, and economic hardship? What do you think kept the colonists motivated? *(Unlike the British, the colonists were fighting for their homes and families. They had come to the colonies to build new lives, away from Britain, or had been born to colonists who already had established themselves. They were motivated to defend their property, their communities, their lives, and their ways of life. They knew that to lose the war might mean to lose everything.)*

Objective 2: Describe the war in the Middle States and Frontier.

Quick Instruction

Project the image of Washington crossing the Delaware. Draw attention to the ice on the river and to the sparse clothing of the colonial soldiers. Guide students to understand that the Battle of Trenton was such a success in part because the British did not expect the colonials to attack. Washington took a bold step in leading his forces across the icy waters.

Apply Concepts How do you think Washington's victory at Delaware impacted the motivation of his troops? *(The victory likely encouraged the troops to keep fighting and helped them to believe that they could win the war.)*

Explain Why did France ally with the United States, and how did that alliance impact the war? *(France chose to ally with the United States after the Battle of Saratoga, at which the British suffered a serious loss. This battle convinced the French that the United States had a chance of winning the war. Benjamin Franklin played a key role in winning the French alliance. French assistance made the war a more equal contest of arms and forces.)*

ELL Use the ELL activity described in the ELL chart.

Further Instruction

Draw Conclusions Why did France and Spain support rebellious colonies in overthrowing the rule of a fellow European power? *(Britain, France, and Spain had long competed for wealth, power, and control of global trade. Each nation had sought to build an empire at the others' expense. Before the American Revolution, Britain had dealt a serious blow to French power. Spain and France likely saw an opportunity to check British power and slow its global expansion by supporting the revolution in its American colonies.)*

Identify Central Issues Why did fighting spread to the frontier? *(After the French and Indian War, Britain had gained lands to the west, and American settlers had rushed to settle those lands. When war broke out between Britain and the colonies, American Indians largely sided with the British to prevent further expansion of American settlements. Fighting spread to the frontier as American Indians tried to push back colonists and Americans sought to secure their claim to the western lands, especially the Ohio River valley.)*

DIGITAL TEXT 3

The War in the South

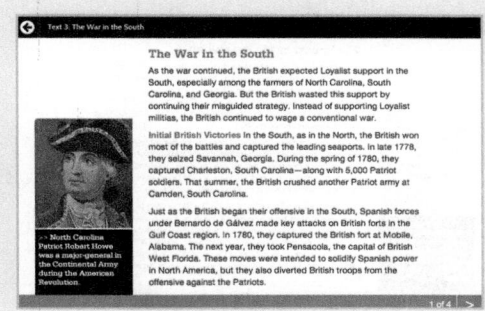

Objective 3: Assess why the British failed to win the war in the South.

Quick Instruction

Project the map of turning points in the war, and draw attention to the battles in the South. Point out that many of these battles took place later in the war. Britain had not won a quick, clear victory in New England or in the Middle Colonies. It turned to the South thinking to find greater support among Loyalists there.

Connect What do you think Britain hoped to gain by winning victories in the South? *(Since Britain could not win the victory that it wanted in the North, it probably hoped to win enough victories in the South to take the colonies there and gain more troops, resources, and bases from which to launch a stronger assault on the Middle and New England Colonies.)*

Further Instruction

Have students continue working in pairs to answer the questions on the Interactive Reading Notepad. Then, review their responses as a class.

Project a map showing the territories held by Britain, France, and Spain at the start of the American Revolution. Point out that Spain held Florida as well as other large territories to the south of what would become the United States. Spain still had a large, powerful navy, and many resources in Central and South America. The alliance of Spain with France posed a serious threat to British forces because Spain could attack British troops from the south as well as at sea.

Be sure to remind students that much of the American Revolution was also fought in naval battles. The alliance of Spain and France helped the United States because these nations were able not only to keep supply lines open to the colonies but also to cut off British forces.

Paraphrase What did one Loyalist mean when he said, "Great Britain has now a hundred enemies, where it had one before"? *(Britain did such a poor job of fighting the war in the South, failing to provided the support needed by Loyalists, that many Loyalists changed sides and many more colonists who had tried to stay out of the war joined the Patriots. Britain had begun by fighting the Patriots, one group of colonists, and had ended up fighting nearly all of them.)*

Draw Conclusions How did the geography of the South help the Patriots? *(Much of the South was agricultural and wild or unsettled. There were vast stretches of countryside through which the British had to travel and fight. The colonists knew these lands but the British did not. Urban centers and transportation lines were not as easy for the British to seize and control. The colonists fought most of the war in the South through militias and through unconventional tactics for which the British were not prepared.)*

DIGITAL TEXT 4

The War Comes to a Conclusion

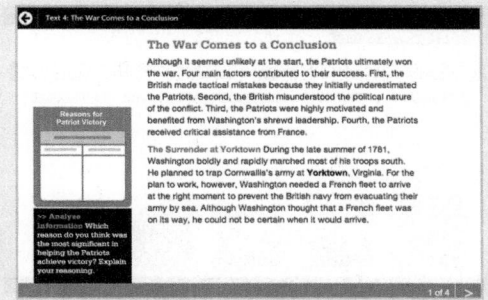

Objective 4: Describe how the British were finally defeated and the terms of the Peace Treaty.

Quick Instruction

Interactive Timeline: Turning Points of the American Revolution Project the Interactive Timeline. Prompt students to explain the importance of each event.

Make Generalizations What factor led Cornwallis to march his troops into a trap? *(From the start, the British underestimated the colonists. The British, especially their military leaders, never believed that the Patriots could defeat them. They placed too much confidence in their methods, their experience, their numbers, and their weapons.)*

Evaluate Information At what point of the war did the United States' victory became certain, and why? *(Possible answer: The American victory became inevitable as soon as France and Spain officially joined the war. At that point, Britain lost the advantages that had sustained its forces up until that point. American forces retained their original advantages and gained additional support and resources. Since Britain had not been able to win before, the empire could not hope to win once the United States had allies.)*

Americans Win the Revolution

INTERACTIVE TIMELINE
Turning Points of the American Revolution

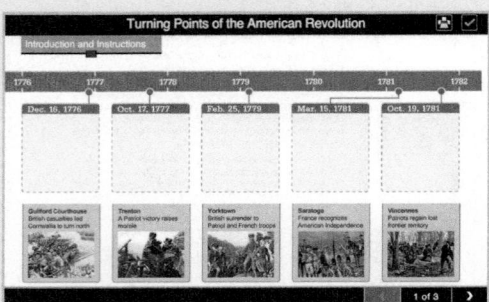

DIGITAL TEXT 5
The Impact of the Revolution

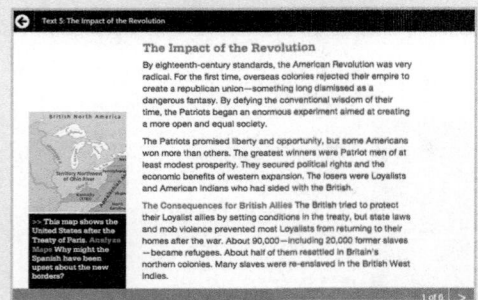

▣ ACTIVE CLASSROOM

Instruct students to form small groups. Tell them that they are to work together as the editorial team for a Patriot or a Loyalist newspaper. Have them use the Made Headlines strategy to write headlines and lead sentences for newspaper articles on each of the events shown on the Interactive Timeline. Display students' work in the classroom or post their work on the class blog.

Further Instruction

Have student pairs continue working together to answer the questions in the Interactive Reading Notepad. Then, review the answers as a class.

Organize students into four groups. Assign each of the groups one of the four factors listed in the opening paragraph of the text:

* First, the British made tactical mistakes because they initially underestimated the Patriots.
* Second, the British misunderstood the political nature of the conflict.
* Third, the Patriots were highly motivated and benefited from Washington's shrewd leadership.
* Fourth, the Patriots received critical assistance from France.

Instruct each group to review the lesson to find supporting evidence and examples for their factor. Then, have the groups read the text together to assess how their factor contributed to the final outcome of the war. Specifically, tell students to explain how their factor contributed to Cornwallis's surrender and the Treaty of Paris. Finally, have each group share their findings with the class.

Explain What part did British citizens in Britain play in the end of the war? *(British citizens grew weary and disenchanted with the war in the colonies as well as tired of the taxes to pay for it. They elected new leadership and demanded an end to the war.)*

Objective 5: Analyze how the Revolution affected Americans and people worldwide.

Quick Instruction
Interactive Map: North America, 1775–1783 Project the interactive map and slide through the images. Prompt students to identify ways in which territorial claims in North America changed as a result of the American Revolution.

Make Predictions What impact might the outcome of the American Revolution have on American Indians? *(Possible answer: The American Revolution will lead to further land losses for American Indians. The colonists would be free to settle former British lands, pushing American Indians farther west and potentially creating more conflict.)*

▣ ACTIVE CLASSROOM

Tell students to use the Wallpaper strategy to record what they have learned about the American Revolution and its impact. Have them draw their piece of the wallpaper and explain its meaning in a short paragraph. Then, post students' completed wall paper. Conduct a "wisdom" walk in which students examine each piece of the wallpaper. Permit them to ask and answer questions about pieces. Finally, have students write one to two paragraphs in which they explain the significance of the American Revolution to either their personal history or to world history.

INTERACTIVE MAP
North America, 1775–1783

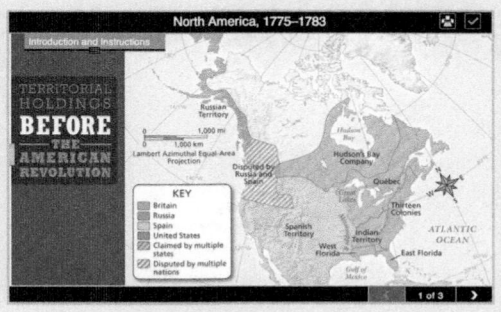

Further Instruction

Instruct students to work alone to answer the questions for the final Interactive Reading Notepad in the lesson. Then, group students to share and revise their responses.

Generate Explanations How did the American Revolution impact nations and peoples outside of its borders? *(The American Revolution became a war for ideals that reverberated around the globe. In the centuries that followed, many other nations would adopt similar democratic and republican principles, forming governments designed to represent the will of their citizens. Though not all of these efforts succeeded or had generally positive outcomes, it represented a fundamental shift in how people viewed their relationship with government.)*

Analyze Information How did the American Revolution both succeed and fail to meet the expectations of the colonists? *(Though the revolution secured a new nation and a new form of government for the Patriots, not all Patriots and not all people in the colonies enjoyed the benefits of this outcome. Women did not gain equal rights with men, despite their contributions to the war effort. Many men did not gain the political rights and economic opportunities for which they had hoped. In the South, slavery only became more entrenched. American Indians, too, suffered losses as more Americans migrated westward.)*

■ SYNTHESIZE

DIGITAL ACTIVITY
The Legacy of the Revolution's Ideas

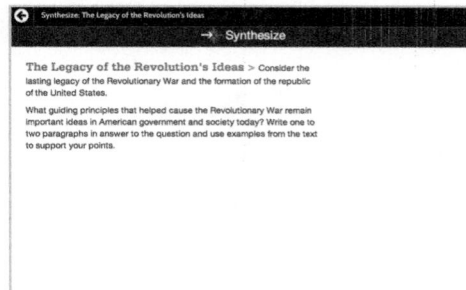

Have students work alone to answer the questions in the digital activity. You may wish to encourage them to list the guiding principles about which they want to write before beginning their paragraphs. Then, tell students to share and discuss their responses in small groups. Ask each group to select one response to share with the class.

Discuss What principles are important to U.S. government today? *(Possible responses: liberty, freedom of press and speech, religious freedom, minority rights, representative government, common good, individual rights, voting rights, democracy, republicanism, popular sovereignty)*

■ DEMONSTRATE

LESSON QUIZ
Lesson Quiz and Class Discussion Board

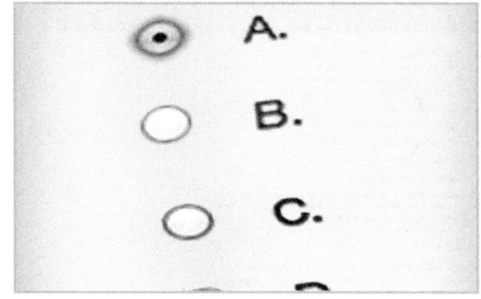

Assign the online Lesson Quiz for this lesson if you haven't already done so. Students will be offered automatic remediation or enrichment based on their score.

Pose these questions to the class on the Discussion Board:

In *Americans Win the Revolution*, you learned about the conduct of the war and examined how the colonial forces overcame British rule. You also explored the terms of the peace and looked at the immediate outcomes and lasting legacy of the American Revolution.

Synthesize How well did the American Revolution deliver on the promises of the Declaration of Independence?

Apply Concepts In what circumstances, if any, is war a justifiable means to secure political change? Explain.

Topic Inquiry
Have students continue their investigations for the Topic Inquiry.

The American Revolution

■ SYNTHESIZE

DIGITAL ESSENTIAL QUESTION ACTIVITY
Reflect on the Essential Question and Topic

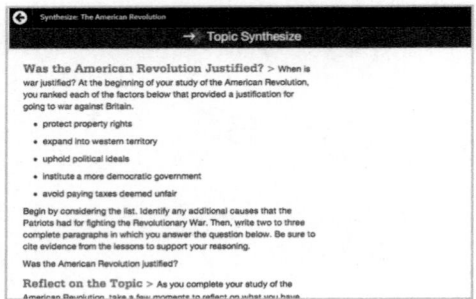

Ask students to consider the Essential Question for the topic: When is war justified? Remind students of the lists of reasons that they ranked at the start of the topic. Recall that reasons for the colonists to go to war included:

- protect property rights
- expand into western territory
- uphold political ideals
- institute a more democratic government
- avoid paying taxes deemed unfair

Have students work in small groups to re-evaluate their rankings. Ask them to re-order their lists, if appropriate, and to add any additional reasons for going to war.

Discuss Were the colonists justified in going to war against Britain? Ask students to cite reasons from the text to explain their positions. You may wish to have students share their responses on the class discussion board. Then, organize students into groups based on their responses and have each group discuss and present their explanation.

Then, ask students to reflect on the topic as a whole. Ask them to write down one to three questions they've thought about. Share an examples like this to prompt their thinking:

- What were three key turning points in the relationship between Britain and its colonies that led to war?
- At what point did the American Revolution become inevitable, and why?

Have students work in pairs and answer one another's questions or ask them to share their responses on the class discussion board.

Topic Inquiry
Have students complete Step 3 of the Topic Inquiry.

■ DEMONSTRATE

DIGITAL TOPIC REVIEW AND ASSESSMENT
The American Revolution

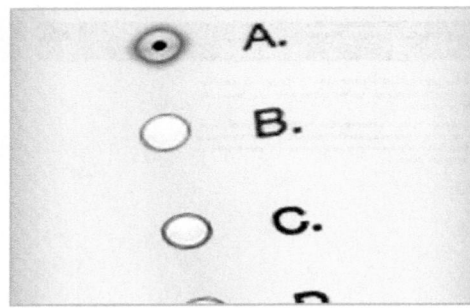

Students can prepare for the Topic Test by answering the questions in the Topic Review and Assessment online or the Assessment questions in the Print Student text. They can also prepare by reviewing their answers to the Interactive Reading Notepad questions or reviewing their notes in the Reading and Notetaking Study Guide.

DIGITAL TOPIC TEST
The American Revolution

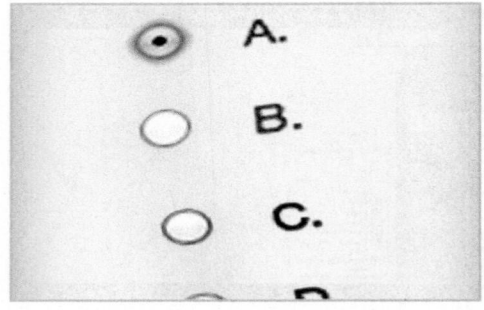

TOPIC TEST
Assign the Topic Test to assess students' understanding of topic content.

BENCHMARK TESTS
Assign these benchmark tests as you complete the relevant topics to monitor student progress toward mastering the course content and as preparation for the End-of-Course Test.

Benchmark Test 1: Topics 1–3
Benchmark Test 2: Topics 4–6
Benchmark Test 3: Topics 7–9
Benchmark Test 4: Topics 10–12
Benchmark Test 5: Topics 13–15
Benchmark Test 6: Topics 16–18
Benchmark Test 7: Topics 19–20

Topic ④

PEARSON
realize™

www.PearsonRealize.com
Access your Digital Lesson

Establishing the New Nation

TOPIC 4 ORGANIZER	PACING: APPROX. 6 PERIODS, 3 BLOCKS
	PACING
Connect	**1 period**
MY STORY VIDEO **Alexander Hamilton, Shaping the New Nation**	10 min.
DIGITAL ESSENTIAL QUESTION ACTIVITY **What Is the Proper Role of Government?**	10 min.
DIGITAL OVERVIEW ACTIVITY **Scene at the Signing of the Constitution of the United States**	10 min.
TOPIC INQUIRY: DOCUMENT-BASED QUESTION **Analyzing Ideas That Influenced the Constitution**	20 min.
Investigate	**1–3 periods**
TOPIC INQUIRY: DOCUMENT-BASED QUESTION **Analyzing Ideas That Influenced the Constitution**	Ongoing
LESSON 1 The Articles of Confederation	30–40 min.
LESSON 2 The Constitutional Convention	30–40 min.
LESSON 3 The Enduring Constitution	30–40 min.
Synthesize	**1 period**
DIGITAL ACTIVITY **Reflect on the Essential Question and Topic**	10 min.
TOPIC INQUIRY: DOCUMENT-BASED QUESTION **Analyzing Ideas That Influenced the Constitution**	20 min.
Demonstrate	**1–2 periods**
DIGITAL TOPIC REVIEW AND ASSESSMENT **Establishing the New Nation**	10 min.
TOPIC INQUIRY: DOCUMENT-BASED QUESTION **Analyzing Ideas That Influenced the Constitution**	20 min.

 **TOPIC INQUIRY: DOCUMENT-BASED QUESTION**

Analyzing Ideas That Influenced the Constitution

In this topic inquiry, students work independently to examine documents that include writings from Enlightenment philosophers, various founding fathers who played a significant role in writing the constitution, and influential persons who debated whether or not to ratify the Constitution. Students will reflect on this information and then write an essay in which they answer the question: How did Enlightenment ideas influence the writing and ratification of the United States Constitution? Developing a deeper understanding of these points of view, the people that held them, and the reasons for their disagreements will contribute to students' understanding of the Essential Question: What is the proper role of government?

STEP 1: CONNECT
Develop Questions and Plan the Investigation

Launch the DBQ Writing Activity
Distribute and introduce the Student Instructions. Then, project the video titled Philadelphia and the Constitutional Convention. Before you start the video, direct students to divide a sheet of paper in half. Have them write "Significant Details" at the top of one column and "Questions" at the top of the second column. Tell students to use this note-taking device to record information as they view the video.

Suggestion: Provide opportunities for multiple viewings to help students gather as much background information as necessary.

Discuss: Have students work with a partner to discuss the video and their questions and observations made while watching the video. Then have each pair answer the questions in their instructions. Tell them to use their individual notes to help them write responses. Ask each pair to post their ideas to the class blog.

Suggestion: Challenge students to explain what they found most surprising, interesting, and confusing about the video segment. Have them share their ideas on the class discussion board.

Suggestion: Encourage students to revisit their notes and questions as they move through the DBQ Inquiry.

Resources
- Student Instructions
- Project Launch Video: "Philadelphia and the Constitutional Convention"

⏻ PROFESSIONAL DEVELOPMENT

Document-Based Question
Be sure to view the Document-Based Question Professional Development resources in the online course.

STEP 2: INVESTIGATE
Apply Disciplinary Concepts and Tools

Analyze the Documents
Students will work individually to read and analyze the six sources related to Enlightenment ideas and their influence on the writing of the United States Constitution. While they should examine each source in detail to grasp key ideas, they should not lose sight of their main goal of answering the question: How did Enlightenment ideas influence the writing and ratification of the United States Constitution? Refer students to helpful resources within the core content of the topic to help answer any lingering questions or to confirm information.

Suggestion: Consider briefly previewing the documents or viewing them as a class to clarify any vocabulary, syntax, or content issues.

Check Your Understanding
Instruct students to work in pairs to read and respond to each document. When students have completed reading the documents and answering the multiple choice and short answer questions, meet as a class to review students' responses.

Suggestion: Encourage students to compare their responses with their notes and questions from the video. Have them identify any conflicting pieces of information, or any information that answers their questions from the start of the inquiry.

Resources
- **Document A:** Excerpts from *The Second Treatise of Civil Government,* John Locke, 1690
- **Document B:** Excerpt from *The Spirit of Laws,* Baron de Montesquieu, 1748
- **Document C:** Excerpt from *Political Discourses,* David Hume, 1752
- **Document D:** Excerpt from *Federalist Paper 10,* James Madison, 1787
- **Document E:** Excerpt from *Centinel, Number 1,* Samuel Bryan, 1787
- **Document F:** Excerpt from *The Major Debates at the Constitutional Convention,* Constitutional Rights Foundation, 2009

STEP 3: SYNTHESIZE
Evaluate Sources and Use Evidence to Formulate Conclusions

Formulate Conclusions

Read aloud the instructions for Step 3 and project the Rubric. Review the expectations outlined in the rubric. Advise students to use the instructions and the rubric as a checklist when they are writing and revising their essays. Provide ample opportunity for students to use the documents and their knowledge of history to write an essay on the following topic: How did Enlightenment ideas influence the writing and ratification of the United States Constitution?

Resources
• Rubric for a DBQ Essay

STEP 4: DEMONSTRATE
Communicate Conclusions and Take Informed Action

Complete and Publish the Writing Projects

Have students revise and submit their essays. Remind students to read over their essays for any errors before turning it in. Hold a class discussion about the question, How did Enlightenment ideas influence the writing and ratification of the United States Constitution? See if the class can reach a consensus on one or more reasons why. Record these reasons on the whiteboard.

Suggestion: Extend the activity by having students conduct library and Internet research to locate additional examples of how Enlightenment ideas influenced the creation of the United States Constitution.

Establishing the New Nation

In 1777, the Articles of Confederation became the first national constitution of the United States. Written during the Revolutionary War, the Articles of Confederation purposely created a weak national government. This government, however, was unable to effectively handle the many issues facing the new nation. The challenge after the war was to determine consensus over the kind of government the new nation needed and how to create it. After much debate, perseverance and dedication, the United States Constitution became the blueprint for the government we know today.

CONNECT

MY STORY VIDEO

Alexander Hamilton, Shaping the New Nation

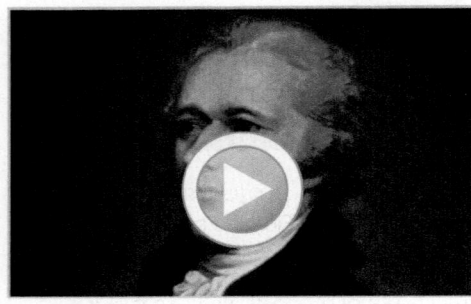

Watch a video about the life of Alexander Hamilton.

Check Understanding What experience during the American Revolution persuaded Hamilton that the United States needed a strong central government? *(the disorganization of the Continental Army)*

Support Ideas with Examples What evidence is there that Hamilton favored a strong central government? *(He helped write the Federalist Papers, urging support for the Constitution. Once in office in George Washington's administration, he established the US Mint and the First Bank of the United States.)*

🔁 FLIP IT!

Assign the My Story video.

DIGITAL ESSENTIAL QUESTION ACTIVITY

What Is the Proper Role of Government?

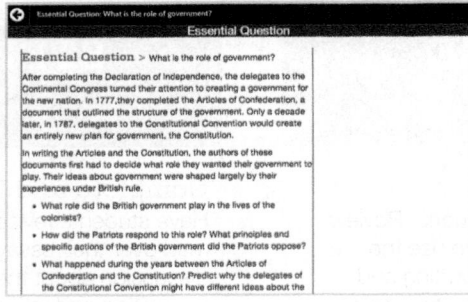

Ask students to think about the Essential Question for this Topic: What is the proper role of government? Explain that determining the power and scope of the federal government has been a struggle throughout American history. Prompt students to suggest factors that might influence Americans' support of a strong or weak federal government.

If students have not already done so, ask them to categorize the roles of government. Then go over the results as a class.

Compare Points of View How did your categorized lists differ from your classmates' lists? How were they the same? What might cause the differences in opinions about the role of government?

Support a Point of View with Evidence In your opinion, what is the most important role of the federal government? Explain. *(Sample answer: Protecting national security is the most important role because all other roles would be impossible to perform if the nation's security is always threatened or under attack.)*

DIGITAL OVERVIEW ACTIVITY

Scene at the Signing of the Constitution of the United States

Display the painting by Howard Chandler Christy titled *Scene at the Signing of the Constitution of the United States*. Point out that many of the men shown had met some 10 years earlier to sign the Declaration of Independence. In 1787, they met again to discuss a new structure of government.

Identify Based on your knowledge of American history, whom do you recognize in the painting? *(Possible responses: George Washington, Alexander Hamilton, Benjamin Franklin, James Madison)*

Hypothesize What relationships do you see depicted in the painting? How might these have helped or hurt debates during the convention? *(Some of the participants seem to be familiar with each other. Hamilton looks like he is telling Franklin something. To the left, some delegates seem to be gazing on Washington with great respect. The professional relationships that developed prior to the Constitutional Convention probably aided in reaching compromises.)*

Topic Inquiry

Launch the Topic Inquiry with students after introducing the topic.

The Articles of Confederation

Supporting English Language Learners

Use with the reading, **The States Create Republics**.

Listening
Read aloud the sections titled *A Preference for Democracy* and *Maintaining Colonial Traditions*. Tell students that you would like them to answer questions to show that they have understood the text.

Beginning Read aloud the section titled *A Preference for Democracy*. Ask: Who wanted state government with strong legislatures and weak governors? Students can answer using a short phrase.

Intermediate Read aloud the section titled *A Preference for Democracy*. Ask: What did the more democratic Patriots want? Encourage students to use complete sentences to answer the question.

Advanced Read aloud the section titled *Maintaining Colonial Traditions*. Ask: Which states chose more conservative constitutions? Have students describe the type of government these states had.

Advanced High Read aloud the section titled *Maintaining Colonial Traditions*. Ask partners to talk about the expanded power of the people under the new constitutions. Encourage them to talk about how this was different from the colonial era.

Use with the reading, **The Northwest Territory**.

Learning
Read aloud the section titled *Governing Western Lands*. Elicit that this section explains the territorial government in the western lands. On the board, draw a flow chart with three boxes connected with arrows. Label the boxes *Appointment*, *5,000 men*, and *60,000 men*.

Beginning Ask partners to work together to write one idea in each box. Tell them that they can use two or three words to describe each idea. Encourage them to go back and look over the section in the text for ideas.

Intermediate Ask partners to work together to write two or three ideas in each box. Then have partners use the chart to discuss their answers using phrases or short sentences.

Advanced Ask partners to work together to include as much information as they can in the chart. Then have them take turns talking about what happened in the territorial government as the population grew.

Advanced High Ask students to include as much information about the territorial government as they can in the chart. Then have them use the chart to write a short paragraph explaining how the government changed as the population grew. Then they can read their paragraph to a partner.

▣ Differentiate Instruction

Use the Differentiated Instruction notes throughout the lesson plan to support the varied skill sets, levels of readiness, and interests in the mixed-ability classroom.

Challenge These notes include suggestions for expanding the activity for advanced students.

On-Level These notes include suggestions for modifying the activity to address different interests or learning styles.

Extra Support These notes include ideas for providing more scaffolding or reading spuport.

Special Needs These notes provide ideas for adapting instruction to support the needs of various special needs students.

■ NOTES

_____

_____

_____

_____

_____

The Articles of Confederation

Objectives

Objective 1: Explain how the states' new constitutions reflected republican ideals.

Objective 2: Describe the structure and powers of the national government under the Articles of Confederation.

Objective 3: Summarize the Congress's plan for the settlement and governance of western lands.

Objective 4: Understand why tensions with foreign countries revealed the weakness of the U.S. government.

Objective 5: List the main weaknesses of the Articles.

LESSON 1 ORGANIZER	PACING: APPROX. 1 PERIOD, .5 BLOCKS		RESOURCES	
	OBJECTIVES	PACING	Online	Print
Connect				
DIGITAL START UP ACTIVITY **The Challenges of the Articles of Confederation**		5 min.	●	
Investigate				
DIGITAL TEXT 1 **The States Create Republics**	Objective 1	10 min.	●	●
DIGITAL TEXT 2 **Union Under the Articles of Confederation**	Objective 2	10 min.	●	●
DIGITAL TEXT 3 **The Northwest Territory**	Objective 3	10 min.	●	●
INTERACTIVE GALLERY **The Northwest Territory**		10 min.	●	
DIGITAL TEXT 4 **Relations with Foreign Powers**	Objective 4	10 min.	●	●
INTERACTIVE CHART **Trade with Great Britain**		10 min.	●	
DIGITAL TEXT 5 **Weaknesses of the Articles of Confederation**	Objective 5	10 min.	●	●
Synthesize				
DIGITAL ACTIVITY **Revisiting the Articles of Confederation**		5 min.	●	
Demonstrate				
DIGITAL QUIZ **Lesson Quiz and Class Discussion Board**		10 min.	●	

PEARSON realize™
www.PearsonRealize.com

Go online to access additional resources including:
Primary Sources • Biographies • Supreme Court cases •
21st Century Skill Tutorials • Maps • Graphic Organizers.

CONNECT

DIGITAL START UP ACTIVITY
The Challenges of the Articles of Confederation

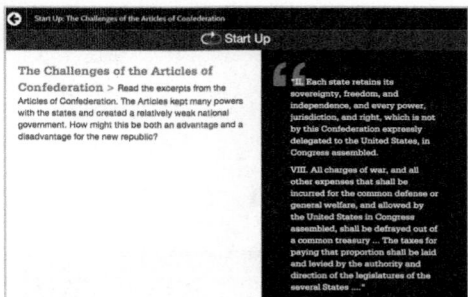

Project the Start Up Activity As students enter and get settled, draw their attention to the excerpts from the Articles of Confederation. Encourage them to take minute to digest the information in the excerpts before they respond to the question. Then have them share their ideas with another student.

Tell students that in this lesson they will be learning about the republican ideals expressed in state constitutions, the strengths and weaknesses of the Articles of Confederation, and Congress's plan for western lands.

Aa Vocabulary Development: Use the Interactive Reading Notepad to preview the Key Terms and Academic Vocabulary in this lesson with students.

⚲ FLIP IT!
Assign the Flipped Video for this lesson.

■ STUDENT EDITION PRINT PAGES: 110–116

INVESTIGATE

DIGITAL TEXT 1
The States Create Republics

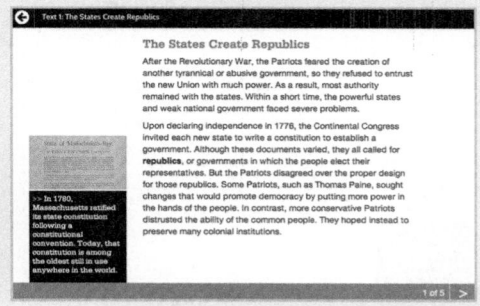

Objective 1: Explain how the states' new constitutions reflected republican ideals.

Quick Instruction
Direct students' attention to the chart showing the advantages and disadvantages of bicameral and unicameral legislatures. Explain that the word *cameral* means of or relating to a legislative or judicial chamber. Ensure students' understanding of bicameral *(lawmaking body made up of two houses)* and unicameral *(lawmaking body made up of a single house)* legislatures. Review the questions and encourage students to discuss the information on the chart.

Compare and Contrast What were the similarities and differences among early state governments? *(Some states had bicameral legislatures while only a few had unicameral legislatures. Voters throughout the states chose the members of both houses of the new legislatures, rather than just the members of the lower house. Also, some states allowed most men over 21 the right to vote. Most states, however, still required the ownership of property as a requirement to vote.)*

ELL Use the ELL activity described in the ELL chart.

Further Instruction
Infer Why might conservatives such as John Adams have preferred to restrict voting to property owners? *(Sample answer: Adams may have equated property ownership with personal and civic responsibility. He probably believed political equality was foolish because only property owners were able to responsibly choose political leaders.)*

Generate Explanations Why did concentration of legislative power trouble conservative Patriots? *(Conservative Patriots were fearful of too much power resting with states' houses of representatives, which were the most democratic of the legislatures. The houses of representatives made representatives more accountable to their constituents, giving voters greater power. Conservative Patriots distrusted the ability of the common people and were afraid of the "tyranny of the majority.")*

Predict Consequences As populations increase, what might happen to the state-established churches in Massachusetts and Connecticut? *(Sample answer: As populations in these states grow and they become more diverse, people not belonging to the established religions will demand religious liberty and pluralism.)*

The Articles of Confederation

DIGITAL TEXT 2

Union Under the Articles of Confederation

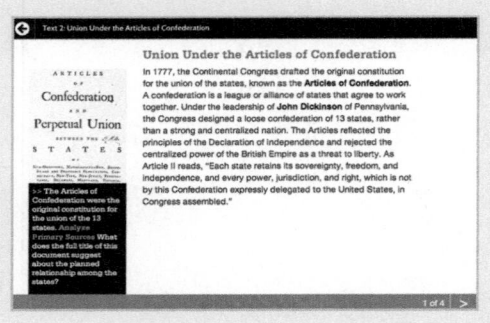

DIGITAL TEXT 3

The Northwest Territory

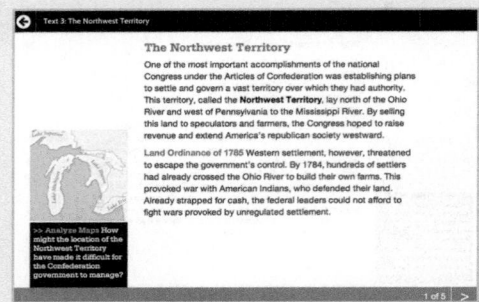

INTERACTIVE GALLERY

The Northwest Territory

Objective 2: Describe the structure and powers of the national government under the Articles of Confederation.

Quick Instruction

Display the image of the Articles of Confederation cover page. Discuss the caption question and invite volunteers to provide responses. Assign Primary Sources: Articles of Confederation and provide opportunities for discussion and clarification of student questions.

Summarize the powers granted Congress under the Articles of Confederation. *(Congress was allowed to declare and conduct war and to manage foreign affairs. However, Congress had few powers beyond those and individual states maintained most of their political autonomy.)*

Further Instruction

Cite Evidence How does the structure of government under the Articles of Confederation reflect the belief that centralized power was a threat to liberty? *(There was no executive branch; rather, executive power and the ability to enforce laws was split between congressional committees. All states, no matter how large or small, had a single vote in Congress.)*

Infer How did the Articles of Confederation ensure that individual states would maintain economic autonomy? *(The new federal government did not have the power to collect taxes, leaving individual states with the option to contribute money as each saw fit.)*

Objective 3: Summarize Congress's plan for the settlement and governance of western lands.

Quick Instruction

The Northwest Territories: Interactive Gallery Project the Interactive Gallery and click on the images to explore the way in which the Northwest Territory was organized. Introduce the activity by asking students to suggest some challenges settlers might face in the Northwest Territory. *(hostile or difficult living conditions; American Indians defending their land)* Explain that in order to entice settlers to the region, Congress established an orderly system for dividing and selling the land and governing the new settlements.

Draw Conclusions How did the land ordinances of 1785 and 1787 affect settlement and development of the Northwest Territory? *(The ordinances provided a sense of confidence in settlers looking to move west. With support from the government, even as weak as it might have been at the time, settlers would be more willing to buy land. Plans for education and a functioning government encouraged settlement in the territory.)*

🖳 ACTIVE CLASSROOM

Conduct a Take a Stand activity. Have students take a stand on the following question: Did the land ordinances of 1785 and 1787 strengthen the United States? Divide students into two groups based on their answer and move to separate areas of the classroom. Have students speak with each other to compare their reasons for answering yes or no. Then ask a representative from each side to present the group's point of view in a larger class discussion.

ELL Use the ELL activity described in the ELL chart.

Further Instruction

Consider using the Interactive Reading Notepad questions as a springboard to continue the discussion of the organization of the Northwest Territory. Assign Primary Sources: Northwest Ordinance to enhance students' understanding.

Summarize the reasons that led Congress to establish the land Ordinances in 1785 and 1787. *(American settlers were moving farther and farther west, provoking war with American Indians. Congressmen feared that the settlers would secede from the Union, form their own states, and turn to the British or the Spanish empire for protection. Congress was also looking for money to fund the government. By selling land in the Northwest Territory to speculators and farmers, Congress hoped to raise revenue and extend America's republican society westward.)*

DIGITAL TEXT 4

Relations with Foreign Powers

INTERACTIVE CHART

Trade with Great Britain

Predict Consequences How might the provision in the Northwest Ordinance of 1787 that barred slavery lead to later domestic conflict? *(The ordinances outlawed slavery in the Northwest Territory, which would shift the balance of power between the free states and the slave states in Congress.)*

Infer What does the organization of the Northwest Territory tell you about the federal government's view of the American Indian populations? *(The government did not consider the needs of the American Indians who already lived in the territories. Congress expected the Indians to give up their lands and relocate elsewhere.)*

Objective 4: Understand why tensions with foreign countries revealed the weakness of the U.S. government.

Quick Instruction

Interactive Chart: Trade with Great Britain Project the Interactive Chart and prompt students to place the tiles in the correct order and to answer the questions. Discuss the information on each tile and clarify any vocabulary and terms with which students might have trouble.

Make Predictions Based on the information in the Interactive Chart, how might Britain's decision to maintain Navigation Act policies affect the American economy if allowed to continue? *(Britain's decision to ban American ships from trading in the West Indies would limit exports and stifle economic growth in its former North American colonies.)*

🖵 ACTIVE CLASSROOM

Conduct a Connect Two activity. List the following terms on the board for students to copy on small pieces of paper: imported goods, British lenders, West Indies, local credit payments, credit limits, American farmers, product ban, foreclosure, American merchants, and debt. Ask students to "connect two" or choose two words they think might belong together, and state the reason, e.g. "I would connect _____ and _____ because _____ ." Invite other students to comment on the connections.

D Differentiate: Extra Support If some students are having difficulty connecting the terms, point them to specific points in the text that will help them define the terms within the context of the lesson.

Further Instruction

Continue the discussion about the economic policies enacted by Britain and Spain and encourage students to explain why the federal government was unable to resolve the issues.

Cite Evidence What Spanish and British actions showed that they did not take the new American nation seriously? *(Both Spain and Britain enacted economic policies that severely restricted U.S. trade freedoms. Spain closed New Orleans to American merchants and Britain returned to the strict policies set out in the Navigation Acts. The British also kept frontier forts on the American side of the boundary set by the peace treaty.)*

Generate Explanations Why did Massachusetts' decision to not allow its exports on British ships fail to change British mercantile policies? *(Massachusetts was acting alone and did not have the support of other states, leaving the British free to continue the same policies with the other remaining states.)*

The Articles of Confederation

DIGITAL TEXT 5

Weaknesses of the Articles of Confederation

Objective 5: List the main weaknesses of the Articles.

Quick Instruction

Direct students' attention to the chart titled *Weaknesses of the Articles of Confederation*. Provide time for student pairs to review and discuss the information in the chart. Ask: Which weakness would likely cause the most problems for the nation over time? Meet as a class and invite each pair to share the rationale for their response.

Identify Central Issues Why did the national government face bankruptcy under the Articles of Confederation? *(Under the Articles, the federal Congress could not establish a common currency, nor could it regulate interstate commerce or levy taxes. For financial support, the Congress relied solely on contributions from the states, which were unreliable.)*

Further Instruction

Support Ideas with Examples What events supported the idea that a stronger national government was necessary? *(The fledgling government had basically gone bankrupt. Open revolts, like Shays' Rebellion, caused great unrest, and the federal government was unable to adequately resolve the severe economic issues throughout the country. The country did not have sufficient funds to pay its debts, but the national Congress lacked power to tax the states or to make them contribute their share of the debt money.)*

Generate Explanations Some states avoided rebellions like the one led by Daniel Shays. Did these states successfully resolve the underlying problems that caused rebellions like this? *(No. The states avoided rebellions by providing relief for those in debt. However, this only upset creditors, who were then not fully paid back. Also, states printed more money, which had the effect of lowering its value.)*

■ SYNTHESIZE

DIGITAL ACTIVITY
Revisiting the Articles of Confederation

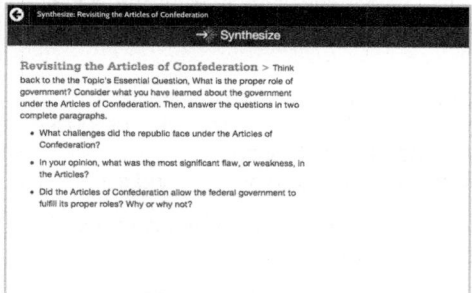

Ask students to think about the Topic Essential Question, "What is the proper role of government?" Have them use the Think Pair Share strategy to create a list of the three most important roles a government performs.

Discuss Before students complete the activity, lead a brief discussion to ensure students understand the fundamentals of the Articles of Confederation. Ask students to think about the advantages and disadvantages of weak and strong national governments. Ask volunteers if the roles they identified are better administered by a weak or a strong government and to explain their thinking.

■ DEMONSTRATE

DIGITAL QUIZ
Lesson Quiz and Class Discussion Board

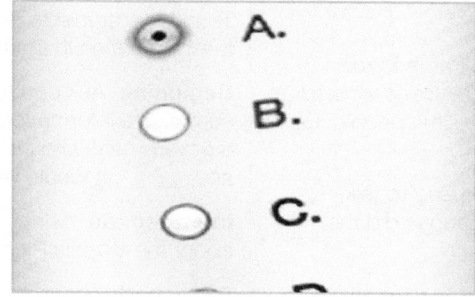

Assign the online Lesson Quiz for this lesson if you haven't already done so. Students will be offered automatic remediation or enrichment based on their score.

Pose these questions to the class on the Discussion Board:

In *The Articles of Confederation*, you read about how the Continental Congress had no intention of replacing one tyrannical government only with another. Consequently, the new nation's leaders wanted to preserve the political autonomy of states. The national government they created, however, was too weak to meet the political and economic challenges the new nation faced.

Identify Central Issues Why did the framers of the Articles of Confederation create a weak national government?

Apply Concepts What additional powers might make the government "stronger" than the one under the Articles of Confederation?

Topic Inquiry
Have students continue their investigations for the Topic Inquiry.

The Constitutional Convention

Supporting English Language Learners

Use with the reading, **Leaders Assemble at the Convention**.

Speaking
Have students read the first three paragraphs of the text silently. Then ask them to use the connecting words *and* and *but* to talk about what they read.

Beginning Ask partners to use the following sentence frame to talk about the powers people wanted Congress to have: Americans wanted Congress to have the power to regulate _____ and _____ the people. Elicit that we use *and* to talk about two separate powers.

Intermediate Ask partners to use the connecting word *and* to talk about Congressional powers. Ask: How many major changes did the people want?

Advanced Ask students to talk about the two major powers Americans wanted Congress to have. Then have them explain why the Federal Convention was delayed. Tell them to use the connecting words *and* and *but* in their explanations.

Advanced High Ask partners to read the section titled *The Delegates Gather* silently. Encourage them to work together to find another connecting word (*so*) and to read aloud the sentences where it is used. Ask partners to say another sentence or two using the connecting word *so*.

Use with the reading, **Constitutional Compromises**.

Reading
Have students read the sections titled *The Virginia Plan* and *The New Jersey Plan* silently. Encourage them to ask questions to clarify meaning. Then have students demonstrate reading comprehension by summarizing the information in the text.

Beginning Ask partners to use the following sentence frames to summarize information about the Virginia Plan. The Virginia Plan proposed a government with power divided among three branches: _____ , _____ , and _____ . It would be a bicameral legislature with a _____ and a _____ .

Intermediate Ask partners to work together to summarize information about the Virginia Plan. Elicit more information as needed.

Advanced Ask students to get a partner. One student summarizes the Virginia Plan and the other summarizes the New Jersey Plan. Then have partners take turns sharing their summaries.

Advanced High Ask partners to take turns summarizing information about the Virginia Plan and the New Jersey Plan. Then have them work together to talk about the differences between the two plans.

�D Differentiate Instruction

Use the Differentiated Instruction notes throughout the lesson plan to support the varied skill sets, levels of readiness, and interests in the mixed-ability classroom.

Challenge These notes include suggestions for expanding the activity for advanced students.

On-Level These notes include suggestions for modifying the activity to address different interests or learning styles.

Extra Support These notes include ideas for providing more scaffolding or reading spuport.

Special Needs These notes provide ideas for adapting instruction to support the needs of various special needs students.

■ NOTES

PEARSON
realize™
www.PearsonRealize.com

Go online to access additional resources including:
Primary Sources • Biographies • Supreme Court cases •
21st Century Skill Tutorials • Maps • Graphic Organizers.

Objectives

Objective 1: Understand the reasons leaders called for the Constitutional Convention.

Objective 2: Summarize the rival plans of government proposed at the convention.

Objective 3: Describe the compromises made in order to reach agreement on the Constitution.

LESSON 2 ORGANIZER		PACING: APPROX. 1 PERIOD, .5 BLOCKS		
			RESOURCES	
	OBJECTIVES	PACING	Online	Print
Connect				
DIGITAL START UP ACTIVITY **Under Pressure**		5 min.	●	
Investigate				
DIGITAL TEXT 1 **Leaders Assemble at the Convention**	Objective 1	10 min.	●	●
INTERACTIVE GALLERY **Delegates of the Constitutional Convention**		10 min.	●	
DIGITAL TEXT 2 **Constitutional Compromises**	Objectives 2, 3	10 min.	●	●
INTERACTIVE CHART **The Great Compromise**		10 min.	●	
Synthesize				
DIGITAL ACTIVITY **Resolving Differences of Opinion**		5 min.	●	
Demonstrate				
DIGITAL QUIZ **Lesson Quiz and Class Discussion Board**		10 min.	●	

The Constitutional Convention

■ CONNECT

DIGITAL START UP ACTIVITY
Under Pressure

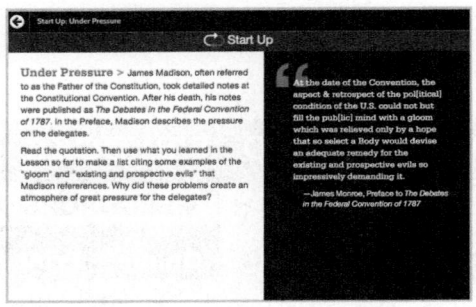

Project the Start Up Activity Ask students to read the quote and answer the questions as they enter and get settled. Then have each of them share ideas with another student, either in class or through a chat or blog.

Discuss Work with students to create a list of examples of "gloom" and "existing and prospective evils" that Madison mentions. Ask: Why were many delegates tense? *(Some of the delegates may have thought that if they could not reach agreement on a lasting structure of government, then the new nation might eventually collapse.)*

Tell students that they will learn how Madison and others worked to produce a document that continues to guide the United States government today.

Aa Vocabulary Development: Use the Interactive Reading Notepad to preview the Key Terms and Academic Vocabulary in this lesson with students.

⚡ FLIP IT!

Assign the Flipped Video for this lesson.

■ STUDENT EDITION PRINT PAGES: 117–122

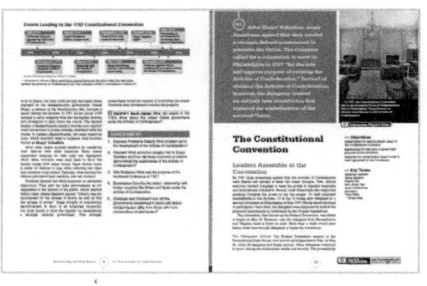

■ INVESTIGATE

DIGITAL TEXT 1
Leaders Assemble at the Convention

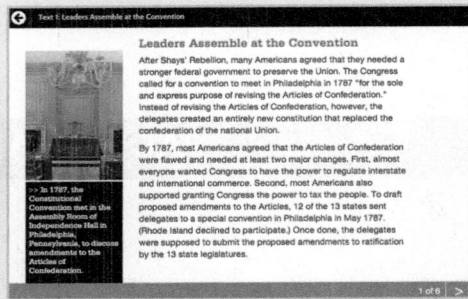

Objective 1: Understand the reasons leaders called for the Constitutional Convention.

Quick Instruction
Interactive Gallery: Delegates of the Constitutional Convention Project the Interactive Gallery. Click on each image to identify an influential delegate to the Constitutional Convention and describe his key contributions. Some of the names may be familiar to students. Ask what they know or think they know about each delegate individually, then reveal his specific contributions.

Summarize Why did leaders call for the Constitutional Convention? *(Most Americans agreed that the Articles of Confederation were flawed and needed at least two major changes, so leaders convened the convention to revise the Articles of Confederation.)*

🖥 ACTIVE CLASSROOM

Conduct a Rank It activity with students. List the following names of delegates on the board: James Madison, Edmund Randolph, William Paterson, Roger Sherman, George Washington, Alexander Hamilton, Benjamin Franklin. Have students rank the delegates based on the impact each had at the convention. Ask students to provide a justification for their decisions. Then ask students to work in pairs to share their rankings and justifications. Poll the class to see if there is agreement on the ranking.

D Differentiate: Challenge/Gifted Ask students to do additional research on additional

INTERACTIVE GALLERY
Delegates of the Constitutional Convention

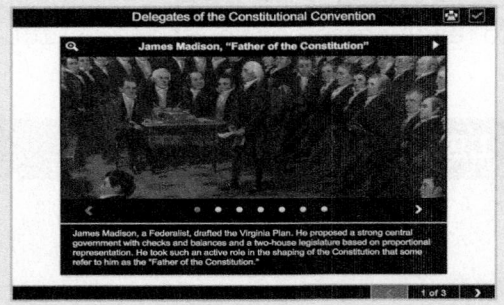

delegates to the Constitutional Convention and share their findings with the class.

ELL Use the ELL activity described in the ELL chart.

Further Instruction
Refocus the discussion of the Constitutional Convention by asking students to review the problems the nation was facing under the Articles of Confederation. *(Possible responses: The national government was going bankrupt; the nation could not effectively deal with British and Spanish trade restrictions and territorial threats.)*

Draw Conclusions How do you think the experiences and backgrounds of the Framers influenced the way the Constitution was shaped? *(Most had government experience working under the Articles of Confederation and knew its weaknesses. The delegates were all familiar with the British Constitution and debate partly centered on how far the new government would stray from that model.)*

Identify Supporting Details What specific changes did leaders look to make to the Articles of Confederation? *(Many delegates wanted Congress to have the power to regulate interstate and international commerce. Many also supported the idea of granting Congress the power to tax.)*

Generate Explanations Why might many delegates disapprove of Alexander Hamilton's ideas about the new structure of the nation's government? *(Hamilton praised the British constitution, including its king and House of Lords, as "the best model the world has ever produced." Many delegates did not want to create a stronger central government too similar to the British model.)*

DIGITAL TEXT 2

Constitutional Compromises

INTERACTIVE CHART

The Great Compromise

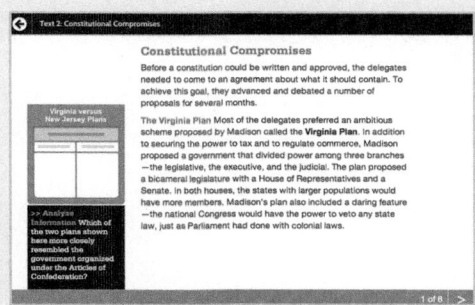

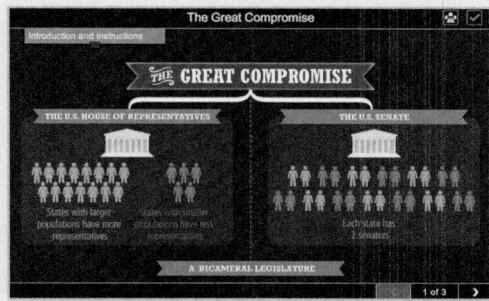

Objectives 2: Summarize the rival plans of government proposed at the convention; 3: Describe the compromises made in order to reach agreement on the Constitution.

Quick Instruction

Interactive Chart: The Great Compromise Project the Interactive Chart. Click on the blue banners to learn more about the Great Compromise of 1787. Prompt students to identify what they think is the most important aspect of the Great Compromise using specific evidence to support their opinion.

Summarize How did the Great Compromise satisfy both the small and large states? *(Each state was given equal representation in the Senate, which satisfied some of the smaller states concerns about unequal representation in Congress. In the House of Representatives, larger states would have more power because representation was based on states' populations.)*

🖳 ACTIVE CLASSROOM

Direct a Conversation with History activity. Ask students to decide if they support or oppose an element of the Great Compromise. Have students conduct their "conversations" with a delegate who disagrees with their stated position on the Great Compromise. Students should write down several questions they would like to ask, then what that person would say to them, and what they would say in response.

ELL Use the ELL activity described in the ELL chart.

Further Instruction

Remind students that the delegates were far from a unanimous decision concerning the structure of the new government. Presented with two strongly supported plans, compromise was necessary to reach an agreement and prevent the convention from ending in a stalemate. Ask students to find examples of key differences among the delegates. *(Delegates were divided over the Virginia and New Jersey plans; delegates argued over federal power versus states' rights; slavery divided the delegates along regional lines, with Southern delegates worrying that Northern domination would threaten the slave system.)*

Draw Conclusions Did the Virginia Plan or the New Jersey Plan represent a more radical departure from the Articles of Confederation? Explain. *(The Virginia Plan was more radical because it included a bicameral legislature, an executive branch, and broader powers of government over the states, all of which were different from the Articles.)*

Generate Explanations Unlike the Declaration of Independence, the Constitution did not proclaim that all men were born free and equal in their rights. In your opinion, why did the Framers not include a similar statement in the Constitution? *(The issue of slavery already divided the Southern and Northern delegates. Omission probably eased the concerns of Southern delegates and helped them reach agreement. The decision also reflected the social and political reality of the time, as not all people were afforded equal rights.)*

The Constitutional Convention

▮ SYNTHESIZE

DIGITAL ACTIVITY
Resolving Differences of Opinion

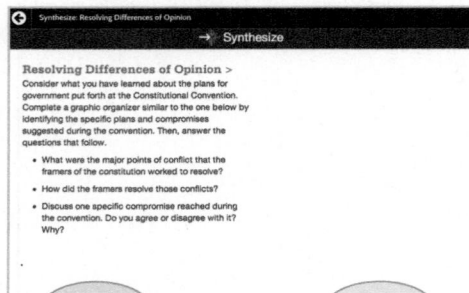

Engage student pairs in completing the graphic organizers. Then have them use the Think Pair Share strategy to discuss the questions in the activity. Ask each student to take five minutes to write down some brief answers to the questions, then share their answers with their partner.

Discuss Have partners think about the following question. What basic principles created during the Constitutional Convention in 1787 have enabled the U.S. Constitution to endure for more than 200 years? Provide opportunities for students to share their responses.

▮ DEMONSTRATE

DIGITAL QUIZ
Lesson Quiz and Class Discussion Board

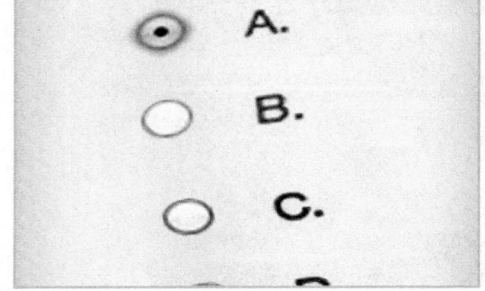

Assign the online Lesson Quiz for this lesson if you haven't already done so. Students will be offered automatic remediation or enrichment based on their score.

Pose these questions to the class on the Discussion Board:

In *The Constitutional Convention*, you read about the Constitutional Convention of 1787 and how the representatives explored the proper role of government in the lives of citizens. After four months, these American leaders created a new constitution based on compromise.

Hypothesize In addition to the two proposed frameworks for a new constitution, what other plan might the delegates have considered?

Connect Identify examples of compromise with which you are familiar in political issues today. In what ways is compromise lacking?

Topic Inquiry
Have students continue their investigations for the Topic Inquiry.

The Enduring Constitution

Supporting English Language Learners

Use with the reading, **The Debate Over Ratification**.

Learning
Read aloud the sections titled *Federalists and Antifederalists Face Off* and *Antifederalists Argue Against a Strong Government*. Ask students to use the information in the text to help them compare and contrast the two groups.

Beginning Ask partners to use the following sentence frames to compare and contrast the Federalists and the Antifederalists: The _____ wanted to ratify the Constitution. The _____ were against ratifying the Constitution.

Intermediate Ask partners to compare and contrast the views of the Federalists and the Antifederalists. Have them name a few of the most famous Federalists.

Advanced Ask partners to talk about the Antifederalists, what they believed, and what their reasons were. Then have partners compare and contrast the Antifederalists with the Federalists.

Advanced High Ask partners to compare and contrast the Federalists and the Antifederalists. Have them talk about views the two groups shared. In the case of opposing views, have them talk about which group's ideas won public support.

Use with the reading, **Ratifying Conventions in the States**.

Listening
Explain to students that they will collaborate with their peers to demonstrate listening comprehension of oral summaries.

Beginning Use simple spoken language to summarize the section titled *The States Ratify the Constitution*. Ask students simple questions about the information in this section, for example, Which group won in Massachusetts? What helped them win? Have students work in small groups to talk about the information they heard and answer the questions.

Intermediate Use simple spoken language to summarize the section titled *The States Ratify the Constitution*. Ask students to listen carefully for information about the promises that helped the Federalists win. Ask partners to collaborate to restate in familiar language the promises and what they achieved.

Advanced Use spoken language to summarize the section titled *The Bill of Rights*. Ask partners to take turns asking and answering questions about the Bill of Rights, such as: What was the Bill of Rights? Who drafted it? How did Madison limit the amendments?

Advanced High Use spoken language to summarize the section titled *The Bill of Rights*. With a partner, talk about what the Bill of Rights included and what it didn't include. Share your ideas about what the Bill of Rights achieved by not declaring all men equal in their creation and rights.

▶ Differentiate Instruction

Use the Differentiated Instruction notes throughout the lesson plan to support the varied skill sets, levels of readiness, and interests in the mixed-ability classroom.

Challenge These notes include suggestions for expanding the activity for advanced students.

On-Level These notes include suggestions for modifying the activity to address different interests or learning styles.

Extra Support These notes include ideas for providing more scaffolding or reading spuport.

Special Needs These notes provide ideas for adapting instruction to support the needs of various special needs students.

■ NOTES

Topic ④ Lesson 3

The Enduring Constitution

Objectives

Objective 1: Summarize the arguments for and against ratification of the Constitution.

Objective 2: Describe how the Constitution was ratified.

Objective 3: Explain the principles of the Constitution.

LESSON 3 ORGANIZER		PACING: APPROX. 1 PERIOD, .5 BLOCKS			
				RESOURCES	
		OBJECTIVES	**PACING**	**Online**	**Print**
Connect					
	DIGITAL START UP ACTIVITY **Benjamin Franklin's Thoughts**		5 min.	●	
Investigate					
	DIGITAL TEXT 1 **The Debate Over Ratification**	Objective 1	10 min.	●	●
	DIGITAL TEXT 2 **Ratifying Conventions in the States**	Objective 2	10 min.	●	●
	INTERACTIVE CHART **Viewpoints on Ratification**		10 min.	●	
	DIGITAL TEXT 3 **Constitutional Principles**	Objective 3	10 min.	●	●
	INTERACTIVE CHART **The Federal System**		10 min.	●	
Synthesize					
	DIGITAL ACTIVITY **Debating the Role of Government**		5 min.	●	
Demonstrate					
	DIGITAL QUIZ **Lesson Quiz and Class Discussion Board**		10 min.	●	

PEARSON
realize™
www.PearsonRealize.com

Go online to access additional resources including:
Primary Sources • Biographies • Supreme Court cases •
21st Century Skill Tutorials • Maps • Graphic Organizers.

CONNECT

DIGITAL START UP ACTIVITY
Benjamin Franklin's Thoughts

Project the Start Up Activity Ask students to read and reflect on Franklin's quote as they enter and get settled. Have students answer the questions and share their responses with another student, either in class or through a chat or blog space.

Discuss Prompt students to discuss what Benjamin Franklin meant when he said, "From such an assembly can a perfect production be expected?" using contextual support from the quote and what they know of the Constitutional Convention to support their responses.

Tell students that in this lesson they will be learning about arguments for and against ratification of the U.S. Constitution and the essential principles upon which the Constitution was written.

Aa Vocabulary Development: Use the Interactive Reading Notepad to preview the Key Terms and Academic Vocabulary in this lesson with students.

⇅ FLIP IT!
Assign the Flipped Video for this lesson.

■ STUDENT EDITION PRINT PAGES: 123–129

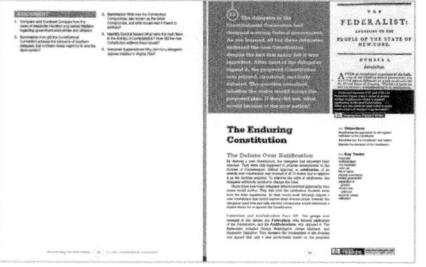

INVESTIGATE

DIGITAL TEXT 1
The Debate Over Ratification

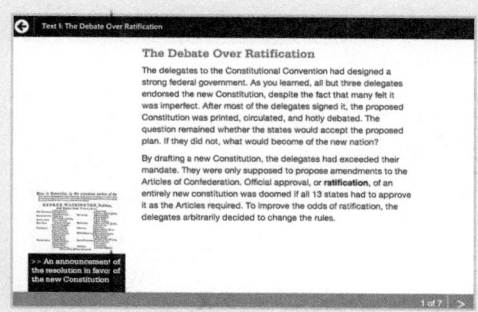

Objective 1: Summarize the arguments for and against ratification of the Constitution.

Quick Instruction
Ensure students' understanding of the requirements for ratification. *(Nine of the thirteen states had to ratify the Constitution.)* Point out that the debate over ratification was often heated. Influential leaders of the time, such as Patrick Henry and James Madison, were on opposing sides and argued effectively for their positions. Work as a class to identify the issues on which Federalists and Antifederalists disagreed. *(Antifederalists thought the Constitution was a retreat from the liberty won by the Revolution. They disliked that the Constitution lacked a bill of rights to protect the states' basic liberties. Federalists supported a stronger federal government, arguing it would protect civil liberties and ensure the success of the nation as a whole.)*

Identify Central Issues What actions did the delegates to the Constitutional Convention take to make ratification easier? *(The delegates determined that approval by nine states rather than all thirteen would suffice. They also took the ratification decision away from the state legislatures and instead ruled that specially elected conventions would determine a state's choice for or against the Constitution.)*

Make Generalizations In what ways did supporters of the Federalists and Antifederalists differ? *(Large numbers of Federalist supporters lived in urban or seaport communities. Those who supported the Antifederalists were mostly rural farmers.)*

ELL Use the ELL activity described in the ELL chart.

Further Instruction
Initiate a discussion about the role of *The Federalist* in the ratification debate. Make sure students are aware of the three leading Federalists—James Madison, Alexander Hamilton, and John Jay, who wrote the essays. To provide depth to the discussion, assign Primary Sources: Federalist Papers (#10, 39, 51) and Primary Sources: Antifederalist Papers.

Determine Point of View In the opinion of the authors of *The Federalist* , what was the true threat to civil liberties? *(The authors insisted that the real threat to liberty came from the state legislatures, which lacked sufficient checks and balances. The new federal government, they argued, would provide checks and balances at the national level.)*

Cite Evidence Why were the Federalists more successful than the Antifederalists in winning support for ratification? *(The Federalists had the support of influential leaders like Benjamin Franklin and George Washington. They were also better organized than the Antifederalists. Federalists were supported by the people living in key cities, where the ratifying conventions were held and where the most influential newspapers were located.)*

The Enduring Constitution

DIGITAL TEXT 2
Ratifying Conventions in the States

INTERACTIVE CHART
Viewpoints on Ratification

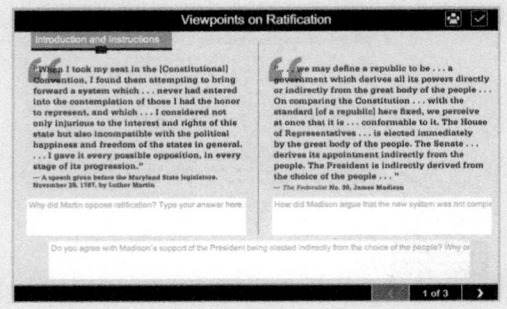

DIGITAL TEXT 3
Constitutional Principles

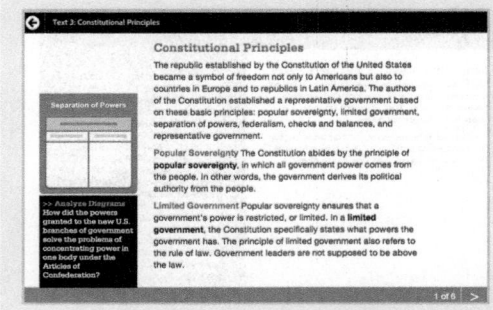

Objective 2: Describe how the Constitution was ratified.

Quick Instruction

Interactive Chart: Viewpoints on Ratification Project the Interactive Chart. Prompt students to understand the essential arguments of the ratification debate in the context of the primary source quotes from Henry and Hamilton. Why was the promise of inclusion of a bill of rights necessary for ratification? *(Adding the Bill of Rights addressed the Antifederalists' concerns of losing individual liberties and convinced them to support ratification.)*

📹 ACTIVE CLASSROOM

Conduct a Take a Stand activity on the issue of ratifying the Constitution. Have students take a stand on the following question: Should the new Constitution be ratified? Ask students to divide into two groups based on their answer and move to separate areas of the classroom. Ask students to talk with each other to compare their reasons for answering yes or no. Ask a representative from each side to present and defend the group's point of view.

ELL Use the ELL activity described in the ELL chart.

Further Instruction

Go through the Interactive Reading Notepad questions and use appropriate questions as a springboard to begin a discussion on the ratification process.

Sequence Events Have students summarize the events that led to the ratification of the Constitution. *(By mid-January 1788, the Federalists had won ratification in Delaware, Pennsylvania, New Jersey, Georgia, and Connecticut. Federalists convinced John Hancock to support ratification and in early February, following Hancock's lead, the Massachusetts convention ratified the Constitution. Federalists then promised to include a bill of rights. Maryland ratified in April; South Carolina, in May; and New Hampshire, in early June. These states provided the required nine states to ensure ratification.)*

Summarize Why did Madison feel it was necessary to add the Ninth Amendment? *(Madison feared that any finite list of rights would later be abused in order to deny rights left unmentioned. Adding the Ninth Amendment provided a way to include additional rights.)*

Objective 3: Explain the principles of the Constitution.

Quick Instruction

Interactive Chart: The Federal System Project the Interactive Chart and invite students to complete the activity. Students may benefit from working with a partner to fill in the charts. Explain that the framers tried to promote democratic principles. They also needed a government that was strong enough to function in the interests of all the states. Remind students that one of the Antifederalist concerns was the potential of the federal government to have too much power relative to the states. Invite students to share what they learned about why the Antifederalists wanted the states to retain as much power as possible.

Generate Explanations How does the concept of federalism relate to the ratification debate? *(Federalism refers to the division of political power between the federal and state governments. The power of the federal government relative to the states was at the heart of the debate over whether or not to ratify the Constitution.)*

INTERACTIVE CHART
The Federal System

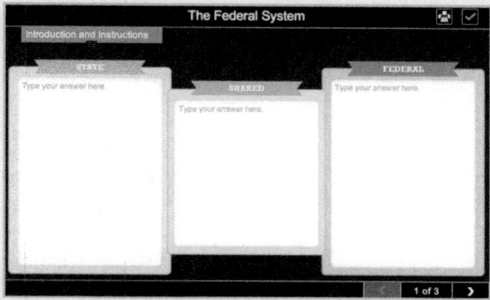

⏸ ACTIVE CLASSROOM

Conduct a Circle Write activity. Break students into groups and provide this writing prompt: Is federalism the most effective form of government for the United States? Why or why not? Have students write as much as they can for one minute then switch with the person on their right. The next person tries to improve or elaborate the response where the other person left off. Continue to switch until the paper comes back to the first person. The group then decides which is the best composition (or response) and shares that with the larger group.

🄳 Differentiate: **Extra Support** Pair students to review the text and the Interactive Chart and write down the distinct powers granted to the states and to the federal government. Have pairs go through their lists and discuss why each power was granted to either the federal government or the states.

Further Instruction
Go through and discuss the Interactive Reading Notepad questions. Ensure students' understanding of the basic principles in the Constitution that established our representative government: popular sovereignty, limited government, separation of powers, federalism, checks and balances, and representative government.

Infer For what reasons might the framers have granted the power to regulate elections to the states? *(The framers were probably concerned that elections were too susceptible to corruption if regulated by the federal government.)*

Connect What relationship exists between popular sovereignty and voting? *(Government derives its political authority from voters. The voters express their will in elections, thereby legitimizing the authority of the government.)*

The Enduring Constitution

■ SYNTHESIZE

DIGITAL ACTIVITY
Debating the Role of Government

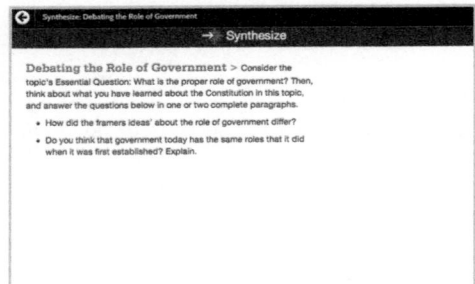

Ask students to recall the Topic Essential Question, "What is the proper role of government?" Have them use the Think Pair Share strategy to reflect on what they have learned about the Constitution. Then have students answer the questions in the Debating the Role of Government Activity individually. Ask them to take five minutes to write down some brief answers to the question below, then share their answers with a talking partner.

Discuss Have partners think about the following question: Do you think that government today has the same roles that it did when it was first established? Explain. Have pairs share their answers with the class.

■ DEMONSTRATE

DIGITAL QUIZ
Lesson Quiz and Class Discussion Board

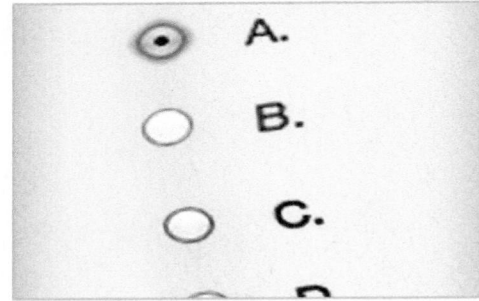

Assign the online Lesson Quiz for this lesson if you haven't already done so. Students will be offered automatic remediation or enrichment based on their score.

Pose these questions to the class on the Discussion Board:

In *The Enduring Constitution* , you read about how America's leaders compromised and balanced the concerns of Federalists and Antifederalists. The Constitution they created has been strong and flexible enough to endure for more than 200 years.

Apply Concepts What are the three branches of the federal government and their powers? Give an example of how one branch might check the power of another.

Connect How do you think the Constitution protects your rights as an individual?

Topic Inquiry
Have students continue their investigations for the Topic Inquiry.

Establishing the New Nation

SYNTHESIZE

DIGITAL ACTIVITY
Reflect on the Essential Question and Topic

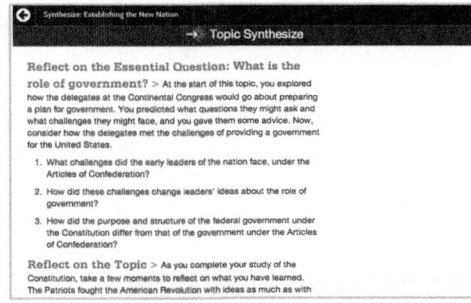

First ask students to reconsider the Essential Question for the Topic: What is the proper role of government? Tell them to review their responses to the Essential Question Activity. Have them revise any parts of the responses as needed.

Organize students into small groups. Direct each group to answer the three questions about how the delegates met the challenges of creating a government for the United States. Call on each group to share their ideas with the class, or post their responses in the class discussion board.

Next, have students reflect on the topic as a whole. Display the questions from the topic Synthesize Activity. Instruct students to jot down notes in response to the three questions. Then, ask students to write a paragraph in which they describe what lessons current and future American political leaders can learn from the experiences of the men who worked so hard to create the Constitution. Tell them to be sure to cite evidence from each lesson in the topic.

Direct students to exchange their paragraphs with a partner. They should read and provide feedback on each other's work. Then, have students revise their paragraphs to submit to the class blog.

Topic Inquiry
Have students complete Step 3 of the Topic Inquiry.

DEMONSTRATE

DIGITAL TOPIC REVIEW AND ASSESSMENT
Establishing the New Nation

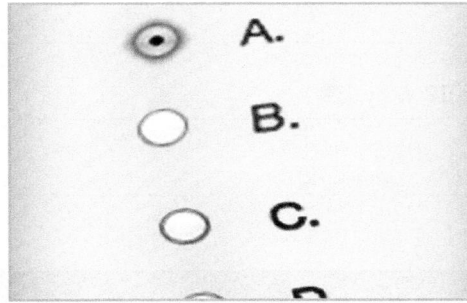

Students can prepare for the Topic Test by answering the questions in the Topic Review and Assessment online or the Assessment questions in the Print Student text. They can also prepare by reviewing their answers to the Interactive Reading Notepad questions or reviewing their notes in the Reading and Notetaking Study Guide.

DIGITAL TOPIC TEST
Establishing the New Nation

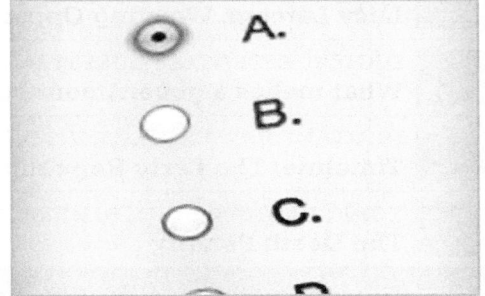

TOPIC TEST
Assign the Topic Test to assess students' understanding of topic content.

BENCHMARK TESTS
Assign these benchmark tests as you complete the relevant topics to monitor student progress toward mastering the course content and as preparation for the End-of-Course Test.

Benchmark Test 1: Topics 1–3

Benchmark Test 2: Topics 4–6

Benchmark Test 3: Topics 7–9

Benchmark Test 4: Topics 10–12

Benchmark Test 5: Topics 13–15

Benchmark Test 6: Topics 16–18

Benchmark Test 7: Topics 19–20

The Early Republic

TOPIC 5 ORGANIZER	PACING: APPROX. 10 PERIODS, 5 BLOCKS
	PACING
Connect	1 period
MY STORY VIDEO **Lucy Larcom, Weaving Opportunity**	10 min.
DIGITAL ESSENTIAL QUESTION ACTIVITY **What makes a government successful?**	10 min.
DIGITAL OVERVIEW ACTIVITY **Timeline: The Early Republic**	10 min.
TOPIC INQUIRY: CIVIC DISCUSSION **The Death Penalty**	20 min.
Investigate	3–7 periods
TOPIC INQUIRY: CIVIC DISCUSSION **The Death Penalty**	Ongoing
LESSON 1 The New Government Finds Its Way	30–40 min.
LESSON 2 Jefferson as President	30–40 min.
LESSON 3 The War of 1812	30–40 min.
LESSON 4 The Beginning of the Industrial Revolution	30–40 min.
LESSON 5 Differences Between North and South Grow	30–40 min.
LESSON 6 Nationalism Influences Policies	30–40 min.
LESSON 7 Jacksonian Democracy	30–40 min.
Synthesize	1 period
DIGITAL ACTIVITY **Reflect on the Essential Question and Topic**	10 min.
TOPIC INQUIRY: CIVIC DISCUSSION **The Death Penalty**	20 min.
Demonstrate	1–2 periods
DIGITAL TOPIC REVIEW AND ASSESSMENT **The Early Republic**	10 min.
TOPIC INQUIRY: CIVIC DISCUSSION **The Death Penalty**	20 min.

TOPIC INQUIRY: CIVIC DISCUSSION

The Death Penalty

In this Topic Inquiry, students work in teams to examine different perspectives on this issue by analyzing several sources, arguing both sides of a Yes/No question, then developing and discussing their own point of view on the question: **Should the death penalty be repealed in the United States?**

STEP 1: CONNECT
Develop Questions and Plan the Investigation

Launch the Civic Discussion

Divide the class into groups of four students. Students can access the materials they'll need in the online course or you can distribute copies to each student. Read the main question and introduction with the students.

Have students complete Step 1 by reading the Discussion Launch and filling in Step 1 of the Information Organizer. The Discussion Launch provides YES and NO arguments on the main question. Students should extract and paraphrase the arguments from the reading in Step 1 of their Information Organizers.

Next, students share within their groups the arguments and evidence they found to support the YES and NO positions. The group needs to agree on the major YES and NO points and each student should note those points in their Information Organizer.

Resources
- Student Instructions
- Information Organizer
- Discussion Launch

STEP 2: INVESTIGATE
Apply Disciplinary Concepts and Tools

Examine Sources and Perspectives

Students will examine sources with the goal of extracting information and perspectives on the main question. They analyze each source and describe the author's perspective on the main question and key evidence the author provides to support that viewpoint in Information Organizer Step 2.

Ask students to keep in mind:

- **Author/Creator:** Who created the source? An individual? Group? Government agency?
- **Audience:** For whom was the source created?
- **Date/Place:** Is there any information that reveals where and when the source was created?
- **Purpose:** Why was the source created? Discuss with students the importance of this question in identifying bias.
- **Relevance:** How does the source support one argument or another?

Suggestion: Reading the source documents and filling in Step 2 of the Information Organizer could be assigned as homework.

Resources
- Student Instructions
- Information Organizer
- Source documents

⏻ PROFESSIONAL DEVELOPMENT

Civic Discussion

Be sure to view the Civic Discussion Professional Development resources in the online course.

The Death Penalty *(continued)*

STEP 3: SYNTHESIZE
Use Evidence to Formulate Conclusions

Formulate Compelling Arguments with Evidence

Now students will apply perspectives and evidence they extracted from the sources to think more deeply about the main question by first arguing one side of the issue, then the other. In this way students become more prepared to formulate an evidence-based conclusion on their own.

Within each student group, assign half of the students to take the position of YES on the main question and the others to take the position of NO. Students will work with their partners to identify the strongest arguments and evidence to support their assigned YES or NO position.

Present Yes/No Positions

Within each group, those assigned the YES position share arguments and evidence first. As the YES students speak, those assigned NO should listen carefully, take notes to fill in the rest of the Compelling Arguments Chart (Step 3 in Information Organizer) and ask clarifying questions.

When the YES side is finished, students assigned the NO position present while those assigned YES should listen, take notes, and ask clarifying questions. Examples of clarifyin questions are:

- I think you just said [x]. Am I understanding you correctly?
- Can you tell me more about [x]?
- Can you repeat [x]? I am not sure I understand, yet.

Suggestion: You may want to set a 5 minute time limit for each side to present. Provide a two-minute warning so that students make their most compelling arguments within the time frame.

Switch Sides

The students will switch sides to argue the opposite point of view. To prepare to present the other position, partners who first argued YES will use the notes they took during the NO side's presentation, plus add any additional arguments and evidence from the reading and sources. The same for students who first argued the NO position.

STEP 4: DEMONSTRATE
Communicate Conclusions and Take Informed Action

Individual Points of View

Now the students will have the opportunity to discuss the main question from their own points of view. To help students prepare for this discussion, have them reflect on the YES/NO discussions they have participated in thus far and fill in Step 4 of their Information Organizers.

After all of the students have shared their points of view, each group should list points of agreement, filling the last portion of Step 4 on their Information Organizers.

Reflect on the Discussion

Ask students to reflect on the civic discussion thinking about:

- The value of having to argue both the YES and NO positions.
- If their individual views changed over the course of the discussion and why.
- What they learned from participating in the discussion.

Resources
- Student Instructions
- Information Organizer

INTRODUCTION

The Early Republic

The early decades of the republic saw an expansion of the federal government's responsibilities, but they also brought new challenges. Americans disagreed over the role of the federal government relative to the states, the best ways to regulate money and pay off debt, and the role the United States should play in foreign affairs. The country expanded dramatically during this time, and conflicts with American Indians over land and other resources intensified. Although the United States fought another war with Britain over trade and territory, the country emerged with a greater sense of purpose and national identity. Divisions between the northern and southern sections of the nation however were deepening as disagreement continued over the economy, states' rights, and the expansion of slavery.

■ CONNECT

MY STORY VIDEO

Lucy Larcom, Weaving Opportunity

Watch a video about Lucy Larcom, a worker in an early 19th century Lowell textile mill.

Check Understanding Where did many of the workers in the early textile mills come from? *(farms)*

Determine Point of View What may have accounted for the change in Lucy Larcom's view of mill work? *(Once she had grown accustomed to mill work, the novelty of it wore off. She grew to dislike the constant noise and refused to become a slave to machines. The tedium of the labor and the need constantly to service the machines no doubt accounted for her change in view.)*

⇅ FLIP IT!

Assign the My Story video.

DIGITAL ESSENTIAL QUESTION ACTIVITY

What makes a government successful?

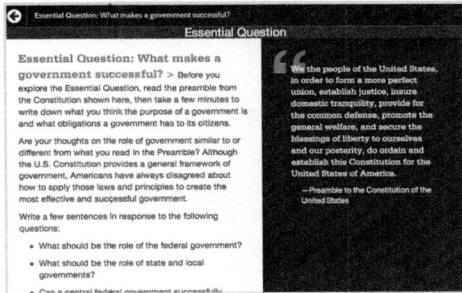

Ask students to think about the Essential Question for this Topic: What makes a government successful? The United States needed to develop a strong government to ensure the success of the nation.

If students have not already done so, ask them to read the preamble and jot down their thoughts about the purpose of government. Then have them answer the questions. Ask students to share their answers with a partner.

Identify Central Issues you think the nation will face in determining the balance of power between federal and state governments.

Hypothesize What challenges will the nation face in securing liberty? What limitations to liberty do you think will persist?

DIGITAL OVERVIEW ACTIVITY

The Early Republic

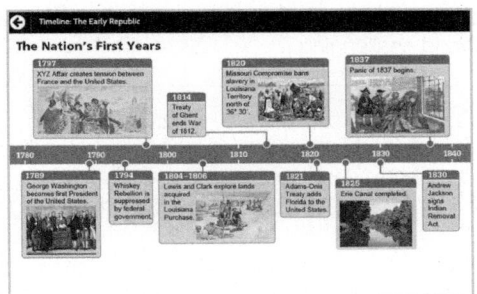

Display the timeline showing the major events that occurred during the early years of the republic. During this topic, students will learn about all of these events and many more, but this timeline will provide a contextual framework into which they can place the events.

Topic Inquiry

Launch the Topic Inquiry with students after introducing the topic.

The New Government Finds Its Way

Supporting English Language Learners

Use with the reading, **Creating a New Government**.

Speaking
Why is it important to use verbs in the correct tense when speaking? Explain that students will monitor their use of verbs in the activities below.

Beginning Have students suppose they are citizens of the newly formed United States. Invite them to say a sentence about their government using a present tense verb. Encourage students to focus on correctly conjugating the verbs they use.

Intermediate Invite students to make affirmative and negative statements about the newly formed United States government using the past tense. Encourage students to focus on correctly conjugating their verbs and self-correcting or asking for assistance as needed.

Advanced Invite pairs of students to describe the formation of the United States government. Encourage them to use any verb conjugations they see fit, and provide them with reference materials that they can use when they are unsure of how to use a verb.

Advanced High Invite pairs of students to describe the formation of the United States government. Encourage them to use any verb conjugations they see fit, employing workarounds when they are unsure of how to use a particular verb. After the discussion, have students look up the verbs they found challenging.

Use with the reading, **Foreign Policy Affects Domestic Politics**.

Listening
Explain to students that when a speaker provides supplemental written materials, they can be used to aid in comprehension. Encourage students to use these materials as support, not as the primary source of input.

Beginning Provide students with a written transcript so they can follow along as you use simple English to tell them about the Alien and Sedition Acts. When you finish, ask students close-ended questions to test their comprehension.

Intermediate Provide students with an outline of key points so they can follow along as you speak to them about the Alien and Sedition Acts. (Signal whenever you shift to a new point on the outline). Then ask students informational questions to test their comprehension.

Advanced Before speaking to students about the Alien and Sedition Acts, display some key words and phrases you will use. Then point to each as you use it in your talk. Ask: What are the benefits of both seeing and hearing key words and phrases?

Advanced High Speak to students about the Alien and Sedition Acts, using additional information not found in the text. Then repeat the same talk. Ask: How did you adjust your listening strategies the second time I spoke?

▢ Differentiate Instruction

Use the Differentiated Instruction notes throughout the lesson plan to support the varied skill sets, levels of readiness, and interests in the mixed-ability classroom.

Challenge These notes include suggestions for expanding the activity for advanced students.

On-Level These notes include suggestions for modifying the activity to address different interests or learning styles.

Extra Support These notes include ideas for providing more scaffolding or reading spuport.

Special Needs These notes provide ideas for adapting instruction to support the needs of various special needs students.

█ NOTES

PEARSON
realize™
www.PearsonRealize.com

Go online to access additional resources including:
Primary Sources • Biographies • Supreme Court cases •
21st Century Skill Tutorials • Maps • Graphic Organizers.

Objectives

Objective 1: Describe how Washington's administration built the federal government.

Objective 2: Analyze Hamilton's plans for the economy and the opposition to them.

Objective 3: Explain how a two-party system emerged in the new nation.

Objective 4: Explain how territorial expansion brought Americans into conflict with the British and with American Indians.

Objective 5: Describe American relations with Britain, France, and Spain.

Objective 6: Analyze how the political parties' debates over foreign policy further divided them.

LESSON 1 ORGANIZER		PACING: APPROX. 1 PERIOD, .5 BLOCKS			
				RESOURCES	
		OBJECTIVES	**PACING**	**Online**	**Print**
Connect					
DIGITAL START UP ACTIVITY **Building a New Nation**			5 min.	●	
Investigate					
DIGITAL TEXT 1 **Creating a New Government**		Objective 1	10 min.	●	●
BEFORE AND AFTER **The United States in 1789 and 2014**			10 min.	●	
DIGITAL TEXT 2 **Addressing the Nation's Debt**		Objective 2	10 min.	●	●
DIGITAL TEXT 3 **Political Divisions Lead to Two Parties**		Objective 3	10 min.	●	●
INTERACTIVE CHART **Federalists versus Republicans**			10 min.	●	
DIGITAL TEXT 4 **Domestic and Foreign Affairs**		Objective 4	10 min.	●	●
DIGITAL TEXT 5 **Foreign Policy Affects Domestic Politics**		Objective 6	10 min.	●	●
Synthesize					
DIGITAL ACTIVITY **Judging the Success of the New Constitution**			5 min.	●	
Demonstrate					
DIGITAL QUIZ **Lesson Quiz and Class Discussion Board**			10 min.	●	

The New Government Finds Its Way

■ CONNECT

DIGITAL START UP ACTIVITY
Building a New Nation

Project the Start Up Activity Ask students to read the activity and write down their thoughts as they enter and get settled. Have students share their responses with a partner, either in class or through a blog space.

Tell students that in this lesson they will be learning about the organization of the early federal government.

Aa Vocabulary Development Use the Interactive Reading Notepad to preview the Key Terms and Academic Vocabulary in this lesson with students.

⇈ FLIP IT!
Assign the Flipped Video for this lesson.

■ STUDENT EDITION PRINT
PAGES: 134–143

■ INVESTIGATE

DIGITAL TEXT 1
Creating a New Government

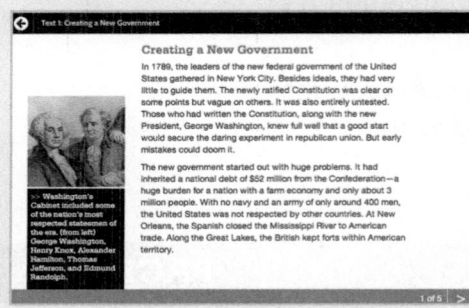

BEFORE AND AFTER
The United States in 1789 and 2014

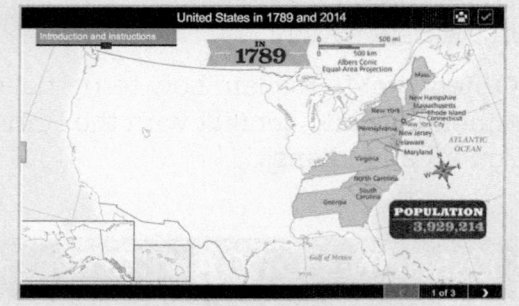

Objective 1: Describe how Washington's administration built the federal government.

Quick Instruction

Before and After: The United States in 1789 and 2014 Project the Before and After and navigate through the contrasting information with the slider to compare the nation in 1789 and 2014. Prompt students to make generalizations about the differences they observe. Then discuss what policies they think the new government had to make in order to enable the nation to grow. For example, what kind of rules did the administration need to set? What new policies were necessary?

Cite Evidence from the text that shows the nation faced significant problems after ratifying the Constitution. (*"Leaders of the new federal government . . . had very little to guide them." "The new government . . . had inherited a national debt of $52 million from the Confederation." "The United States was not respected by other countries." "The Spanish closed the Mississippi River to American trade." "The British kept forts within American territory." "The nation had a farm economy, a small population, no navy, and an army of about 400."*)

📖 ACTIVE CLASSROOM

Conduct a Connect Two activity. Write the following words on the board for students to copy on small pieces of paper: Constitution, experiment, president, administration, Congress, precedent, Cabinet, court system, executive branch, judiciary, departments. Read the list of words with students. Ask students to choose two words they think might belong together and state the reason. Have students provide textual evidence to support or refute their connections.

ELL Use the ELL activity described in the ELL chart.

Further Instruction

Go through the Interactive Reading Notepad questions and discuss the answers with the class. Assign Government Basics: Executive Branch and Government Basics: Serving on a Jury Tutorial.

Support Ideas with Examples Give an example of a precedent that Washington set during his presidency and explain its importance to the nation. (*Washington formed a Cabinet, a group of leaders to head major departments. Having a Cabinet ensured that important functions of the executive branch were fulfilled and gave presidents access to key advisers.*)

Summarize the Judiciary Act of 1789. (*It established a judiciary, or a system of courts. This system included one federal district court per state. Circuit courts heard appeals from the state courts. The Supreme Court decided contested cases and cases involving states or foreign affairs. There was also an office to try cases on behalf of the federal government.*)

DIGITAL TEXT 2

Addressing the Nation's Debt

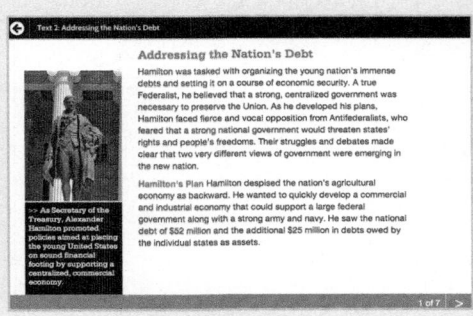

Text 2: Addressing the Nation's Debt

Addressing the Nation's Debt

Hamilton was tasked with organizing the young nation's immense debts and setting it on a course of economic security. A true Federalist, he believed that a strong, centralized government was necessary to preserve the Union. As he developed his plans, Hamilton faced fierce and vocal opposition from Antifederalists, who feared that a strong national government would threaten states' rights and people's freedoms. Their struggles and debates made clear that two very different views of government were emerging in the new nation.

Hamilton's Plan Hamilton despised the nation's agricultural economy as backward. He wanted to quickly develop a commercial and industrial economy that could support a large federal government along with a strong army and navy. He saw the national debt of $52 million and the additional $25 million in debts owed by the individual states as assets.

>> As Secretary of the Treasury, Alexander Hamilton promoted policies aimed at placing the young United States on sound financial footing by supporting a centralized, commercial economy.

1 of 7

Objective 2: Analyze Hamilton's plans for the economy and the opposition to them.

Quick Instruction

Summarize Hamilton's plan to alleviate the debt. *(Hamilton wanted to shift the economy from agriculture to commerce and industry. He planned to sell government bonds and proposed excise taxes and high tariffs to pay interest on the bonds, raise government revenue, and protect American manufacturers. He also suggested a Bank of the United States to regulate state banks, strengthen the federal government, and align business with the government.)*

Identify Central Issues What were the main arguments against Hamilton's plan? *(It taxed southern farmers to pay northern merchants. Southern states had paid off much of their debts and did not want their tax dollars going to the northeast. They worried that a national bank would benefit the North at the expense of the South.)*

Further Instruction

Go through the Interactive Reading Notepad questions. Prompt students to understand that disagreements over the role of the federal government in managing the nation's economy will lead to political divisions and contribute to the rise of a two-party system.

Compare Points of View Compare the views of Alexander Hamilton and antifederalists on the role of the federal government in managing the nation's economy. *(Hamilton believed the federal government should play a significant role in reducing debt. Antifederalists, on the other hand, thought a strong federal government threatened states' rights and individual freedoms.)*

Generate Explanations Explain why the nation's capital was moved to Washington, D.C. *(Hamilton agreed to move the capital to a southern location to get southerners to agree to assume state debts.)*

DIGITAL TEXT 3

Political Divisions Lead to Two Parties

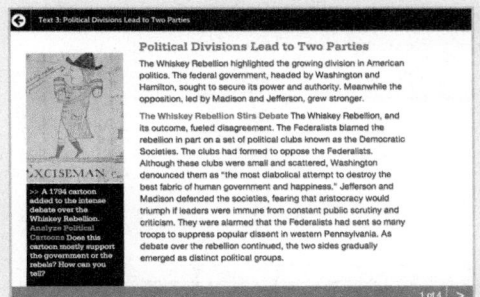

Text 3: Political Divisions Lead to Two Parties

Political Divisions Lead to Two Parties

The Whiskey Rebellion highlighted the growing division in American politics. The federal government, headed by Washington and Hamilton, sought to secure its power and authority. Meanwhile the opposition, led by Madison and Jefferson, grew stronger.

The Whiskey Rebellion Stirs Debate The Whiskey Rebellion, and its outcome, fueled disagreement. The Federalists blamed the rebellion in part on a set of political clubs known as the Democratic Societies. The clubs had formed to oppose the Federalists. Although these clubs were small and scattered, Washington denounced them as "the most diabolical attempt to destroy the best fabric of human government and happiness." Jefferson and Madison defended the societies, fearing that aristocracy would triumph if leaders were immune from constant public scrutiny and criticism. They were alarmed that the Federalists had sent so many troops to suppress popular dissent in western Pennsylvania. As debate over the rebellion continued, the two sides gradually emerged as distinct political groups.

>> A 1794 cartoon added to the intense debate over the Whiskey Rebellion. Analyze Political Cartoons Does this cartoon mostly support the government or the rebels? How can you tell?

1 of 4

Objective 3: Explain how a two-party system emerged in the new nation.

Quick Instruction

Interactive Chart: Federalists versus Republicans Project the Interactive Chart. Have students state in their own words the key differences between Federalists and Republicans. Which party would a southern farmer likely support? What about a northern merchant? Explain your reasoning. *(A southern farmer would likely be a Democratic Republican because that party promoted an agricultural economy and state power. A northern merchant would likely be a Federalist because that party favored a strong federal government to promote industry and trade.)*

Compare Points of View What were Democratic Societies? Compare the views of those in favor and opposed to these groups. *(The Democratic Societies were clubs that organized to oppose the Federalists. Washington blamed them for the Whiskey Rebellion and thought they threatened the government. Jefferson and Madison defended the societies, saying it was important to scrutinize the government and express criticisms in order to prevent the aristocracy from becoming too powerful.)*

The New Government Finds Its Way

INTERACTIVE CHART
Federalists versus Republicans

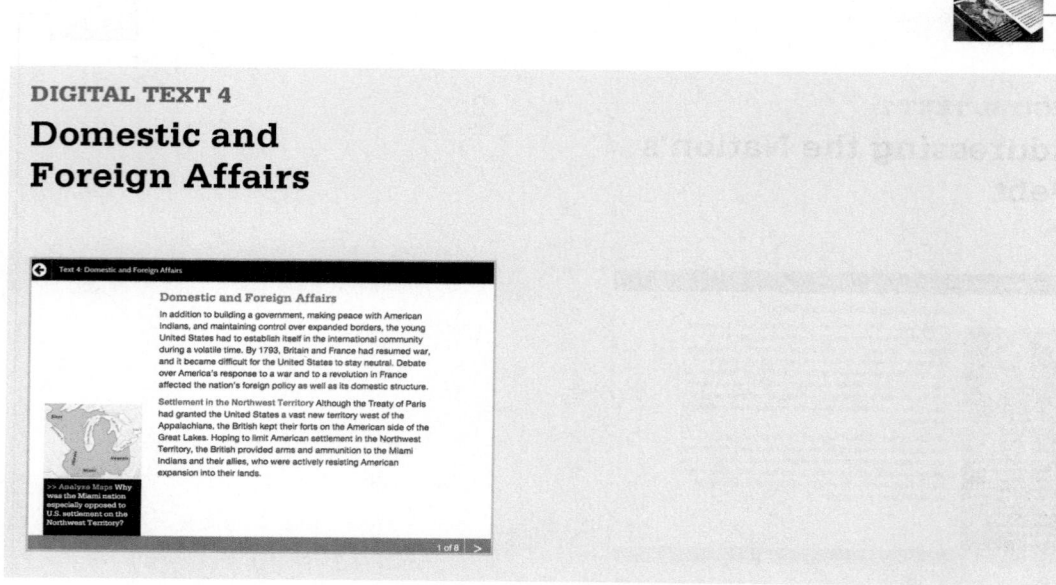

DIGITAL TEXT 4
Domestic and Foreign Affairs

📖 ACTIVE CLASSROOM
Conduct a Plus/Minus/Interesting activity. Group students. Give each group a three-column organizer with the headings Plus/Minus/Interesting. Have groups use the organizer to record their responses to the following questions: 1. What are the positive ideas about the emergence of a two-party system? 2. What are the negative ideas about this? 3. What is interesting about this? Have groups share their responses with the class.

Further Instruction
Go through the Interactive Reading Notepad questions and discuss the answers with the class. Be sure students understand the key similarities and differences between the Federalists and Republicans and the reasons the two parties emerged.

Draw Conclusions How did the Whiskey Rebellion reflect the growing tension between Federalists and Democratic Republicans? *(Washington and Hamilton argued that the federal government needed to put down the rebellion in order to secure its powers. Others, led by Jefferson and Madison, opposed such a strong show of force against popular dissent over a federal government policy. The disagreement strengthened the divisions between the two emerging parties.)*

Objective 4: Explain how territorial expansion brought Americans into conflict with the British and with American Indians.

Quick Instruction
Project the map titled *American Indians in the Northwest Territory, c.1787.* Remind students that the Treaty of Paris gave the United States territory west of the Appalachians. However the British still kept forts on the American side. American Indian groups also lived in the territories the United States had claimed. Ask students to predict the tensions that might result over this territory.

Identify Cause and Effect Identify the causes and effects of the Treaty of Greenville. *(Causes—conflict escalated between American settlers and American Indians. Little Turtle and his troops, aided by the British, initially defeated American forces, but federal troops won a decisive victory at the Battle of Fallen Timbers, leading to the treaty. Effects—American Indians ceded most of present-day Ohio to the United States. The Northwest Territory was opened to settlement.)*

Support Ideas with Evidence How did American expansion affect the economy? *(Westward expansion led to economic improvements. The federal government was able to pay off some of its debt by selling land to settlers.)*

Further Instruction
Go through the Interactive Reading Notepad questions and discuss the answers with the class. Assign the Primary Sources: Washington's Farewell Address and the Declaration of the Rights of Man. Be sure students understand the impact of the French Revolution on American foreign policy.

Compare Points of View Compare and contrast the views of the Federalists and the Democratic Republicans on the French Revolution. *(Federalists—opposed the revolution; viewed the revolutionaries as bloody anarchists; feared that both the French and the Democratic Republicans wanted to destroy social order. Democratic Republicans—regretted the executions but supported the French Republic; favored the revolutionaries to the monarchy they had replaced. Both—did not want to enter the conflict between Britain and France.)*

Generate Explanations Why did the United States try to remain neutral during the war in Europe? *(The United States was too weak to fight another war. It did not have a strong army or navy, or sufficient funds. Entering the conflict would bankrupt the federal government, and the United States could not afford to alienate any of its trade partners.)*

DIGITAL TEXT 5

Foreign Policy Affects Domestic Politics

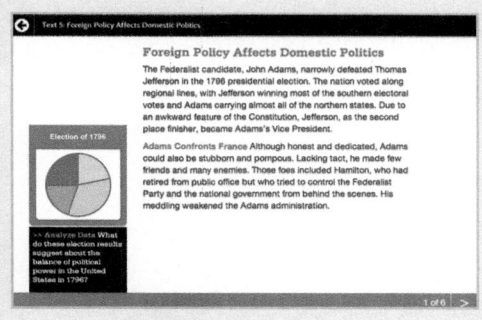

Text 5: Foreign Policy Affects Domestic Politics

Foreign Policy Affects Domestic Politics

The Federalist candidate, John Adams, narrowly defeated Thomas Jefferson in the 1796 presidential election. The nation voted along regional lines, with Jefferson winning most of the southern electoral votes and Adams carrying almost all of the northern states. Due to an awkward feature of the Constitution, Jefferson, as the second place finisher, became Adams's Vice President.

Adams Confronts France Although honest and dedicated, Adams could also be stubborn and pompous. Lacking tact, he made few friends and many enemies. Those foes included Hamilton, who had retired from public office but who tried to control the Federalist Party and the national government from behind the scenes. His meddling weakened the Adams administration.

Election of 1796

>> Analyze Data What do these election results suggest about the balance of political power in the United States in 1796?

1 of 6

Objective 6: Analyze how the political parties' debates over foreign policy further divided them.

Quick Instruction

Project the political cartoon of the XYZ affair. Explain that while the United States tried to remain neutral, France began seizing American ships and humiliated the United States with its demands. Review the divisions in American politics during this time. Ask how and why the XYZ affair united the nation—at least temporarily.

Identify Steps in a Process How was the United States drawn into war with France? *(In response to the Jay Treaty of 1794, France started taking American merchant ships. Adams tried to negotiate peace but the French officials demanded humiliating terms, including exorbitant bribes. Public opinion turned against France. Congress voted to expand the army and to authorize a small navy to fight against French ships.)*

D Differentiate: Extra Support Explain that an *alien* is a foreigner and *sedition* is an action or speech that inspires people to rebel against the government. Have students use these definitions to describe the Alien and Sedition Acts in their own words and explain why many people found these laws unfair.

ELL Use the ELL activity described in the ELL chart.

Further Instruction

Go through the Interactive Reading Notepad questions and discuss the answers with the class. Review the chain of events, including the French Revolution, the XYZ Affair, the Alien and Sedition Acts, and the Virginia and Kentucky Resolutions. Be sure students understand how the United States became involved in the conflict with France and the effect this had on domestic policies.

Draw Conclusions What political advantage would enacting new laws such as the Alien and Sedition Acts have given the Federalists? *(The Federalists took advantage of the war to weaken the Democratic Republicans. They deported non-citizens who criticized the government and made it more difficult for non-citizens to attain citizenship. Because many non-citizens were Democratic Republicans, these policies weakened the opposition.)*

Identify Cause and Effect Identify the causes of the Virginia and Kentucky Resolutions. Then make a prediction about what you think their effects will be. *(Causes— the Sedition Act made it a crime to publicly criticize the federal government. Jefferson and Madison passed resolutions declaring the act unconstitutional. They hinted that states could nullify federal laws that were unconstitutional. However, the doctrine of nullification will not be upheld. States will have to follow federal law and will not be able to pass resolutions that contradict the federal government.)*

The New Government Finds Its Way

SYNTHESIZE

DIGITAL ACTIVITY
Judging the Success of the New Constitution

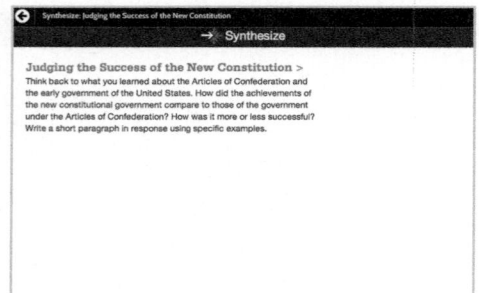

Have students brainstorm ideas and write a paragraph comparing the new constitutional government to the government under the Articles of Confederation. Remind them to use specific examples and then exchange paragraphs with a partner to review.

Discuss Ask students to consider the increased powers that the Constitution gave the federal government. Have them give examples of how these powers affected foreign and domestic policy during the presidencies of Washington and Adams. What Constitutional limits to federal power remained?

DEMONSTRATE

DIGITAL QUIZ
Lesson Quiz and Class Discussion Board

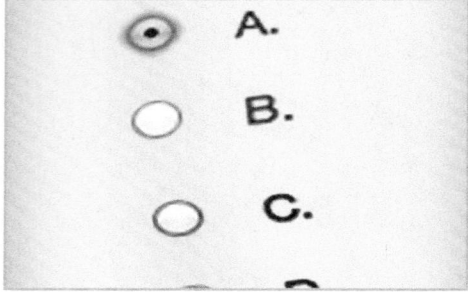

Assign the online Lesson Quiz for this lesson if you haven't already done so. Students will be offered automatic remediation or enrichment based on their score.

Pose these questions to the class on the Discussion Board:

In *The New Government Finds its Way*, you read about the political tensions that led to the establishment of political parties in the United States, as well as domestic and foreign challenges that faced the young nation.

Evaluate Arguments Do you agree with the authors of the Constitution that early political parties were factions that threatened the unity of the nation? Why or why not?

Summarize the major political divisions that emerged in the early nation and explain the reasons for disagreement.

Topic Inquiry
Have students continue their investigations for the Topic Inquiry.

Jefferson as President

Supporting English Language Learners

Use with the reading, **John Marshall Shapes the Supreme Court**.

Speaking
Remind students that many English words have multiple meanings. Explain that they will practice using specific meanings of such words in context.

Beginning Display the word *decision*, and use it in familiar contexts with students (e.g., I made a decision about what to eat). Explain the specific meaning of *decision* in regard to the Supreme Court. Guide students to use the word in this context.

Intermediate Ask: What does *power* mean in the sentence, *There was no power after the storm?* Then read the section titled *The Power of the Judicial Branch*. Ask students to define *power* in this context and practice using it to speak about the Supreme Court.

Advanced Invite pairs of students to read the text's first paragraph together and discuss the meanings of *court* and *decision* in context. Then have them use these two words to describe the career of John Marshall.

Advanced High Invite pairs of students to discuss the impact of John Marshall on the Supreme Court using these words: appointment, power, court, decision. Ask: How do you use these words in everyday conversations? How are those uses like and unlike the uses of these words in the text?

Use with the reading, **Foreign Difficulties Challenge Jefferson**.

Reading
Tell students that one way to better understand the meanings of words is to compare and contrast them with other words they know.

Beginning Read the text's third paragraph together and point out the words *spread* and *expand*. With students, use words and gestures to discuss their meanings and how they are related. Ask: Did the reexport trade help the U.S. economy expand?

Intermediate Point out the verbs *picked up* and *unloaded* in the text's fourth paragraph. Ask: What does each verb mean? How are the meanings related? Invite students to practice using the words in sentences.

Advanced Invite pairs of students to locate the phrasal verb *picked up* in the text's fourth paragraph and discuss its meaning. Then have them locate a verb in the same paragraph that means the opposite (unloaded). Ask students to practice using both verbs in sentences about the text.

Advanced High Invite pairs of students to locate these verb pairs in the text: *spread* and *expand* (paragraph 3), *picked up* and *unloaded* (paragraph 4), *threatened* and *attacked* (paragraph 9). For each verb pair, have students discuss and compare the verbs' meanings. Then have them practice using them to discuss the text.

▶ Differentiate Instruction

Use the Differentiated Instruction notes throughout the lesson plan to support the varied skill sets, levels of readiness, and interests in the mixed-ability classroom.

Challenge These notes include suggestions for expanding the activity for advanced students.

On-Level These notes include suggestions for modifying the activity to address different interests or learning styles.

Extra Support These notes include ideas for providing more scaffolding or reading spuport.

Special Needs These notes provide ideas for adapting instruction to support the needs of various special needs students.

■ NOTES

Jefferson as President

Objectives

Objective 1: Understand why some saw Jefferson's election as a "Democratic Republican revolution."

Objective 2: Explain the impact of John Marshall's tenure as Chief Justice of the United States.

Objective 3: Identity the importance of the Louisiana Purchase.

Objective 4: Analyze Jefferson's foreign policies.

LESSON 2 ORGANIZER		PACING: APPROX. 1 PERIOD, .5 BLOCKS			
		OBJECTIVES	PACING	Online	Print
Connect					
(icon) DIGITAL START UP ACTIVITY **President Thomas Jefferson**			5 min.	●	
Investigate					
(icon) DIGITAL TEXT 1 **A New Direction for American Government**		Objective 1	10 min.	●	●
(icon) DIGITAL TEXT 2 **John Marshall Shapes the Supreme Court**		Objective 2	10 min.	●	●
(icon) DIGITAL TEXT 3 **A Growing Nation Looks Westward**		Objective 3	10 min.	●	●
(icon) INTERACTIVE GALLERY **On the Trail with Lewis and Clark**			10 min.	●	
(icon) DIGITAL TEXT 4 **Foreign Difficulties Challenge Jefferson**		Objective 4	10 min.	●	●
(icon) INTERACTIVE CARTOON **The Embargo Act of 1807**			10 min.	●	
Synthesize					
(icon) DIGITAL ACTIVITY **Reflecting on Jefferson's Presidency**			5 min.	●	
Demonstrate					
(icon) DIGITAL QUIZ **Lesson Quiz and Class Discussion Board**			10 min.	●	

PEARSON
realize™
www.PearsonRealize.com

Go online to access additional resources including:
Primary Sources • Biographies • Supreme Court cases •
21st Century Skill Tutorials • Maps • Graphic Organizers.

CONNECT

DIGITAL START UP ACTIVITY
President Thomas Jefferson

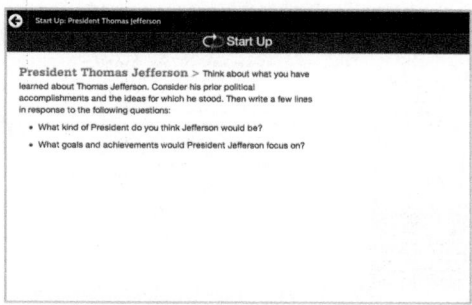

Project the Start Up Activity Ask students to answer the questions as they enter and get settled. Have students share their answers with a partner.

Discuss What kind of President do you think Jefferson would be? What goals and achievements would President Jefferson focus on? *(He would be more focused on creating a strong agrarian economy than his Federalist predecessors. He would also be concerned with reducing the reach of the federal government.)*

Tell students that in this lesson they will be learning about Jefferson's presidency, including the importance of the Louisiana Purchase and his foreign policy decisions, as well as the impact of John Marshall on the U.S. Supreme Court.

Vocabulary Development Use the Interactive Reading Notepad to preview the Key Terms and Academic Vocabulary in this lesson with students.

⟳ FLIP IT!
Assign the Flipped Video for this lesson.

▊ STUDENT EDITION PRINT
PAGES: 144–150

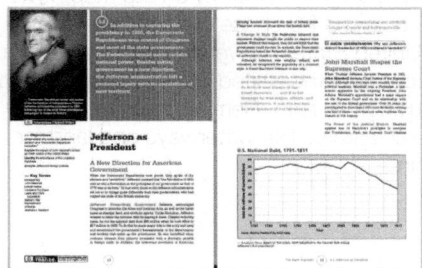

INVESTIGATE

DIGITAL TEXT 1
A New Direction for American Government

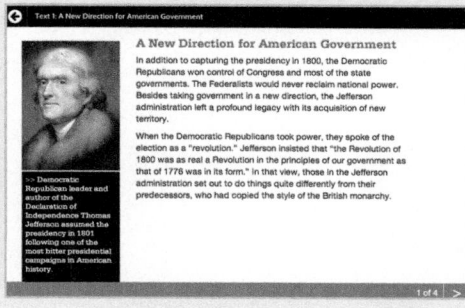

Objective 1: Understand why some saw Jefferson's election as a "Democratic Republican revolution."

Quick Instruction
Explain that although Jefferson was very wealthy, he promoted a popular, common style. Prompt students to see how Jefferson's approach to the presidency differed from that of his predecessors with specific examples. *(Jefferson encouraged the government to end the Alien and Sedition Acts and taxes on stamps, land, and spirits. He cut the army and navy and limited bureaucracy in order to pay down the national debt.)*

Further Instruction
Go through the Interactive Reading Notepad questions and discuss the answers with the class. Be sure students understand how Jefferson's election took the country in a new direction.

Compare and Contrast How did Jefferson address the national debt? Compare his policies to Hamilton's. *(Jefferson wanted to pay down the debt. He did this by cutting government spending, including limiting the army and navy and streamlining bureaucracy. He also raised money by increasing foreign trade and selling federal lands to Americans moving west. In contrast, Hamilton did not focus on paying down the debt. He sold government bonds to investors in order to create economic growth in commercial and industrial sectors.)*

Generate Explanations Explain how Jefferson's policies reflected the principles of the Democratic Republicans. *(Democratic Republicans wanted to limit federal government and were critical of the aristocracy, which they felt held too much political power. Towards that end, Jefferson cut government spending and reduced bureaucracy, limiting the reach of the federal government.)*

Jefferson as President

DIGITAL TEXT 2

John Marshall Shapes the Supreme Court

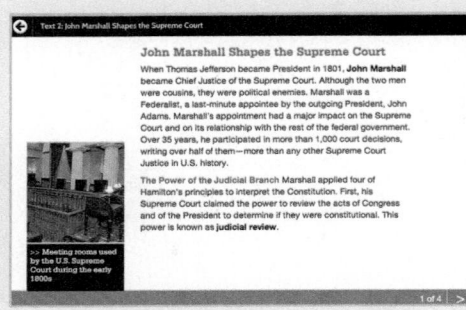

Text 2: John Marshall Shapes the Supreme Court

John Marshall Shapes the Supreme Court

When Thomas Jefferson became President in 1801, **John Marshall** became Chief Justice of the Supreme Court. Although the two men were cousins, they were political enemies. Marshall was a Federalist, a last-minute appointee by the outgoing President, John Adams. Marshall's appointment had a major impact on the Supreme Court and on its relationship with the rest of the federal government. Over 35 years, he participated in more than 1,000 court decisions, writing over half of them—more than any other Supreme Court Justice in U.S. history.

The Power of the Judicial Branch Marshall applied four of Hamilton's principles to interpret the Constitution. First, his Supreme Court claimed the power to review the acts of Congress and of the President to determine if they were constitutional. This power is known as **judicial review.**

>> Meeting rooms used by the U.S. Supreme Court during the early 1800s

1 of 4 >

DIGITAL TEXT 3

A Growing Nation Looks Westward

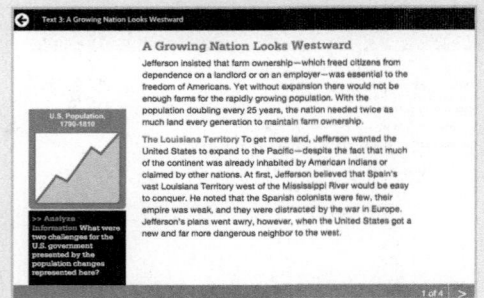

Text 3: A Growing Nation Looks Westward

A Growing Nation Looks Westward

Jefferson insisted that farm ownership—which freed citizens from dependence on a landlord or on an employer—was essential to the freedom of Americans. Yet without expansion there would not be enough farms for the rapidly growing population. With the population doubling every 25 years, the nation needed twice as much land every generation to maintain farm ownership.

The Louisiana Territory To get more land, Jefferson wanted the United States to expand to the Pacific—despite the fact that much of the continent was already inhabited by American Indians or claimed by other nations. At first, Jefferson believed that Spain's vast Louisiana Territory west of the Mississippi River would be easy to conquer. He noted that the Spanish colonists were few, their empire was weak, and they were distracted by the war in Europe. Jefferson's plans went awry, however, when the United States got a new and far more dangerous neighbor to the west.

>> Analyze Information What were two challenges for the U.S. government presented by the population changes represented here?

U.S. Population, 1790-1810

1 of 4 >

Objective 2: Explain the impact of John Marshall's tenure as Chief Justice of the United States.

Quick Instruction

Project the flowchart titled *The Process of Judicial Review* and outline the essential process of judicial review, or the power of the Supreme Court to decide whether executive action or congressional legislation is constitutional.

Distinguish How did Marshall's idea of determining the constitutionality of legislation differ from the 1798 Kentucky and Virginia Resolutions? *The 1798 Kentucky and Virginia Resolutions had hinted that states could nullify federal laws they deemed unconstitutional, but the Constitution itself was silent on the matter. Marshall, however, thought the responsibility for doing so fell to a federal judicial body.*

Paraphrase the paragraphs under the heading "The Power of the Judicial Branch." What four principles did Marshall use to interpret the Constitution? *(Marshall claimed the power of judicial review, said federal laws took precedent over state laws, broadly interpreted the Constitution, and limited the power of sate governments to interfere with business.)*

ELL Use the ELL activity described in the ELL chart.

Further Instruction

Go through the Interactive Reading Notepad questions. Assign Government Basics: Judicial Branch and Landmark Supreme Court: *Marbury* v. *Madison*. Be sure students understand the significance of judicial review and can explain how this ruling affected the balance of powers in the federal government.

Express Problems Clearly How did the Court's decision in *Marbury* v. *Madison* create judicial precedent for the Court to determine the constitutionality of legislative action? *(After the election of 1800, incoming Secretary of State James Madison refused to deliver appointment papers to William Marbury, a Federalist justice appointed by the outgoing President Adams. Marbury complained to the Court. The Court ruled that part of the Judiciary Act of 1789 was unconstitutional, which denied Marbury his appointment while establishing judicial precedent that the Court could rule legislation unconstitutional.)*

Support Ideas with Evidence What evidence from the text supports the idea that John Marshall strengthened the national government? *(Marshall established judicial review, which strengthened the power of the courts by giving them the authority to overrule the executive and legislative branches. Judicial review also strengthened the position of the national government over the states by affirming that the court, not states, can declare laws unconstitutional.)*

Objective 3: Identify the importance of the Louisiana Purchase.

Quick Instruction

Interactive Gallery: On the Trail with Lewis and Clark Project the Interactive Gallery and have students navigate through the images. Explain that in 1803 Jefferson purchased the Louisiana Territory from France, nearly doubling the size of the United States. Why did Jefferson want to expand the United States? *(The country's population was growing. In order for the American population to maintain the same level of farm ownership, the nation needed more land.)*

Sequence Events leading up to the Louisiana Purchase. *(Bonaparte forced Spain to give him the Louisiana Territory. France then threatened to block American access to the strategic port city of New Orleans. To avoid war with France, Jefferson offered to buy the Louisiana Territory. After a rebellion in Haiti, Bonaparte agreed to sell the Louisiana Territory and give up his imperial ambitions in the Americas.)*

D Differentiate: Extra Support Have students locate the Louisiana Territory on a map. Ask them to show on the map how the Louisiana Purchase changed the size of the United States. Have students brainstorm reasons why the United States benefited from acquiring this land. Remind them to look for natural features like waterways and land for farming.

INTERACTIVE GALLERY
On the Trail with Lewis and Clark

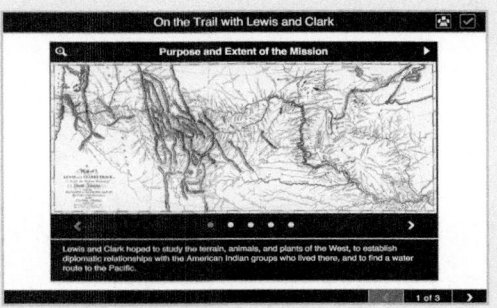

DIGITAL TEXT 4
Foreign Difficulties Challenge Jefferson

INTERACTIVE CARTOON
The Embargo Act of 1807

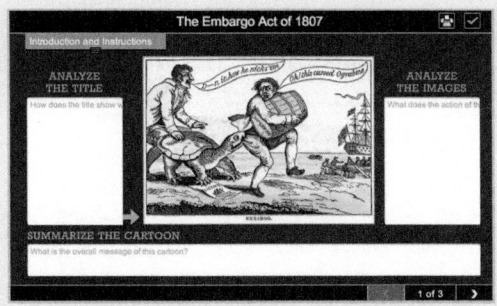

📷 ACTIVE CLASSROOM
Conduct a Conversation activity. Have students imagine they are having a conversation with Lewis and Clark after they reached the Pacific. Have students write down a question they'd like to ask, then what Lewis or Clark would say to them, and what they would say in response.

Further Instruction
Go through the Interactive Reading Notepad questions and discuss the answers with the class. Have students make a prediction about how they think the Louisiana Purchase will change the United States.

Cite Evidence explaining why Jefferson encouraged Americans to own farms. *("Jefferson insisted that farm ownership—which freed citizens from dependence on a landlord or on an employer—was essential to the freedom of Americans.")*

Identify Cause and Effect Identify one cause and one effect of the Louisiana Purchase. *(Cause—France lost the army it would have needed to occupy Louisiana and maintain an empire in North America. Effect—The United States expanded westward.)*

Objective 4: Analyze Jefferson's foreign policies.

Quick Instruction
Interactive Cartoon: The Embargo Act of 1807 Project the Interactive Cartoon on the whiteboard and have students describe the image. Explain that in 1807, Jefferson ordered an embargo to suspend trade with Britain. Prompt students to imagine how many Americans reacted to the embargo, using evidence from the Interactive Cartoon for support.

Identify Cause and Effect Identify the causes and effects of the Embargo Act of 1807. *(Causes—Britain impressed American sailors, confiscated American merchant ships trading with France, and attacked an American warship. Effects—Britain was not forced to end its abuses. Instead it found other markets in South America, putting American farmers, merchants, and businesses out of work.)*

📷 ACTIVE CLASSROOM
Have students make a headline capturing one of the foreign difficulties that challenged Jefferson during his presidency, such as the Barbary War, the reexport trade, impressment, or the Embargo Act of 1807. Have students exchange their headlines with a partner to review.

ELL Use the ELL activity described in the ELL chart.

Further Instruction
Go through the Interactive Reading Notepad questions and discuss the answers with the class. Be sure students understand how foreign difficulties affected the final years of Jefferson's presidency.

Summarize the benefits and challenges of the reexport trade. *(The British had banned American ships from traveling between the French West Indies and France. However, the United States wanted to expand its overseas markets and trade with France. American merchants worked around Britain's ban by picking up cargoes in the French colonies. They took the cargoes to the United States, unloaded them, and shipped them to France as if they were American products. This system allowed the United States to keep up its trade with France, but it led Britain to seize American ships in retaliation.)*

Draw Conclusions How did westward expansion shape American foreign policy? *(Americans moved west to own more farmland. The nation then needed to increase its overseas trade to provide markets for its crops. American foreign policy then focused on increasing trade with Britain and France while protecting American businesses.)*

Jefferson as President

SYNTHESIZE

DIGITAL ACTIVITY
Reflecting on Jefferson's Presidency

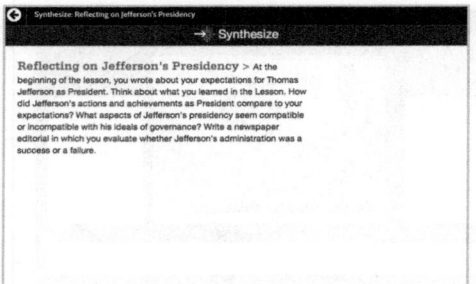

Have students review their answers to the questions at the beginning of the lesson. Then have them write a newspaper editorial evaluating Jefferson's administration. Have students share their editorials with a partner and compare their views of Jefferson's presidency.

Discuss Prompt students to explain how Jefferson's presidency reflected the ideals of the Democratic Republican party. Discuss the extent to which the country shifted away from Federalist ideology during this time.

DEMONSTRATE

DIGITAL QUIZ
Lesson Quiz and Class Discussion Board

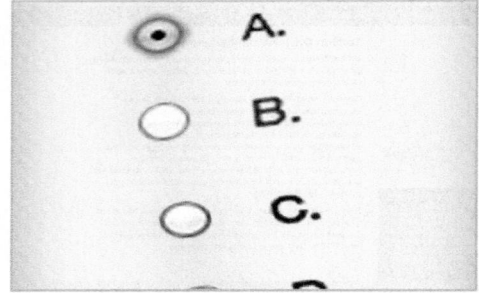

Assign the online Lesson Quiz for this lesson if you haven't already done so. Students will be offered automatic remediation or enrichment based on their score.

Pose these questions to the class on the Discussion Board:

In *Jefferson as President*, you read about the political significance of Jefferson's election and some of his foreign and domestic accomplishments, such as the Louisiana Purchase. You also read about Chief Justice John Marshall's impact on the Supreme Court.

Evaluate Arguments Why was the election of 1800 considered a "revolution"? Do you agree with this assessment? Explain your reasoning.

Draw Conclusions How did American economic growth shape domestic and foreign policy during Jefferson's presidency?

Topic Inquiry
Have students continue their investigations for the Topic Inquiry.

The War of 1812

Supporting English Language Learners

Use with the reading, **War with Britain**.

Learning
Ask: When you are speaking and cannot think of a word you need, what can you do? Invite students to brainstorm answers to this question.

Beginning Ask students to make statements about the war between Britain and the United States. Encourage them to ask you or their classmates for assistance when they cannot think of a word or pronounce it.

Intermediate Invite students to sit in a circle and take turns adding sentences to a narration of the War of 1812. Encourage them to ask one another for assistance, or to use non-verbal cues, when they cannot think of a word.

Advanced Invite pairs of students to describe the events in Detroit during the War of 1812. If they cannot think of a word during their discussion, encourage students to ask their partner for assistance, use non-verbal cues, or come up with another way to express the same idea.

Advanced High Invite pairs of students to analyze the preparedness and effectiveness of the U.S. military during the War of 1812. If they cannot think of a word during their discussion, encourage students to use synonyms and circumlocution to express the idea in another way.

Use with the reading, **The Impact of the War of 1812**.

Listening
Review how to form and use a gerund. Explain that sometimes gerunds stand alone in a sentence, while other times they are part of a gerund clause.

Beginning Read aloud the text's fifth (one-sentence) paragraph, and ask students to identify the gerund clause in it. Then display the sentence and discuss the meaning of the clause *drawing back from the brink*.

Intermediate Display three gerund clauses found in the text's fourth paragraph. Then encourage students to listen for these clauses as you read the paragraph aloud. Discuss their meanings together.

Advanced Place students in pairs and have them take turns reading aloud the text's first and third paragraphs. While one partner speaks, encourage the other to identify the gerund clause in the paragraph. Then have partners discuss the meaning of each gerund clause.

Advanced High Invite pairs of students to use gerunds as they discuss the impact of the War of 1812. Encourage them to identify the gerunds their partner uses and explain their meanings.

⒟ Differentiate Instruction

Use the Differentiated Instruction notes throughout the lesson plan to support the varied skill sets, levels of readiness, and interests in the mixed-ability classroom.

Challenge These notes include suggestions for expanding the activity for advanced students.

On-Level These notes include suggestions for modifying the activity to address different interests or learning styles.

Extra Support These notes include ideas for providing more scaffolding or reading spuport.

Special Needs These notes provide ideas for adapting instruction to support the needs of various special needs students.

■ NOTES

The War of 1812

Objectives

Objective 1: Identify the events that led to the War Hawks' call for war.

Objective 2: Analyze the major battles and conflicts of the War of 1812.

Objective 3: Explain the significance of the War of 1812.

LESSON 3 ORGANIZER		OBJECTIVES	PACING	RESOURCES	
				Online	Print
Connect					
	DIGITAL START UP ACTIVITY **Burning the Capital**		5 min.	●	
Investigate					
	DIGITAL TEXT 1 **The Road to War**	Objective 1	10 min.	●	●
	INTERACTIVE CHART **Is War Against Great Britain Justified?**		10 min.	●	
	DIGITAL TEXT 2 **War with Britain**	Objective 2	10 min.	●	●
	INTERACTIVE MAP **The War of 1812**		10 min.	●	
	DIGITAL TEXT 3 **The Impact of the War of 1812**	Objective 3	10 min.	●	●
Synthesize					
	DIGITAL ACTIVITY **Evaluating the War of 1812**		5 min.	●	
Demonstrate					
	DIGITAL QUIZ **Lesson Quiz and Class Discussion Board**		10 min.	●	

PACING: APPROX. 1 PERIOD, .5 BLOCKS

PEARSON
realize™
www.PearsonRealize.com

Go online to access additional resources including:
Primary Sources • Biographies • Supreme Court cases •
21st Century Skill Tutorials • Maps • Graphic Organizers.

■ CONNECT

DIGITAL START UP ACTIVITY
Burning the Capital

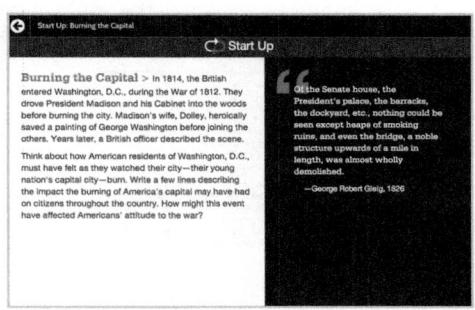

Project the Start Up Activity Ask students to read the quote and answer the questions as they enter and get settled. Have students share their responses with a partner, either in class or through a blog space.

Discuss Write a few lines describing the impact the burning of America's capital may have had on citizens throughout the country. *(Americans were probably shocked and upset by the burning of the capital. They may have feared the country seemed less strong and secure.)* How might this event have affected Americans' attitude to the war? *(Americans may have rallied behind the war effort.)*

Tell students that in this lesson they will be learning about the causes, effects, and significance of the War of 1812.

Aa Vocabulary Development Use the Interactive Reading Notepad to preview the Key Terms and Academic Vocabulary in this lesson with students.

⊾ FLIP IT!
Assign the Flipped Video for this lesson.

■ STUDENT EDITION PRINT
PAGES: 151–155

■ INVESTIGATE

DIGITAL TEXT 1
The Road to War

INTERACTIVE CHART
Is War Against Great Britain Justified?

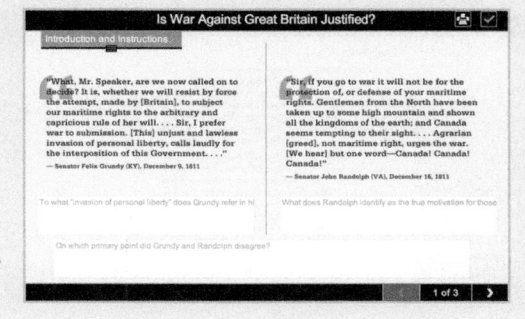

Objective 1: Identify the events that led to the War Hawks' call for war.

Quick Instruction
Interactive Chart: Is War Against Great Britain Justified? Project the Interactive Chart and prompt students to discuss whether the war with Britain was justifed, based on the quotations.

Summarize the conflicts leading up to the Battle of Tippecanoe. *(As settlers moved west, two Shawnee Indian brothers launched an armed resistance against American expansion and the use of dishonest treaties to take their lands. American troops attacked the brothers' village and burned it down.)*

Determine Point of View Who were the War Hawks and what did they want? *(The War Hawks were a group of young politicians led by Calhoun and Clay who represented farmers and settlers from the South and West. Strongly nationalist, they wanted war to uphold America's honor and drive British forces from North America.)*

🗨 ACTIVE CLASSROOM
Conduct a Take a Stand activity using the following question: Were the War Hawks right to want war? Ask students to divide into two groups based on their answer and move to separate areas of the classroom. Ask students to talk with each other to compare their reasons for answering yes or no. Have a representative from each side present and defend the group's point of view.

D Differentiate: Extra Support Have students list the conflicts the United States faced with Britain and France. Ask what problems the United States experienced in trying to trade with both countries. Discuss why it was important for the United States to sell its goods abroad.

Further Instruction
Identify Steps in a Process Describe the progression from the Embargo Act to the Nonintercourse Act and Macon's Bill No. 2. *(The Embargo Act suspended trade with Britain. When that failed to stop British abuses and harmed American businesses, Congress passed the Nonintercourse Act, in which the United States would trade with either Britain or France if one of them lifted their restrictions on American shipping. Macon's Bill No. 2 relaxed the previous legislation and restored trade with both Britain and France. It added that if one country recognized American neutrality, the United States would stop trading with the country that did not.)*

The War of 1812

DIGITAL TEXT 2
War with Britain

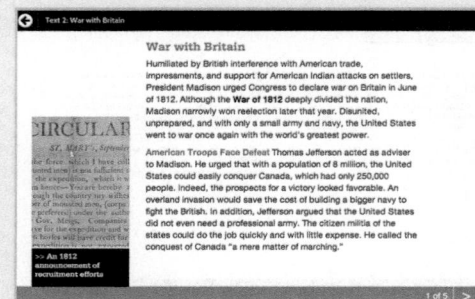

INTERACTIVE MAP
The War of 1812

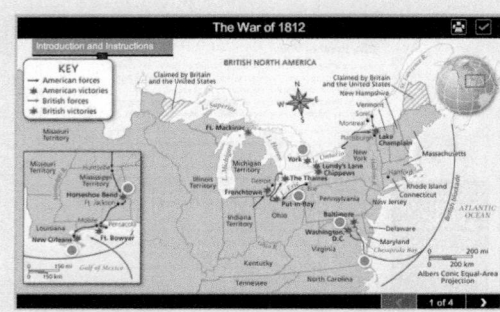

DIGITAL TEXT 3
The Impact of the War of 1812

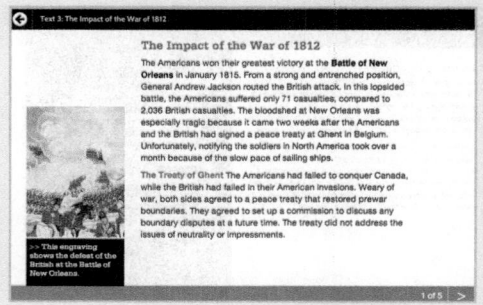

Objective 2: **Analyze the major battles and conflicts of the War of 1812.**

Quick Instruction
Interactive Map: The War of 1812 Project the Interactive Map and navigate through the images with students. Have students locate the main areas of fighting in the War of 1812. Guide students to identify the geographic factors such as waterways that influenced the location of battles and the British and American lines of attack.

Identify Central Issues that led the United States to go to war in the War of 1812. *(Britain had been interfering with American trade, impressing Americans at sea, and supporting American Indian attacks on settlers. War Hawks urged the United States to fight back by conquering Canada, pushing the British out of North America, and forcing Britain to relax its trade restrictions.)*

📷 ACTIVE CLASSROOM
Conduct a Closer Look activity. Use a whiteboard tool to divide the Interactive Map into three numbered sections: the Great Lakes, the Eastern Seaboard, and the Gulf of Mexico. Have students count off 1 to 3. Then have them look closely at the part of the image in their sections. Have them tell you what they see and what they learned as a result of their focus on this part of the image. Collect insights for each section.

ELL Use the ELL activity described in the ELL chart.

Further Instruction
Go through the Interactive Reading Notepad questions. Discuss the key battles of the War of 1812. Be sure students understand the military setbacks and the reasons for the country's eventual success.

Support Ideas with Evidence Jefferson believed that conquering Canada would be an easy task. Provide evidence that this view was incorrect. *(State militias from the United States had no professional training and were not successful fighters. Some generals proved to be ineffectual. British and Indian forces in Canada repeatedly defeated U.S. troops.)*

Make Predictions Make a prediction about how Jackson's victories in Alabama and Florida will shape the nation after the war. *(Jackson's victories were against the Creek Indians, the Seminole Indians, and the Spanish. He made the survivors surrender their lands and seized Spanish territories. As a result, his victories will likely lead to increased American expansion and further loss of land for American Indians and the Spanish.)*

Objective 3: **Explain the significance of the War of 1812.**

Quick Instruction
Explain that the Treaty of Ghent ended the War of 1812 and restored prewar boundaries. Prompt students to think of reasons that explain why Americans might have considered the War of 1812 a victory even though the treaty did not address the issues of neutrality and impressment that had led to war. *(Many Americans still considered the outcome of the war a successful defense against British encroachment on foreign trade and remembered the well-publicized victory against the British at New Orleans.)*

Determine Relevance Why was the defeat of Napoleon in France relevant to the peace treaty between the United States and Britain? *(The Treaty of Ghent did not address the issue of impressment or British interference with American trade with France. However, after the defeat of Napoleon, Britain was no longer at war with France and did not need to obstruct France's trade with the United States and other countries.)*

Generate Explanations Explain how the War of 1812 encouraged further westward expansion. *(American victories temporarily ended American Indian resistance east of the Mississippi and opened up southern land for settlement. Increased settlement led new states to enter the union.)*

ELL Use the ELL activity described in the ELL chart.

SYNTHESIZE

DIGITAL ACTIVITY

Evaluating the War of 1812

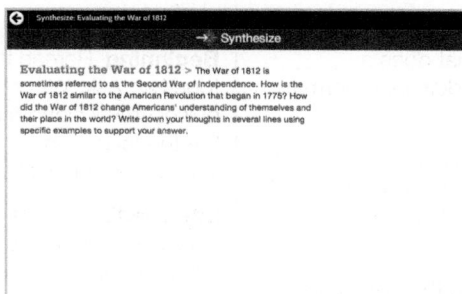

Have students answer the questions using specific examples for support. Have students share their responses with a partner and compare their views.

Discuss Ask students whether they think the war fulfilled the aims of the War Hawks. Have them provide examples from the reading for support.

DEMONSTRATE

DIGITAL QUIZ

Lesson Quiz and Class Discussion Board

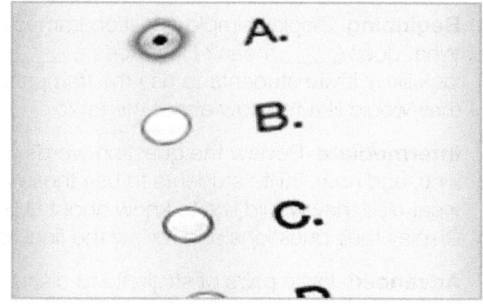

Assign the online Lesson Quiz for this lesson if you haven't already done so. Students will be offered automatic remediation or enrichment based on their score.

Pose these questions to the class on the Discussion Board:

In *The War of 1812*, you read about causes, major battles, and significance of the War of 1812.

Summarize How did the United States win the war? What did it achieve through its victory?

Identify Cause and Effect Identify the impact of the War of 1812 on American politics, economics, geography, and society.

Topic Inquiry
Have students continue their investigations for the Topic Inquiry.

Further Instruction
Go through the Interactive Reading Notepad questions and discuss the answers with the class. Have students consider the impact of the War of 1812 and make a prediction about how feelings of nationalism will affect the United States following the war.

Identify Cause and Effect How did the War of 1812 affect the Federalist party? *(The war contributed to the end of the party. The Federalists looked weak for having opposed the war. They tried to make a separate peace with Britain when it turned out the war had already ended. As a result, they were embarrassed as traitors and lost the next elections.)*

Make Generalizations Make a generalization about feelings of nationalism and national identity in the United States before and after the war. *(Before the war, Americans were largely divided between political parties and between those who were for and against the conflict. After Jackson's victory in New Orleans, Americans strongly supported the war and felt proud for defeating the British again.)*

The Beginning of the Industrial Revolution

Supporting English Language Learners

Use with the reading, **New Technology Revolutionizes Transportation**.

Speaking
Brainstorm characteristics of a good question with students, as well as the importance of asking questions well.

Beginning Display simple question frames related to the text, such as: What does _____ mean? How does a _____ work? What does a _____ look like? Invite students to use the frames to ask for additional information they would like to know about the topic.

Intermediate Review the question words *who*, *what*, *when*, *where*, *why*, and *how*. Invite students to use these words to ask questions about what else they would like to know about U.S. transportation in the 1800s. Display their questions and review the final list.

Advanced Invite pairs of students to discuss what else they would like to know about U.S. transportation in the 1800s. Have them shape their ideas into effective questions and record them in a list.

Advanced High Invite students to write five questions about what else they would like to know about U.S. transportation in the 1800s. Then have partners read their questions to each other and discuss where they might find answers to them.

Use with the reading, **Innovations in Industry and Agriculture**.

Reading
Ask: What are some ways of making sure you understand what you read? Explain that students will demonstrate their comprehension by retelling or summarizing a text.

Beginning Reread the section titled *Morse Improves Communication* together. Ask: Which sentence best summarizes the section: (a) Electric pulses travel along metal wires, (b) Ships could not carry letters over land like the telegraph, or (c) Morse invented a telegraph that allowed for nearly instant communication?

Intermediate Invite students to silently read the section titled *Morse Improves Communication*. Then ask them to volunteer a one-sentence summary of the section. Display students' sentences and compare and contrast them together.

Advanced Place students in pairs and invite partners to take turns adding sentences to an oral retelling of the text. Encourage them to include key details but not every detail. Ask: How well did you remember details from the text? How did you decide which details to retell?

Advanced High Invite students to write a summary of the text based on what they remember. Then have partners read and compare their summaries. Ask them to discuss these questions: How well did you understand the text? What information should you have included or omitted?

▣ Differentiate Instruction

Use the Differentiated Instruction notes throughout the lesson plan to support the varied skill sets, levels of readiness, and interests in the mixed-ability classroom.

Challenge These notes include suggestions for expanding the activity for advanced students.

On-Level These notes include suggestions for modifying the activity to address different interests or learning styles.

Extra Support These notes include ideas for providing more scaffolding or reading spuport.

Special Needs These notes provide ideas for adapting instruction to support the needs of various special needs students.

■ NOTES

PEARSON
realize™
www.PearsonRealize.com

Go online to access additional resources including:
Primary Sources • Biographies • Supreme Court cases •
21st Century Skill Tutorials • Maps • Graphic Organizers.

Objectives

Objective 1: Summarize the key developments in the transportation revolution of the early 1800s.

Objective 2: Analyze the rise of industry in the United States in the early 1800s.

Objective 3: Describe some of the leading inventions and industrial developments in the early 1800s.

LESSON 4 ORGANIZER		PACING: APPROX. 1 PERIOD, .5 BLOCKS			
				RESOURCES	
		OBJECTIVES	PACING	Online	Print
Connect					
	DIGITAL START UP ACTIVITY **A New Way of Life**		5 min.	●	
Investigate					
	DIGITAL TEXT 1 **New Technology Revolutionizes Transportation**	Objective 1	10 min.	●	●
	INTERACTIVE MAP **Major Canals, Roads, and Railroads, 1840–1850**		10 min.	●	
	DIGITAL TEXT 2 **The Industrial Revolution**		10 min.	●	●
	3-D MODEL **Early Textile Mill**	Objective 2	10 min.	●	
	INTERACTIVE ILLUSTRATION **The Lowell System**		10 min.	●	
	DIGITAL TEXT 3 **Inventions in Industry and Agriculture**	Objective 3	10 min.	●	●
Synthesize					
	DIGITAL ACTIVITY **Transportation and Industry**		5 min.	●	
Demonstrate					
	DIGITAL QUIZ **Lesson Quiz and Class Discussion Board**		10 min.	●	

The Beginning of the Industrial Revolution

■ CONNECT

DIGITAL START UP ACTIVITY
A New Way of Life

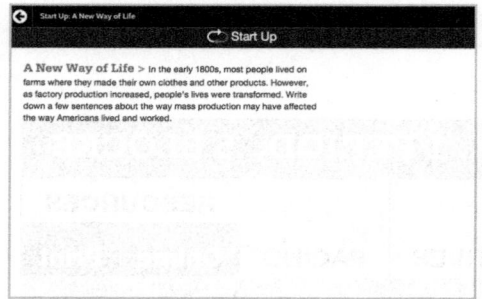

Project the Start Up Activity Ask students to read the activity and write down their thoughts as they enter and get settled. Have students share their responses with a partner.

Discuss Write a few sentences about the way mass production may have affected the way Americans lived and worked. *(Products were made cheaply and more quickly, allowing some Americans to purchase clothes and shoes rather than making them themselves. Americans who moved to urban areas to find factory found their lives regulated by the clock.)*

Tell students that in this lesson they will be learning about the beginning of the Industrial Revolution in the early 1800s, including innovations in transportation and manufacturing.

Aa Vocabulary Development Use the Interactive Reading Notepad to preview the Key Terms and Academic Vocabulary in this lesson with students.

↑↓ FLIP IT!
Assign the Flipped Video for this lesson.

■ STUDENT EDITION PRINT
PAGES: 156–160

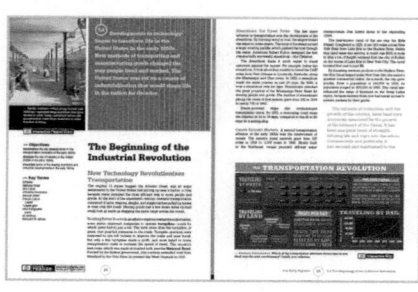

■ INVESTIGATE

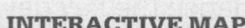

DIGITAL TEXT 1
New Technology Revolutionizes Transportation

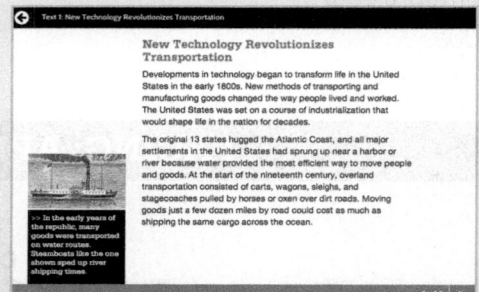

INTERACTIVE MAP
Major Canals, Roads, and Railroads, 1840–1850

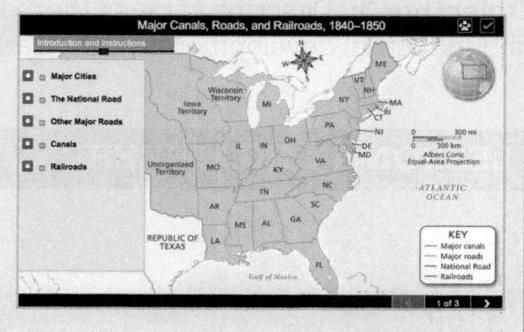

Objective 1: **Summarize the key developments in the transportation revolution of the early 1800s.**

Quick Instruction
Interactive Map: Major Canals, Roads, and Railroads, 1840–1850 Project the Interactive Map on the whiteboard and navigate through the layers with students. Discuss how people traveled and transported goods before the transportation revolution. Prompt students to describe some of the major innovations in transportation and explain their impact on American society. How did the steamboat affect trade in the United States? *(The steamboat increased trade by making it easier to travel upstream. People could move goods along major rivers like the Ohio and the Mississippi.)*

Infer How did the increasing U.S. population shape developments in transportation in the early 1800s? *(As the population increased, people moved west—away from the Atlantic coast. The country therefore had to develop more efficient means of transportation to connect people and transfer goods overland, without relying on the Atlantic seaboard.)*

■ ACTIVE CLASSROOM
Conduct a Rank It activity. List the following developments on the board: roads, canals, steamboats, railroads. Have students rank the developments according to which changed the nation the most. Ask students to provide a justification for the ranking decisions they made. Then ask students to work in pairs to share their rankings and justifications. Poll the class to see if there is agreement on the ranking.

ELL Use the ELL activity described in the ELL chart.

Further Instruction
Go through the Interactive Reading Notepad questions and discuss the answers with the class.

Identify Cause and Effect How did the construction of the Erie Canal contribute to the growth of New York City and surrounding areas? *(The Erie Canal made it possible to ship Hudson Valley produce to New York City, allowing the city to support a growing population. The canal also made farmland in the Great Lakes region more desirable because it gave farmers better access to eastern markets.)*

Make Predictions How do you think the rise of the American rail network will shape settlement in the United States? Explain your reasoning. *(The rail network will make it possible for people to move increasingly westward. It will open up new areas for settlement and allow people to build up farms and industries. More Americans will live farther from eastern cities while still accessing markets across the country.)*

DIGITAL TEXT 2

The Industrial Revolution

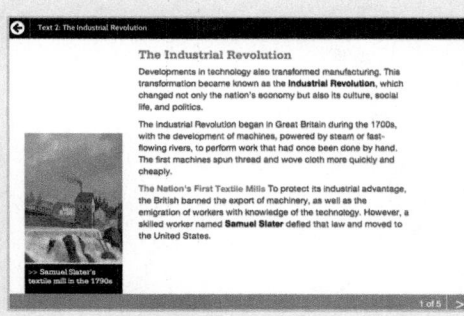

3-D MODEL

Early Textile Mill

INTERACTIVE ILLUSTRATION

The Lowell System

Objective 2: Analyze the rise of industry in the United States in the early 1800s.

Quick Instruction

3-D Model: Early Textile Mill Project the 3-D Model and drag your cursor to view the textile mill. Then click on the circles to view the machinery. Ask students what examples of new technology they see and how they think that technology was used. Prompt students to explain what a water-powered textile mill was. *(Water-powered textile mills used machines powered by steam or fast-moving rivers. These machines performed tasks that had once been done by hand. They spun thread and weaved cloth faster and more efficiently than individuals could.)*

🗣 ACTIVE CLASSROOM

Conduct a See-Think-Wonder activity. Ask students to closely examine the 3-D Model and have them answer the following questions: What do you see? What does that make you think? What are you wondering about now that you've seen this? Ask volunteers to share their insights with the class.

Interactive Illustration: The Lowell System Project the Interactive Illustration and navigate through the images with students. Encourage students to reflect on the economic effects of the Lowell System by citing evidence that explains how the Lowell mills changed the speed and volume of production. *(Lowell built mills "in which all operations in the manufacture of cloth occurred—instead of just the production of thread.")*

🗣 ACTIVE CLASSROOM

Conduct a Conversation with History activity. Ask students to imagine that they are having a conversation with one of the Lowell girls. Have them write down a question they would like to ask, then what the Lowell girl would say to them, and what they would say in response.

D Differentiate: Challenge Have students read more about the Lowell girls and the first textile mills online or in a biography. Have students prepare a short presentation for the class describing how textile mills changed the lives of young workers. Challenge students in their presentations to consider both the benefits and drawbacks of factory work.

Further Instruction

Summarize how the rise of factories changed the lives of American workers. *(Factories increased the pace of work. They also changed the kind of work that was done. Rather than making one product from start to finish, each worker completed a single small task. This meant workers did not have to be skilled or well trained and could therefore be paid less.)*

Hypothesize What was the garment trade and how do you think it affected New York City? *(In the garment trade, individuals used the cloth and thread from textile factories to make finished clothes. This industry probably provided a lot of work to poor New Yorkers. As the industry developed, more workers would have been attracted to the city.)*

The Beginning of the Industrial Revolution

DIGITAL TEXT 3

Inventions in Industry and Agriculture

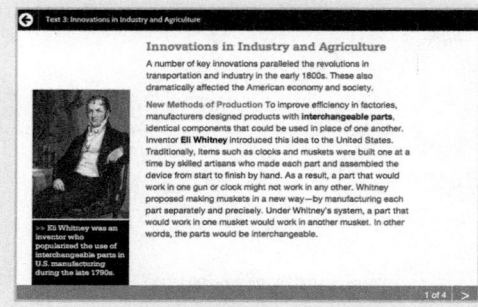

Objective 3: Describe some of the leading inventions and industrial developments in the early 1800s.

Quick Instruction

In the early 1800s, innovations in manufacturing and communications set off rapid changes in American society. Ask students to explain in their own words how innovation quickened the pace of life. *(The use of interchangeable parts increased the speed of manufacturing. The invention of the telegraph increased the speed of communcation.)*

Identify Cause and Effect Identify the factors that facilitated an increase in farm production. *(New farms in the Midwest were more fertile. Farmers adopted better methods for planting, tending, and harvesting crops and for raising livestock. Large farms also began using new machines like the steel plow and mechanical reaper.)*

📷 ACTIVE CLASSROOM

Conduct a Wallpaper activity. Have students review what they have learned about the beginning of the Industrial Revolution and design a piece of wallpaper that encapsulates key aspects of the shift from manual labor to mechanized work. Ask students to post their wallpaper and take a gallery walk around the room to note what others have written or drawn. Conclude with a brief discussion in which students note their observations.

ELL Use the ELL activity described in the ELL chart.

Further Instruction

Go through the Interactive Reading Notepad questions and discuss the answers with the class. Assign Economics Basics: Supply and Economics Basics: Demand to help students understand the economic effect of technological innovations.

Hypothesize How do you think the invention of the telegraph affected American industries? *(Businesses could communicate instantly, allowing markets to stay more closely connected. Factories could be in touch with sellers and suppliers, improving efficiency across all stages of production.)*

Generate Explanations Explain how the development of interchangeable parts made the Industrial Revolution possible. *(Interchangeable parts were identical components that were used in place of one another. This invention was necessary to bring about the shift from manual to machine labor that characterized the Industrial Revolution. Items could be made by manufacturing each part in the same way every time. Individual parts could be made faster and more efficiently than by hand.)*

■ SYNTHESIZE

DIGITAL ACTIVITY

Transportation and Industry

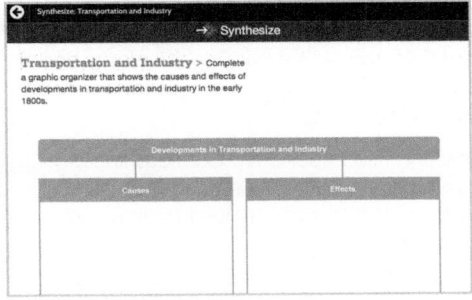

Have students complete the graphic organizer. Have students exchange organizers with a partner to review their responses.

Discuss Ask students to make a generalization about the major causes and effects of the Industrial Revolution. Then ask them which developments in transportation and industry they think had the greatest effects on the country, citing evidence from the lesson for support.

■ DEMONSTRATE

DIGITAL QUIZ

Lesson Quiz and Class Discussion Board

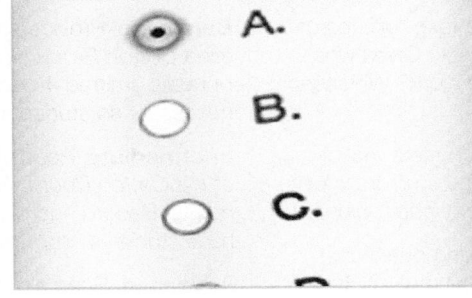

Assign the online Lesson Quiz for this lesson if you haven't already done so. Students will be offered automatic remediation or enrichment based on their score.

Pose these questions to the class on the Discussion Board:

In *The Beginning of the Industrial Revolution*, you read about significant innovations in transportation and the rise of industrial production that transformed the U.S. economy and the lives of many Americans.

Support Ideas with Examples Select one of the major inventions of the early 1800s and explain how it impacted American industry and society during this time.

Identify Central Issues that you think might arise in the United States as a result of industrialization.

Topic Inquiry
Have students continue their investigations for the Topic Inquiry.

Differences Between North and South Grow

Supporting English Language Learners

Use with the reading, **Industrialization Changes Northern Society**.

Learning
Display the term *labor union*. Tell students that they will use prior knowledge to explore the meaning of this term.

Beginning Read the definition of *labor unions* from the text: "groups of workers who unite to seek better pay and conditions." Ask: Given what you already know, which word in *labor unions* relates to work? Which word relates to uniting, or joining together?

Intermediate Read the definition of *labor unions* from the text. Ask: Which part of the definition does labor refer to? What about unions? Invite students to create new sentences using *labor*, *union*, and *labor union*.

Advanced Invite pairs of students to discuss the following questions: What do *united* (in United States) and *labor* (in Labor Day) mean? How does this information help you to understand the term *labor union*?

Advanced High Invite students to write down definitions, variants, and sample sentences for the words *labor* and *union*. Then have partners discuss their notes and connect them to the meaning of *labor union*. Ask: Given what you know, what do you think *labor party* means in politics?

Use with the reading, **Agriculture Drives Southern Society**.

Listening
Discuss the benefits of taking notes while reading or rereading a text with students.

Beginning Provide students with a bullet-point outline for the section titled *Cotton Production and Slavery Increase* that has several words and phrases omitted. Read aloud the section, pausing and/or rereading when necessary so students can complete the outline.

Intermediate Read aloud the section titled *Economic Consequences of the Cotton Boom*. After each paragraph, have students identify its key points. Record and display this information in a bullet-point outline and have students copy the notes onto paper.

Advanced Read aloud the section titled *Economic Consequences of the Cotton Boom*, pausing periodically so students can add notes to a bullet-point outline. After you are done reading, encourage students to read over their notes and then revise, organize, and create subheadings as needed.

Advanced High Place students in pairs. Invite students to take turns reading paragraphs of the text, while their partners listen for key points and record them on a joint outline. Then have partners read over their outline and work together to revise and organize it as needed.

▶ Differentiate Instruction

Use the Differentiated Instruction notes throughout the lesson plan to support the varied skill sets, levels of readiness, and interests in the mixed-ability classroom.

Challenge These notes include suggestions for expanding the activity for advanced students.

On-Level These notes include suggestions for modifying the activity to address different interests or learning styles.

Extra Support These notes include ideas for providing more scaffolding or reading spuport.

Special Needs These notes provide ideas for adapting instruction to support the needs of various special needs students.

■ NOTES

Objectives

Objective 1: Analyze why industrialization took root in the northern part of the United States.

Objective 2: Describe the impact of industrialization on northern life.

Objective 3: Analyze the reasons that agriculture and slavery became entrenched in the South.

LESSON 5 ORGANIZER		PACING: APPROX. 1 PERIOD, .5 BLOCKS			
				RESOURCES	
		OBJECTIVES	PACING	Online	Print
Connect					
	DIGITAL START UP ACTIVITY **A Nation of Farming and Industry**		5 min.	●	
Investigate					
	DIGITAL TEXT 1 **Industrialization Takes Hold in the North**	Objective 1	10 min.	●	●
	DIGITAL TEXT 2 **Industrialization Changes Northern Society**	Objective 2	10 min.	●	●
	INTERACTIVE CHART **Immigration to the United States, 1820–1850**		10 min.	●	
	DIGITAL TEXT 3 **Agriculture Drives Southern Society**		10 min.	●	●
	3-D MODEL **The Cotton Gin**	Objective 3	10 min.	●	
	INTERACTIVE GALLERY **The Closed World of the Plantation**		10 min.	●	
Synthesize					
	DIGITAL ACTIVITY **Sectional and National Politics**		5 min.	●	
Demonstrate					
	DIGITAL QUIZ **Lesson Quiz and Class Discussion Board**		10 min.	●	

Differences Between North and South Grow

CONNECT

DIGITAL START UP ACTIVITY
A Nation of Farming and Industry

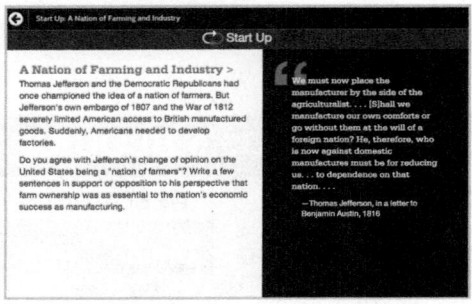

Project the Start Up Activity Ask students to read the quote and write down a few sentence for or against Jefferson's view. Have students share their responses with a partner, either in class or through a blog space.

Discuss Do you agree with Jefferson's change of opinion on the United States being a "nation of farmers"? *(Jefferson noted that manufacturing is as essential to the nation as agriculture. The United States needs to produce its own goods in order to maintain economic growth and become more self-sufficient.)*

Tell students that in this lesson they will be learning how industrialization led to economic and social change in the North and how the southern economy grew increasingly dependent on agriculture and slavery.

Aa Vocabulary Development Use the Interactive Reading Notepad to preview the Key Terms and Academic Vocabulary in this lesson with students.

↳ FLIP IT!
Assign the Flipped Video for this lesson.

▮ STUDENT EDITION PRINT
PAGES: 161–166

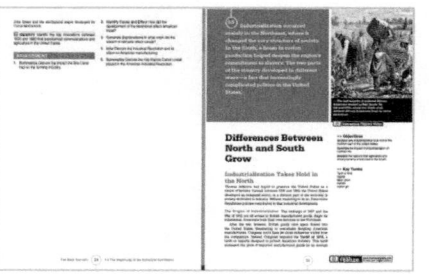

INVISTIGATE

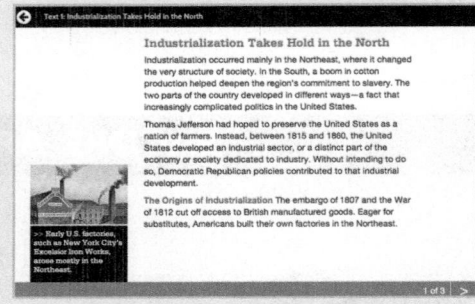

DIGITAL TEXT 1
Industrialization Takes Hold in the North

Objective 1: Analyze why industrialization took root in the northern part of the United States.

Quick Instruction
Review what students have learned about the development of mechanized labor and manufacturing in the early 1800s. Prompt students to see a connection between the trade embargoes and foreign policy decisions associated with the War of 1812 that encouraged an increase in domestic manufacturing. Explain why the United States developed an industrial economy in the early 1800s. *(The United States stopped trading for British manufactured goods during the War of 1812. As a result, American factories had to produce their own goods. When the war ended, Congress imposed a tariff to keep American industries competitive.)*

Summarize Why did factories develop in the Northeast rather than in the South? *(The Northeast had capital to invest in manufacturing, abundant cheap labor, and swift-moving rivers to power factories. The South had a strong agricultural economy, which led people to invest in land and slave labor rather than factories.)*

D Differentiate: Extra Support Explain that a tariff is a tax. To help students understand why the United States passed a tariff on British imports, have them brainstorm the expenses associated with starting up a factory. Discuss why American manufactured goods were more expensive than British imports when industrialization first took hold in the North.

Further Instruction
Compare and Contrast how a northern manufacturer and a southern farmer would have viewed the Tariff of 1816. Explain your reasoning. *(Northern manufacturers benefited from the tariff. It made British goods more expensive, which made American goods more competitive in comparison. Southern farmers were hurt by the tariff. The tariff didn't help them earn more money to pay the higher prices for manufactured goods.)*

DIGITAL TEXT 2
Industrialization Changes Northern Society

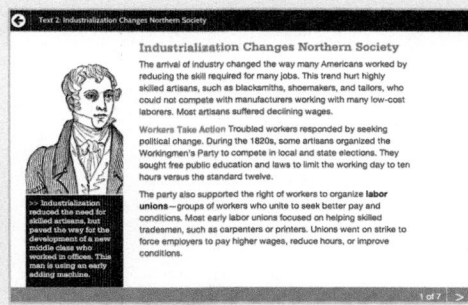

INTERACTIVE CHART
Immigration to the United States, 1820–1850

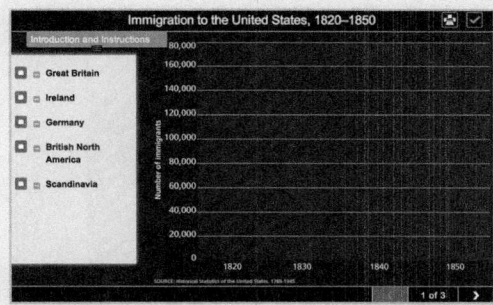

DIGITAL TEXT 3
Agriculture Drives Southern Society

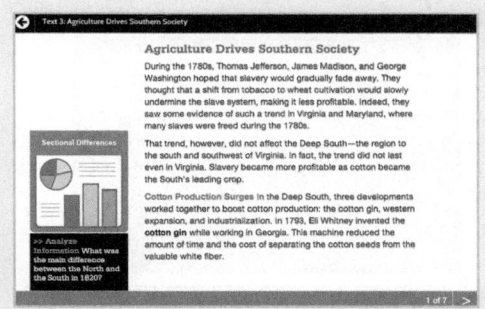

Objective 2: Describe the impact of industrialization on northern life.

Quick Instruction

Interactive Chart: Immigration to the United States, 1820–1850 Project the Interactive Chart and navigate through the layers with students. Prompt students to make generalizations about immigration trends throughout the 1800s. Identify the central issues that led immigrants from Germany and Ireland to the United States. What further issues did they face on their arrival? *(Immigrants from Ireland came to escape the potato famine. German immigrants were fleeing a failed political revolution. Many immigrants were poor and had difficulties finding work when they arrived. Riots occurred over religious differences and wages as the increase in immigrants created competition for jobs and housing. Nativist politicians campaigned to curb immigration and deny immigrants political rights.)*

Identify Cause and Effect Identify three effects of industrialization on northern life. *(Artisan wages declined; labor unions formed; the middle class expanded; immigrants arrived in search of work.)*

📷 ACTIVE CLASSROOM

Conduct a See-Think-Wonder activity with each layer of the Interactive Chart. Project each layer and ask: What do you see? What does that make you think? What are you wondering about now that you've seen this? Prompt students to share their insights with the class.

ELL Use the ELL activity described in the ELL chart.

Further Instruction

Support Ideas with Evidence What evidence supports the claim that industrialization changed settlement patterns in northern cities. *(Industrialization helped increase the size of the middle class, which could afford to move away from more dense urban areas and the noise of factories. Neighborhoods became segregated by economic class, as working class and middle class families lived in separate places.)*

Objective 3: Analyze the reasons that agriculture and slavery became entrenched in the South.

Quick Instruction

The new inventions of the Industrial Revolution changed life in both the North and the South. Summarize the reasons why cotton production surged in the South. *(The invention of the cotton gin made cotton cultivation much more profitable. Western expansion led planters to build new cotton plantations. Industrialization in the North created demand for cotton and cotton textiles.)*

Differences Between North and South Grow

3-D MODEL
The Cotton Gin

INTERACTIVE GALLERY
The Closed World of the Plantation

ELL Use the ELL activity described in the ELL chart.

Quick Instruction

3-D Model: The Cotton Gin Project the 3-D Model on the whiteboard and click on the circles. Ask students to explain the new process in their own words and prompt them to consider the economic impact the Cotton Gin would have: How did inventions like the cotton gin and the sewing machine affect the supply of textiles in the United States? *(These inventions made it possible to produce clothing quickly and cheaply, therefore increasing supply.)*

Quick Instruction

Interactive Gallery: The Closed World of the Plantation Project the Interactive Gallery and navigate through the images with students, prompting them to contrast the plantation with northern cities, using the images for support. Why were houses like this one part of southern culture? *(The architecture showed the plantation owner's privilege. Houses conveyed nobility and grandeur, emphasizing the order entrenched in southern society and the wealth that came from agriculture.)*

Further Instruction

Draw Conclusions How did the economy of the North encourage the increase of slavery in the South? *(Northern textile mills relied on cotton from the South to manufacture cotton goods, which they sold and exported.)*

Support Ideas with Examples What evidence supports the idea that cotton production limited regional development in the South? *(Because the South depended on one crop, planters were devastated when prices dropped. Plantations also kept the population dispersed so that the South did not develop the urban centers and commercial towns needed for industrial growth and a more diversified economy. The restricted economy did not attract workers or investors, which limited growth. Two fifths of the population was enslaved, and many African Americans and whites remained poor and uneducated.)*

SYNTHESIZE

DIGITAL ACTIVITY
Sectional and National Politics

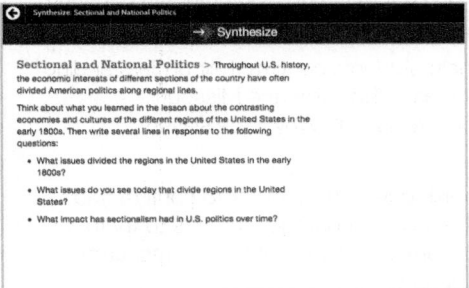

Have students consider the regional or sectional differences in the country and answer the questions. Have students exchange answers with a partner to review their responses.

Discuss Ask students to summarize the factors that gave rise to sectionalism in the 1800s. Discuss the major differences that emerged between North and South during this time. Then ask students how they think sectionalism will continue to affect the country throughout the century.

DEMONSTRATE

DIGITAL QUIZ
Lesson Quiz and Class Discussion Board

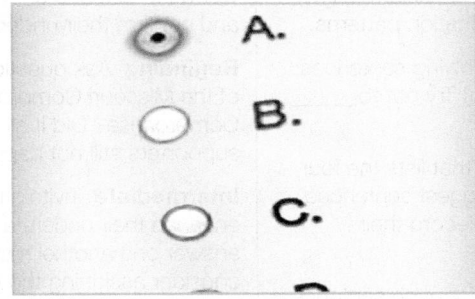

Assign the online Lesson Quiz for this lesson if you haven't already done so. Students will be offered automatic remediation or enrichment based on their score.

Pose these questions to the class on the Discussion Board:

In *Differences Between North and South Grow*, you read about the reasons why industrialization developed in the North, why agriculture continued to dominate the South's economy, and how these differences further encouraged a social and economic division between the two regions.

Compare and Contrast the northern and southern economies and societies during the Industrial Revolution, using examples for support.

Identify Cause and Effect What factors caused major economic differences between North and South to emerge? What will be the effects of these differences?

Topic Inquiry
Have students continue their investigations for the Topic Inquiry.

Nationalism Influences Policies

Supporting English Language Learners

Use with the reading, **The Influence of Nationalism on Domestic Affairs**.

Speaking
Review the four sentence types (declarative, interrogative, exclamatory, imperative) with students, including their usage and intonation patterns.

Beginning Invite students to complete and say the following sentences: _____ is a bust? A bust is when _____. Prices are _____! Try not to _____. Then ask students to identify the sentence types.

Intermediate Display a two-column chart titled *Boom* that lists the four sentence types in the first column. Invite students to suggest sentences about booms that correspond to each sentence type. Record their examples in the chart.

Advanced Invite pairs of students to create examples for each sentence type, first about booms and then about busts. For declarative and interrogative sentences, students can state or ask for information. For exclamatory and imperative sentences, they can make up quotations from people living through booms and busts.

Advanced High Invite pairs of students to create a dialogue about a boom that turns into a bust (or vice versa). Encourage each of them to use all four sentence types in the skit. Provide time for pairs to recite their dialogues for one another.

Use with the reading, **Slavery and the Missouri Compromise**.

Reading
Explain that engaging with classmates and teachers to discuss a text, as well as to ask and answer questions about it, can help students enhance and confirm their understanding of a text.

Beginning Ask questions that help students confirm their understanding of the Missouri Compromise, such as: Who wrote the Missouri Compromise? Did it allow slavery in Missouri? Why were slavery supporters still not happy?

Intermediate Invite students to ask questions in order to confirm and enhance their understanding of the text. Encourage students to try to answer one another's questions. If any questions entail extra research, consider assigning the task to students.

Advanced Place students in pairs and invite them to take turns asking each other factual questions about the text (at least three questions each). Then have them discuss these questions: Was it harder to ask or to answer questions? How did this process help you better understand what you read?

Advanced High Invite students to write down three questions based on the text but requiring deeper analysis (e.g., drawing conclusions, forming opinions, comparing and contrasting). Have partners discuss each other's questions. Ask: How did discussing these questions help to deepen your understanding of the text?

▣ Differentiate Instruction

Use the Differentiated Instruction notes throughout the lesson plan to support the varied skill sets, levels of readiness, and interests in the mixed-ability classroom.

Challenge These notes include suggestions for expanding the activity for advanced students.

On-Level These notes include suggestions for modifying the activity to address different interests or learning styles.

Extra Support These notes include ideas for providing more scaffolding or reading spuport.

Special Needs These notes provide ideas for adapting instruction to support the needs of various special needs students.

■ NOTES

PEARSON
realize™
www.PearsonRealize.com

Go online to access additional resources including:
Primary Sources • Biographies • Supreme Court cases •
21st Century Skill Tutorials • Maps • Graphic Organizers.

Objectives

Objective 1: Analyze the causes and effects of nationalism on domestic policy during the years following the War of 1812.

Objective 2: Describe the impact of nationalism on the nation's foreign policy.

Objective 3: Summarize the struggle over the issue of slavery as the nation grew.

LESSON 6 ORGANIZER		PACING: APPROX. 1 PERIOD, .5 BLOCKS			
				RESOURCES	
		OBJECTIVES	**PACING**	**Online**	**Print**
Connect					
	DIGITAL START UP ACTIVITY **Nationalism**		5 min.	●	
Investigate					
	DIGITAL TEXT 1 **The Influence of Nationalism on Domestic Affairs**	Objective 1	10 min.	●	●
	INTERACTIVE GALLERY **American Art of the Mid-1800s**		10 min.	●	
	DIGITAL TEXT 2 **Nationalism Leads to American Expansion**	Objective 2	10 min.	●	●
	DIGITAL TEXT 3 **Slavery and the Missouri Compromise**	Objective 3	10 min.	●	●
Synthesize					
	DIGITAL ACTIVITY **Nationalism and Sectionalism**		5 min.	●	
Demonstrate					
	DIGITAL QUIZ **Lesson Quiz and Class Discussion Board**		10 min.	●	

Nationalism Influences Policies

▪ CONNECT

DIGITAL START UP ACTIVITY
Nationalism

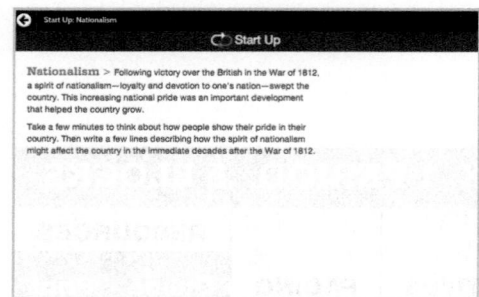

Project the Start Up Activity Ask students to read the prompt and write down a few sentences in response. Have students share their answers with a partner, either in class or through a blog space.

Discuss How might nationalism affect the country in the decades after the War of 1812? *(Congress might pass tariffs to protect American industries. Americans might continue westward expansion in an effort to grow the country.)*

Tell students that in this lesson they will be learning about how stronger feelings of nationalism influenced both domestic issues and foreign policy decisions in the decades after the War of 1812, as well as the intensifying political struggle over slavery.

Aa Vocabulary Development Use the Interactive Reading Notepad to preview the Key Terms and Academic Vocabulary in this lesson with students.

↿⇂ FLIP IT!
Assign the Flipped Video for this lesson.

▪ STUDENT EDITION PRINT PAGES: 167–171

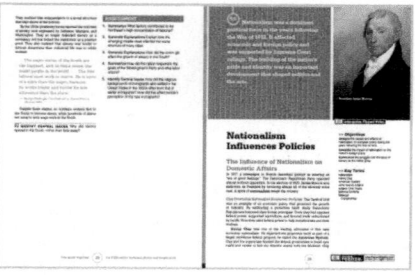

▪ INVESTIGATE

DIGITAL TEXT 1
The Influence of Nationalism on Domestic Affairs

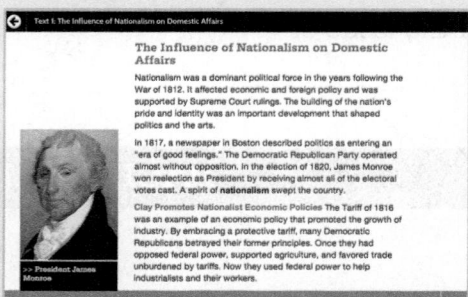

INTERACTIVE GALLERY
American Art of the Mid-1800s

Objective 1: Analyze the causes and effects of nationalism on domestic policy during the years following the War of 1812.

Quick Instruction
Interactive Gallery: American Art of the Mid-1800s Project the Interactive Gallery and navigate through the images with students. Discuss how Americans developed new styles of painting, music, and literature. Prompt students to describe the relationship between each example of artwork and increasingly strong feelings of nationalism in the nation.

Support Ideas with Examples What examples from the text show the development of economic nationalism in the United States? *(The federal government increasingly regulated commerce, banking, and contracts. More consistent economic policies were established throughout the nation, creating a larger integrated domestic market.)*

📷 ACTIVE CLASSROOM
Conduct a Sticky Notes activity. Ask students to spend three minutes jotting down their response to this question on sticky notes: How did American art reflect a stronger sense of nationalism in the 1800s? Ask students to post their Sticky Notes on the board or on chart paper. Have students look at all the various responses, then discuss similarities and differences in the responses as a group.

ELL Use the ELL activity described in the ELL chart.

Further Instruction
Go through the Interactive Reading Notepad questions and discuss the answers with the class. Assign Culture Basics: The Arts and Landmark Cases: *McCulloch v. Maryland* and *Gibbons v. Ogden*.

Support Ideas with Examples Give three examples of how Chief Justice Marshall expanded federal power. *(In Marbury v. Madison, Marshall claimed the Court had the power to review acts of Congress and the President to determine their constitutionality. In Dartmouth College v. Woodward and Fletcher v. Peck, he limited the power of state governments to interfere with business contracts. In McCulloch v. Maryland, he upheld federal law over state law, ruling that Congress had the power to charter a national bank that states could not interfere with.)*

Identify Cause and Effect Identify a cause and effect of the boom and bust cycles of the 1800s. *(Cause—the emergence of national markets and interconnected businesses meant that downturns in one area affected all aspects of the economy. Effect—during a panic, workers lost their jobs and farmers and planters went bankrupt.)*

PEARSON
realize™
www.PearsonRealize.com
Access your Digital Lesson

DIGITAL TEXT 2

Nationalism Leads to American Expansion

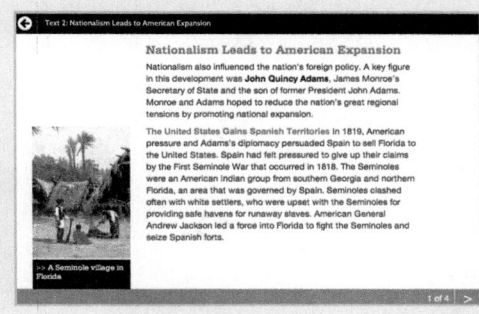

Text 2: Nationalism Leads to American Expansion

Nationalism Leads to American Expansion

Nationalism also influenced the nation's foreign policy. A key figure in this development was **John Quincy Adams**, James Monroe's Secretary of State and the son of former President John Adams. Monroe and Adams hoped to reduce the nation's great regional tensions by promoting national expansion.

The United States Gains Spanish Territories In 1819, American pressure and Adams's diplomacy persuaded Spain to sell Florida to the United States. Spain had felt pressured to give up their claims by the First Seminole War that occurred in 1818. The Seminoles were an American Indian group from southern Georgia and northern Florida, an area that was governed by Spain. Seminoles clashed often with white settlers, who were upset with the Seminoles for providing safe havens for runaway slaves. American General Andrew Jackson led a force into Florida to fight the Seminoles and seize Spanish forts.

>> A Seminole village in Florida

1 of 4 >

Objective 2: Describe the impact of nationalism on the nation's foreign policy.

Quick Instruction

Project the image of Andrew Jackson's 1818 Florida campaign. Explain that Jackson led troops to fight the Seminoles, an American Indian group, and seize Spanish forts. Discuss the reasons why the United States wanted to claim Florida. The growing population was looking for more land to settle, and white settlers were upset with the Seminoles for protecting runaway slaves. The United States also wanted to force Spain and other European countries out of North America.

Cite Evidence from the text explaining why the United States looked to expand. (*"Monroe and Adams hoped to reduce the nation's great regional tensions by promoting national expansion."*)

Generate Explanations Why was the Monroe Doctrine a significant statement even though the United States could do little to enforce it at the time? *The Monroe Doctrine was a reflection of American nationalism. The United States didn't have the military to support the Monroe Doctrine at the time, but the federal government was projecting a clear message that represented the country as a whole.)*

D Differentiate: Extra Support Define a doctrine as a statement of government policy. Have students summarize what the Monroe Doctrine stated and what this did and did not allow the United States to do. Ask why the United States made such a declaration. Guide students to see that the Monroe Doctrine was an important symbol that will take on increasing significance in the coming decades.

Further Instruction

Interpret Review the quote from James Monroe's address to Congress. How was nationalism expressed in this passage? *(Monroe declares that the Americas are not to be colonized by European powers. This shows that the United States is a strong and independent nation with a growing desire for influence in the region. The country is looking to protect its rights and interests and sees itself as powerful enough to assert those rights and interests over others.)*

Summarize How did the Adams-Onís Treaty contribute to U.S. expansion? *(The treaty ended Spanish control over the territories of Florida and Oregon, opening the areas to U.S. expansion and trade.)*

DIGITAL TEXT 3

Slavery and the Missouri Compromise

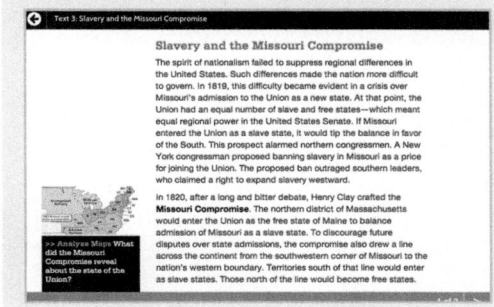

Text 3: Slavery and the Missouri Compromise

Slavery and the Missouri Compromise

The spirit of nationalism failed to suppress regional differences in the United States. Such differences made the nation more difficult to govern. In 1819, this difficulty became evident in a crisis over Missouri's admission to the Union as a new state. At that point, the Union had an equal number of slave and free states—which meant equal regional power in the United States Senate. If Missouri entered the Union as a slave state, it would tip the balance in favor of the South. This prospect alarmed northern congressmen. A New York congressman proposed banning slavery in Missouri as a price for joining the Union. The proposed ban outraged southern leaders, who claimed a right to expand slavery westward.

In 1820, after a long and bitter debate, Henry Clay crafted the **Missouri Compromise**. The northern district of Massachusetts would enter the Union as the free state of Maine to balance admission of Missouri as a slave state. To discourage future disputes over state admissions, the compromise also drew a line across the continent from the southwestern corner of Missouri to the nation's western boundary. Territories south of that line would enter as slave states. Those north of the line would become free states.

>> Analyze Maps What did the Missouri Compromise reveal about the state of the Union?

Objective 3: Summarize the struggle over the issue of slavery as the nation grew.

Quick Instruction

Project the digital map of the Missouri Compromise. Prompt students to use the map to explain why the admission of Missouri to the Union as a new state sparked controversy. Summarize the terms of the Missouri Compromise. (*Maine entered the Union as a free state and Missouri as a slave state to maintain the balance of power in the Union. A line was then drawn west across the continent from southwestern Missouri. Territories south of that line entered the nation as slave states and those north of the line were free.)*

Identify Patterns How did westward expansion increase regional tensions in the United States? *(The Union had an equal number of slave and free states. This balance of power was disrupted as the country expanded and added new states. Southerners wanted to admit Missouri as a slave state. Northerners wanted to ban slavery there, which outraged southerners.)*

ELL Use the ELL activity described in the ELL chart.

Further Instruction

Identify Cause and Effect How did Denmark Vesey's planned revolt affect sectional divisions between North and South? *(The planned revolt deepened the divide between North and South. Southerners felt threatened by northern attacks on slavery. They blamed the debates over Missouri for inspiring Vesey to plan a revolt and argued that debates over slavery should end.)*

Nationalism Influences Policies

SYNTHESIZE

DEMONSTRATE

DIGITAL ACTIVITY
Nationalism and Sectionalism

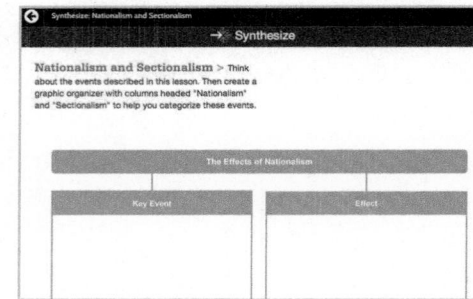

DIGITAL QUIZ
Lesson Quiz and Class Discussion Board

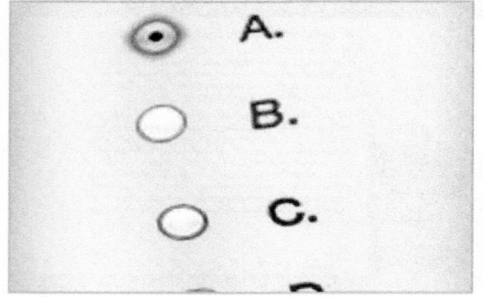

Evaluate Arguments Henry Clay believed the Missouri Compromise would solve the issue of how to admit the new state of Missouri. Was this an effective solution? *(Although it tried to maintain the balance of power between slave and free states, it did not end the divisions between North and South. The country remained divided over whether to allow slavery at all, and disagreements between northerners and southerners continued. The Compromise also did not end the question of whether new states should allow slavery or not. New problems would continue to emerge.)*

Have students complete the graphic organizer. Have students exchange organizers with a partner to be sure they have covered key events.

Discuss Ask students why the "era of good feelings" emerged after the War of 1812 and whether they think this description still characterized the country by the mid-1800s. Discuss how the rise of sectionalism affected feelings of nationalism in the country.

Assign the online Lesson Quiz for this lesson if you haven't already done so. Students will be offered automatic remediation or enrichment based on their score.

Pose these questions to the class on the Discussion Board:

In *Nationalism Influences Policies*, you read about the effects of nationalism on the nation's domestic and foreign policies and the way in which western expansion prompted an increasingly bitter debate over slavery across the nation.

Support Ideas with Examples How did federal power increase following the War of 1812? Provide examples for support.

Identify Cause and Effect What factors contributed to the rise of sectionalism in the country?

Topic Inquiry
Have students continue their investigations for the Topic Inquiry.

Jacksonian Democracy

Supporting English Language Learners

Use with the reading, **American Indian Removal**.

Learning
Review what a timeline is, and explain that students will be using a timeline to better understand the events described in the text.

Beginning Display a timeline that includes brief captions of events described in the text but that is missing dates. Invite students to read aloud the captions and search the text for their corresponding dates. Record their responses on the timeline.

Intermediate Display a timeline that includes either a date or a caption for each event described in the text. Invite students to volunteer information to complete the timeline, referring to the text as needed. Then read aloud the timeline together in chronological order.

Advanced Provide pairs of students with a timeline that only includes dates from the text. Have them collaborate to write a caption for each date. Then invite them to read the timeline in chronological order. Ask: How does creating a timeline help you identify key information in a text?

Advanced High Invite pairs of students to create a timeline for the text. Remind them to account for events that happen in specific years as well as over a span of years. Have pairs share and compare their completed timelines.

Use with the reading, **Economic Change Leads to the Bank War**.

Listening
Discuss with students when it might be necessary to ask a speaker for clarification, as well as how to do it in an appropriate way.

Beginning Display and discuss these clarifying questions: What does _____ mean? Could you repeat that? Could you say that a different way? Using simpler language, retell the section titled *Jackson Fights the National Bank*. Pause periodically so students can practice seeking clarification using the above questions.

Intermediate Read aloud the section titled *Jackson Fights the National Bank*. Pause periodically so students can ask you what a word means, to repeat or restate something, or to explain a concept more deeply.

Advanced Retell the section titled *Jackson Fights the National Bank*, adding additional information not found in the text. Pause periodically so students can ask clarifying questions about what you have said.

Advanced High Retell the section titled *Jackson Fights the National Bank*, adding additional information not found in the text. While you are speaking, encourage students to jot down any questions that arise. Then have partners share their questions and try to answer them together.

▣ Differentiate Instruction

Use the Differentiated Instruction notes throughout the lesson plan to support the varied skill sets, levels of readiness, and interests in the mixed-ability classroom.

Challenge These notes include suggestions for expanding the activity for advanced students.

On-Level These notes include suggestions for modifying the activity to address different interests or learning styles.

Extra Support These notes include ideas for providing more scaffolding or reading spuport.

Special Needs These notes provide ideas for adapting instruction to support the needs of various special needs students.

■ NOTES

Jacksonian Democracy

Objectives

Objective 1: Analyze the movement toward greater democracy under Andrew Jackson.

Objective 2: Summarize the causes and effects of the removal of American Indians in the early 1800s.

Objective 3: Evaluate the significance of the debate over tariffs and the idea of nullification.

Objective 4: Summarize the key events of the conflict over the second Bank of the United States in the 1830s.

Objective 5: Analyze the political environment in the United States after Andrew Jackson.

LESSON 7 ORGANIZER		PACING: APPROX. 1 PERIOD, .5 BLOCKS			
				RESOURCES	
		OBJECTIVES	PACING	Online	Print
Connect					
DIGITAL START UP ACTIVITY **Expanding Democracy**			5 min.	●	
Investigate					
DIGITAL TEXT 1 **Andrew Jackson Enters National Politics**		Objective 1	10 min.	●	●
DIGITAL TEXT 2 **American Indian Removal**		Objective 2	10 min.	●	●
INTERACTIVE TIMELINE **The Trail of Tears**			10 min.	●	
DIGITAL TEXT 3 **The Debate Over Nullification**		Objective 3	10 min.	●	●
DIGITAL TEXT 4 **Economic Change Leads to the Bank War**		Objective 4	10 min.	●	●
INTERACTIVE CHART **Evaluate Andrew Jackson's Actions**			10 min.	●	
DIGITAL TEXT 5 **National Politics After Jackson**		Objective 5	10 min.	●	●
Synthesize					
DIGITAL ACTIVITY **Evaluating the Jackson Legacy**			5 min.	●	
Demonstrate					
DIGITAL QUIZ **Lesson Quiz and Class Discussion Board**			10 min.	●	

PEARSON realize™
www.PearsonRealize.com

Go online to access additional resources including:
Primary Sources • Biographies • Supreme Court cases •
21st Century Skill Tutorials • Maps • Graphic Organizers.

■ CONNECT

DIGITAL START UP ACTIVITY
Expanding Democracy

Project the Start Up Activity Ask students to read the prompt and write down a few sentences in response. Have students share their answers with a partner.

Discuss How might the expansion of democracy under Jackson have affected national politics? *(Individual voters had a stronger voice in national politics, which may have made politicians more representative of and concerned with ordinary citizens.)*

Tell students that in this lesson they will be learning about significant events during Andrew Jackson's presidency, including American Indian removal policies, and debates over tariffs and the Bank of the United States.

Aa Vocabulary Development Use the Interactive Reading Notepad to preview the Key Terms and Academic Vocabulary in this lesson with students.

⇵ FLIP IT!

Assign the Flipped Video for this lesson.

■ STUDENT EDITION PRINT
PAGES: 172–180

■ INVESTIGATE

DIGITAL TEXT 1
Andrew Jackson Enters National Politics

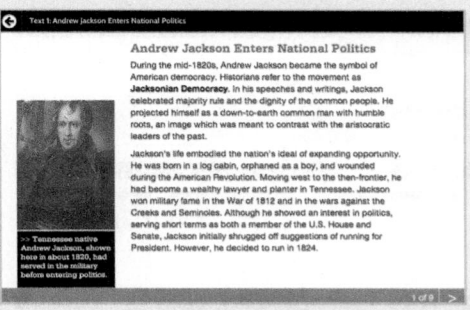

Objective 1: Analyze the movement toward greater democracy under Andrew Jackson.

Quick Instruction
Project the digital chart showing the results of the 1824 presidential election. Prompt students to see the relationship between the results and the political climate of the time. Why did the House of Representatives decide the winner in the 1824 presidential election, and what effects did this decision have? *(Cause—four Democratic Republicans ran and none won a majority of the electoral votes. Effects—John Quincy Adams won but his victory generated strong opposition. Jackson accused him of winning in a corrupt bargain with Henry Clay, who was appointed Secretary of State after he supported Adams for President. These criticisms weakened Adams's presidency.)*

Generate Explanations How did the fact that more states were allowing a popular vote to choose presidential electors affect Andrew Jackson and the election of 1828? *(Many states were rewriting their constitutions to allow more men to vote. Male voter turnout increased, and the majority of these voters favored Jackson. Jackson traveled the country building support among voters. As a result, he won clear victories in the popular vote and the electoral college.)*

Further Instruction
Go through the Interactive Reading Notepad questions and discuss the answers with the class. Assign Biographies: Andrew Jackson.

Summarize the movement known as Jacksonian Democracy. *(Andrew Jackson and his followers based their political philosophy around the interests of the common people and strove to limit the role of the federal government. This movement celebrated ordinary Americans and majority rule, rather than the aristocracy.)*

Support Ideas with Evidence What evidence supports the idea that the elections of 1824 and 1828 saw a shift in American political and social life? *(A new political party, the Democrats, emerged in 1824. With Jackson's victory in 1828, the Democrats turned politics toward a more democratic style. They promised to return to strong states and a weak federal government that would not interfere with slavery. The Democrats also developed a system of local and state committees and conventions, rewarding those who supported the party and casting out those who did not.)*

Jacksonian Democracy

DIGITAL TEXT 2
American Indian Removal

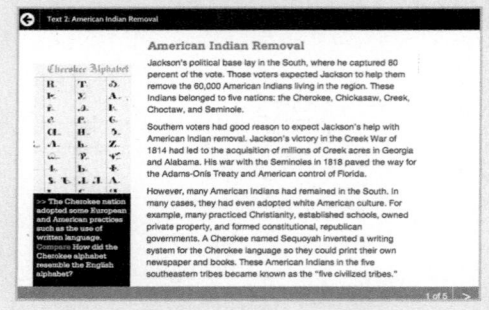

INTERACTIVE TIMELINE
The Trail of Tears

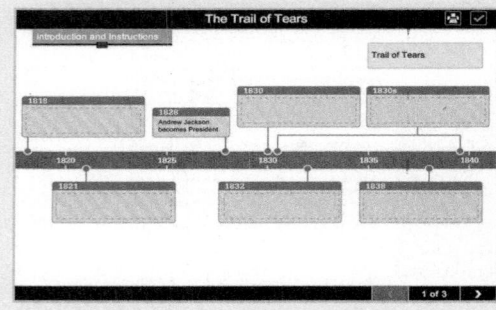

DIGITAL TEXT 3
The Debate Over Nullification

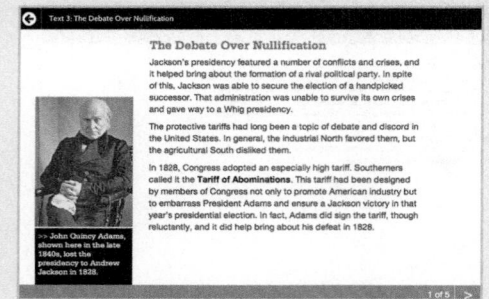

Objective 2: Summarize the causes and effects of the removal of American Indianss in the early 1800s.

Quick Instruction

Interactive Timeline: The Trail of Tears Project the Interactive Timeline and navigate through the images with students. Remind students that Jackson had won victories against American Indian groups in Georgia, Alabama, and Florida. Discuss the desire for land that led southern voters to demand Jackson remove American Indians from the area. How did the Trail of Tears affect American Indians and southern whites? *(16,000 Cherokees were forced to leave their land in the Southeast and walk to Oklahoma. At least 4,000 died. Those who survived had to rebuild their lives in an unfamiliar place. Southern whites expanded into Cherokee land to form new settlements and plantations.)*

🎙️ ACTIVE CLASSROOM

Conduct a Quick Write activity. Have students take one minute to write what they know abut the removal of American Indians from the southeastern United States. Ask volunteers to share what they've written with the class.

D Differentiate: Extra Support Ask students why they think the forced march of many American Indians from their homes in the Southeast was known as the Trail of Tears. Have them describe the forced march in their own words and explain why it occurred. Ask students what difficulties they think the Cherokee Indians faced when they arrived in Indian Territory.

ELL Use the ELL activity described in the ELL chart.

Further Instruction

Summarize Marshall's ruling in *Worcester v. Georgia*. How did Jackson respond to this decision, and why? *(Marshall ruled that Georgia's attempts to seize American Indian land was unconstitutional. The federal government had treaties with American Indians that states could not violate. Jackson ignored the decision, knowing that Marshall could not enforce it. He urged Congress to pass the Indian Removal Act and continued to take American Indian land.)*

Interpret How did Jackson view the government's actions toward American Indians, based on his message to Congress? *(Jackson's message suggests that he believed the government's actions were generous and fair. He argued that because American Indians did not conform to white society, they were better off being moved. He described the Indian Removal Act as an act of kindness, despite the fact that the Trail of Tears killed thousands.)*

Objective 3: Evaluate the significance of the debate over tariffs and the idea of nullification.

Quick Instruction

Project the digital image titled *The Nullification Crisis of 1833*. Remind students that the Kentucky and Virginia Resolutions had hinted that states could nullify federal laws, or declare them unconstitutional. Under what concept was the authority to do so already granted to the Supreme Court? *(judicial review).* Prompt students to place the nullification issue within the larger historical debate of the federal government's power relative to that of the states.

Compare and Contrast the views of secessionists and nationalists over nullification. *(Secessionists—supported nullification; favored states' rights; believed states should be able to separate from the Union if the federal government used force against them. Nationalists—opposed nullification; upheld the power of the federal government; wanted to keep the Union together.)*

Evaluate Arguments Why did many southerners refer to the 1828 tariff as the *Tariff of Abominations*? *(Southerners were outraged by the tariff. It was very high and hurt the South, where people had to pay more for manufactured goods without getting any of the profits.)*

Further Instruction

Go through the Interactive Reading Notepad questions and discuss the answers with the class. Be sure students can define nullification and understand how protective tariffs and ongoing debates over slavery created tensions within the Union.

DIGITAL TEXT 4

Economic Change Leads to the Bank War

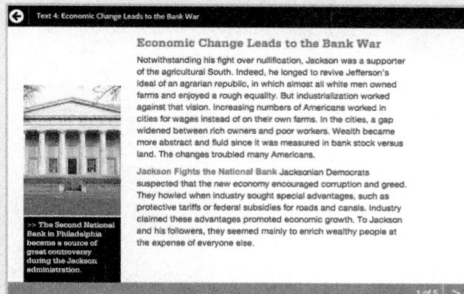

INTERACTIVE CHART

Evaluate Andrew Jackson's Actions

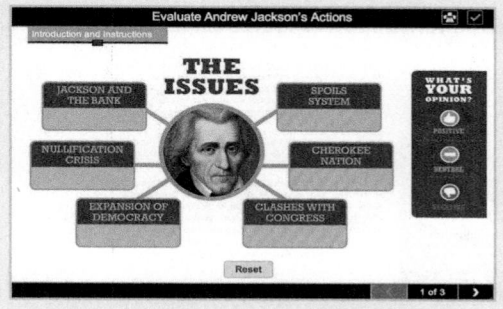

Generate Explanations Why did southern leaders such as John C. Calhoun connect the issue of whether to allow slavery with the larger issue of states' rights? *(Calhoun was from South Carolina and supported slavery. The Missouri controversy led him to believe that states needed stronger rights to protect against federal intervention. For Calhoun, slavery was a state issue that the national government could not decide.)*

Identify Cause and Effect What caused South Carolina to threaten secession? *(Congress passed a high tariff that Jackson modified but did not eliminate. South Carolina passed a law that nullified the protective tariff and said the state would not pay federal tariff duties. The legislature then threatened to secede if the federal government used force against it in response to nullification.)*

Objective 4: Summarize the key events of the conflict over the second Bank of the United States in the 1830s.

Quick Instruction

Interactive Chart: Evaluate Andrew Jackson's Actions Project the Interactive Chart and poll the class to determine an overall opinion on each issue. Ask volunteers to defend their opinions with specific evidence.

Summarize Describe the new economy that emerged in the 1800s. What was it based on? What benefits and drawbacks did it pose? *(The United States was becoming more industrial and less agrarian. An increasing number of Americans worked in cities rather than on farms. As the economy became more focused on money and bank stocks, divisions grew between owners and workers. The country generated more wealth, but many Americans feared that industry and protective tariffs served the wealthy and were leading to the creation of a new aristocracy.)*

📖 ACTIVE CLASSROOM

Conduct a Make Headlines activity. Ask students to make two headlines announcing Jackson's veto, one from the perspective of a Democratic newspaper and one from the perspective of a Whig newspaper. Have students exchange headlines with a partner to review.

ELL Use the ELL activity described in the ELL chart.

Further Instruction

Go through the Interactive Reading Notepad questions and discuss the answers with the class. Assign Economics Basics: Money, Banking, and International Trade. Be sure students understand the debates around the second Bank of the United States. Review the arguments for and against chartering the Bank.

Evaluate Arguments Why did Jackson oppose the second Bank of the United States? *(Jackson viewed the bank as unconstitutional and a threat to states' rights. He argued that the Bank served only rich investors and would hurt the American economy. Jackson feared that government support for the Bank helped some Americans get rich at the expense of the ordinary Americans whom he supported.)*

Identify Cause and Effect What caused the emergence of the Whigs? What were the effects of this formation? *(Cause—Jackson vetoed the charter for the second Bank. Bank supporters were shocked and argued that Jackson was infringing on the rights of Congress. Bank supporters led by Henry Clay and Daniel Webster formed a new political party in favor of a strong federal government to manage the economy. Effects—two parties again dominated the political system. The Whigs ran against the Democrats.)*

Jacksonian Democracy

DIGITAL TEXT 5
National Politics After Jackson

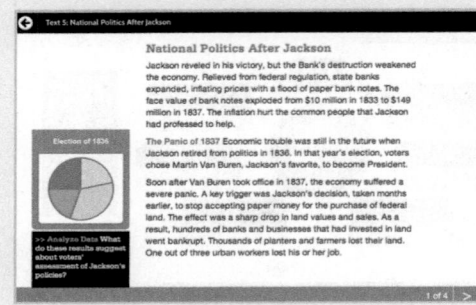

SYNTHESIZE

DIGITAL ACTIVITY
Evaluating the Jackson Legacy

DEMONSTRATE

DIGITAL QUIZ
Lesson Quiz and Class Discussion Board

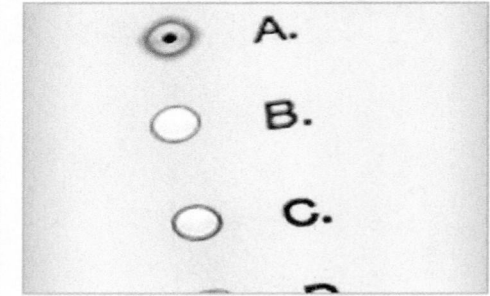

Objective 5: Analyze the political environment in the United States after Andrew Jackson.

Quick Instruction
Project the presidential election results of 1836 and of 1840. Ask students what changed in the leadership of the country during those four years. Ask them to make a prediction about what factors they think caused this political shift.

Identify Steps in a Process Explain how vetoing the second Bank hurt the American economy. *(Without federal regulation, state banks grew and flooded the market with paper money, causing inflation to increase.)*

Summarize the events surrounding the Panic of 1837. *(Jackson stopped accepting paper money to buy federal land. Land values and sales dropped, bankrupting banks and businesses that had invested in land. Planters and farmers lost their land, wages dropped, and urban workers lost their jobs.)*

Further Instruction
Go through the Interactive Reading Notepad questions and discuss the answers with the class. Be sure students understand the factors that gave rise to an economic depression in the 1830s and how this affected the nation.

Draw Conclusions How did the country's economic struggles impact the 1840 presidential election? *(The depression helped put the Whigs in office. They defeated the Democrats by portraying Van Buren as a corrupt, ineffective aristocrat and Harrison as in touch with common Americans. Given the country's economic problems, Americans were probably looking for new leadership and a change in policy.)*

Have students read the quote and write several lines evaluating whether Jackson's presidency was a success. Have students exchange answers with a partner to review.

Discuss Ask students whether they agree or disagree with Feller's assessment of Andrew Jackson. Discuss why students think the Age of Jackson has come to be viewed as such a significant period, given Jackson's policies.

Assign the online Lesson Quiz for this lesson if you haven't already done so. Students will be offered automatic remediation or enrichment based on their score.

Pose these questions to the class on the Discussion Board:

In *Jacksonian Democracy*. you read about the significant debates and events of Andrew Jackson's presidency and the way in which these debates continued to influence American politics and society.

Evaluate Arguments Do you think Jackson was right to veto the second Bank? Why or why not?

Determine Point of View How did Jackson view the power of the federal government? In what ways did his actions sometimes contract his ideals? Give at least one example for support.

Topic Inquiry
Have students continue their investigations for the Topic Inquiry.

The Early Republic

■ SYNTHESIZE

DIGITAL ACTIVITY
Reflect on the Essential Question and Topic

First ask students to reconsider the Essential Question for this topic: What makes a government successful? Have students think about the continuing political divisions in the United States and then answer the questions using examples for support.

Ask students, "In what ways can political disagreements among parties make government successful? In what ways can they cause difficulties?" Discuss their responses as a class or ask students to post their answers on the Class Discussion Board.

Next ask students to reflect on the topic as a whole. Have students write down three important questions they have thought about during the topic and their answers to those questions. Have students consider the following examples to help them get started:

1. How might the federal government have helped reduce the effects of growing sectionalism in the country?
2. Did the emergence of political parties strengthen or weaken our country's political process?
3. Should the Supreme Court have had such a strong influence on congressional legislation?

Topic Inquiry
Have students complete Step 3 of the Topic Inquiry.

■ DEMONSTRATE

DIGITAL TOPIC REVIEW AND ASSESSMENT
The Early Republic

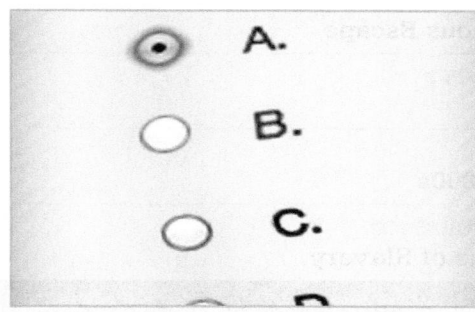

Students can prepare for the Topic Test by answering the questions in the Topic Review and Assessment online or the Assessment questions in the Print Student text. They can also prepare by reviewing their answers to the Interactive Reading Notepad questions or reviewing their notes in the Reading and Notetaking Study Guide.

DIGITAL TOPIC TEST
The Early Republic

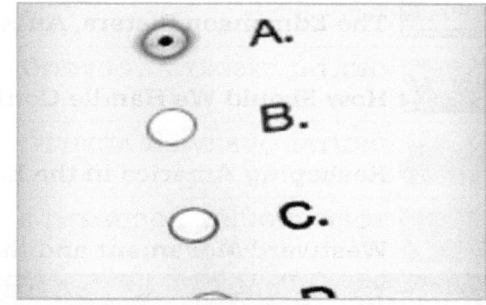

TOPIC TEST
Assign the Topic Test to assess students' understanding of topic content.

BENCHMARK TESTS
Assign these benchmark tests as you complete the relevant topics to monitor student progress toward mastering the course content and as preparation for the End-of-Course Test.

Benchmark Test 1: Topics 1–3
Benchmark Test 2: Topics 4–6
Benchmark Test 3: Topics 7–9
Benchmark Test 4: Topics 10–12
Benchmark Test 5: Topics 13–15
Benchmark Test 6: Topics 16–18
Benchmark Test 7: Topics 19–20

Topic 6

Reshaping America in the Early 1800s

TOPIC 6 ORGANIZER	PACING: APPROX. 9 PERIODS, 4.5 BLOCKS
	PACING
Connect	1 period
MY STORY VIDEO **The Edmonson Sisters, An Audacious Escape**	10 min.
DIGITAL ESSENTIAL QUESTION ACTIVITY **How Should We Handle Conflict?**	10 min.
DIGITAL OVERVIEW ACTIVITY **Reshaping America in the Early 1800s**	10 min.
TOPIC INQUIRY: DOCUMENT-BASED QUESTION **Westward Movement and the Issue of Slavery**	20 min.
Investigate	3–6 periods
TOPIC INQUIRY: DOCUMENT-BASED QUESTION **Westward Movement and the Issue of Slavery**	Ongoing
LESSON 1 Moving West	30–40 min.
LESSON 2 Texas and the Mexican-American War	30–40 min.
LESSON 3 America Achieves Manifest Destiny	30–40 min.
LESSON 4 A Religious Awakening Sparks Reform	30–40 min.
LESSON 5 The Abolition Movement	30–40 min.
LESSON 6 Women Work for Change	30–40 min.
Synthesize	1 period
DIGITAL ACTIVITY **Reflect on the Essential Question and Topic**	10 min.
TOPIC INQUIRY: DOCUMENT-BASED QUESTION **Westward Movement and the Issue of Slavery**	20 min.
Demonstrate	1–2 periods
DIGITAL TOPIC REVIEW AND ASSESSMENT **Reshaping America in the Early 1800s**	10 min.
TOPIC INQUIRY: DOCUMENT-BASED QUESTION **Westward Movement and the Issue of Slavery**	20 min.

TOPIC INQUIRY: DOCUMENT-BASED QUESTION

Westward Movement and the Issue of Slavery

In this Topic Inquiry, students work independently to examine documents that demonstrate how Americans—through social and political avenues—handled the conflict over slavery as the pressures of westward expansion increased. Students will reflect on this information and their knowledge of history to write an essay in which they answer the question: How did westward expansion affect the debate over slavery and abolition?

STEP 1: CONNECT
Develop Questions and Plan the Investigation

Launch the DBQ Writing Activity
Distribute and introduce the Student Instructions. Then, project the Debating Slavery video. Before you start the video, suggest to students that they use a note-taking device to record information as they view the video. After you have watched the video, discuss the questions as a class or have students work with partners.

Suggestion: If your class has limited access to the Internet, have students watch the video on their own outside of class.

Generate Questions
Before students begin their independent work, provide additional context and depth about the debate over slavery by discussing the John Brown and Frederick Douglass excerpts in class. Alternatively, students might wish to use the Think-Pair-Share strategy with a partner. Students may benefit from keeping their responses to help them later when writing their essays.

Resources
- Student Instructions
- Video

STEP 2: INVESTIGATE
Apply Disciplinary Concepts and Tools

Analyze the Documents
Students will work individually to read and analyze the six sources relating to the issues of slavery and abolition during westward expansion. Before students begin, review the 21st Century Skill Tutorials Evaluate Existing Arguments and Distinguish Between Fact and Opinion. Remind students that they should not lose sight of their main goal of answering the question, How did westward expansion affect the debate over slavery and abolition?

Suggestion: Consider briefly previewing the documents or viewing them as a class to clarify any vocabulary, syntax, or content issues.

Check Your Understanding
Students may benefit from working with a partner to read and respond to each document. Meet as a class to review students' responses.

Resources
- Document A: Excerpt from the Argument of John Quincy Adams, Before the Supreme Court of the United States: in the Case of the United States, Appellants, vs. Cinque, and Others, Africans, Captured in the schooner Amistad, by Lieut. Gedney, 1841
- Document B: Congressional Scales. A True Balance, political cartoon by Nathaniel Currier, 1850
- Document C: Excerpt from The Seventh of March Speech, Daniel Webster, 1850
- Document D: Excerpts from The Missouri Compromise, 1820 and Scott v. Sandford, U.S. Supreme Court, 1856
- Document E: Forcing Slavery Down The Throat of a FreeSoiler, political cartoon, by John L. Magee, 1856
- Document F: Excerpt from West India Emancipation, speech by Frederick Douglass, 1857
- 21st Century Skill Tutorials Evaluate Existing Arguments and Distinguish Between Fact and Opinion.

Westward Movement and the Issue of Slavery *(continued)*

STEP 3: SYNTHESIZE
Evaluate Sources and Use Evidence to Formulate Conclusions

Write Your Essay
Read aloud the instructions for Step 3 and project the Rubric. Review the expectations outlined in the rubric. Advise students to use the instructions and the rubric as a checklist when they are writing and revising their essays.

Resources
• Rubric for a DBQ Essay

STEP 4: DEMONSTRATE
Communicate Conclusions and Take Informed Action

Review and Publish the DBQ Writing Projects
Have students revise and submit their essays. Remind students to read over their essays for any errors before turning it in. Hold a class discussion about the question, How did westward expansion affect the debate over slavery and abolition?

Suggestion: To make sure students reread and revise their essays, you may want to provide time in class. You can also give them time to proofread their essays one last time before turning them in or work with partners to elicit peer review.

INTRODUCTION

Reshaping America in the Early 1800s

Even before victory in the Mexican-American War opened new territories to U.S. expansion, Americans began moving in large numbers westward across the Great Plains. Westward expansion, however, intensified the debate over slavery and eroded the spirit of nationalism that swept the nation in the early 1800s. Many Americans worked to end slavery, while other reformers forged new movements to address social concerns such as equal rights for women, prison reform, and the reduction of alcohol abuse.

■ CONNECT

MY STORY VIDEO

The Edmonson Sisters, An Audacious Escape

Watch a video about the struggles of Mary and Emily Edmonson to escape enslavement.

Check Understanding How did the Edmonson sisters try to escape from captivity? *(by hiding in a small vessel that sailed down the Potomac from Washington, D.C.)*

Identify Central Issues What role did the story of the Edmonson sisters play in the abolition movement? *(Harriet Beecher Stowe and other abolitionists took up the cause of the sisters. By describing their efforts to escape slavery, Stowe and others were able to advance the abolitionist cause.)*

DIGITAL ESSENTIAL QUESTION ACTIVITY

How Should We Handle Conflict?

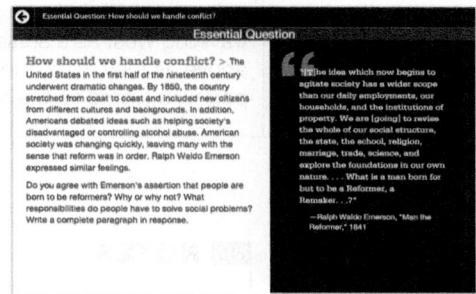

Ask students to think about the Essential Question for this topic: How should we handle conflict? Explain that by 1850, the United States stretched from coast to coast and included citizens from different cultures and backgrounds, which often led to a clash of ideas and lifestyles. Ask students to suggest how these differences might lead to conflict. *(Possible response: differences in culture, religion, and ways of life might create conflict because some Americans might feel threatened or might want their own culture to dominate.)*

Invite a volunteer to read the excerpt from Ralph Waldo Emerson. Have students respond to the questions on the interactivity. Invite students to share their paragraphs with the class.

Generate Explanations Select at least two of the areas of society that Emerson names that reformers are going to "revise" *(the state, the school, religion, marriage, trade, science)* and suggest possible reasons for the reforms.

Connect In your opinion, what local or national issue today do you think ordinary citizens or lawmakers need to address? Why?

DIGITAL OVERVIEW ACTIVITY

Reshaping America in the Early 1800s

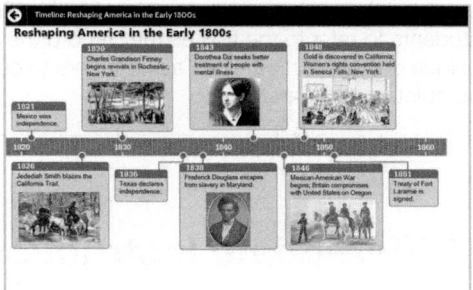

Display the timeline showing major events from 1820–1860. Have students identify and describe events that they have already studied. Preview the Topic by pointing out that students will explore key events and social movements in the United States that reshaped the country in the mid-1800s. Encourage students to use this timeline as a reference to guide their studies.

D Differentiate: Extra Support Encourage students to draw their own timelines for the Topic. Have them copy events from the Digital Timeline. Then, tell them to add other key events as they move through the topic.

Draw Conclusions Which events reflect the growing territorial expansion of the United States? *(Jedediah Smith blazes the California Trail, Texas declares independence, Britain compromises with United States on Oregon, Gold is discovered in California, Treaty of Fort Laramie is signed.)*

Topic Inquiry
Launch the Topic Inquiry with students after introducing the topic.

Moving West

Supporting English Language Learners

Use with the reading, **The Borderlands of Northern Mexico**.

Learning
Display a blank three-circle Venn diagram. Explain how the circles work together to compare and contrast three separate things.

Beginning Label the Venn diagram circles as follows: Pueblo, Apache, Comanche. Then say key words or phrases pertaining to one or more of these American Indian groups and have students identify in which part of the diagram each belongs.

Intermediate Label the Venn diagram circles as follows: Pueblo, Apache, Comanche. Then ask questions that prompt students to suggest information for the diagram's various sections (e.g., What is unique to the Apache? What do the Apache and Comanche have in common?).

Advanced Have pairs of students draw a three-circle Venn diagram and label the circles as follows: New Mexico, Texas, California. Invite partners to discuss these three settlements and record their shared and unique characteristics on the diagram.

Advanced High Have students draw a three-circle Venn diagram and label the circles as follows: New Mexico, Texas, California. Invite students to refer to the text as they record the settlements' shared and unique characteristics. Then ask partners to compare and discuss their completed diagrams.

Use with the reading, **Settling New Lands in the West**.

Listening
Display basic vocabulary that is essential to discussing the text's content (e.g., journey, wagon, travel, desert, mountains, plains, adventure, danger). Review the words' meanings with students.

Beginning Say simple true or false statements about the text that use the basic vocabulary above (e.g., Emigrants never had to travel through a desert). Ask students to identify the statements as true or false and correct them if necessary.

Intermediate Ask questions about the text that use the basic vocabulary above and require responses of varying length and depth (e.g., Why did men think the journey was an adventure?). Encourage students to answer using the same vocabulary and complete sentences.

Advanced Invite pairs of students to recount the journey that a typical emigrant might experience. Have them take turns adding sentences to the narration, building on what the other says and using all of the basic vocabulary words above.

Advanced High Invite pairs of students to debate the pros and cons of traveling west as a settler. Encourage them to use the basic vocabulary above as they make their points, as well as to listen closely to their partner's words so they can effectively refute them.

▷ Differentiate Instruction

Use the Differentiated Instruction notes throughout the lesson plan to support the varied skill sets, levels of readiness, and interests in the mixed-ability classroom.

Challenge These notes include suggestions for expanding the activity for advanced students.

On-Level These notes include suggestions for modifying the activity to address different interests or learning styles.

Extra Support These notes include ideas for providing more scaffolding or reading spuport.

Special Needs These notes provide ideas for adapting instruction to support the needs of various special needs students.

■ NOTES

PEARSON
realize™
www.PearsonRealize.com

Go online to access additional resources including:
Primary Sources • Biographies • Supreme Court cases •
21st Century Skill Tutorials • Maps • Graphic Organizers.

Objectives

Objective 1: Summarize the settlement and development of the Spanish borderlands.

Objective 2: Explain the concept of Manifest Destiny and how it influenced westward expansion.

Objective 3: Analyze the causes and challenges of westward migration.

LESSON 1 ORGANIZER		PACING: APPROX. 1 PERIOD, .5 BLOCKS			
				RESOURCES	
		OBJECTIVES	**PACING**	**Online**	**Print**
Connect					
DIGITAL START UP ACTIVITY **A Pioneer Family Heads West**			5 min.	●	
Investigate					
DIGITAL TEXT 1 **The Borderlands of Northern Mexico**		Objective 1	10 min.	●	●
INTERACTIVE CHART **The Spanish Borderlands**			10 min.	●	
DIGITAL TEXT 2 **America Looks to the West**		Objective 2	10 min.	●	●
3-D MODEL **The Covered Wagon**			10 min.	●	
DIGITAL TEXT 3 **Settling New Lands in the West**		Objective 3	10 min.	●	●
INTERACTIVE MAP **Trails to the West**			10 min.	●	
Synthesize					
DIGITAL ACTIVITY **A Pioneer's Journal**			5 min.	●	
Demonstrate					
DIGITAL QUIZ **Lesson Quiz and Class Discussion Board**			10 min.	●	

Moving West

▮ CONNECT

DIGITAL START UP ACTIVITY
A Pioneer Family Heads West

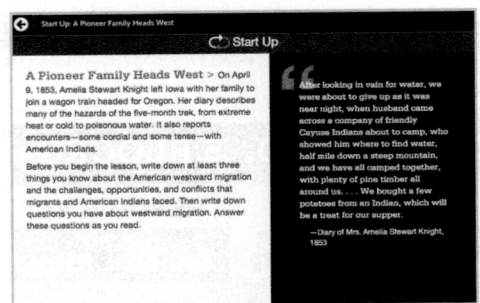

Project the Start Up Activity Ask students to read the diary entry as they enter and get settled. Have students discuss the accounts described in the entry. Then have them share their ideas with another student.

Discuss Ask students: If you were a poor farmer in 1850, would you have chosen to join a wagon train to the West? Why or why not? Invite volunteers to share their responses with the class.

Tell students that in this lesson they will be learning about the various factors that motivated thousands of Americans to endure the challenging journey to settle in the West.

Aa Vocabulary Development: Use the Interactive Reading Notepad to preview the Key Terms and Academic Vocabulary in this lesson with students.

⚙ FLIP IT!

Assign the Flipped Video for this lesson.

▮ STUDENT EDITION PRINT PAGES: 186–191

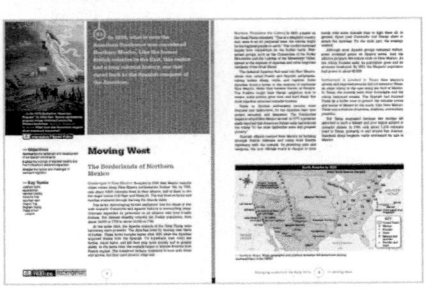

▮ INVESTIGATE

DIGITAL TEXT 1
The Borderlands of Northern Mexico

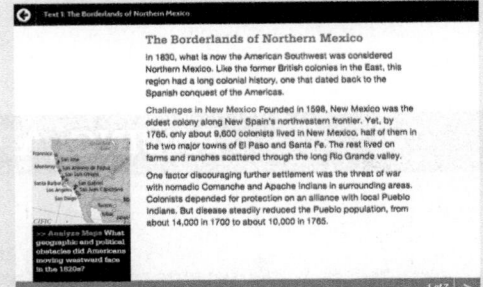

INTERACTIVE CHART
The Spanish Borderlands

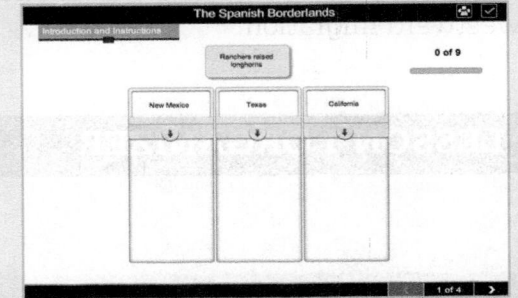

Objective 1: Summarize the settlement and development of the Spanish borderlands.

Quick Instruction

Interactive Chart: The Spanish Borderlands Project the Interactive Chart. Prompt students to place the tiles in the correct locations and answer the questions. Invite volunteers to briefly summarize the unique characteristics of the various colonies in the Spanish borderlands. Based on the information in the interactivity, what logistical issue did settlers in the colonies in the Spanish borderlands face? *(The colonies were located great distances from markets and from frontier forts that provided protection for the colonies.)*

Contrast Unlike the other borderland colonies, what factors allowed Father Junípero Serra and other Franciscans to establish successful missions in California? *(The local American Indians in California lacked guns and horses, which limited their ability to resist development of Spanish missions.)*

👥 ACTIVE CLASSROOM

Conduct a Connect Two activity. List the following terms on the board for students to copy on small pieces of paper: settlers, Gulf of Mexico, Russian settlement, California, Pueblos, livestock and crops, Texas, Comanche raids, New Mexico. Read the list of words with students. Ask students to "connect two" or choose two words they think might belong together, and state the reason, e.g. "I would connect ____ and ____ because. . . ." Ask volunteers to share their sentences and prompt other students to provide textual evidence that supports or refutes their connections.

ELL Use the ELL activity described in the ELL chart.

Further Instruction

Determine Relevance What long-term effects did the introduction of horses and firearms have on American Indians in the West? *(Horses provided a more effective means of transportation for the American Indians. Indian groups could travel farther and much faster for hunting and raiding. Firearms made the Indians much more powerful as they tried to defend and protect their traditional homelands from Spanish and American settlers.)*

Identify Cause and Effect How might Spain's reasons for founding the colony of Texas have hindered its development? *(The Spanish did not allocate the resources or attention to developing Texas because they looked at the colony mainly as a buffer zone to protect the valuable towns and mines of Mexico to the south. The Spanish did not view Texas as a valuable resource-rich acquisition.)*

DIGITAL TEXT 2
America Looks to the West

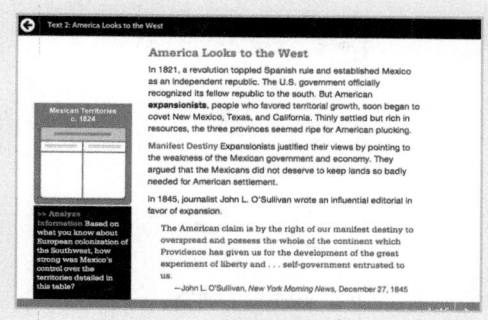

3-D MODEL
The Covered Wagon

DIGITAL TEXT 3
Settling New Lands in the West

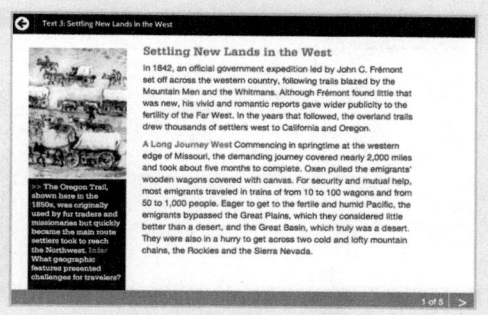

Objective 2: Explain the concept of Manifest Destiny and how it influenced westward expansion.

Quick Instruction

3-D Model: The Covered Wagon Project the 3-D Model and encourage students to examine the covered wagon by manipulating the cursor. Call on students to share their thoughts about what travel in a covered wagon would have been like. Explain that the typical trip west took many months and that the pioneers traveled in groups of covered wagons called wagon trains.

Draw Conclusions Do you think the covered wagons were used primarily to ride in or for hauling supplies? Explain. *(Based on the information in the 3-D Model, it looks like the wagons would have been used mostly for carrying things. There doesn't appear to be much room for passengers inside the wagon.)*

👥 ACTIVE CLASSROOM

Conduct a Conversation with a Pioneer activity. Tell students to imagine that they are having a conversation with a person who is migrating to the West in a wagon train. Direct each student to write down a question he or she would like to ask, then how the pioneer would respond, and then what the student would say in response.

Further Instruction

Ask students to identify some of the causes of and reasons for westward migration. *(Many Americans thought the western lands were needed for American settlement. Southern expansionists hoped to add more slave states in the West to strengthen their political position in Congress. In addition, trade and migration promoted economic growth in the border provinces. Many Americans were looking for better farmland in Oregon.)*

Determine Point of View Who might have agreed with the idea of Manifest Destiny? Who might have disagreed? *(Young people who wanted to start new lives in the West would have been enthusiastic supporters of Manifest Destiny. Also American businesses looking to expand their markets or looking for new opportunities also would have supported it. American Indians and Mexicans would have been opposed to the idea of Manifest Destiny.)*

Summarize the significance of Jedediah Smith's explorations of the West. *(Smith blazed the first trail across the Great Basin and the Sierra Nevada to reach California. Smith's route became the California Trail, linking the United States with the Pacific coast.)*

Objective 3: Analyze the causes and challenges of westward migration.

Quick Instruction

Interactive Map: Trails to the West Project the Interactive Map and click through the hot spots with students to explore the major overland trails over which Americans migrated westward during the 1840s. Introduce the map activity by telling students that the journey west on one of the key overland trails took about five months and presented great challenges. Invite students to speculate about the obstacles pioneers faced on their travels westward and to rank the obstacles according to the difficulty they presented.

Analyze Information How did the Treaty of Fort Laramie affect American Indians? *(The treaty didn't have much of an immediate impact on the American Indians. They continued their mobile way of life, pursuing buffalo across all artificial boundaries.)*

👥 ACTIVE CLASSROOM

Conduct a Make Headlines activity for each trail depicted in the Interactive Map. Ask: If you were to write a headline for each trail that captured the most important aspect of the trail that should be remembered, what would that headline be? Emphasize to students that their headlines should capture why each trail is significant. Allow them to use subheadings if they would like. Have students pass their headlines to a partner for them to review.

Moving West

INTERACTIVE MAP
Trails to the West

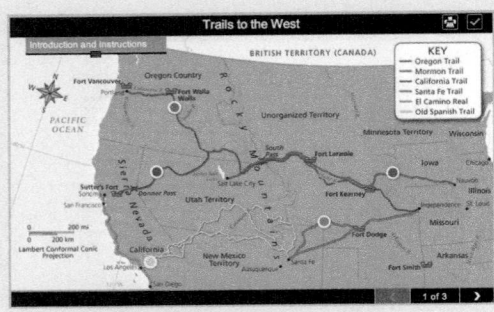

D Differentiate: **Challenge** Ask students to do additional research on the overland trails and present their findings.

ELL Use the ELL activity described in the ELL chart.

Further Instruction
Go through the Interactive Reading Notepad questions and discuss the answers with the class. To extend the lesson, assign 21st Century Skill Tutorials: Read Special-Purpose Maps and Geography Core Concepts: Forces on Earth's Surface.

Use Context Clues to develop a definition for the word "exodus." *(The Mormons were being persecuted and quickly left their homes. I think "exodus" means a large group of people moving—a large migration—to escape harm.*

▪ SYNTHESIZE

DIGITAL ACTIVITY
A Pioneer's Journal

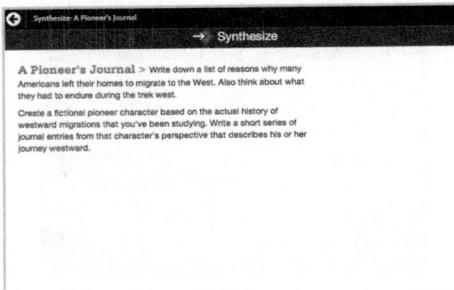

Discuss Before students begin their journal entries, direct students to review their notes from the Start Up Activity. Encourage them to correct or enhance their notes and to make sure their questions about westward migration have been answered. Students may benefit from working with a partner to answer any unanswered questions.

Consider providing opportunities for students to share and discuss their fictional journal entries. Remind students to incorporate information learned in the lesson, including reasons for westward migration, forms and routes of travel, challenges faced on the journey, and the opportunities awaiting at the final destinations.

▪ DEMONSTRATE

DIGITAL QUIZ
Lesson Quiz and Class Discussion Board

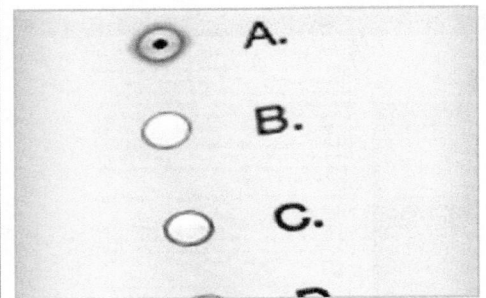

Assign the online Lesson Quiz for this lesson if you haven't already done so. Students will be offered automatic remediation or enrichment based on their score.

Pose these questions to the class on the Discussion Board:

In *Moving West*, you read about how the United States looked to western regions for new opportunities and wealth. Large numbers of Americans and immigrants moving to the West transformed the country, but they encroached on Mexican- and American Indian-controlled territories.

Make Predictions How might the settling of western territories impact the United States' relationship with Mexico? *(The settling of lands near Mexico's territories will eventually threaten Mexico and lead to conflict over control of those regions.)*

Topic Inquiry
Have students continue their investigations for the Topic Inquiry.

Texas and the Mexican-American War

Supporting English Language Learners

Use with the reading, **Texas Fights for Independence**.

Speaking
Explain that students will quiz each other on the content of the text—but the emphasis will be on the questions, not the answers. Brainstorm the importance of being able to ask clear questions.

Beginning Arrange students in a circle and provide them with simple question frames to use with the text. Invite one student to pose a question to the student on his or her right. After that student answers, have him or her pose a question to the student on the right. Continue around the circle.

Intermediate Ask pairs of students to ask each other five questions about the text, beginning each with *who, what, when, where, why,* or *how.* If their partner does not understand a question, encourage them to restate it.

Advanced Have students write a fact from the text on each of five index cards. Then place students in pairs and have them take turns forming questions for the "answers" on their partner's cards.

Advanced High Place students in pairs and have them take turns asking each other open-ended questions about the text. After their partner responds, encourage them to ask a follow-up question that is based on the answer given.

Use with the reading, **The Mexican-American War**.

Reading
Explain that a compound adjective is made up of two or more words, often joined by one or more hyphens. Hyphens are used to make the intended meaning clear to a reader.

Beginning Point out the phrase *long-standing border dispute* in the text's first paragraph. Ask: What is the compound adjective? Does long-standing mean (a) very tall, (b) lasting a long time, or (c) standing alongside?

Intermediate Point out the phrase *long-standing border dispute* in the text's first paragraph. Ask: What is the compound adjective? What does it describe? What does it mean? What would it mean without the hyphen?

Advanced Point out the phrase *long-standing border dispute* in the text's first paragraph and discuss its meaning. Then ask pairs of students to locate two other compound adjectives in the text and discuss their meanings (e.g., one-sided, short-lived).

Advanced High Ask pairs of students to locate three compound adjectives in the text (e.g., long-standing, one-sided, short-lived). Have them discuss their meanings, as well as how their meanings could be misunderstood without the hyphens. Then invite them to create an original sentence about the text that contains a compound adjective.

▣ Differentiate Instruction

Use the Differentiated Instruction notes throughout the lesson plan to support the varied skill sets, levels of readiness, and interests in the mixed-ability classroom.

Challenge These notes include suggestions for expanding the activity for advanced students.

On-Level These notes include suggestions for modifying the activity to address different interests or learning styles.

Extra Support These notes include ideas for providing more scaffolding or reading spuport.

Special Needs These notes provide ideas for adapting instruction to support the needs of various special needs students.

▮ NOTES

Texas and the Mexican-American War

Objectives

Objective 1: Describe how Texas was settled and how it won independence from Mexico.

Objective 2: Explain the debate around the annexation of Texas.

Objective 3: Identify the causes and outcome of the Mexican-American War.

LESSON 2 ORGANIZER		PACING: APPROX. 1 PERIOD, .5 BLOCKS			
				RESOURCES	
		OBJECTIVES	**PACING**	**Online**	**Print**
Connect					
DIGITAL START UP ACTIVITY **Comparing the United States and Mexico, 1840**			5 min.	●	
Investigate					
DIGITAL TEXT 1 **Texas Fights for Independence**		Objective 1	10 min.	●	●
DIGITAL TEXT 2 **The Expansion Debate**		Objective 2	10 min.	●	●
INTERACTIVE CHART **Compare Viewpoints: The Annexation of Texas**			10 min.	●	
DIGITAL TEXT 3 **The Mexican-American War**		Objective 3	10 min.	●	●
INTERACTIVE MAP **Growth of the United States, 1783 to 1853**			10 min.	●	
Synthesize					
DIGITAL ACTIVITY **Return to the Essential Question**			5 min.	●	
Demonstrate					
DIGITAL QUIZ **Lesson Quiz and Class Discussion Board**			10 min.	●	

PEARSON

realize™

www.PearsonRealize.com

Go online to access additional resources including:
Primary Sources • Biographies • Supreme Court cases •
21st Century Skill Tutorials • Maps • Graphic Organizers.

▉ CONNECT

DIGITAL START UP ACTIVITY
Comparing the United States and Mexico, 1840

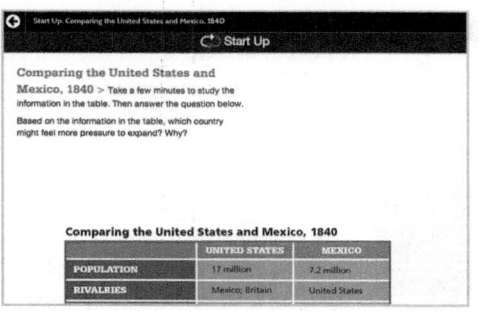

Project the Start Up Activity Ask students to examine the information in the table and answer the question as they enter and get settled. Have students share their response with a partner.

Discuss What features or characteristics of Texas made the region such a desirable territory? Would acquiring Texas through war be worth the costs? Explain. *(Possible answers: Texas had land suitable for farming and ranching and access to the Gulf of Mexico. Texas had such great potential that the benefits outweighed the costs.)*

Tell students that in this lesson they will be learning about how Texas became the focus of a territorial dispute that led to war.

Aa Vocabulary Development: Use the Interactive Reading Notepad to preview the Key Terms and Academic Vocabulary in this lesson with students.

⇅ FLIP IT!
Assign the Flipped Video for this lesson.

▉ STUDENT EDITION PRINT
PAGES: 192–196

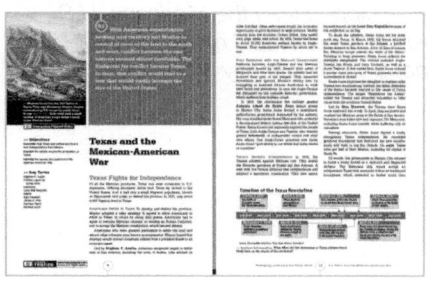

▉ INVESTIGATE

DIGITAL TEXT 1
Texas Fights for Independence

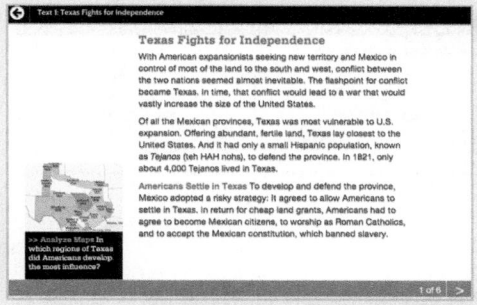

Objective 1: Describe how Texas was settled and how it won independence from Mexico.

Quick Instruction
Display the map titled *Empresario Land Grants in Texas, 1820s–1830s* . Ensure understanding of the map itself by reviewing the term *empresario* and the locations of major Anglo-Texan settlements. Challenge students to explain the factors that might have influenced Americans to settle in those regions of Texas. *(Possible responses: open fertile lands, near good water sources and routes)*

Infer Why was Mexico's strategy of allowing Americans to settle in Texas "risky"? *(Mexico's immigration policy enticed large numbers of American settlers to Texas, eventually leading to the new Anglo-Texans outnumbering Tejanos by about six to one. Also, there was no way Mexico could guarantee that the Anglo-Texans would abide the conditions of the policy and assimilate.)*

Identify Central Issues What aspects of their culture did American settlers in Texas refuse to change? *(The Anglo-Texans refused to become Roman Catholics and remained Protestants. They also ignored Mexico's slavery ban by smuggling in enslaved African Americans to work their farms and plantations.)*

ELL Use the ELL activity described in the ELL chart.

Further Instruction
Go through the Interactive Reading Notepad questions and use appropriate questions as a springboard to discuss the growing conflict between the Mexican government and the Anglo-Texans.

Identify Causes and Effects In what way was the fighting in Texas caused by both the Anglo-Texans and the Mexican government? *(Despite their oaths of allegiance and their land grants, the settlers had not honored their part of the bargain. This angered the Mexican government. The Mexican government, however, was taken over by Antonio López de Santa Anna , who favored a centralized, authoritarian government dominated by the military. Santa Anna's rule especially angered the people of Texas, both Anglo-Texans and Tejanos, who wanted greater autonomy, or independent control over their own affairs. These issues eventually led to fighting.)*

Draw Conclusions What actions did Santa Anna take that inspired Anglo-Texans to fight even harder for independence? *(Santa Anna ordered the execution of the Anglo-Texan and Tejano defenders of the Alamo and Goliad.)*

Texas and the Mexican-American War

DIGITAL TEXT 2

The Expansion Debate

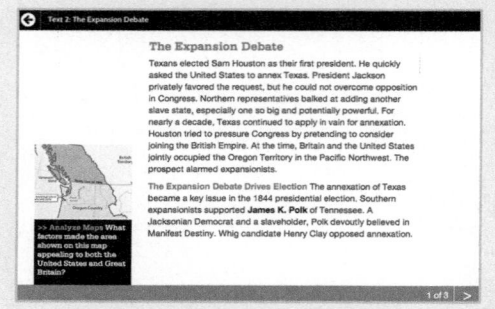

INTERACTIVE CHART

Compare Viewpoints: The Annexation of Texas

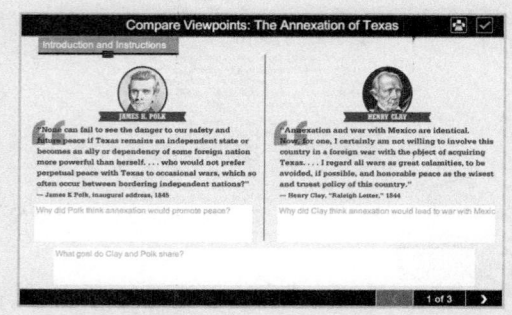

DIGITAL TEXT 3

The Mexican-American War

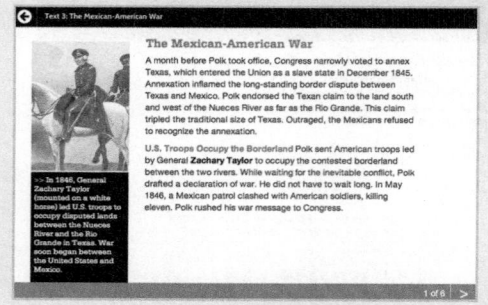

Objective 2: Explain the debate around the annexation of Texas.

Quick Instruction

Interactive Chart: Compare Viewpoints: The Annexation of Texas Project the Interactive Chart with the quotes from James Polk and Henry Clay. Invite two volunteers to read the quotes. Discuss each, ensuring student understanding. Invite volunteers to briefly summarize the key points in each quote and then answer the questions.

Express Problems Clearly What goal did both Polk and Clay have in the annexation debate? *(They both wanted peace.)*

🗣 ACTIVE CLASSROOM

Conduct a Graffiti Concepts activity. Ask students to reflect on the conflicting viewpoints in the debate on the annexation of Texas and create a visual image and/or phrase that represents each viewpoint. (Allow approximately 3–5 minutes.) Ask students to post their "graffiti" on the board or on chart paper, then have them look at all the various viewpoints and discuss them as a group.

Further Instruction

Infer Why did Polk and northerners consider the Oregon Territory a "prize"? *(Annexing the Oregon Territory would have made it possible to create free states to offset the annexation of Texas, which would enter the union as a slave state.)*

Draw Conclusions What did one Ohio Democrat mean when stating, "The administration is Southern, Southern, Southern!"? *(The Ohio Democrat believed that Polk's administration put the interests of the southern slave states ahead of the northern free states.)*

Objective 3: Identify the causes and outcome of the Mexican-American War.

Quick Instruction

Interactive Map: Growth of the United States, 1783 to 1853 Project the Interactive Map and click on the checkboxes to see the major acquisitions that led to westward expansion. Introduce the map activity by reminding students that in seventy years the United States had almost tripled in size. For each acquisition, ask the following questions: From whom did the United States acquire the territory? What impact did it have on the United States?

Make Generalizations How did the Louisiana Purchase heighten U.S. interests in the West? *(The Louisiana Purchase pushed the U.S. boundaries past the Mississippi River for the first time. It opened up the West to Americans, who were looking to expand and develop the great amounts of natural resources in the new lands.)*

Support a Point of View with Evidence What was the most significant advantage the United States had in the Mexican-American War? Explain. *(American forces were much better equipped than the Mexicans. U.S. soldiers had better and more powerful weapons and had many more soldiers.)*

INTERACTIVE MAP
Growth of the United States, 1783 to 1853

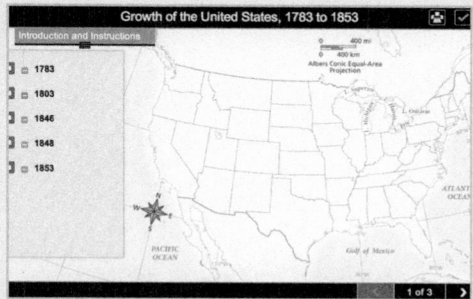

ACTIVE CLASSROOM

Conduct a Make Headlines activity for the expansion of the United States from 1783 to 1853. Ask: If you were to write a headline for the key acquisitions of the United States that captured the most important aspect that should be remembered, what would that headline be? Allow students to use subheadings to communicate more information. Encourage them to present their expansion headlines as part of the concept of Manifest Destiny. Have students pass their headlines to a partner for review.

D Differentiate: **Challenge** Ask students to do additional research on one of the territorial acquisitions and present their findings.

ELL Use the ELL activity described in the ELL chart.

Further Instruction

Initiate a discussion about the causes of the Mexican-American War. Make sure students can identify how Congress voted to annex Texas, inflaming the long-standing border dispute between Texas and Mexico. Mexicans refused to recognize the annexation. Students should also note the U.S. occupation of the borderlands and the clash between the Mexican patrol and American soldiers. Then ask students to identify key figures and battles of the war. To provide depth to the discussion, assign *21st Century Skill Tutorials: Draw Conclusions*.

Compare Points of View Why did most northerners tend to oppose the Mexican-American War while most southerners tended to support it? *(Most southerners thought that the conquered territories might become slave states, increasing southern power in Congress. Most northerners did not want to see any expansion of slavery in the new territories.)*

Texas and the Mexican-American War

SYNTHESIZE

DIGITAL ACTIVITY
Return to the Essential Question

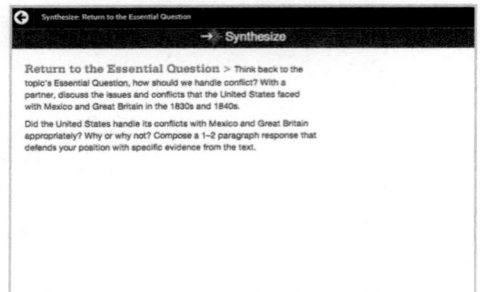

Ask students to recall the Topic Essential Question, "How should we handle conflict?" Have them use the Think Pair Share strategy to answer the questions in the Return to the Essential Question Activity. Ask them to take five minutes to write down some brief answers to the questions below then share their answers with a talking partner.

Have partners think about the following question. How did the U.S. government handle the conflicts with Mexico and Great Britain differently? Have pairs share their answers with the class.

Discuss Ask students to think about the question they thought about and answered at the beginning of this topic. Ask if they would change their response now that they have learned more about Texas and the Mexican-American War.

DEMONSTRATE

DIGITAL QUIZ
Lesson Quiz and Class Discussion Board

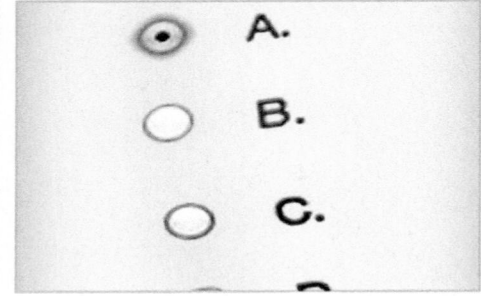

Assign the online Lesson Quiz for this lesson if you haven't already done so. Students will be offered automatic remediation or enrichment based on their score.

Pose these questions to the class on the Discussion Board:

In *Texas and the Mexican-American War*, you read about how American expansionist goals ignited conflict between Mexico and the United States. Debate began over control of Texas and its borderlands and the issue of annexation. Eventually, the hostilities over the southwestern boundary of Texas led to war with Mexico.

Summarize How did the revolution in Texas lead to war with Mexico?

Draw Conclusions Do you think the U.S. declaration of war against Mexico was justified? Why or why not?

Topic Inquiry
Have students continue their investigations for the Topic Inquiry.

America Achieves Manifest Destiny

Supporting English Language Learners

Use with the reading, **Realizing Manifest Destiny**.

Learning
Point out the words *treaty*, *purchase*, and *proviso* in the text. Explain that by relating these words to their own life, students will better understand and use them in other contexts.

Beginning Display the words *treaty*, *purchase*, and *proviso*. Invite students to match each word to a hypothetical yet plausible life experience (e.g., My parents will give me their old car if I pay for my own insurance). Then restate the life experiences to include the vocabulary words.

Intermediate Pair a word from above with a setting familiar to students (e.g., *purchase* and *mall*). Invite students to explain the word in the context of the setting. Repeat for all three words, using multiple settings if time allows.

Advanced Place students in pairs and have each partner choose either *treaty* or *proviso*. Invite students to relate a real or hypothetical life experience to their partner that both uses and centers on their vocabulary word.

Advanced High Ask students to write three paragraphs, each narrating a real or hypothetical life experience that both uses and centers on one of the vocabulary words above. Provide time for partners to read and discuss one of the paragraphs they wrote.

Use with the reading, **The California Gold Rush**.

Listening
Discuss the pros and cons of seeking clarification when someone is speaking (e.g., increases comprehension but interrupts the speaker), as well as why the pros outweigh the cons.

Beginning Provide students with question stems they can use to ask for clarification (e.g., What does _____ mean?). Then briefly describe aloud the three mining methods from the text (placer, hydraulic, hard rock). Pause periodically so students can use the frames to ask questions about what you have said.

Intermediate Using extra details not found in the text, describe aloud the *placer*, *hydraulic*, and *hard rock* mining methods. Pause periodically and invite students to ask questions about what you have said.

Advanced Have pairs of students research one mining method mentioned in the text (placer, hydraulic, or hard rock). Then have them share their research aloud with another pair, pausing periodically so the other pair can ask clarifying questions about what was said.

Advanced High Have students research one mining method mentioned in the text (placer, hydraulic, or hard rock). Then have them share their research aloud with a partner, pausing periodically so the partner can ask clarifying questions about what was said.

▣ Differentiate Instruction

Use the Differentiated Instruction notes throughout the lesson plan to support the varied skill sets, levels of readiness, and interests in the mixed-ability classroom.

Challenge These notes include suggestions for expanding the activity for advanced students.

On-Level These notes include suggestions for modifying the activity to address different interests or learning styles.

Extra Support These notes include ideas for providing more scaffolding or reading spuport.

Special Needs These notes provide ideas for adapting instruction to support the needs of various special needs students.

▪ NOTES

America Achieves Manifest Destiny

Objectives

Objective 1: Explain how the Mexican-American War helped the United States achieve the goal of Manifest Destiny.

Objective 2: Identify the causes and effects of the California Gold Rush.

LESSON 3 ORGANIZER	PACING: APPROX. 1 PERIOD, .5 BLOCKS			
			RESOURCES	
	OBJECTIVES	PACING	Online	Print
Connect				
DIGITAL START UP ACTIVITY **Seeking a Mountain of Gold**		5 min.	●	
Investigate				
DIGITAL TEXT 1 **Realizing Manifest Destiny**	Objective 1	10 min.	●	●
DIGITAL TEXT 2 **The California Gold Rush**		10 min.	●	●
INTERACTIVE GALLERY **California Gold Rush**	Objective 2	10 min.	●	
BEFORE AND AFTER **The Growth of San Francisco**		10 min.	●	
Synthesize				
DIGITAL ACTIVITY **Identify Cause and Effect**		5 min.	●	
Demonstrate				
DIGITAL QUIZ **Lesson Quiz and Class Discussion Board**		10 min.	●	

PEARSON **realize.**
www.PearsonRealize.com

Go online to access additional resources including:
Primary Sources • Biographies • Supreme Court cases •
21st Century Skill Tutorials • Maps • Graphic Organizers.

CONNECT

DIGITAL START UP ACTIVITY
Seeking a Mountain of Gold

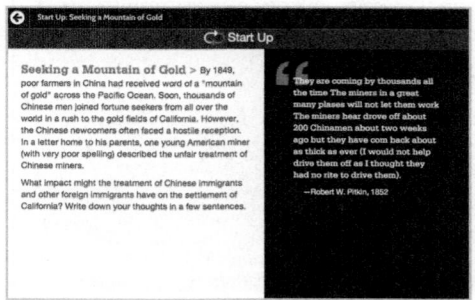

Project the Start Up Activity Ask students to consider the activity as they enter and get settled. Then have them share their sentences with another student, either in class or through a chat or blog space.

Discuss Discuss with students how the discovery of and rush to find gold might have increased the tensions between ethnic groups in gold fields and towns of California. Invite volunteers to discuss ways in which individuals can take a stand against discrimination against minorities.

Tell students that in this lesson they will be learning how the California Gold Rush affected individuals, California, and the country as a whole.

Aa **Vocabulary Development:** Use the Interactive Reading Notepad to preview the Key Terms and Academic Vocabulary in this lesson with students.

🔃 FLIP IT!
Assign the Flipped Video for this lesson.

■ STUDENT EDITION PRINT PAGES: 197–200

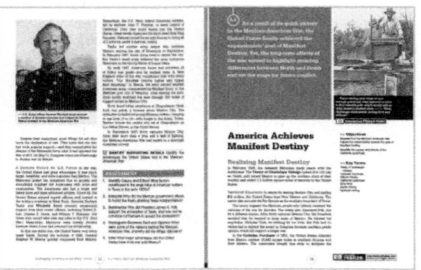

INVESTIGATE

DIGITAL TEXT 1
Realizing Manifest Destiny

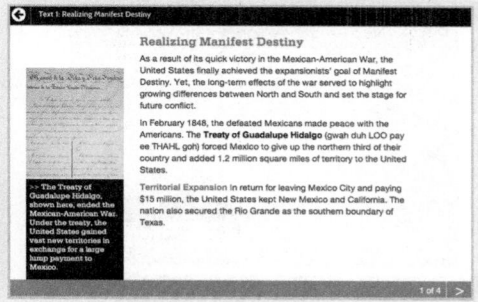

Objective 1: Explain how the Mexican-American War helped the United States achieve the goal of Manifest Destiny.

Quick Instruction
Direct students' focus to the image of the Treaty of Guadalupe Hidalgo. Invite volunteers to briefly review and discuss the reasons the United States and Mexico went to war. *(disputes between Mexico and the United States over the U.S. annexation of Texas and Texas' exact borders)* Explain to students that the treaty was signed at Villa de Guadalupe Hidalgo, a neighborhood of Mexico City in which the peace negotiations were held. Make sure that students understand that under the treaty the United States gained vast new territories in exchange for a large lump payment to Mexico.

Apply Concepts How did the Treaty of Guadalupe Hidalgo settle the chief issues that led to the Mexican-American War? *(Mexico was forced to accept that Texas was part of the United States and that the Rio Grande was the southern boundary of Texas.)*

ELL Use the ELL activity described in the ELL chart.

Further Instruction
Determine Relevance What effect did the Gadsden Purchase have on the idea of Manifest Destiny? *(With the Gadsden Purchase, the United States acquired territory that completed U.S. control of the Southwest. This land made possible a railroad across the continent.)*

Express Problems Clearly How did the Wilmot Proviso weaken the major political parties in the United States? *(Debate over the Wilmot Proviso divided members within each political party along regional lines. Most northerners and southerners split with their respective parties and supported the position supported by regional views rather than the views of their political parties.)*

America Achieves Manifest Destiny

DIGITAL TEXT 2

The California Gold Rush

INTERACTIVE GALLERY

California Gold Rush

BEFORE AND AFTER

The Growth of San Francisco

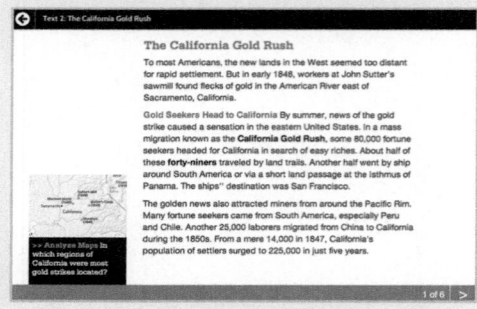

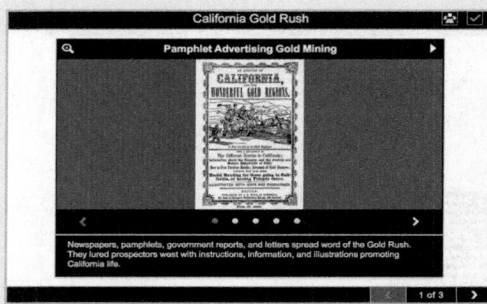

Objective 2: Identify the causes and effects of the California Gold Rush.

Quick Instruction

Interactive Gallery: California Gold Rush Project the Interactive Gallery and navigate through the images with students. What does the inclusion of "temporary population" figures suggest about the lasting effects of the California Gold Rush? *(It suggests that much of the population increase due to the gold rush was short-lived. Mining was so difficult that many miners eventually left California.)*

📷 ACTIVE CLASSROOM

Conduct a Wallpaper activity in which students review information about the California Gold Rush. Have students design a piece of "wallpaper" with text and images that encapsulates a key aspect of the gold rush and its significance on San Francisco. Post the wallpaper and have students take a gallery walk to note what others have written or illustrated.

Before and After: The Growth of San Francisco Project the Before and After and have students manipulate the slider to investigate the rapid growth of California by contrasting San Francisco before and after 1849. In your opinion, what will happen to San Francisco when the mines run out of gold or the miners lose their jobs because of more efficient means of mechanical mining?

(I think San Francisco will still be an important city because of the new businesses that were created and because of its location as an important ocean port.)

📷 ACTIVE CLASSROOM

Conduct a See-Think-Wonder activity. Ask: What do you see? What does that make you think? What are you wondering about now that you've seen this? Prompt volunteers to share their insights with the class.

🅓 **Differentiate: On Level** If time allows, ask students to highlight significant words and phrases in the Interactivities that describe the long-term effects of the California Gold Rush.

ELL Use the ELL activity described in the ELL chart.

Further Instruction

Initiate a discussion about how the California Gold Rush effected individuals. Ask students to identify groups of people who were impacted by the discovery of gold. *(Americans, Chinese, South American, and Mexican miners who headed to California to mine or start businesses; Californios and American Indians who were already living in the region)* Invite volunteers to describe the positive and negative effects on each group of people listed. To extend the discussion, assign Geography Core Concepts: Migration.

Make Generalizations Who benefited most from the California Gold Rush? Who benefited least? *(Mine owners or wealthy investors rather than common miners enjoyed the profits from the mines. Shrewd traders who sold goods to the miners at high prices also benefited greatly. Minorities, including Chinese, Mexican Americans (Californios), and American Indians benefited the least from the gold rush.)*

Draw Conclusions How did the settlement of California by gold seekers affect the lives of the people already settled there? *(American Indians were terrorized and killed by the thousands. Many lost their lands and homes and had to become workers on farms and ranches. Californios, or Mexican Californians, also lost most of their land.)*

SYNTHESIZE

DIGITAL ACTIVITY
Identify Cause and Effect

Instruct students to break the assignment into two basic parts before starting. Encourage students to work with a partner to discuss westward expansion as a topic before moving onto the Gold Rush.

Discuss Invite students to discuss how the causes and effects of westward expansion and the Gold Rush are similar or different.

DEMONSTRATE

DIGITAL QUIZ
Lesson Quiz and Class Discussion Board

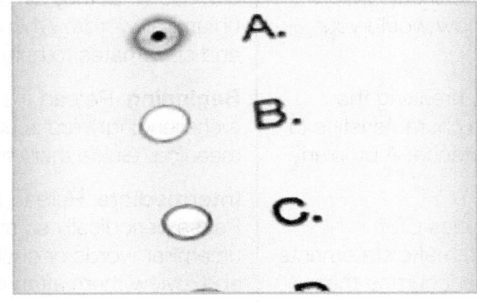

Assign the online Lesson Quiz for this lesson if you haven't already done so. Students will be offered automatic remediation or enrichment based on their score.

Pose these questions to the class on the Discussion Board:

In *America Achieves Manifest Destiny*, you read the territorial disputes between Mexico and the United States that eventually resulted in war. Victory in the Mexican-American War allowed the United States to finally fulfill the ideals of Manifest Destiny.

Draw Conclusions What were the effects of the Mexican-American War and the California Gold Rush?

Support a Point of View with Evidence Were American expansionists justified in their pursuit of Manifest Destiny? Why or why not?

Topic Inquiry
Have students continue their investigations for the Topic Inquiry.

A Religious Awakening Sparks Reform

Supporting English Language Learners

Use with the reading, **Utopias and Transcendentalism**.

Speaking
Point out some of the key content-area vocabulary from the text: utopian community, cooperative society, Transcendentalist, conscience, Civil Disobedience. Ask: If you didn't grasp this vocabulary, how would your understanding of the text be affected?

Beginning Review the meaning of *utopian community*, breaking the term into individual words. Then have students describe characteristics of a utopian community by completing and saying this sentence: A utopian community was _____.

Intermediate Display a Venn diagram, and label the circles *Civil Disobedience* and *Transcendentalism* . Invite students to make statements that compare and contrast these two movements, and encourage them to use content-area vocabulary from the text to do so. Record their responses on the diagram.

Advanced Ask pairs of students to identify which movement from the text they consider the most worthwhile. Then have them use content-area vocabulary to discuss the strengths of that movement and weaknesses of the others.

Advanced High Invite pairs of students to define and discuss the term conscience. Then have them answer this question: To what extent did the idea of conscience influence the formation and appeal of each movement mentioned in the text?

Use with the reading, **Public Education Reform**.

Reading
Tell students that as they reread the paragraphs about Horace Mann, they can use what they already know about the topic to help them decode unfamiliar words. When that does not work, they can rely on their teacher and classmates to help them understand the text.

Beginning Reread the paragraphs about Horace Mann together. When a challenging word is encountered, pause and ask students to guess its meaning. Guide them to understand the word in context.

Intermediate Reread the paragraphs about Horace Mann together. Pause periodically so students have the opportunity to ask about unfamiliar words or challenging phrasing. Record these words and phrases and review them afterward.

Advanced Invite pairs of students to reread the paragraphs about Horace Mann together. Have them discuss these words as they are encountered: reformers, inadequate, championed, chair, oversight, abolish. Ask: How can discussing a word's meaning with a partner help you reach an understanding you might not have reached on your own?

Advanced High Ask students to individually reread the paragraphs about Horace Mann. As they read, have them write down the words or phrases they do not understand. Then have partners work to understand the items on each list.

▶ Differentiate Instruction

Use the Differentiated Instruction notes throughout the lesson plan to support the varied skill sets, levels of readiness, and interests in the mixed-ability classroom.

Challenge These notes include suggestions for expanding the activity for advanced students.

On-Level These notes include suggestions for modifying the activity to address different interests or learning styles.

Extra Support These notes include ideas for providing more scaffolding or reading spuport.

Special Needs These notes provide ideas for adapting instruction to support the needs of various special needs students.

■ NOTES

PEARSON
realize™
www.PearsonRealize.com

Go online to access additional resources including:
Primary Sources • Biographies • Supreme Court cases •
21st Century Skill Tutorials • Maps • Graphic Organizers.

Objectives

Objective 1: Explain how the Second Great Awakening affected the United States.

Objective 2: Describe the discrimination that some religious groups suffered from in the mid-1800s.

Objective 3: Trace the emergence of the utopian and transcendentalism movements.

Objective 4: Analyze the goals and methods of the public school movement.

Objective 5: Evaluate the effectiveness of the prison reform and temperance movement.

LESSON 4 ORGANIZER		PACING: APPROX. 1 PERIOD, .5 BLOCKS			
		OBJECTIVES	PACING	**RESOURCES** Online	Print
Connect					
DIGITAL START UP ACTIVITY **A Great Awakening**			5 min.	●	
Investigate					
DIGITAL TEXT 1 **The Second Great Awakening**		Objective 1	10 min.	●	●
DIGITAL TEXT 2 **Religious Discrimination and Intolerance**		Objective 2	10 min.	●	●
DIGITAL TEXT 3 **Utopias and Transcendentalism**		Objective 3	10 min.	●	●
INTERACTIVE GALLERY **Religious and Spiritual Movements of the Early 1800s**			10 min.	●	
DIGITAL TEXT 4 **Public Education Reform**		Objective 4	10 min.	●	●
DIGITAL TEXT 5 **Social Reform Movements**		Objective 5	10 min.	●	●
INTERACTIVE GALLERY **Mid-Nineteenth Century Reform Movements**			10 min.	●	
Synthesize					
DIGITAL ACTIVITY **Fighting for Reforms**			5 min.	●	
Demonstrate					
DIGITAL QUIZ **Lesson Quiz and Class Discussion Board**			10 min.	●	

A Religious Awakening Sparks Reform

CONNECT

DIGITAL START UP ACTIVITY
A Great Awakening

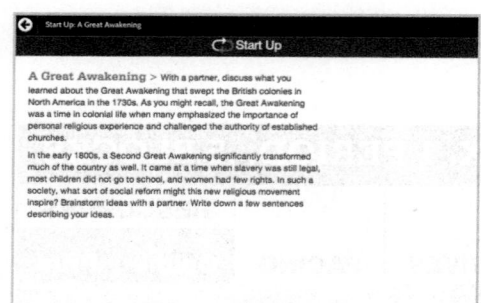

Start Up: A Great Awakening

Start Up

A Great Awakening > With a partner, discuss what you learned about the Great Awakening that swept the British colonies in North America in the 1730s. As you might recall, the Great Awakening was a time in colonial life when many emphasized the importance of personal religious experience and challenged the authority of established churches.

In the early 1800s, a Second Great Awakening significantly transformed much of the country as well. It came at a time when slavery was still legal, most children did not go to school, and women had few rights. In such a society, what sort of social reform might this new religious movement inspire? Brainstorm ideas with a partner. Write down a few sentences describing your ideas.

Project the Start Up Activity Pair students and ask them to make a list of the important changes brought about by the Great Awakening that swept the British colonies in North America in the 1730s. Have student pairs share their ideas in class or through a chat or blog space.

Tell students that in this lesson they will be learning about another religious revival—the Second Great Awakening—that significantly transformed much of the country as well.

Discuss What sort of social reform might this new religious movement inspire? Encourage students to provide context for their responses based on their knowledge of American society at the time.

Aa Vocabulary Development: Use the Interactive Reading Notepad to preview the Key Terms and Academic Vocabulary in this lesson with students.

⇪ FLIP IT!

Assign the Flipped Video for this lesson.

■ STUDENT EDITION PRINT PAGES: 201–210

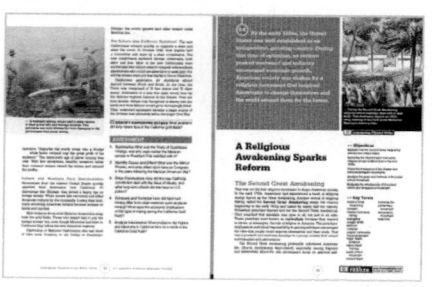

INVESTIGATE

DIGITAL TEXT 1
The Second Great Awakening

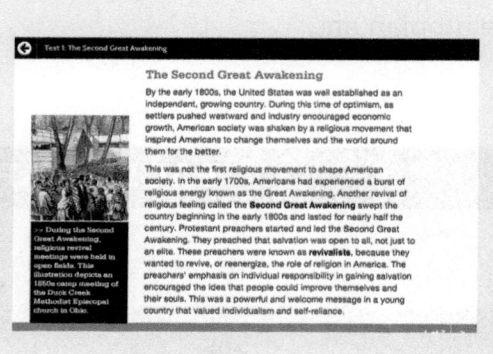

Text 1: The Second Great Awakening

The Second Great Awakening

By the early 1800s, the United States was well established as an independent, growing country. During this time of optimism, as settlers pushed westward and industry encouraged economic growth, American society was shaken by a religious movement that inspired Americans to change themselves and the world around them for the better.

This was not the first religious movement to shape American society. In the early 1700s, Americans had experienced a burst of religious energy known as the Great Awakening. Another revival of religious feeling called the **Second Great Awakening** swept the country beginning in the early 1800s and lasted for nearly half the century. Protestant preachers started and led the Second Great Awakening. They preached that salvation was open to all, not just to an elite. These preachers were known as **revivalists**, because they wanted to revive, or reenergize, the role of religion in America. The preachers' emphasis on individual responsibility in gaining salvation encouraged the idea that people could improve themselves and their souls. This was a powerful and welcome message in a young country that valued individualism and self-reliance.

>> During the Second Great Awakening, religious revival meetings were held in open fields. This illustration depicts an 1850s camp meeting of the Duck Creek Methodist Episcopal church in Ohio.

Objective 1: Explain how the Second Great Awakening affected the United States.

Quick Instruction

Direct students' attention to the illustration of the religious revival or "camp meeting." Invite students to review and discuss the Great Awakening of the 1730s and 1740s. *(a religious movement in the English colonies that was heavily inspired by evangelical preachers)* Explain that in the early 1800s another revival of religious feeling called the Second Great Awakening swept the country. Preachers known as revivalists tried to revive, or re-energize, Americans' faith.

Infer Why do you think the religious messages of the Second Great Awakening affected so many Americans? *(Many Americans were concerned about personal salvation and were attracted to the idea of spiritual improvement.)*

Further Instruction

Draw Conclusions What were some of the positive aspects of the Second Great Awakening on the United States? *(Many Americans were inspired by the Second Great Awakening to work for a wide variety of social reforms.)*

Generate Explanations How did the Second Great Awakening lead to the widening of religious diversity in the 1800s? *(Many Americans inspired by the Second Great Awakening sought new interpretations of religious meaning in their lives. Although they shared basic Christian beliefs, the new religions diverged from established religious creeds.)*

DIGITAL TEXT 2
Religious Discrimination and Intolerance

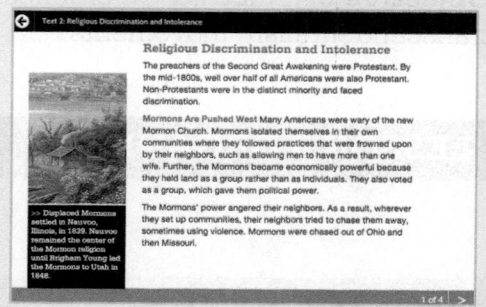

Text 2: Religious Discrimination and Intolerance

Religious Discrimination and Intolerance

The preachers of the Second Great Awakening were Protestant. By the mid-1800s, well over half of all Americans were also Protestant. Non-Protestants were in the distinct minority and faced discrimination.

Mormons Are Pushed West Many Americans were wary of the new Mormon Church. Mormons isolated themselves in their own communities where they followed practices that were frowned upon by their neighbors, such as allowing men to have more than one wife. Further, the Mormons became economically powerful because they held land as a group rather than as individuals. They also voted as a group, which gave them political power.

The Mormons' power angered their neighbors. As a result, wherever they set up communities, their neighbors tried to chase them away, sometimes using violence. Mormons were chased out of Ohio and then Missouri.

>> Displaced Mormons settled in Nauvoo, Illinois, in 1839. Nauvoo remained the center of the Mormon religion until Brigham Young led the Mormons to Utah in 1846.

1 of 4 >

Objective 2: Describe the discrimination that some religious groups suffered from in the mid-1800s.

Quick Instruction

Project the illustration that shows the Nauvoo settlement in 1839. Review the founding of the Church of Jesus Christ of Latter-day Saints with students. *(After claiming to have had visions directing him to found a new religious group, Joseph Smith and a few followers organized the Church of Jesus Christ of Latter-day Saints, whose members are commonly called the Mormons.)* Explain that because of their beliefs the Mormons were chased out of Ohio and Missouri before settling on the Mississippi River in Illinois and founding the town of Nauvoo.

Summarize why many Americans were wary of the new Mormon Church. *(The Mormons isolated themselves in their own communities where they followed practices that their neighbors did not support, such as allowing men to have more than one wife. The Mormons also became economically powerful because they held land as a group rather than as individuals. They also voted as a group, which gave them political power.)*

Further Instruction

Go through the Interactive Reading Notepad questions and use appropriate questions to begin a discussion about the causes and effects of discrimination based on religious beliefs. Invite volunteers to share what they know about cases of discrimination they learned about in their past readings, from current events, or from their own personal experiences.

DIGITAL TEXT 3
Utopias and Transcendentalism

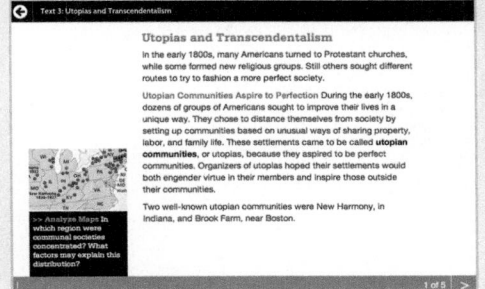

INTERACTIVE GALLERY
Religious and Spiritual Movements of the Early 1800s

Compare Points of View Why was Catholic loyalty to the United States questioned while the loyalty of Protestants was not? *(The Catholic Church was led by a powerful Pope, in Rome. Protestants did not have a similar centralized leader.)*

Cite Evidence What constitutional right were Jewish people denied until the late nineteenth century in many states? *(Jews were barred from holding office even though Article VI of the U.S. Constitution states that no religious test shall ever be required as a qualification to any office.)*

Objective 3: Trace the emergence of the utopian and transcendentalism movements.

Quick Instruction
Interactive Chart: Religious and Spiritual Movements of the Early 1800s Project the Interactive Chart. Click on each image and guide the class to determine the key information for each religious and spiritual movement. Then guide the discussions into one about how these movements changed everyday life in the United States.

Analyze Information What did the Transcendentalists and people who founded utopias have in common? *(Both movements moved away from mainstream religious beliefs and doctrines and sought different routes to try to fashion a more perfect society.)*

👥 ACTIVE CLASSROOM
Direct students to have a Conversation with History with a member from one of the religious or spiritual movements shown in the gallery. Have students imagine that they are having a conversation with their selected individual. Students should write down a question they would like to ask, then what that person would say to them, and what they would say in response.

D **Differentiate: Challenge** Ask students to do additional research on the additional aspects of one of the religious or spiritual movements and present their findings.

ELL Use the ELL activity described in the ELL chart.

Further Instruction
Express Problems Clearly What aspect of Shaker communities hindered their long-term viability? *(Men and women in Shaker communities did not marry or have children. The communities grew only when adults joined or when the group took in orphans.)*

Connect What did Transcendentalist philosophy share with the Enlightenment philosophy? *(Both philosophies proposed that self-knowledge is acquired through experience and reason and that individuals are able to learn the truth about the universe without relying on religious doctrines.)*

A Religious Awakening Sparks Reform

DIGITAL TEXT 4
Public Education Reform

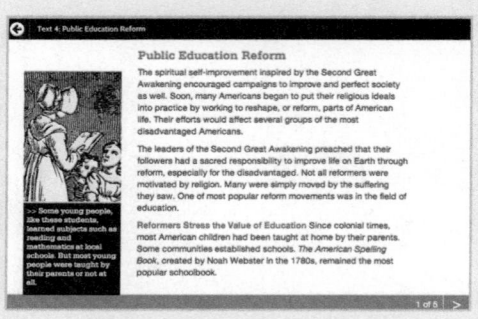

Text 4: Public Education Reform

Public Education Reform

The spiritual self-improvement inspired by the Second Great Awakening encouraged campaigns to improve and perfect society as well. Soon, many Americans began to put their religious ideals into practice by working to reshape, or reform, parts of American life. Their efforts would affect several groups of the most disadvantaged Americans.

The leaders of the Second Great Awakening preached that their followers had a sacred responsibility to improve life on Earth through reform, especially for the disadvantaged. Not all reformers were motivated by religion. Many were simply moved by the suffering they saw. One of most popular reform movements was in the field of education.

Reformers Stress the Value of Education Since colonial times, most American children had been taught at home by their parents. Some communities established schools. *The American Spelling Book*, created by Noah Webster in the 1780s, remained the most popular schoolbook.

>> Some young people, like these students, learned subjects such as reading and mathematics at local schools. But most young people were taught by their parents or not at all.

1 of 5 >

DIGITAL TEXT 5
Social Reform Movements

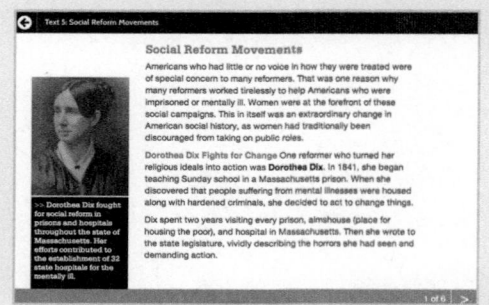

Text 5: Social Reform Movements

Social Reform Movements

Americans who had little or no voice in how they were treated were of special concern to many reformers. That was one reason why many reformers worked tirelessly to help Americans who were imprisoned or mentally ill. Women were at the forefront of these social campaigns. This in itself was an extraordinary change in American social history, as women had traditionally been discouraged from taking on public roles.

Dorothea Dix Fights for Change One reformer who turned her religious ideals into action was **Dorothea Dix**. In 1841, she began teaching Sunday school in a Massachusetts prison. When she discovered that people suffering from mental illnesses were housed along with hardened criminals, she decided to act to change things.

Dix spent two years visiting every prison, almshouse (place for housing the poor), and hospital in Massachusetts. Then she wrote to the state legislature, vividly describing the horrors she had seen and demanding action.

>> Dorothea Dix fought for social reform in prisons and hospitals throughout the state of Massachusetts. Her efforts contributed to the establishment of 32 state hospitals for the mentally ill.

1 of 6 >

Objective 4: Analyze the goals and methods of the public school movement.

Quick Instruction

Direct students' attention to the image of an early American schoolroom. Invite a volunteer to explain what the image might symbolize about the view of education in nineteenth century America. *(Education looked very basic and structured; the students are separated by gender and they are in uniforms. Students look like they are not active participants. Rather, they are being read to.)* Point out that most young people did not attend formal schools. Instead they were taught by their parents or not at all. Encourage discussion about the advantages and disadvantages of home schooling in the 19th century.

Determine Point of View According to reformers, how would the public school movement help America's government and economy? *(Reformers argued that expanding education would give Americans the knowledge and intellectual tools they needed to make decisions as citizens of a democracy. Education would promote economic growth by supplying knowledgeable workers and help keep wealthy, educated people from oppressing the uneducated poor.)*

ELL Use the ELL activity described in the ELL chart.

Further Instruction

Apply Concepts How does Horace Mann's background and work on education reform reflect the ideal of America as a land of opportunity? *(Mann grew up poor and had firsthand experience with inadequate schooling, yet with hard work he ended up educated and successful. Mann believed that all young people could do the same if given the proper education and opportunities.)*

Summarize the role women played in the education reforms of the 19th century. *(Many women tried to persuade local legislatures to support public education. Many others became teachers in the new schools. Others opened schools for women.)*

Objective 5: Evaluate the effectiveness of the prison reform and temperance movement.

Quick Instruction

Interactive Gallery: Mid-Nineteenth Century Reform Movements Project the Interactive Gallery and click through the images as the class discusses the key social problems that reformers in the mid-nineteenth century worked to solve. Invite volunteers to discuss the state of these social problems today. Encourage open discussion and invite all students to participate and share their opinions. Ask: What role should religion and government play in social reform movements? What role should individual citizens play? Extend the discussion by assigning *Culture Core Concepts: Belief* .

Analyze Images What does Image Four (Temperance Movement) tell you about the differences in how men and women viewed the issue? *(The image suggests that more women viewed the consumption of alcohol as a problem than did men. The men in the image look as though they are blocking the entrance as if to warn the women to stay away.)*

📖 ACTIVE CLASSROOM

Conduct a Sticky Notes activity. Have students take three minutes to jot down their ideas about how social reformers in the mid-nineteenth century changed life in the United States. Then ask, "Were the reformers successful and did their work make the country better?" Have students post their stickies on a wall, then sort and discuss their responses as a group.

■ **SYNTHESIZE**

■ **DEMONSTRATE**

INTERACTIVE GALLERY
Mid-Nineteenth Century Reform Movements

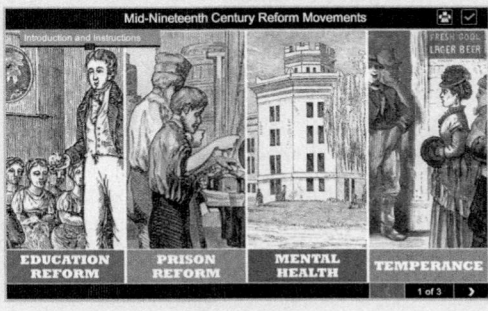

DIGITAL ACTIVITY
Fighting for Reforms

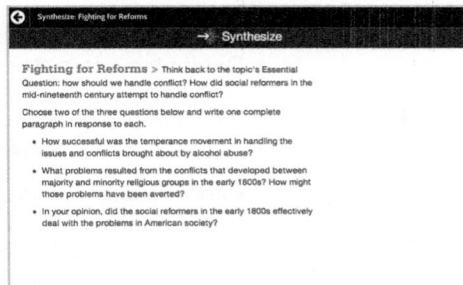

DIGITAL QUIZ
Lesson Quiz and Class Discussion Board

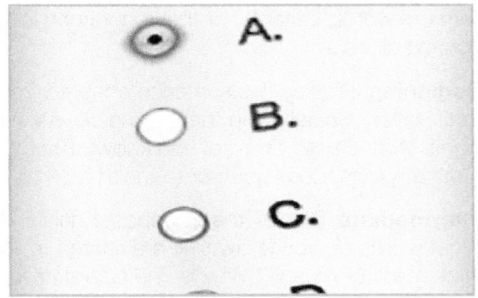

Further Instruction

Briefly discuss how the growing influence of women in American society affected the social reform movements in the mid-nineteenth century. Ask students to find examples of prominent women who were leaders in the social reform movements discussed in the Lesson. *(Dorothea Dix, Catharine Beecher, Elizabeth Blackwell and Ann Preston, Emma Willard)*

Support a Point of View with Evidence
How effective do you think the penitentiary movement was? Explain. *In general, the penitentiary movement was somewhat successful. It changed the way people thought about inmates. Before the movement, people viewed prisons as a means to punish criminals. Reformers viewed prisons as a way to make criminals feel penitence, or sorrow for their crimes, with the hope of rehabilitation. Treatment of prisoners changed greatly because of the work of the penitentiary movement.)*

Analyze Information How did the leaders of the temperance movement try to solve the problems of crime and poverty? *(Temperance movement leaders thought that alcohol consumption caused a great deal of the crime and poverty in society. Consequently, they worked to limit the availability of alcohol and in some cases tried to ban it altogether.)*

Ask students to recall the Topic Essential Question, "How Should We Handle Conflict?" Have them use the Think Pair Share strategy to answer the question, "How did social reformers in the mid-nineteenth century attempt to handle conflict"? Ask them to take five minutes to write down some brief notes and then share their answers with a talking partner.

Discuss Before students write their brief paragraphs, hold a quick round table in which students identify a religious, spiritual, or social reform movement of the 1800s. For each, have students describe the problems the movement sought to address and its goals.

Assign the online Lesson Quiz for this lesson if you haven't already done so. Students will be offered automatic remediation or enrichment based on their score.

Pose these questions to the class on the Discussion Board:

In *A Religious Awakening Sparks Reform*, you explored how a renewed focus on religious life inspired many Americans to build social reform movements to address pressing problems in American life. Others formed their own churches and adopted new ways of worship. Some embraced non-traditional ways to learn about and understand the natural world.

Draw Conclusions How did the Second Great Awakening affect daily life in the United States?

Make Predictions How might the Second Great Awakening and the social reform movements of the mid-nineteenth century affect the escalating conflicts over the issue of slavery?

Topic Inquiry

Have students continue their investigations for the Topic Inquiry.

The Abolition Movement

Supporting English Language Learners

Use with the reading, **The Antislavery Movement Grows**.

Learning
Tell students that when they do not understand the meaning of a word, what they already know can often help. For example, they might be familiar with the word's variants, or their prior knowledge might help them interpret context clues.

Beginning Display this sentence adapted from the text: The American Anti-Slavery Society said that having slaves was counter to most religious ideals. Ask: Based on what you know about this antislavery group and most religions, does *counter to* mean "for" or "against"?

Intermediate Display the newspaper name *The Liberator*. Ask: What words do you know that are related to *liberator*? What do you think *liberator* means? Why is *The Liberator* a good name for an antislavery newspaper?

Advanced Ask pairs of students to locate the word *implemented* in the text's second-to-last paragraph. Have them discuss the word's meaning based on their understanding of abolitionists and their tactics.

Advanced High Have students examine the first word of the text, *misgivings*, and write a definition of it using what they already know to help them. Ask pairs of students to discuss their decoding strategies and definitions.

Use with the reading, **The Backlash Against Abolition**.

Listening
Ask: How do you know if you are listening well? How do you make sure you understand what a speaker says? Together, brainstorm answers to these questions.

Beginning Make simple statements about either abolitionists or defenders of slavery, without identifying the group (e.g., They believed the economy depended on slavery). Ask students to identify the group being described and repeat the key words that led to their answer.

Intermediate Summarize the text aloud for students. Pause periodically to ask students to restate what you just said or answer a brief question about it. Afterward, discuss how students can adapt this activity to monitor their listening at other times.

Advanced Talk to students about possible arguments that refute pro-slavery rationalizations. After you counter each point mentioned in the text, invite pairs of students to discuss what you said and ask clarifying questions to improve their understanding (as needed).

Advanced High Place students in pairs, and invite each partner to select one pro-slavery rationalization and argue against it. After each student speaks, have the partner summarize what he or she heard and ask clarifying questions as needed.

▣ Differentiate Instruction

Use the Differentiated Instruction notes throughout the lesson plan to support the varied skill sets, levels of readiness, and interests in the mixed-ability classroom.

Challenge These notes include suggestions for expanding the activity for advanced students.

On-Level These notes include suggestions for modifying the activity to address different interests or learning styles.

Extra Support These notes include ideas for providing more scaffolding or reading spuport.

Special Needs These notes provide ideas for adapting instruction to support the needs of various special needs students.

■ NOTES

PEARSON ...
realize.™
www.PearsonRealize.com

Go online to access additional resources including:
Primary Sources • Biographies • Supreme Court cases •
21st Century Skill Tutorials • Maps • Graphic Organizers.

Objectives

Objective 1: Describe the hardships of the lives of enslaved African Americans and the ways in which they coped.

Objective 2: Explain the struggles and successes of free African Americans in the mid-1800s.

Objective 3: Identify the leaders and tactics of the abolition movement.

Objective 4: Summarize the positions and tactics of those opposed to abolition.

LESSON 5 ORGANIZER	PACING: APPROX. 1 PERIOD, .5 BLOCKS			
			RESOURCES	
	OBJECTIVES	PACING	Online	Print
Connect				
DIGITAL START UP ACTIVITY **Slavery and the Abolition Movement in America**		5 min.	●	
Investigate				
DIGITAL TEXT 1 **Life as an Enslaved African American**	Objective 1	10 min.	●	●
INTERACTIVE GALLERY **Resisting Slavery**		10 min.	●	
DIGITAL TEXT 2 **Free African Americans**	Objective 2	10 min.	●	●
DIGITAL TEXT 3 **The Antislavery Movement Grows**	Objective 3	10 min.	●	●
INTERACTIVE GALLERY **The Movement to End Slavery**		10 min.	●	
DIGITAL TEXT 4 **The Backlash Against Abolition**	Objective 4	10 min.	●	●
Synthesize				
DIGITAL ACTIVITY **Resisting Slavery**		5 min.	●	
Demonstrate				
DIGITAL QUIZ **Lesson Quiz and Class Discussion Board**		10 min.	●	

The Abolition Movement

■ CONNECT

DIGITAL START UP ACTIVITY
Slavery and the Abolition Movement in America

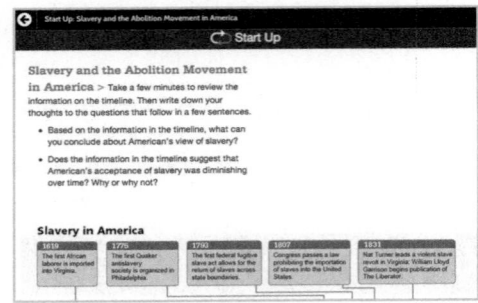

Project the Start Up Activity As students enter and get settled, draw their attention to the timeline. Encourage them to take a few minutes to digest the information the timeline provides before they answer the questions.

Discuss When they have completed their answers, consider working together as a group to reach a consensus answer on each question using information gleaned from the timeline. Direct students to use specific information from the timeline to support their responses.

Tell students that in this lesson they will explore the effects of slavery on African Americans and the key organizations and individuals involved in the debate about abolition.

Aa Vocabulary Development: Use the Interactive Reading Notepad to preview the Key Terms and Academic Vocabulary in this Lesson with students.

⇅ FLIP IT!
Assign the Flipped Video for this lesson.

■ STUDENT EDITION PRINT
PAGES: 211–217

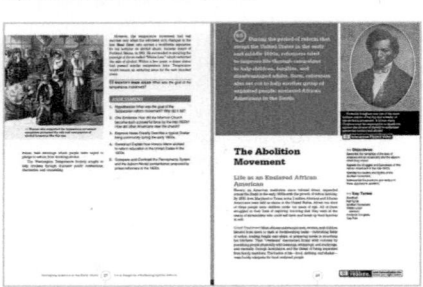

■ INVESTIGATE

DIGITAL TEXT 1
Life as an Enslaved African American

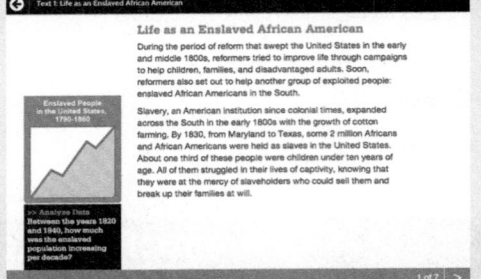

INTERACTIVE GALLERY
Resisting Slavery

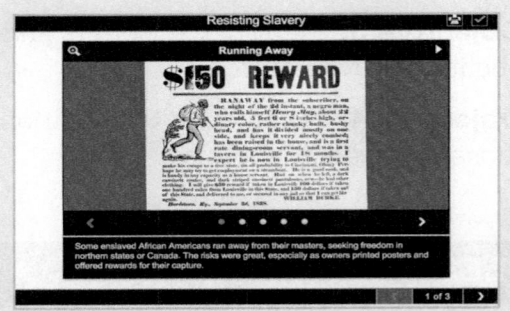

Objective 1: Describe the hardships of the lives of enslaved African Americans and the ways in which they coped.

Quick Instruction
Interactive Gallery: Resisting Slavery
Project the Interactive Gallery and navigate through the images with students to reveal information about how enslaved African Americans resisted slavery. Encourage students to hypothesize about why some enslaved African Americans were motivated to lead armed resistance movements while others were not. Suggest students think about the role of education, religion, and personal experiences of enslaved people when formulating their responses.

Cite Evidence What role did religion play in the lives of enslaved African Americans? *(Many enslaved people maintained their hope and their dignity by turning to religion to help them cope with their difficult lives.)*

▶ ACTIVE CLASSROOM
Conduct a Make Headlines activity for the Nat Turner and Denmark Vesey uprisings. Ask: If you were to write a headline for each uprising that captured the most important aspect that should be remembered, what would that headline be? Emphasize to students that their headlines should capture why each rebellion is significant. Allow them to use subheadings if they would like. Have students pass their headlines to a partner for them to review.

D Differentiate: Challenge Ask students to do additional research on Solomon Northup and present their findings.

Further Instruction
Initiate a discussion of the lives of enslaved African Americans by asking students to find examples of everyday conditions. *(Men, women, and children labored from dawn to dusk at backbreaking tasks; enslaved people were often punished physically with beatings, whippings, and maimings, and mentally, through humiliation and the threat of being separated from family members; food, clothing, and shelter were barely adequate.)*

Draw Conclusions How successful were slave revolts in helping enslaved African Americans resist slavery? *(The revolts were not very successful. The fear inspired by the revolts usually led to even harsher treatment of enslaved African Americans.)*

DIGITAL TEXT 2

Free African Americans

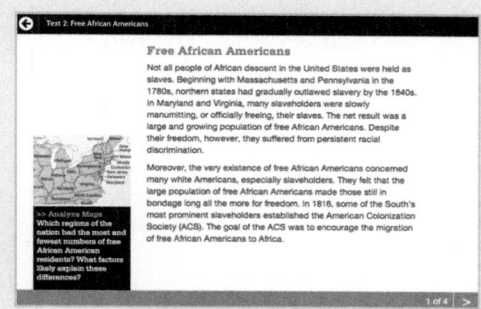

Text 2: Free African Americans

Free African Americans

Not all people of African descent in the United States were held as slaves. Beginning with Massachusetts and Pennsylvania in the 1780s, northern states had gradually outlawed slavery by the 1840s. In Maryland and Virginia, many slaveholders were slowly manumitting, or officially freeing, their slaves. The net result was a large and growing population of free African Americans. Despite their freedom, however, they suffered from persistent racial discrimination.

Moreover, the very existence of free African Americans concerned many white Americans, especially slaveholders. They felt that the large population of free African Americans made those still in bondage long all the more for freedom. In 1816, some of the South's most prominent slaveholders established the American Colonization Society (ACS). The goal of the ACS was to encourage the migration of free African Americans to Africa.

>> Analyze Maps Which regions of the nation had the most and fewest numbers of free African American residents? What factors likely explain these differences?

1 of 4 >

DIGITAL TEXT 3

The Antislavery Movement Grows

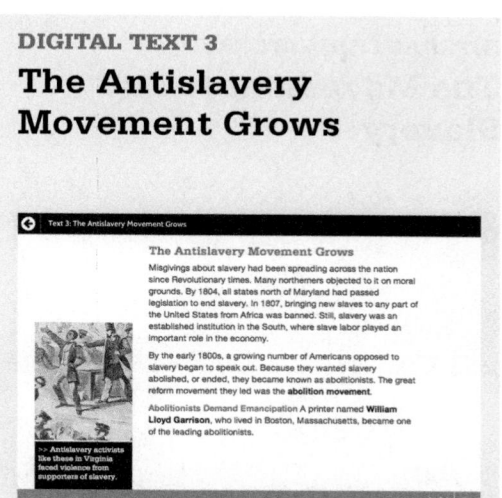

Text 3: The Antislavery Movement Grows

The Antislavery Movement Grows

Misgivings about slavery had been spreading across the nation since Revolutionary times. Many northerners objected to it on moral grounds. By 1804, all states north of Maryland had passed legislation to end slavery. In 1807, bringing new slaves to any part of the United States from Africa was banned. Still, slavery was an established institution in the South, where slave labor played an important role in the economy.

By the early 1800s, a growing number of Americans opposed to slavery began to speak out. Because they wanted slavery abolished, or ended, they became known as abolitionists. The great reform movement they led was the **abolition movement**.

Abolitionists Demand Emancipation A printer named **William Lloyd Garrison**, who lived in Boston, Massachusetts, became one of the leading abolitionists.

>> Antislavery activists like these in Virginia faced violence from supporters of slavery.

1 of 4 >

Objective 2: Explain the struggles and successes of free African Americans in the mid-1800s.

Quick Instruction

Present the map showing the population of Free African Americans in 1850. Ask students to describe trends on the map. Ask them to generate explanations of why Maryland would have more free African Americans per square mile than Massachusetts. *(Possible response: Maryland would have had a larger number of African Americans than Massachusetts because of the type of economy in Maryland.)*

Further Instruction

Go through the Interactive Reading Notepad questions and use appropriate questions to begin a discussion about free African Americans. Ask students to identify the challenges free African Americans faced. *(persistent racial discrimination)*

Evaluate Arguments According to David Walker, what would be the effect of the abolition of slavery on the country? *(Walker basically states that if slavery is abolished, all previous injustice would be forgotten. If treated equally, African Americans would become productive citizens and the country would become united.)*

Apply Concepts How did the Second Great Awakening influence the work of free African Americans trying to help those still enslaved? *(The religious views embraced during the Second Great Awakening, such as tolerance and equality for all, were fundamentally incompatible with the institution of slavery. Many people, regardless of race, supported the partial or full ending of slavery.)*

Objective 3: Identify the leaders and tactics of the abolition movement.

Quick Instruction

Interactive Gallery: The Movement to End Slavery Project the Interactive Gallery and select the hot spots as students read quotes from key abolitionists and learn more about their views. What argument does Angelina Grimké use to promote the abolitionist cause? *(Grimké uses the traditional philosophical "Golden Rule" to argue her case: Treat others as you would like to be treated.)*

▣▣ ACTIVE CLASSROOM

Conduct a Circle Write activity. Have students break into groups to address the prompt, "How did the views of prominent abolitionists differ?" Have students write as much as they can for one minute and then switch with the person on their right. The next person tries to improve or elaborate the response where the other person left off. Continue to switch until the paper comes back to the first person. The group decides which is the best composition and shares it with the class.

Summarize William Lloyd Garrison's role in the Abolition Movement. *(Garrison started his own antislavery newspaper, The Liberator . Garrison's publication was notable for its use of dramatic language and moral suasion. He also formed the American Anti-Slavery Society,*

The Abolition Movement

INTERACTIVE GALLERY

The Movement to End Slavery

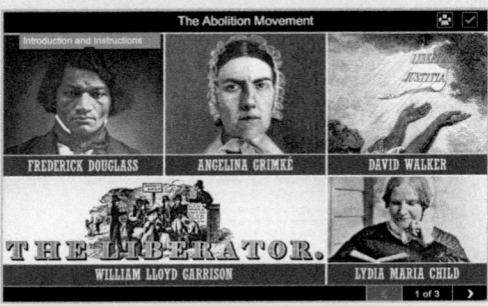

DIGITAL TEXT 4

The Backlash Against Abolition

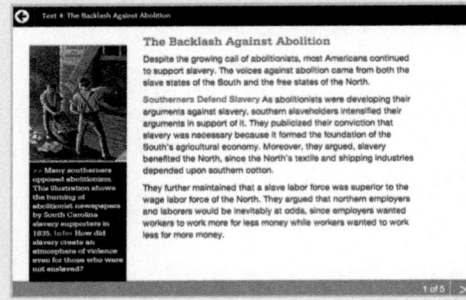

an abolitionist association which boasted over 150,000 members across the nation. He advocated immediate emancipation and the extension of full political and social rights to African Americans.

Contrast How did Theodore Weld's tactics differ from those of William Lloyd Garrison? *(Although Weld shared Garrison's belief in the power of moral suasion, Weld chose to work through the churches rather than resorting to public confrontation as Garrison did.).*

ELL Use the ELL activity described in the ELL chart.

Further Instruction

Initiate a discussion by asking students to think about their personal experiences in trying to persuade someone to change their opinions or point of view. Invite volunteers to describe specific instances and the methods of persuasion they used and if they were successful. Discuss how various methods of persuasion can affect the outcome of a disagreement.

Infer Why might Frederick Douglass have had more of an impact than other abolitionists? *(Douglass was a former slave who could give personal accounts of the cruel treatment of enslaved African Americans, making his arguments much more persuasive.)*

Compare What similarities were there in the way the American Anti-Slavery Society and the evangelical preachers of the Second Great Awakening spread their messages? *(Both stressed religious ideals to people at large camp meetings and other public gatherings.)*

Objective 4: Summarize the positions and tactics of those opposed to abolition.

Quick Instruction

Direct students' attention to the illustration depicting the burning of Elijah Lovejoy's printing press in 1837. Be sure students understand that many northerners as well as southerners were opposed to abolition. Point out that Elijah Lovejoy's printing operation was located in the free state of Illinois. Ask students to locate other examples of northern opposition to abolition. *(William Lloyd Garrison was chased through the streets by an angry mob as a result of his antislavery views. In Philadelphia in 1838, the Grimké-Weld wedding, attended by both white and black guests, so infuriated local residents that they burned down the antislavery meeting hall. A passive acceptance of slavery was widespread.)*

Determine Point of View According to many southern supporters of slavery, how did the North benefit from slavery? *(They claimed that slavery benefited the North because the North's textile and shipping industries depended upon southern cotton.)*

ELL Use the ELL activity described in the ELL chart.

Further Instruction

Go through the Interactive Reading Notepad questions and use appropriate questions to begin a discussion about the resistance to the Abolition Movement. Be sure students understand the concept of manumission *(officially freeing enslaved people)*

Identify Cause and Effect What led to the decline of manumission in the South? *(Southern spokespeople stepped up their arguments about the value of slavery, and southern slaveholders tried to prevent southerners from reading abolitionist publications. Post offices refused to deliver abolitionist newspapers.)*

Summarize the reason many white northern workers did not support the Abolition Movement. *(Many white workers feared that African Americans would take their jobs.)*

A.
B.
C.

SYNTHESIZE

DIGITAL ACTIVITY
Resisting Slavery

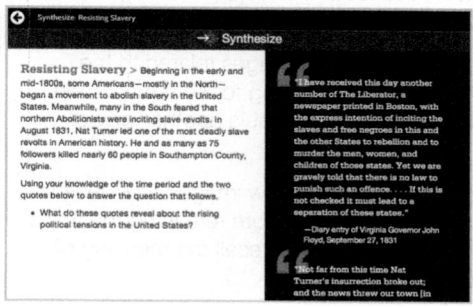

Call on two students to read aloud the quotes. Ask students to discuss the following question in small groups: What do these quotes reveal about the rising political tensions in the United States? Have groups share their ideas in response. Direct students to highlight key phrases or words that support their positions.

Discuss Challenge students to Take a Stand and determine whether they agree or disagree with Governor John Floyd's statement at the end of his quote. (". . . If this is not checked it must lead to a separation of these states.") Split the room into groups according to their responses, and instruct groups to discuss their rationales. Then, have each group appoint a spokesperson to present their position and reasoning.

DEMONSTRATE

DIGITAL QUIZ
Lesson Quiz and Class Discussion Board

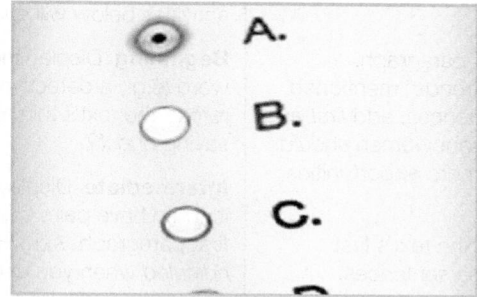

Assign the online Lesson Quiz for this lesson if you haven't already done so. Students will be offered automatic remediation or enrichment based on their score.

Pose these questions to the class on the Discussion Board:

In *The Abolition Movement*, you learned about the forces that sparked the Abolition Movement in the 1800s. You also examined the roles of key organizations and individuals in the Abolition Movement and their motivations and goals.

Generate Explanations Supporters of abolition used a variety of tactics to persuade fellow Americans to support the ending of slavery. In your opinion, which tactics were most effective? Explain.

Predict Consequences What will result from many northerner's passive acceptance of slavery?

Topic Inquiry
Have students continued their investigations for their Topic Inquiry.

Women Work for Change

Supporting English Language Learners

Use with the reading, **Women Seek Expanded Rights**.

Speaking
Explain to students that *conjunctions* can make spoken communication more effective. Define *conjunctions* as words and phrases that connect ideas and show the relationship between them.

Beginning Point out *first* and *second* in the text's first paragraph. Explain that these words introduce the "two historical trends" mentioned previously. Then have students order the following sentences, add *first* and *second* to two of them and say them aloud: They thought women should be treated equally. They thought women should have more opportunities. Reformers had many ideas about women's rights.

Intermediate Point out the use of *first* and *second* in the text's first paragraph. Then have students complete and say these sentences: Reformers had many ideas about women's rights. First, _____ . Second, _____.

Advanced Point out the use of *although* and *however* in the text. Ask: What is the purpose of these words? How are they similar and different? Guide students to practice using each conjunction as they make statements about the text.

Advanced High Point out the conjunctions *although* and *however* in the text. Have pairs of students compare and contrast their meanings and usage. Then have them use these conjunctions as they discuss the core issues of the women's movement.

Use with the reading, **The Seneca Falls Convention**.

Reading
Explain that forming mental images of words—through pictures or role-play, for example—can help students to recall the words' meanings. The activities below will encourage the formation of mental images.

Beginning Display the word *quest* , along with images related to the word (e.g., a detective, a knight). Act out its meaning for students. Then reread the text's third paragraph together. Ask: What is another way of saying *quest*?

Intermediate Display the word *ridiculed* , and show images that depict it. Then have pairs of students act out the word before rereading the text's first paragraph. Ask: How did this activity help you recall the meaning of *ridiculed* when you encountered it?

Advanced Display the word *illustrious*, and discuss its meaning. Invite students to draw pictures that depict this word. Have students share their pictures with one another and then reread the text's first paragraph.

Advanced High Ask students to look up the definitions of *attracted* and *illustrious*, reread the text's first paragraph, and then draw a single picture that depicts both words and relates to the text. Ask: How did this activity add more meaning to the text?

▣ Differentiate Instruction

Use the Differentiated Instruction notes throughout the lesson plan to support the varied skill sets, levels of readiness, and interests in the mixed-ability classroom.

Challenge These notes include suggestions for expanding the activity for advanced students.

On-Level These notes include suggestions for modifying the activity to address different interests or learning styles.

Extra Support These notes include ideas for providing more scaffolding or reading spuport.

Special Needs These notes provide ideas for adapting instruction to support the needs of various special needs students.

◼ NOTES

PEARSON
realize™
www.PearsonRealize.com

Go online to access additional resources including:
Primary Sources • Biographies • Supreme Court cases •
21st Century Skill Tutorials • Maps • Graphic Organizers.

Objectives

Objective 1: Identify the limits faced by American women in the early 1800s.

Objective 2: Trace the development of the women's movement.

Objective 3: Describe the Seneca Falls Convention and its effects.

LESSON 6 ORGANIZER		PACING: APPROX. 1 PERIOD, .5 BLOCKS			
				RESOURCES	
		OBJECTIVES	**PACING**	**Online**	**Print**
Connect					
DIGITAL START UP ACTIVITY **Equality for Women**			5 min.	●	
Investigate					
DIGITAL TEXT 1 **Women Fight for Reforms**		Objective 1	10 min.	●	●
DIGITAL TEXT 2 **Women Seek Expanded Rights**		Objective 2	10 min.	●	●
INTERACTIVE TIMELINE **The Early Women's Rights Movement**			10 min.	●	
DIGITAL TEXT 3 **The Seneca Falls Convention**		Objective 3	10 min.	●	●
INTERACTIVE CHART **Analyzing Primary Sources on Women's Rights**			10 min.	●	
Synthesize					
DIGITAL ACTIVITY **Women's Movement Leaders**			5 min.	●	
Demonstrate					
DIGITAL QUIZ **Lesson Quiz and Class Discussion Board**			10 min.	●	

Women Work for Change

■ CONNECT

DIGITAL START UP ACTIVITY
Equality for Women

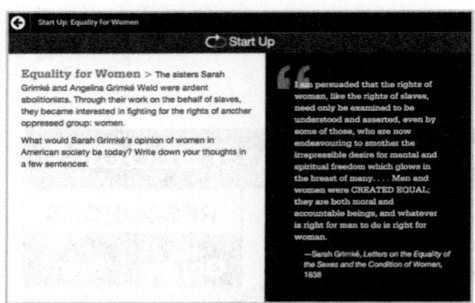

Project the Start Up Activity Ask students to read and reflect on the excerpt from Sarah Grimké as they enter and get settled. Have student partners think about and discuss their views on the role of women in American society today. Then have students answer the question on the interactivity individually and share their responses with another student, either in class or through a chat or blog space.

Discuss Ask: If you were a woman in the mid-1800s, how would you have felt about being denied basic rights like voting, property ownership, and equal access to education and economic opportunities? What would you have done to address your concerns?

Aa **Vocabulary Development:** Use the Interactive Reading Notepad to preview the Key Terms and Academic Vocabulary in this lesson with students.

⮏ FLIP IT!
Assign the Flipped Video for this lesson.

■ STUDENT EDITION PRINT
PAGES: 218–222

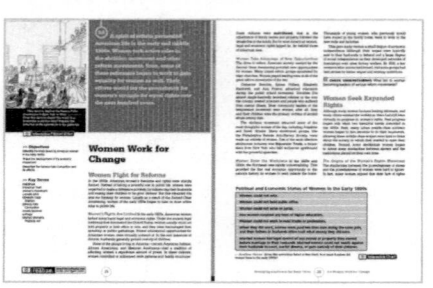

■ INVESTIGATE

DIGITAL TEXT 1
Women Fight for Reforms

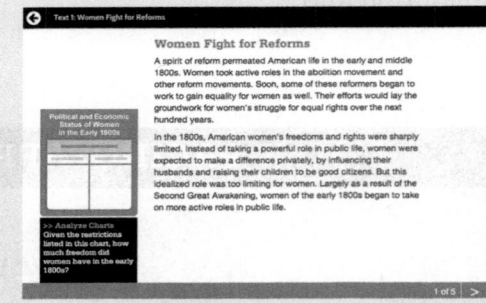

Objective 1: Identify the limits faced by American women in the early 1800s.

Quick Instruction

Direct students' focus to the photograph of Catharine Beecher. Explain that Beecher was an American author and educator who focused on equal education opportunities for women. Invite volunteers to share what they learned about the educational opportunities available to women in the 19th century and why many viewed education as such an important issue for women to address. *(Education provided a person with greater knowledge, better and more financial and social status, as well as independence.)* Ensure student understanding of the concepts of *patrilineal (inheritance of family names and property following the male line in a family)*, *matrilineal (inheritance of family names and property following the female line in a family)* and *primogeniture (traditional feudal rule by which family estates passed to the eldest son)*.

Infer Why do you think women's rights were so limited in the early years of the country? *(The United States was still greatly influenced by British legal traditions under which women usually could not hold property or hold office or vote, and they usually were discouraged from speaking in public gatherings.)*

Further Instruction

Continue the discussion about the limits faced by American women in the early 1800s by reviewing the progress women made because of the Second Great Awakening and the role women played in many of the social reform movements. *(Students might mention the growing power women displayed in the prison, educational, temperance, and abolition movements and the emergence of influential activists, such as Dorothea Dix, Elizabeth Blackwell, Ann Preston, Angelina and Sarah Grimké, and Emma Willard.)*

Generate Explanations How did industrialization in the United States increase opportunities for women? *(The larger workforce needed to operate factories created opportunities for women to work outside the home. This gave women their first real economic opportunity in the nation's history and gave many women a small degree of economic and social independence.)*

Draw Conclusions How did the rights of women in the 1800s go against modern interpretations of the Constitution? *(Women were not treated equally; they did not have the same opportunities because of gender discrimination, which is counter to the view today that the Constitution protects these rights.)*

DIGITAL TEXT 2

Women Seek Expanded Rights

INTERACTIVE TIMELINE

The Early Women's Rights Movement

DIGITAL TEXT 3

The Seneca Falls Convention

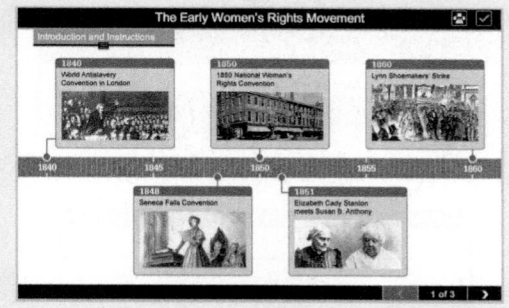

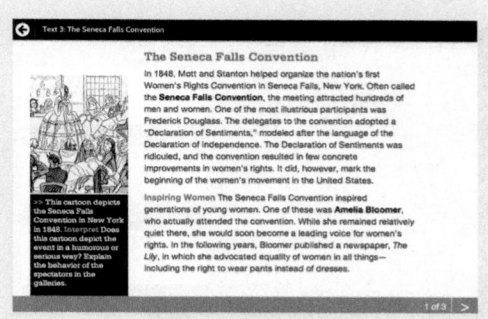

Objective 2: Trace the development of the women's movement.

Quick Instruction

Interactive Timeline: The Early Women's Rights Movement Project the Interactive Timeline and navigate through the images with students, prompting them to explain the significance of each event. Begin by challenging students to make generalizations about women's roles in American society in the mid-1880s. *(Possible generalizations include that women had limited rights and educational opportunities, and restricted personal freedoms, and so on.)* Tell students that the timeline helps trace the historical development of the early civil rights movement for women in the 19th century.

▶ ACTIVE CLASSROOM

Conduct a Make a Headline activity for an event from the timeline. Have each student select one historical figure or event. Ask: If you were to write a headline for your chosen individual or event that captured the most important aspect that should be remembered, what would that headline be? Encourage students to use subheadings to convey the significance of their event or individual. Have students pass their headlines to a partner for them to review.

ELL Use the ELL activity described in the ELL chart.

Further Instruction

Compare What similar ideas did abolitionists and women's rights reformers hold? *(Both groups of reformers argued that God made all people equal and that therefore men and women should be treated equally. Many also argued for equality on moral grounds, proposing that all human beings have rights, because they are moral beings.)*

Determine Relevance What effect did the international abolitionists' convention in London in 1840 have on Elizabeth Cady Stanton and Lucretia Mott? *(Stanton and Mott were outraged that women were refused full participation at a meeting to discuss the promotion of human decency and equality. The experience inspired them to take a dramatic step to advance women's rights by organizing the nation's first Women's Rights Convention in Seneca Falls, New York, in 1848, marking the beginning of the women's movement in the United States.)*

Objective 3: Describe the Seneca Falls Convention and its effects.

Quick Instruction

Interactive Chart: Analyzing Primary Sources on Women's Rights Project the Interactive Chart. Discuss each quote and work through each with students to clarify any vocabulary or syntax that is unclear. Ask students to paraphrase key ideas in each quote in their own words. Ask students whether they agree with each decision, and why.

Connect How did the creators of the Seneca Falls Declaration of Sentiments and Resolutions try to appeal to the ideals of American Democracy to advance their cause? *(The Declaration of Sentiments and Resolutions was written in language modeled on that of the Declaration of Independence.)*

▶ ACTIVE CLASSROOM

Conduct a Sticky Notes activity. Have students take three minutes to jot down their ideas about Frederick Douglass's arguments for equal rights and opportunities for women in American society. Then ask, "Which argument is the most persuasive?" Have students post their stickies on a wall, then sort and discuss their responses as a group.

Women Work for Change

INTERACTIVE CHART
Analyzing Primary Sources on Women's Rights

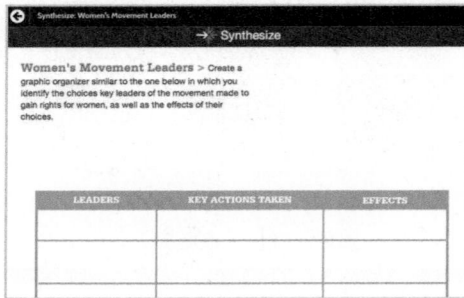

SYNTHESIZE

DIGITAL ACTIVITY
Women's Movement Leaders

DEMONSTRATE

DIGITAL QUIZ
Lesson Quiz and Class Discussion Board

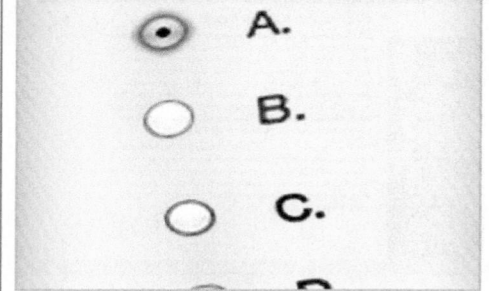

D **Differentiate: Extra Support** Some students may struggle with the style of writing Douglass uses. Provide opportunities for these students to work with a partner or work individually with students to ensure understanding.

ELL Use the ELL activity described in the ELL chart.

Further Instruction
Go through the Interactive Reading Notepad questions and use appropriate questions as a springboard to begin a discussion about the Seneca Falls Convention. To enhance students' understanding of the convention and of using primary source materials, assign Primary Sources: Seneca Falls Declaration of Sentiments and Resolutions.

Distinguish How did the Married Women's Property Act break from the traditional view of property rights for women? *(The New York state law guaranteed many property rights for women that had been denied them in the past. At the time, many women were only able to own property through their husbands and were not allowed to inherit property.)*

Discuss Before students begin their graphic organizers, lead a brief discussion to ensure student understanding of the limits faced by American women in the early 1800s and the basic rights that they were denied.

Assign the online Lesson Quiz for this lesson if you haven't already done so. Students will be offered automatic remediation or enrichment based on their score.

Pose these questions to the class on the Discussion Board:

In *Women Work for Change*, you read about how in the wake of the Second Great Awakening, women took advantage of new educational and employment opportunities. Full equality, however, had not been realized. To achieve this goal, reformers of both genders forged a lasting movement that laid the foundation for the modern women's rights movement.

Cite Evidence What steps did American women take to advance their rights in the mid-1800s?

Support Ideas with Evidence Have women achieved full equality in American society today? Give evidence for your position.

Topic Inquiry
Have students continue their investigations for the Topic Inquiry.

Reshaping America in the Early 1800s

■ SYNTHESIZE

DIGITAL ACTIVITY
Reflect on the Essential Question and Topic

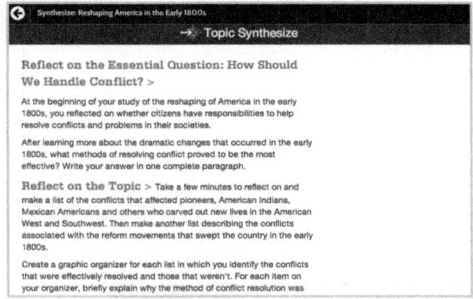

First ask students to reconsider the Essential Question for the topic: How should we handle conflict? Tell them to review their responses to the Essential Question Activity. Have them revise any parts of the responses as needed.

Organize students into small groups. Direct each group to identify two social problems reformers worked to solve and the methods they used. Then direct students to work individually to answer the question, What methods of resolving conflict proved to be the most effective? Call on volunteers to share their ideas with the class, or post their responses in the class discussion board.

Next ask students to reflect on the Topic as a whole and jot down 1-3 questions they've thought about during the Topic. Share these examples if students need help getting started:

- How might Spanish and American colonists have avoided conflict with American Indians in the Southwest?
- Was Manifest Destiny morally justified? Why or why not?
- What motivates someone to lead or take part in a reform movement?

You may ask students to share their questions and answers on the Class Discussion Board.

Topic Inquiry
Have students complete Step 3 of the Topic Inquiry.

■ DEMONSTRATE

DIGITAL TOPIC REVIEW AND ASSESSMENT
Reshaping America in the Early 1800s

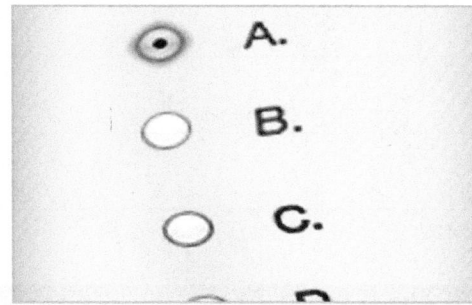

Students can prepare for the Topic Test by answering the questions in the Topic Review and Assessment online or the Assessment questions in the Print Student text. They can also prepare by reviewing their answers to the Interactive Reading Notepad questions or reviewing their notes in the Reading and Notetaking Study Guide.

DIGITAL TOPIC TEST
Reshaping America in the Early 1800s

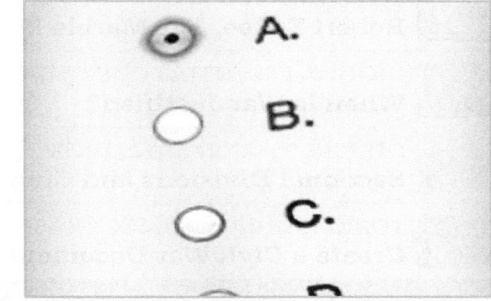

TOPIC TEST
Assign the Topic Test to assess students' understanding of topic content.

BENCHMARK TESTS
Assign these benchmark tests as you complete the relevant topics to monitor student progress toward mastering the course content and as preparation for the End-of-Course Test.

Benchmark Test 1: Topics 1–3
Benchmark Test 2: Topics 4–6
Benchmark Test 3: Topics 7–9
Benchmark Test 4: Topics 10–12
Benchmark Test 5: Topics 13–15
Benchmark Test 6: Topics 16–18
Benchmark Test 7: Topics 19–20

Topic 7

Sectional Divisions and Civil War

TOPIC 7 ORGANIZER	PACING: APPROX. 10 PERIODS, 5 BLOCKS
	PACING
Connect	1 period
MY STORY VIDEO **Robert E. Lee, The Marble Man**	10 min.
DIGITAL ESSENTIAL QUESTION ACTIVITY **When Is War Justified?**	10 min.
DIGITAL TIMELINE ACTIVITY **Sectional Divisions and Civil War**	10 min.
TOPIC INQUIRY: PROJECT-BASED LEARNING **Create a Civil War Documentary**	20 min.
Investigate	3–7 periods
TOPIC INQUIRY: PROJECT-BASED LEARNING **Create a Civil War Documentary**	Ongoing
LESSON 1 Slavery Divides the Nation	30–40 min.
LESSON 2 Violence Escalates	30–40 min.
LESSON 3 The Civil War Begins	30–40 min.
LESSON 4 African Americans and the War	30–40 min.
LESSON 5 Everyday Life During the War	30–40 min.
LESSON 6 Key Civil War Battles	30–40 min.
LESSON 7 Impact of the Civil War	30–40 min.
Synthesize	1 period
DIGITAL ACTIVITY **Reflect on the Essential Question and Topic**	10 min.
TOPIC INQUIRY: PROJECT-BASED LEARNING **Create a Civil War Documentary**	20 min.
Demonstrate	1–2 periods
DIGITAL ACTIVITY **Reflect on the Essential Question and Topic**	10 min.
TOPIC INQUIRY: PROJECT-BASED LEARNING **Create a Civil War Documentary**	20 min.

realize™

TOPIC INQUIRY: PROJECT-BASED LEARNING

Create a Civil War Documentary

In this Topic Inquiry, students work in teams to research the lives of Americans who lived during the Civil War and to create a documentary based on those subjects. Learning how the war impacted specific individuals will contribute to students' ability to answer the Topic Essential Question: When is war justified?

STEP 1: CONNECT
Develop Questions and Plan the Investigation

Launch the Project
Read the *Project Launch* with the class and watch the video. Then, divide the class into five teams and have them review the *Student Instructions*. Allow students to ask clarifying questions about the project.

Prepare the Investigation
Allow teams time to review the *Project Contract* and begin to organize the workload. Post in the classroom for student reference the Guiding Question: How did ordinary citizens experience the Civil War and explain the justifications for war? Have teams generate their own questions and answer the example questions from Step 1B of the *Student Instructions*.

Suggestion: Review the *Rubric for a Civil War Documentary* as a class to make sure students know what is expected from the project. If time is limited, have students create questions as homework and combine their questions as a team during class time.

Resources
- Project Launch
- Student Instructions
- Project Contract
- Rubric for a Civil War Documentary

⏻ PROFESSIONAL DEVELOPMENT

Project-Based Learning
Be sure to view the Project-Based Learning Professional Development resources in the online course.

STEP 2: INVESTIGATE
Apply Disciplinary Concepts and Tools

Assign Roles and Conduct Research
If you have not already done so, divide students into five teams and have each team choose a project manager. Then, have teams turn to the *Project Tracker* to assign the remaining roles.

Suggestion: Address the sensitivities of assigning roles of different races by discussing the atmosphere of discrimination and prejudice of the Civil War era. Instruct students who are assigned to African American and American Indian roles to be sure to include in their reenactments the effects of the added challenge of facing the overwhelming inequality that existed throughout the nation.

Have teams review the *Student Instructions* and begin research. Guide teams to divide research either by person or by type. For example, one student might search for pertinent maps while another searches for primary source quotations.

Suggestion: Students should use the list of sources as a starting point for research. As they visit each site, they can search it for relevant sources.

Review Your Artifact Choices
Have teams review the criteria and choose artifacts based on their evaluations. Tell students to also keep in mind how well the artifacts will present in a documentary.

Write an Outline for Your Storyboard
Have Storyboard Writers lead the team discussion as members work together to outline the storyboard for the documentary. Tell Storyboard Writers to be sure to take thorough notes as they create outlines.

Resources
- Student Instructions
- Project Tracker

 TOPIC INQUIRY: PROJECT-BASED LEARNING

Create a Civil War Documentary *(continued)*

STEP 3: SYNTHESIZE
Create a Storyboard, Script, and Edited Documentary

Create and Revise Your Storyboard
Have Storyboard Writers consult the outline from Step 2 to create a fleshed-out storyboard for the team documentary. Instruct students to read the questions in Step 3A of the *Student Instructions* to guide their work. Then, have Storyboard Writers present their work to their teams, allowing time for input and adjustment.

Write Your Script
Decide as a team if you want to create a strict script that reenactors will memorize or if you want to create a concept script that guides reenactors as they improvise "personal" answers that align with the subject and time period.

Suggestion: Before finalizing the script, teams should read everything aloud to make sure the writing does not sound stilted or uncomfortable.

Create and Edit Your Documentary
Discuss the school's policies concerning photography and distribute media resources as necessary. Point out that most documentaries go through extensive editing, so students should not expect to get the final work in "one shot."

Suggestion: If media resources are not available for filming, have teams practice a stage version of the documentary.

Resources
• Student Instructions

STEP 4: DEMONSTRATE
Communicate Conclusions and Take Informed Action

Present Your Documentary and Reflect on the Project
Schedule a "film festival" in which teams introduce documentaries, show their work, and answer questions afterward. Suggest that students post their films on a class website or blog.

After students have completed and shared their documentaries, lead a class discussion in which students reflect on what they have learned and share the opinions they have formed and the reasoning behind those opinions. Ask students how they predict this new-found understanding of how war affects individual's lives will impact their perspectives on the justifications for historical and present-day wars.

Suggestion: As an extension activity, have students debate their responses to the Essential Question: When is war justified?

Resources
• Student Instructions

INTRODUCTION

Sectional Divisions and Civil War

The years leading up to the Civil War were marked by sectionalism and tension over the issues of states' rights and slavery. Abraham Lincoln's victory in the presidential election of 1860 prompted southern states to secede from the Union. When Lincoln took office in 1861, he did all that he could to prevent war but was unsuccessful. A brilliant statesman, Lincoln negotiated the war years with steadfast resolve to preserve the Union. In the end, the Union was victorious, though the country was left in shambles and faced with the challenges of reunification and rebuilding.

CONNECT

MY STORY VIDEO

Robert E. Lee, The Marble Man

Watch a video about Robert E. Lee's leadership at the Battle of Chancellorsville.

Check Understanding How was Robert E. Lee able to win victory at Chancellorsville? *(His risky decision to divide his forces resulted in a major victory for the South. However, the Confederate side suffered many casualties, among them General Stonewall Jackson.)*

Determine Point of View When the Civil War broke out, Robert E. Lee was offered command of the Union forces, but he chose to fight for the South. Why do you think he made that decision? *(A native Virginian, his desire to defend his home state from Union attack no doubt overruled his desire to see the Union be kept intact.)*

DIGITAL ESSENTIAL QUESTION ACTIVITY

When Is War Justified?

Ask students to think about the Essential Question for this Topic: When is war justified? Countries often enter war for religious beliefs, political differences, and border disputes.

If students have not already done so, have them read the quotation and record their responses to the questions.

Express Ideas Clearly In your own words, summarize Lincoln's argument. *(Because the Constitution has no provision for the government's termination, any state that tries to undermine the federal government should be seen as a revolutionary and must be stopped.)*

Evaluate Arguments Is Lincoln's reasoning sound? Explain. *(Possible response: Yes. He establishes the argument that the Constitution does not allow for the federal government's termination by the states that comprise that government.)*

Generate Explanations How might a state that had seceded respond to this argument? *(Possible response: Because the federal government no longer provided protection and threatened harm to the economy and way of life, it was no longer a guiding authority and should be abandoned.)*

DIGITAL TIMELINE ACTIVITY

Sectional Divisions and Civil War

Display the timeline of major events in the Civil War. During this Topic, students will learn about all these events and many more. This timeline will provide a framework into which students can place the events they learn about as they study the topic.

Analyze Information What do the Compromise of 1850 and the Kansas-Nebraska Act have in common? *(They attempted to address the equality between free and slaveholding states in the Union.)*

Topic Inquiry

Launch the Topic Inquiry with students after introducing the topic.

Slavery Divides the Nation

Supporting English Language Learners

Use with the text reading, **Slavery's Effect on the 1848 Election**.

Learning
Discuss the benefits and challenges of monitoring one's speaking effectiveness, either while speaking or after the fact.

Beginning Read aloud the last paragraph of the text, pausing after each phrase so students can repeat after you. Encourage them to imitate both your pronunciation and your intonation. Afterward, have students reflect on their efforts.

Intermediate Invite students to record themselves reading the text's last paragraph and then to listen to the recording. Ask: What did you notice about your reading as you were reading? What did you notice as you were listening to the recording? What aspect of speaking will you try to improve upon?

Advanced Invite pairs of students to record a discussion of each political party's position in the 1848 election. Have them assess their speaking efforts before and after listening to the recording. Ask: What strengths and weaknesses did you notice about your speaking?

Advanced High Invite pairs of students to discuss the importance of the Free-Soil Party, including how things might have been different if it had not existed. As they speak, have students jot down difficulties and successes regarding their speaking efforts. Afterward, have them review their notes.

Use with the reading, **The Compromise of 1850 Averts a Crisis**.

Listening
Explain that one way for students to monitor their listening comprehension is periodically to retell or summarize what they think a speaker is saying, either silently or back to the speaker for confirmation.

Beginning In a few simple sentences, tell students how California became a state. Then help students to summarize what you said with these questions: What subject did I speak about? What did I say about it?

Intermediate Tell students about the Compromise of 1850, including some details not found in the text. Next, have them summarize what you said. Begin by asking them for your main point and then ask them to follow up with specific details.

Advanced Invite pairs of students to take turns telling about either Calhoun's or Webster's position on Henry Clay's proposal. After each student speaks, have his or her partner retell what was said.

Advanced High Place students in pairs, and invite each partner to choose either Calhoun's or Webster's position on Henry Clay's proposal. Have them research their chosen topic, looking for details not found in the text. Then have them present their research aloud to each other, while their partner retells what was said.

▣ Differentiate Instruction

Use the Differentiated Instruction notes throughout the lesson plan to support the varied skill sets, levels of readiness, and interests in the mixed-ability classroom.

Challenge These notes include suggestions for expanding the activity for advanced students.

On-Level These notes include suggestions for modifying the activity to address different interests or learning styles.

Extra Support These notes include ideas for providing more scaffolding or reading spuort.

Special Needs These notes provide ideas for adapting instruction to support the needs of various special needs students.

▮ NOTES

PEARSON
realize™
www.PearsonRealize.com

Go online to access additional resources including:
Primary Sources • Biographies • Supreme Court cases •
21st Century Skill Tutorials • Maps • Graphic Organizers.

Objectives

Objective 1: Contrast the economies, societies, and political views of the North and the South.

Objective 2: Describe the role of the Free-Soil Party in the election of 1848.

Objective 3: Analyze why slavery in the territories was a divisive issue between North and South and how Congress tried to settle the issue in 1850.

Objective 4: Analyze why the Fugitive Slave Act increased tensions between the North and South.

LESSON 1 ORGANIZER		PACING: APPROX. 1 PERIOD, .5 BLOCKS			
				RESOURCES	
		OBJECTIVES	**PACING**	**Online**	**Print**
Connect					
DIGITAL START UP ACTIVITY **Slavery and States' Rights**			5 min.	●	
Investigate					
DIGITAL TEXT 1 **Different Perspectives on the Issue of Slavery**		Objective 1	10 min.	●	●
DIGITAL TEXT 2 **Slavery's Effect on the 1848 Election**		Objective 2	10 min.	●	●
DIGITAL TEXT 3 **The Compromise of 1850 Averts a Crisis**		Objective 3	10 min.	●	●
INTERACTIVE CHART **Causes and Effects of Sectional Issues in the 1800s**			10 min.	●	
DIGITAL TEXT 4 **Northern Resistance to Slavery Increases**		Objective 4	10 min.	●	●
INTERACTIVE MAP **The Underground Railroad**			10 min.	●	
Synthesize					
DIGITAL ACTIVITY **Contrasting Opinions Over Slavery in the Union**			5 min.	●	
Demonstrate					
DIGITAL QUIZ **Lesson Quiz and Discussion Board**			10 min.	●	

Slavery Divides the Nation

■ CONNECT

DIGITAL START UP ACTIVITY

Slavery and States' Rights

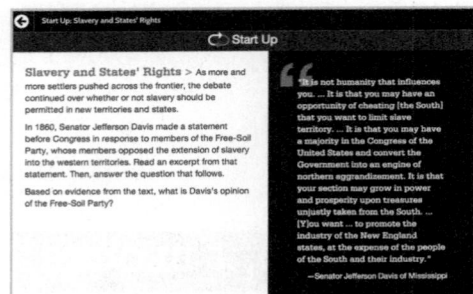

Project the Start Up Activity Have students read the quotation and answer the question as they enter the classroom. Then ask them to share and discuss their ideas with partners.

Discuss Based on evidence from the text, what is Davis's opinion of the Free-Soil Party? *(He believes the Free-Soil Party is not so much antislavery as anti-South.)*

Tell students that in this lesson they will be learning about the economic and political differences between the North and the South, the role of the Free-Soil Party in the 1848 election, and how the issue of slavery continued to divide the country.

Aa Vocabulary Development: Use the Interactive Reading Notepad to preview the Key Terms and Academic Vocabulary in this lesson with students.

⇅ FLIP IT!

Assign the Flipped Video for this lesson.

■ STUDENT EDITION PRINT PAGES: 228–236

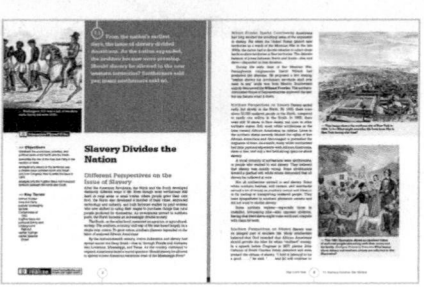

■ INVESTIGATE

DIGITAL TEXT 1

Different Perspectives on the Issue of Slavery

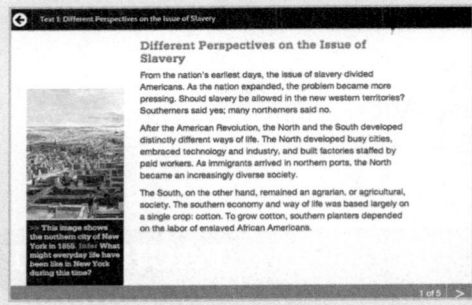

Objective 1: Contrast the economies, societies, and political views of the North and the South.

Quick Instruction

Explain to students that the differences between the North and the South are often simplified into pro- and antislavery, but the issues were more complex than that. Discuss some of the key differences, contrasting the North's industrial, wage-labor economy with the South's agricultural, slave-based economy. Point out that many northerners were not abolitionists but generally wanted to contain slavery in the southern states.

Draw Conclusions How could northerners benefit from slavery when it was not practiced in the North? *(Northerners relied on raw goods produced in the South by slave labor, such as cotton and tobacco, to supplement northern industrial production.)*

D Differentiate: Extra Support Prompt students to understand that the southern economy relied on slave labor. As a result, it was important for the states in the South to have enough representation in the federal government to protect their economic interests.

Further Instruction

Compare Points of View How did many people in the North and South feel about slavery? *(People in the North were divided on the issue of slavery. A few abolitionists wanted it to end, but most wanted to contain the institution in the South. The freedom of many African Americans in the North, however, was limited, and they were often perceived as inferior. Many in the South supported slavery on economic grounds. Many southerners viewed any attempt to limit slavery as an attack on the southern way of life.)*

Infer Why was the Wilmot Proviso so controversial? *(The Wilmot Proviso tried to limit the spread of slavery by declaring territory won from Mexico during the war "free." Southerners, however, feared the political balance of power in the nation would swing to the free states if the proviso was accepted.)*

DIGITAL TEXT 2

Slavery's Effect on the 1848 Election

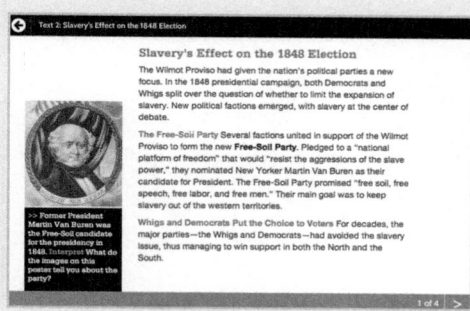

DIGITAL TEXT 3

The Compromise of 1850 Averts a Crisis

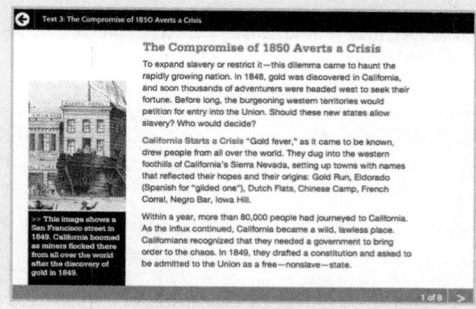

Objective 2: Describe the role of the Free-Soil Party in the election of 1848.

Quick Instruction

Explain that the issue of slavery was at the forefront of the presidential election of 1848. The Free-Soil candidate Martin Van Buren took enough votes to cost the Democrats the election, leaving the Whig Party's candidate Zachary Taylor as the winner.

Connect What relationship did the Free-Soil Party have with the idea of popular sovereignty in the 1848 election? *(The Free-Soil Party openly supported keeping slavery out of the western territories, as shown by their embrace of the Wilmot Proviso. With the Free-Soil Party making slavery an issue in the election, the Whigs and Democrats reluctantly stepped into the public debate over slavery. Instead of choosing sides in the issue, both older parties simply supported the idea of popular sovereignty to shift the burden of choosing one side or another to individual states.)*

Hypothesize How can a losing third party affect the balance in an election? *(Even though the party does not win, it garners enough support to weaken one of the other parties, allowing the party furthest from its interest a victory.)*

ELL Use the ELL activity described in the ELL chart.

Further Instruction

Predict Consequences How will Taylor's victory affect the balance of power between slave and free states? *(Possible response: He will support the expansion of slavery in the western territories because he is a slaveholder. His victory will potentially give slave states more political power in Congress.)*

Objective 3: Analyze why slavery in the territories was a divisive issue between the North and South and how Congress tried to settle the issue in 1850.

Quick Instruction

Interactive Chart: Causes and Effects of Sectional Issues in the 1800s Display the Interactive Chart and prompt students to match the causes and effects. Place the Fugitive Slave Act in the context of the ongoing debate over the Wilmot Proviso, the rise of the Free-Soil Party, and the idea of popular sovereignty. Point out that the enforcement of the Fugitive Slave Act was one provision in the Compromise of 1850.

Identify Cause and Effect What effect did California's request for admission to the Union have on the slavery debate? *(California petitioned to be admitted to the union as a free state. In turn, sectarian tensions rose considerably as many southerners were concerned that the political balance in Congress would tip in favor of the free states.)*

📖 ACTIVE CLASSROOM

Conduct a Word Wall activity. Ask students to chose one of the following terms and create a visual image with a definition: Compromise of 1850, popular sovereignty, Wilmot Proviso, Free-Soil Party, Fugitive Slave Act. Allow approximately three to five minutes. Have students post their words on the board or on chart paper. Ask students to look at all the various responses then discuss similarities and differences in the responses as a group.

Slavery Divides the Nation

INTERACTIVE CHART
Causes and Effects of Sectional Issues in the 1800s

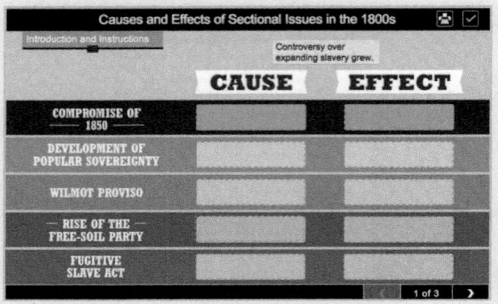

DIGITAL TEXT 4
Northern Resistance to Slavery Increases

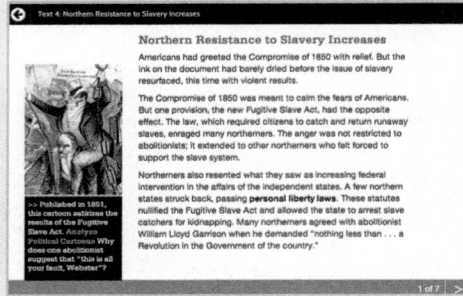

INTERACTIVE MAP
The Underground Railroad

ELL Use the ELL activity described in the ELL chart.

Further Instruction

Support Ideas with Evidence What evidence supports the idea that Henry Clay's compromise addressed some political concerns of both free and slave states? *(Clay's compromise entailed allowing California to enter the Union as a free state but strengthening the Fugitive Slave law. The Utah and New Mexico territories would decide for themselves if they would accept slavery.)*

Evaluate Arguments John Calhoun argued that the Compromise of 1850 did not protect the South and that if the South's demands were not met, they should consider secession. Daniel Webster argued for the acceptance of the Compromise in order to save the Union. Which argument proved more effective at the time? *(After considerable debate, Webster's argument convinced a majority of Congress to adopt Clay's proposal, so his argument was the more effective of the two.)*

Objective 4: **Analyze why the Fugitive Slave Act increased tensions between the North and South.**

Quick Instruction

Interactive Map: The Underground Railroad Project the Interactive Map and navigate through the images with students. Explain that the new Fugitive Slave Act angered many northerners, many of whom defied the law. Some refused to return runaways to their owners; others helped enslaved people escape from the South. Point out the risks that "conductors" of the Underground Railroad took in order to help enslaved people.

Predict Consequences What risks did the runaways take by attempting to gain their freedom? *(They risked their lives, as well as the security and lives of their family, who were often unable to leave at the same time.)*

ACTIVE CLASSROOM

Use the See-Think-Wonder strategy to explore the Interactive Map. Pair students and have them discuss their answers to these questions: What do you see? What does it make you think? What are you wondering about now that you have seen this? After pairs finish discussion, reconvene as a class and allow students time to share new insights.

Further Instruction

Connect What essential idea did personal liberty laws and the concept of popular sovereignty have in common? *(Both personal liberty laws and popular sovereignty share an essential argument that individual states should have a significant amount of political autonomy relative to the federal government.)*

Determine Author's Purpose Several authors wrote books about the slave experience. What was their purpose in presenting realistic characters and their struggles in slavery? *(Some authors, such as Harriet Beecher Stowe, used fiction to expose the horrors of slavery, hoping to sway public opinion and encourage condemnation of the practice. Other authors wrote fiction that directly contradicted Stowe's book, portraying slavery in a softer light.)*

SYNTHESIZE

DIGITAL ACTIVITY

Contrasting Opinions Over Slavery in the Union

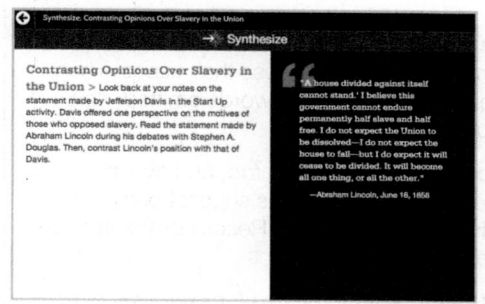

Allow students time to review the Start Up activity quotation and their answers to the question. Then, have them read the quotation and write their responses comparing and contrasting the ideas presented in each.

Discuss Invite volunteers to paraphrase each of the quotes and then make their comparisons based on the summaries.

DEMONSTRATE

DIGITAL QUIZ

Lesson Quiz and Discussion Board

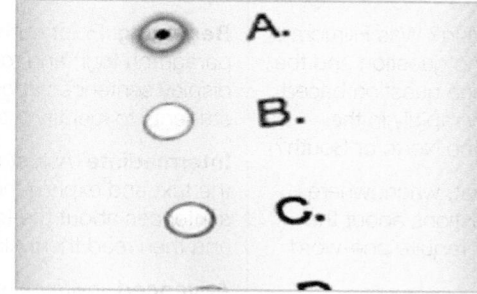

Assign the online Lesson Quiz for this lesson if you haven't already done so. Students will be offered automatic remediation or enrichment based on their score.

In *Slavery Divides the Nation*, you learned about the differences in the North and South that added to sectional conflict. At the forefront of these was the perspective on slavery, which fueled debate about the standing of new territories and states added to the Union. Though the Compromise of 1850 tried to restore unity, in practice it ended in deeper division.

Post these questions to the class on the Discussion Board:

Contrast How did the economies, societies, and politics of the North and South differ?

Draw Conclusions What were the provisions of the Compromise of 1850? How did the compromise appease both North and South? How did it inflame both regions?

Topic Inquiry
Have students continue their investigations for the Topic Inquiry.

Violence Escalates

Supporting English Language Learners

Use with the text reading, **Regional Tension Affects National Politics**.

Speaking
Ask students why we ask questions. Explain that questions can be asked in different ways in order to elicit different types of responses.

Beginning Display these questions: Was Fillmore a Whig? Was Fillmore a Whig or a Republican? Point out that the first is a yes/no question and the second is a choice question. Have students ask a choice question based on this yes/no question: Did the Republican Party grow rapidly in the North? (e.g., Did the Republican Party grow rapidly in the North or South?)

Intermediate Review these question words: who, what, when, where, why, how. Then have students ask—and answer—questions about the text using these words. Point out how some questions require one-word answers, while others are more in-depth answers.

Advanced Discuss what makes a question close-ended or open-ended, as well as when you might use each. Then place students in pairs and have partners take turns asking each other both close-ended and open-ended questions about the text.

Advanced High Point out the series of three questions in the section titled *The Know-Nothings*. Discuss the purpose of these rhetorical questions. Then have pairs of students use rhetorical questions as they discuss the influence of political parties mentioned in the text.

Use with the reading, **The Raid on Harpers Ferry**.

Reading
Display the words *to*, *too*, and *two*. Review their pronunciations and meanings.

Beginning Point out examples of the preposition *to*, as well as *two* (in paragraph four) and *too* (in paragraph seven). Discuss their usage. Then display sentences about the text with one of these words omitted. Ask students to identify the missing word.

Intermediate Ask students to find examples of *to*, *too*, and *two* in the text and explain their usage. Then have students suggest original sentences about the text that include these words. Record their sentences and then read them aloud together.

Advanced Invite pairs of students to search the text for examples of *to*, *too*, and *two*, as well as to identify two common uses of *to* (to introduce an infinitive verb or a prepositional phrase). Then discuss these uses of *to* and have pairs create original sentences about the text with them.

Advanced High Remind students that *to* can be used to introduce an infinitive verb or a prepositional phrase. Have them write a paragraph about the text that includes *too*, *two*, and both uses of *to*. Invite partners to read each other's paragraphs and check for correct usage of these three words.

▶ Differentiate Instruction

Use the Differentiated Instruction notes throughout the lesson plan to support the varied skill sets, levels of readiness, and interests in the mixed-ability classroom.

Challenge These notes include suggestions for expanding the activity for advanced students.

On-Level These notes include suggestions for modifying the activity to address different interests or learning styles.

Extra Support These notes include ideas for providing more scaffolding or reading spuport.

Special Needs These notes provide ideas for adapting instruction to support the needs of various special needs students.

■ NOTES

Objectives

Objective 1: Assess how the Kansas-Nebraska Act was seen differently by the North and South.

Objective 2: Explain why fighting broke out in Kansas and the effects of that conflict.

Objective 3: Analyze how deepening sectional distrust affected the nation's politics.

Objective 4: Compare the positions of Abraham Lincoln and Stephen Douglas on the issue of slavery.

Objective 5: Explain the effect of John Brown's raid on the slavery debate.

LESSON 2 ORGANIZER		PACING: APPROX. 1 PERIOD, .5 BLOCKS			
		OBJECTIVES	PACING	Online	Print
Connect					
DIGITAL START UP ACTIVITY **Compromises Over Slavery Prove Contentious**			5 min.	●	
Investigate					
DIGITAL TEXT 1 **The Kansas-Nebraska Act and "Bleeding Kansas"**		Objectives 1, 2	10 min.	●	●
INTERACTIVE CARTOON **Forcing Slavery Down the Throat of a Freesoiler**			10 min.	●	
DIGITAL TEXT 2 **Regional Tension Affects National Politics**			10 min.	●	●
DIGITAL TEXT 3 **Sectional Divisions Split the Country**		Objective 3	10 min.	●	●
INTERACTIVE MAP **Territories Open to Slavery**			10 min.	●	
DIGITAL TEXT 4 **Lincoln and Douglas Debate Slavery**		Objective 4	10 min.	●	●
DIGITAL TEXT 5 **The Raid on Harpers Ferry**		Objective 5	10 min.	●	●
Synthesize					
DIGITAL ACTIVITY **The Events That Led to War**			5 min.	●	
Demonstrate					
DIGITAL QUIZ **Lesson Quiz and Discussion Board**			10 min.	●	

Violence Escalates

■ CONNECT

DIGITAL START UP ACTIVITY
Compromises Over Slavery Prove Contentious

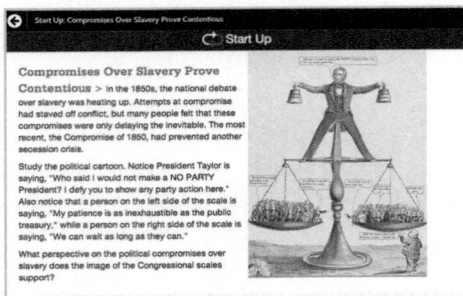

Project the Start Up Activity Have students view the cartoon and answer the question as they enter the classroom. Then ask them to share and discuss their ideas with partners.

Discuss What perspective on the political compromises over slavery does the image of the Congressional scales support? *(The compromise between free and slave states has been difficult to achieve and could easily fall in favor of one side or the other, resulting in further conflict. Neither side seems willing to compromise further.)*

Tell students that this lesson further examines the slavery debate, describing the sectionalism that divided the nation and the escalation in violence that resulted between pro- and antislavery factions.

Aa Vocabulary Development: Use the Interactive Reading Notepad to preview the Key Terms and Academic Vocabulary in this lesson with students.

⇗ FLIP IT!

Assign the Flipped Video for this lesson.

■ STUDENT EDITION PRINT PAGES: 237–244

■ INVESTIGATE

DIGITAL TEXT 1
The Kansas-Nebraska Act and "Bleeding Kansas"

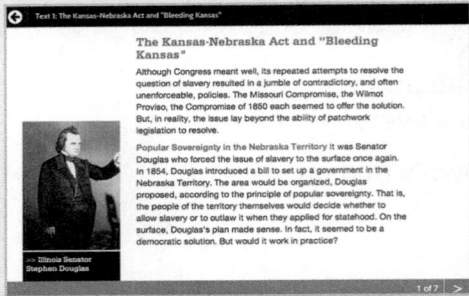

Objectives 1: Assess how the Kansas-Nebraska Act was seen differently by the North and South; 2: Explain why fighting broke out in Kansas and the effects of that conflict.

Quick Instruction

Interactive Cartoon: Forcing Slavery Down the Throat of a Freesoiler Project the Interactive Cartoon and prompt students to complete the graphic organizer as you discuss the cartoon's elements. Ask: Why are Douglas and Pierce depicted as the people forcing an African American man down the giant's throat? *(Douglas amended the petition for statehood, dividing the Nebraska territory into two regions, and President Pierce supported accepting Kansas as a slave state.)*

Summarize How did the Kansas-Nebraska Act contribute to sectional tension in the 1850s? *(The Kansas-Nebraska Act divided the Nebraska territory into two sections, Kansas and Nebraska. The supposition was that Kansas would enter the Union as a slave state and Nebraska as a free state. However, many Freesoilers did not want Kansas to be slave territory. As a result, tempers ran high and proslavery factions fought antislavery factions, creating what came to be known as "Bleeding Kansas.")*

INTERACTIVE CARTOON
Forcing Slavery Down the Throat of a Freesoiler

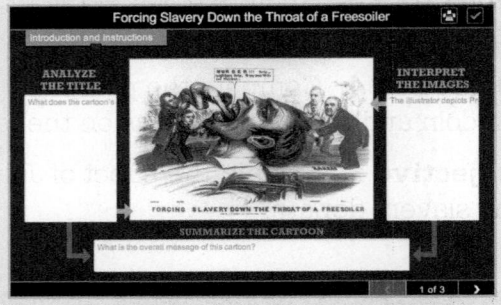

🎥 ACTIVE CLASSROOM

Conduct a Sticky Notes activity. Ask students to jot down questions, comments, or observations about the cartoon on sticky notes and post them on the wall alongside a copy of the cartoon. Sort and discuss the notes as a group. Encourage students to elaborate on their own comments and expand on or challenge others' interpretations of the cartoon.

Further Instruction

Identify Central Issues Who were the Border Ruffians and what was their agenda? *(The border ruffians were a proslavery faction that moved to Kansas to establish political power there. They wanted to ensure that Kansas was admitted to the Union as a slave state.)*

Support Ideas with Examples How is the metaphor "Bleeding Kansas" an accurate description of the situation there in the mid-1850s? *(Clashes between proslavery border ruffians and those opposed to slavery over the political fate of Kansas quickly escalated into violence. In retaliation for border ruffian raids in Lawrence, Kansas, abolitionist John Brown and others were responsible for the murder of five proslavery settlers.)*

DIGITAL TEXT 2

Regional Tension Affects National Politics

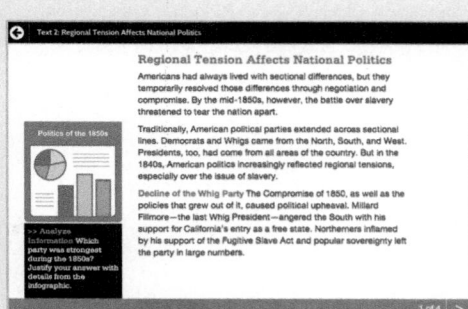

DIGITAL TEXT 3

Sectional Divisions Split the Country

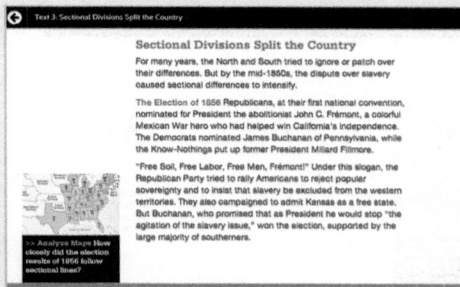

INTERACTIVE MAP

Territories Open to Slavery

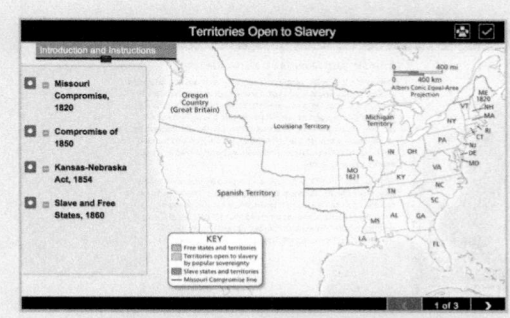

Objective 3: Analyze how deepening sectional distrust affected the nation's politics.

Quick Instruction

Interactive Map: Territories Open to Slavery Project the Interactive Map and navigate through the layers with students. Prompt students to note each piece of legislation and its impact on sectionalism. Ask: How did the Kansas-Nebraska Act violate the Missouri Compromise? *(It allowed for the possibility of slavery in a territory that was previously deemed free.)*

Generate Explanations How did the political parties in the 1856 election reflect the larger sectional divisions over slavery in the nation? *(The Whig party was in decline, but the Republican party was born on the platform of abolition. The Know-Nothings, a nativist party, gained some support. The Democrats remained strong and won the election with proslavery candidate James Buchanan.)*

🖳 ACTIVE CLASSROOM

Conduct an Audio Tour activity. Have students investigate the layers of the Interactive Map. Pair students and have the first student give the second a verbal "tour" of the map. The guide should describe what the map shows. Then, the second student should give the first an explanation of what the description means. Have pairs repeat the process with each layer of the map.

ELL Use the ELL activity described in the ELL chart.

Further Instruction

Assign Landmark Cases: *Dred Scott* v. *Sandford* for students to further investigate the details of the Dred Scott case.

Infer Why was the Supreme Court decision in the Dred Scott case so controversial? *(The ruling that enslaved people and their descendants were property, not citizens, suggested that all African Americans were denied the benefits of U.S. citizenship, including the right to sue for redress of harm. It also ruled the Missouri Compromise unconstitutional.)*

Violence Escalates

DIGITAL TEXT 4

Lincoln and Douglas Debate Slavery

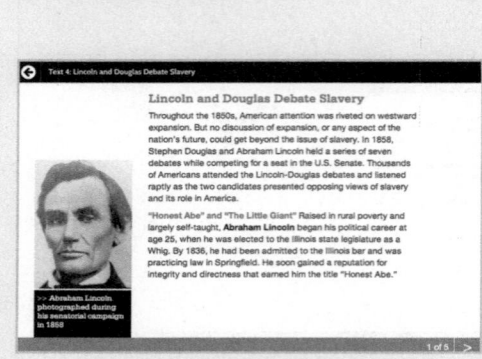

DIGITAL TEXT 5

The Raid on Harpers Ferry

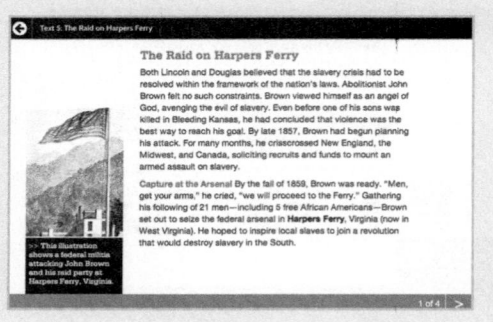

Objective 4: Compare the positions of Abraham Lincoln and Stephen Douglas on the issue of slavery.

Quick Instruction

Introduce students to Abraham Lincoln and Stephen Douglas, explaining that Lincoln was antislavery and Douglas was sympathetic to slavery. As the two men participated in a series of debates in the 1858 campaign for Senate, each man expressed his opinions openly. Though Douglas's motives were often in question, he ended up winning the Senate seat. However, Lincoln won a devout following that would lead him to the White House in the next presidential election.

Contrast the reasons behind Lincoln's and Douglas's respective positions on slavery. *(Lincoln spoke out more forcefully against slavery as an institution. Although Douglas did not personally own slaves, he believed in the principle of popular sovereignty, arguing the individual states should decide whether or not to legalize slavery. Lincoln however was against popular sovereignty in this case.)*

Further Instruction

Assign Primary Sources: Abraham Lincoln, House Divided Speech for students to read in order to better understand Lincoln's perspective on the impact of slavery in the country.

Interpret What did Lincoln predict would happen in the debate over slavery? *(Either proslavery policies would expand to the North or antislavery policies would expand to the South. He believed the political balance between pro- and antislavery states would not be maintained.)*

Objective 5: Explain the effect of John Brown's raid on the slavery debate.

Quick Instruction

Display the abolitionist painting of John Brown on the way to the gallows. Remind students that John Brown was a fanatical abolitionist who believed that violence was the only way to end slavery. He was responsible for organizing the retaliatory execution of proslavery settlers in Kansas and then went on to plan a raid on Harpers Ferry, a government arsenal. His attempted raid failed and he was sentenced to death. His actions furthered stirred emotions and violence surrounding the slavery issue, yet many people saw him as a courageous martyr in the cause of abolition.

Analyze Images What perspective of John Brown is conveyed in this painting? *(He is portrayed as a loving, gentle man on his way to death. He is the quintessential martyr for the cause.)*

ELL Use the ELL activity described in the ELL chart.

Further Instruction

Determine Relevance Why did John Brown's raid and capture have a significant effect on the slavery debate and sectional tension in the country? *(The event inflamed sectional tension, involved the federal government, and resulted in further distrust between the differing factions.)*

SYNTHESIZE

DIGITAL ACTIVITY
The Events That Led to War

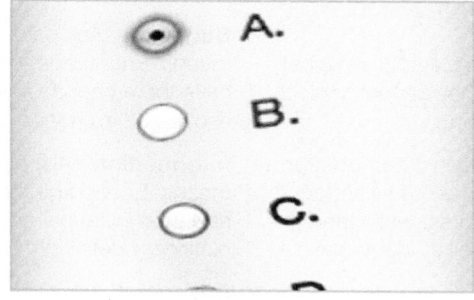

Discuss each entry in the sequence of events, evaluating the impact of each on the country as a whole. Then, allow students time to record their responses and explanations.

Discuss Poll the class to see if there is agreement on the turning point. Then, invite volunteers to share their explanations. Guide students as they discuss and debate their ideas.

DEMONSTRATE

DIGITAL QUIZ
Lesson Quiz and Discussion Board

Assign the online Lesson Quiz for this lesson if you haven't already done so. Students will be offered automatic remediation or enrichment based on their score.

In *Violence Escalates*, you learned about the Kansas-Nebraska Act that created a "Bleeding Kansas" and the regional tension resulting from sectionalism. The Lincoln-Douglas debates personified much of the tension over the political autonomy of states and the legality of slavery.

Post these questions to the class on the Discussion Board:

Generate Explanations How did the Kansas-Nebraska Act contribute to a "Bleeding Kansas"?

Support a Point of View with Evidence Did John Brown's violent tactics in Kansas and attempted raid on Harpers Ferry help or harm the abolitionist's cause?

Topic Inquiry
Have students continue their investigations for the Topic Inquiry.

The Civil War Begins

Supporting English Language Learners

Use with the text reading, **Resources and Strategies**.

Learning
Brainstorm strategies for students to use when they cannot think of the words needed to express themselves (e.g., asking for help; using non-verbal cues, synonyms, and circumlocution).

Beginning Display the photograph of the Union warship and its rowboat. Ask students to identify what they see in the image. If they cannot think of a word, have them ask for help from their teacher or peers.

Intermediate Label both familiar and unfamiliar objects in the photograph of the Union warship and its rowboat. Then ask a volunteer to select an object and describe it using alternative words and gestures, while the other students try to identify it. Repeat the activity until all students have described an object.

Advanced Place students in pairs and ask partners to take turns describing objects in the photograph of the Union warship and its rowboat and guessing which objects are being described. Encourage them to rely mostly on synonyms and circumlocution in their descriptions.

Advanced High Have pairs of students discuss the photograph of the Union warship and its rowboat. In the course of their discussion, encourage them to describe the details of the photograph using exact terms, synonyms, and circumlocution as needed.

Use with the reading, **The First Year of the Civil War**.

Listening
With students, brainstorm ways that they can demonstrate strong listening skills when collaborating with one another.

Beginning Ask pairs of students to discuss what the verb *stonewall* means. Encourage them to use the text to support their discussion and have them choose from these possibilities: (1) to climb over walls during an escape, (2) to honor, or (3) not to do what the other side wants.

Intermediate Ask pairs of students to discuss what the verb *stonewall* means. Encourage them to use the text to support their discussion and then invite pairs to share their definitions. Compare their ideas to a dictionary definition.

Advanced Ask pairs of students to discuss why there might be two names for one battle (Battle of Bull Run, Battle of Manassas). Have them address these questions: Who names a battle? Which should be the official name for this battle? Why?

Advanced High Ask pairs of students to discuss the role of American Indian groups in the first year of the Civil War. Have them address these questions: Why do you think loyalties shifted over time? Why was it important to have the loyalties of these groups?

▣ Differentiate Instruction

Use the Differentiated Instruction notes throughout the lesson plan to support the varied skill sets, levels of readiness, and interests in the mixed-ability classroom.

Challenge These notes include suggestions for expanding the activity for advanced students.

On-Level These notes include suggestions for modifying the activity to address different interests or learning styles.

Extra Support These notes include ideas for providing more scaffolding or reading spuport.

Special Needs These notes provide ideas for adapting instruction to support the needs of various special needs students.

■ NOTES

PEARSON
realize™
www.PearsonRealize.com

Go online to access additional resources including:
Primary Sources • Biographies • Supreme Court cases •
21st Century Skill Tutorials • Maps • Graphic Organizers.

Objectives

Objective 1: Compare the candidates in the election of 1860 and analyze the results.

Objective 2: Analyze why southern states seceded from the Union.

Objective 3: Contrast the resources and strategies of the North and South.

Objective 4: Describe the outcomes and effects of the early battles of the Civil War.

LESSON 3 ORGANIZER		PACING: APPROX. 1 PERIOD, .5 BLOCKS			
				RESOURCES	
		OBJECTIVES	**PACING**	**Online**	**Print**
Connect					
	DIGITAL START UP ACTIVITY Different Perspectives Over the Right to Secede		5 min.	●	
Investigate					
	DIGITAL TEXT 1 Sectional Politics in the Election of 1860	Objective 1	10 min.	●	●
	DIGITAL TEXT 2 The Collapse of the Union	Objective 2	10 min.	●	●
	INTERACTIVE CHART South Carolina Declaration of Causes of Secession		10 min.	●	
	DIGITAL TEXT 3 Resources and Strategies	Objective 3	10 min.	●	●
	DIGITAL TEXT 4 The First Year of the Civil War	Objective 4	10 min.	●	●
	DIGITAL TEXT 5 A Stalemate in the East		10 min.	●	●
	INTERACTIVE TIMELINE Early Battles of the Civil War		10 min.	●	
Synthesize					
	DIGITAL ACTIVITY Justification for War		5 min.	●	
Demonstrate					
	DIGITAL QUIZ Lesson Quiz and Discussion Board		10 min.	●	

The Civil War Begins

▮ CONNECT

DIGITAL START UP ACTIVITY
Different Perspectives Over the Right to Secede

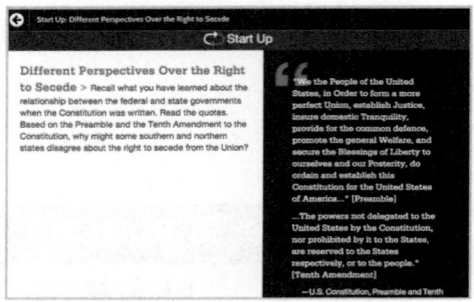

Project the Start Up Activity Have students read the quotations and complete the writing as they enter the classroom. Then ask them to share and discuss their ideas with partners.

Discuss Based on the Preamble and the Tenth Amendment to the Constitution, why might some southern and northern states disagree about the right to secede from the Union? *(Those who cite the Constitution might focus on the existence of the Union, whereas those who argued for secession might cite the Tenth Amendment, claiming it is best for the individual states.)*

Tell students that this lesson examines the reasons behind the collapse of the Union, the beginning of the Civil War, and the resources and strategies of each side.

Vocabulary Development: Use the Interactive Reading Notepad to preview the Key Terms and Academic Vocabulary in this lesson with students.

↻ FLIP IT!
Assign the Flipped Video for this lesson.

▮ STUDENT EDITION PRINT
PAGES: 245–255

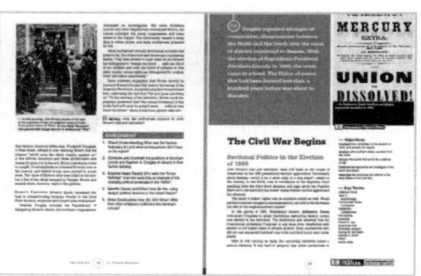

▮ INVESTIGATE

DIGITAL TEXT 1
Sectional Politics in the Election of 1860

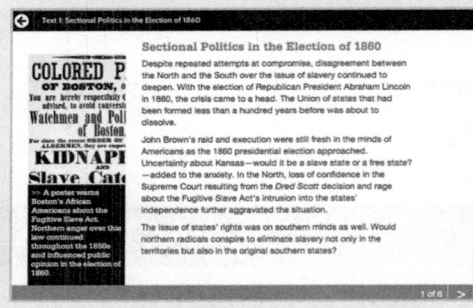

Objective 1: Compare the candidates in the election of 1860 and analyze the results.

Quick Instruction
Display the political cartoon showing the different 1860 presidential candidates trying to open the door to the White House. Prompt students to understand the way in which many of the candidates are portrayed shows their inability to win the White House. Contrast those images with Lincoln, who looks confident and prepared. Ask: Why is Lincoln portrayed as the watchman, while the other candidates look like they're trying to break into the White House? *(Lincoln was the presumptive favorite to win the presidency, as the Democratic and Constitutional Union parties could not rally enough popular support behind one candidate.)*

Support Ideas with Evidence How did the 1860 elections illustrate the stark political divisions within the United States? *(The North and the South voted independently, it seemed, for the next U.S. President. Republican Abraham Lincoln won the election with 40 percent of the popular vote, but he did not even appear on many ballots in the South. Other candidates won in regions in which their political party's platforms were accepted, but no other regions.)*

Summarize Why did the Democratic Party split into Northern Democrats and Southern Democrats? *(At the Democratic Convention, southerners fought for protection of slavery in the territories, while northerners fought for popular sovereignty. When the northern candidate Stephen Douglas, a supporter of popular sovereignty, won the nomination, the southerners formed their own convention and selected another nominee for president, John Breckinridge.)*

Further Instruction
Assign Biographies: Jefferson Davis. Explain that Jefferson Davis was instrumental in persuading Congress to pass regulations in favor of states' rights and protection of slavery. Point out that he would become the President of the Confederacy when the South seceded.

Draw Conclusions Why were Southerners concerned that the antislavery movement supported free territories? *(They believed that the movement would not stop at the territories but would try to abolish slavery in the South as well, thereby undermining the southern economy.)*

PEARSON
realize™ www.PearsonRealize.com
Access your Digital Lesson

DIGITAL TEXT 2

The Collapse of the Union

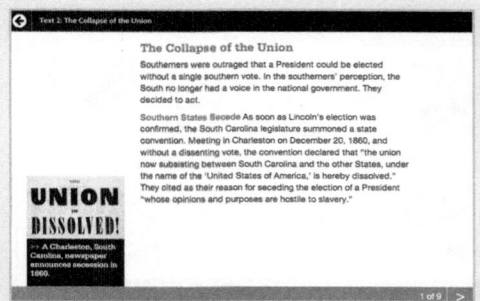

Text 2: The Collapse of the Union

The Collapse of the Union

Southerners were outraged that a President could be elected without a single southern vote. In the southerners' perception, the South no longer had a voice in the national government. They decided to act.

Southern States Secede As soon as Lincoln's election was confirmed, the South Carolina legislature summoned a state convention. Meeting in Charleston on December 20, 1860, and without a dissenting vote, the convention declared that "the union now subsisting between South Carolina and the other States, under the name of the 'United States of America,' is hereby dissolved." They cited as their reason for seceding the election of a President "whose opinions and purposes are hostile to slavery."

UNION DISSOLVED!

>> A Charleston, South Carolina, newspaper announces secession in 1860.

1 of 9 >

INTERACTIVE CHART

South Carolina Declaration of Causes of Secession

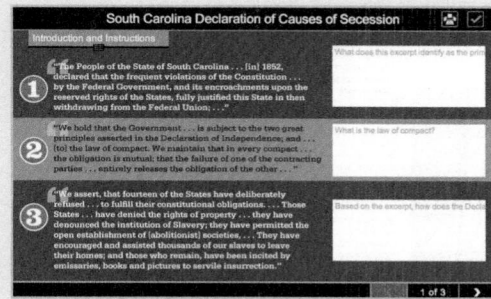

South Carolina Declaration of Causes of Secession

Introduction and Instructions

1 "The People of the State of South Carolina ... [in] 1852, declared that the frequent violations of the Constitution ... by the Federal Government, and its encroachments upon the reserved rights of the States, fully justified this State in then withdrawing from the Federal Union ..."

2 "We hold that the Government ... is subject to the two great principles asserted in the Declaration of Independence; and ... [to] the law of compact. We maintain that in every compact ... the obligation is mutual; that the failure of one of the contracting parties ... entirely releases the obligation of the other ..."

3 "We assert, that fourteen of the States have deliberately refused ... to fulfill their constitutional obligations.... Those States ... have denied the rights of property ... they have denounced the institution of Slavery; they have permitted the open establishment of [abolitionist] societies, ... They have encouraged and assisted thousands of our slaves to leave their homes; and those who remain, have been incited by emissaries, books and pictures to servile insurrection."

1 of 3 >

DIGITAL TEXT 3

Resources and Strategies

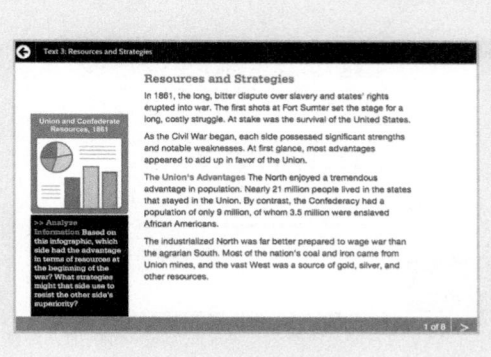

Text 3: Resources and Strategies

Resources and Strategies

In 1861, the long, bitter dispute over slavery and states' rights erupted into war. The first shots at Fort Sumter set the stage for a long, costly struggle. At stake was the survival of the United States.

As the Civil War began, each side possessed significant strengths and notable weaknesses. At first glance, most advantages appeared to add up in favor of the Union.

The Union's Advantages The North enjoyed a tremendous advantage in population. Nearly 21 million people lived in the states that stayed in the Union. By contrast, the Confederacy had a population of only 9 million, of whom 3.5 million were enslaved African Americans.

The industrialized North was far better prepared to wage war than the agrarian South. Most of the nation's coal and iron came from Union mines, and the vast West was a source of gold, silver, and other resources.

Union and Confederate Resources, 1861

>> Analyze Information Based on this infographic, which side had the advantage in terms of resources at the beginning of the war? What strategies might that side use to resist the other side's superiority?

1 of 8 >

Objective 2: Analyze why southern states seceded from the Union.

Quick Instruction

Interactive Chart: South Carolina Declaration of Causes of Secession Project the Interactive Chart and discuss the content and context of the quotations with students. Prompt students to understand that many southerners were shocked that a U.S. President could win election without electoral support from the southern region of the country. As a result, the South Carolina state government convened to make a list of the reasons for secession.

Paraphrase What cause for secession does the first quotation cite? *(The Federal Government has usurped states' rights.)* The second? *(The Federal Government has failed to honor the Constitution, so the state is released from its constitutional obligations)* The third? *(Northern states denied the right to own slaves and are doing what they can to discourage the institution as such.)*

📖 ACTIVE CLASSROOM

Conduct a Rank It activity. Ask students to summarize and rank the reasons why South Carolina chose to secede from the Union according to the order of their importance. Ask students to provide a justification for the ranking decisions they made. Then divide students into pairs to share their rankings and justifications. Poll the class to see if there is agreement on the ranking.

Further Instruction

South Carolina and several other states seceded before Abraham Lincoln took office. President Buchanan did nothing to stop the division, but upon inauguration, Lincoln claimed that no state had the right to secede from the Union. Assign *Primary Source: First Inaugural Address* so students can read exactly what Lincoln claimed. Then, have students read *Biography: Abraham Lincoln.*

Infer Why did Lincoln begin his inaugural address by assuring the South that he had no plans to eliminate slavery where it existed? *(Though Lincoln was antislavery, he was staunchly pro-Union and was willing to compromise in order to preserve the unity of the country.)*

Objective 3: Contrast the resources and strategies of the North and South.

Quick Instruction

Display the infographic titled *Union and Confederate Resources, 1861.* Discuss the advantages and weaknesses of each faction. Prompt students to understand that the North had significant advantages in population, industrial production, military forces, and an experienced government. On the other hand, the South had the advantage of fighting a defensive war on native soil for a cause in which many of its people whole-heartedly believed.

Distinguish What weaknesses and disadvantages did each side have? *(The North had the disadvantage of lack of support for the war. It also had the disadvantage of needing to fight a defensive war on foreign ground. The South had the disadvantage of lack of population, industry, and military, as well as lack of experience with government.)*

ELL Use the ELL activity described in the ELL chart.

Further Instruction

Infer Why did Lincoln declare that he had no plan to free slaves in border states? *(Although the economies of many border states were not as dependent on slavery as other states farther south, Lincoln still hoped to appease these states and convince them to join the war on the side of the Union.)*

Summarize What was the Anaconda Plan? *(Devised by General Winfield Scott, the Anaconda plan involved blockading southern ports and taking control of the Mississippi, thereby dividing Confederate forces and supply lines.)*

The Civil War Begins

DIGITAL TEXT 4

The First Year of the Civil War

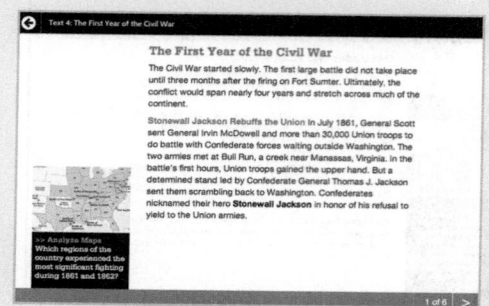

DIGITAL TEXT 5

A Stalemate in the East

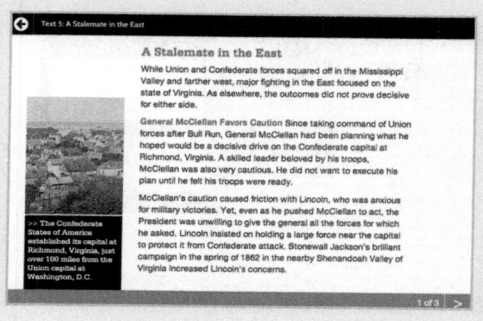

INTERACTIVE TIMELINE

Early Battles of the Civil War

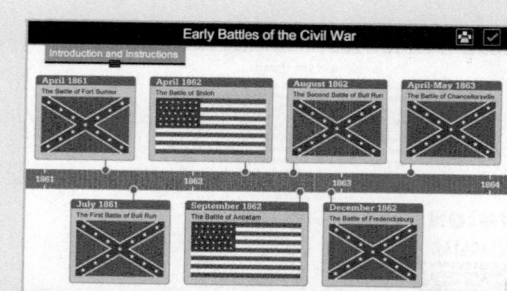

Objective 4: Describe the outcomes and effects of the early battles of the Civil War.

Quick Instruction

Interactive Timeline: Early Battles of the Civil War Project the Interactive Timeline and navigate through the images with students. Guide students to understand the importance of each of the early battles of the Civil War. Ask: Why did it take three months after the Battle of Fort Sumter to stage another major battle in the war? *(Possible response: The warring factions needed time to create a strategy, build a military, and train soldiers.)*

ACTIVE CLASSROOM

Conduct a Rank It activity. Have students rank the list of early battles based on their impact, whether psychological, strategic, or physical. Ask students to provide justification for the ranking decisions they made. Pair students and have them share their rankings and justifications. Finally, poll the class to see if there is agreement on ranking.

ELL Use the ELL activity described in the ELL chart.

Further Instruction

Generate Explanations What factors contributed to the Union defeat at Richmond? *(General McClellan did not feel his troops were ready to attack Richmond, but President Lincoln was anxious for military success. McClellan attacked Richmond without the troops and resources for which he asked, and Lee was able to hold the Confederate capital.)*

SYNTHESIZE

DIGITAL ACTIVITY
Justification for War

After students read the quotations, discuss them as a class to make sure students understand the key points in each. Then, allow them time to answer the question.

Discuss Invite volunteers to share their paragraphs with the class. Allow students time to respond to and discuss the volunteers' ideas and share their own concerning the legitimacy of going to war.

DEMONSTRATE

DIGITAL QUIZ
Lesson Quiz and Discussion Board

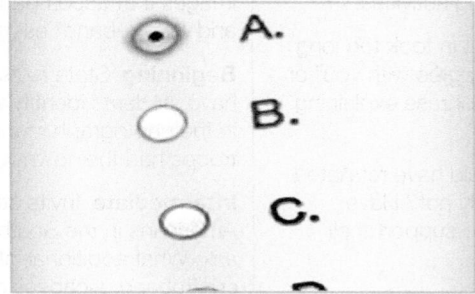

Assign the online Lesson Quiz for this lesson if you haven't already done so. Students will be offered automatic remediation or enrichment based on their score.

In *The Civil War Begins*, you learned about the sectional politics in the election of 1860 and Lincoln's victory, which spurred the collapse of the Union. You also learned about the resources and strategies of the North and the South and how the first year of the Civil War ended in a stalemate in the East.

Post these questions to the class on the Discussion Board:

Summarize Identify the political parties, their candidates, and their platforms for the 1860 election.

Compare and Contrast What advantages and disadvantages did the North and the South have as they entered war?

Topic Inquiry
Have students continue their investigations for the Topic Inquiry.

African Americans and the War

Supporting English Language Learners

Use with the reading, **Emancipation and the Civil War**.

Speaking
Review the difference between a fact and an opinion. Tell students that they will be speaking about their opinions in the following activities.

Beginning State opinions regarding the text (e.g., Lincoln took too long to free the slaves). Have students respond by saying "I agree with you" or "I do not agree with you." Challenge students to add a phrase explaining their opinion.

Intermediate Ask: Do you think the border states would have retaliated if Lincoln had not reversed Frémont's order? Why or why not? Have students answer with a yes or no, as well as a reason to support their opinion.

Advanced Ask pairs of students to offer an opinion about the following question: Would it have been worthwhile to fight the Civil War only for preservation of the Union (i.e., without emancipation)? Why or why not? Encourage partners to support their opinions with facts.

Advanced High Have pairs of students discuss this question: Why do you think Lincoln downplayed the issue of slavery? Encourage them to consider political, economic, and societal angles, as well as Lincoln's personal beliefs. Also encourage partners to pick apart each other's opinions in order to draw out stronger supporting details.

Use with the reading, **African Americans Join the Fight**.

Reading
Have students read or reread the text if necessary. Then display these images that accompany the text: soldiers of the 4th U.S. Colored Infantry, and "contraband" escapees from the South.

Beginning State facts about African American troops in the Civil War and have students identify whether the information can be found in the text, in the photograph of the soldiers, or in both (e.g., Some African American troops had their own weapons and uniforms).

Intermediate Invite students to state facts from the text about African Americans in the South during the Civil War. Display these in a list. Then ask: What additional information or understanding does the photograph of contraband escapees give you about the situation of African Americans?

Advanced Invite pairs of students to examine the two photographs and describe what they see. Then have them discuss this question: How do these photographs help you better understand how the situations of northern and southern African Americans were similar and different during the Civil War?

Advanced High Invite students to create a Venn diagram comparing African American troops and contraband escapees according to information found in the text. Then have them add additional information to the Venn diagram that is found only in the photographs.

▶ Differentiate Instruction

Use the Differentiated Instruction notes throughout the lesson plan to support the varied skill sets, levels of readiness, and interests in the mixed-ability classroom.

Challenge These notes include suggestions for expanding the activity for advanced students.

On-Level These notes include suggestions for modifying the activity to address different interests or learning styles.

Extra Support These notes include ideas for providing more scaffolding or reading spuport.

Special Needs These notes provide ideas for adapting instruction to support the needs of various special needs students.

◼ NOTES

PEARSON
realize™
www.PearsonRealize.com

Go online to access additional resources including:
Primary Sources • Biographies • Supreme Court cases •
21st Century Skill Tutorials • Maps • Graphic Organizers.

Objectives

Objective 1: Analyze why Lincoln decided to issue the Emancipation Proclamation and what it achieved.

Objective 2: Assess the different roles that African Americans played in the Civil War.

LESSON 4 ORGANIZER		PACING: APPROX. 1 PERIOD, .5 BLOCKS			
				RESOURCES	
		OBJECTIVES	PACING	Online	Print
Connect					
DIGITAL START UP ACTIVITY **The Will to Fight**			5 min.	●	
Investigate					
DIGITAL TEXT 1 **Emancipation and the Civil War**		Objective 1	10 min.	●	●
INTERACTIVE GALLERY **The Road to the Emancipation Proclamation**			10 min.	●	
DIGITAL TEXT 3 **African Americans Join the Fight**		Objective 2	10 min.	●	●
INTERACTIVE GALLERY **African Americans and the Civil War**			10 min.	●	
Synthesize					
DIGITAL ACTIVITY **Emancipation-Era Headlines**			5 min.	●	
Demonstrate					
DIGITAL QUIZ **Lesson Quiz and Discussion Board**			10 min.	●	

African Americans and the War

■ CONNECT

DIGITAL START UP ACTIVITY
The Will to Fight

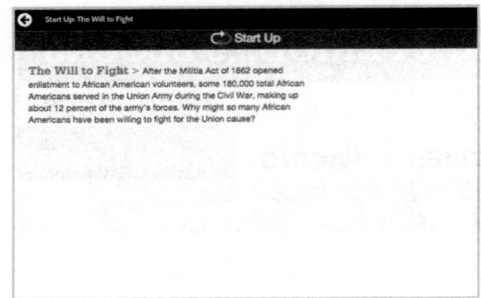

Project the Start Up Activity Have students complete the activity as they enter the classroom. Then ask them to share and discuss their ideas with partners.

Discuss Why might so many African Americans have been willing to fight for the Union cause? *(Possible answers include a desire to end the practice of slavery throughout the country and free any relatives or friends still living as slaves in the Confederacy.)*

Aa Vocabulary Development: Use the Interactive Reading Notepad to preview the Key Terms and Academic Vocabulary in this lesson with students.

⇧ FLIP IT!
Assign the Flipped Video for this lesson.

■ STUDENT EDITION PRINT
PAGES: 256–260

■ INVESTIGATE

DIGITAL TEXT 1
Emancipation and the Civil War

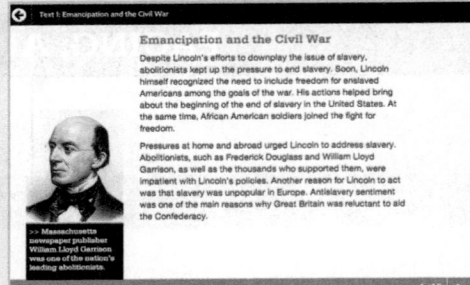

Objective 1: Analyze why Lincoln decided to issue the Emancipation Proclamation and what it achieved.

Quick Instruction
Interactive Gallery: The Road to the Emancipation Proclamation Project the Interactive Gallery and navigate through the images with students. Ask: What theme connects these images? *(All the images depict scenes in which the fate of African Americans, both free and enslaved, was determined.)* Prompt students to understand that the Emancipation Proclamation, announced in September 1862, did not go into effect until January 1, 1863. Also, it did not free all slaves—only those in the Confederate states, which were not under Union control. Though it was an inspiration and a step forward for enslaved people, it was also published to convince African Americans in the North to join the Union forces and to convince states in the Confederacy to surrender before the Proclamation went into effect.

👥 ACTIVE CLASSROOM
Conduct an If Images Could Talk activity. Ask the following questions about each image in the gallery: What do you think a person from this image would say if they could speak from the picture? What's your evidence? Invite volunteers to share their responses and discuss the ideas as a class.

INTERACTIVE GALLERY
The Road to the Emancipation Proclamation

ELL Use the ELL activity described in the ELL chart.

Further Instruction
To further extend the lesson, assign Primary Sources: Emancipation Proclamation.

Draw Conclusions Why did President Lincoln wait for a Union victory to announce his plan? *(The decree would have seemed like a desperate ploy to get African Americans to fight with the Union and signalled to the Confederate states that the Union was clearly facing defeat.)*

Identify Cause and Effect What was the primary effect of the announcement of the Emancipation Proclamation? *(It inspired some African Americans to fight with the Union and boosted morale of African Americans and abolitionists.)*

DIGITAL TEXT 3

African Americans Join the Fight

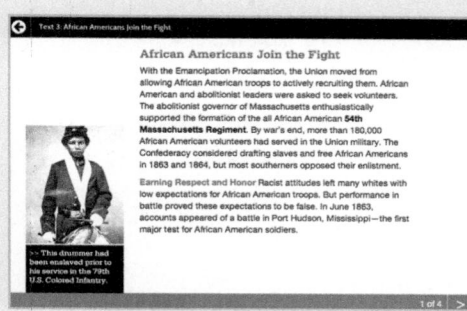

INTERACTIVE GALLERY

African Americans and the Civil War

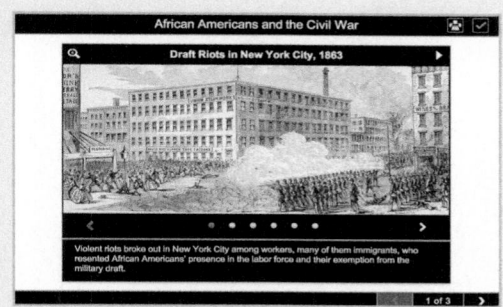

Objective 2: Assess the different roles that African Americans played in the Civil War.

Quick Instruction

Interactive Gallery: African Americans and the Civil War Project the Interactive Gallery and navigate through the images with students, discussing the significance of each.

Predict Consequences How do you think African American participation in the war affected racial prejudice at the time? *(Possible response: Racial prejudice ran so deeply that their participation probably did little to change those perceptions on the whole. However the sacrifices of African American soldiers did not go unrecognized.)*

ACTIVE CLASSROOM

Conduct a Conversation with History activity. Tell students to imagine they are having a conversation with one of the people depicted—an African American soldier, Harriet Tubman, or Martin R. Delany. Have students record a question they would like to ask, what the person would answer, and what they would say in response. Invite volunteers to share their conversations with the class.

ELL Use the ELL activity described in the ELL chart.

D Differentiate: **Challenge** Have students choose an African American historical figure from the Civil War to investigate. For example, students might choose Harriet Tubman, Martin R. Delany, a member of the 54th Massachusetts Regiment, or Frederick Douglass. After students conduct research, allow time for them to give mini-presentations on their chosen subjects to the rest of the class.

Further Instruction

Summarize How did enslaved people support the Union? *(On abandoned plantations, they produced food for Union troops. They served as spies and scouts, and they formed their own militias.)*

African Americans and the War

▌ SYNTHESIZE

DIGITAL ACTIVITY
Emancipation-Era Headlines

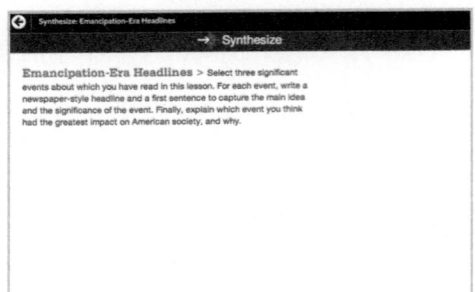

Discuss as a class some of the main events students learned about in this lesson. Then, allow students time to write their headlines and first sentences.

Discuss Invite volunteers to share their headlines with the class and discuss the importance of the events.

▌ DEMONSTRATE

DIGITAL QUIZ
Lesson Quiz and Discussion Board

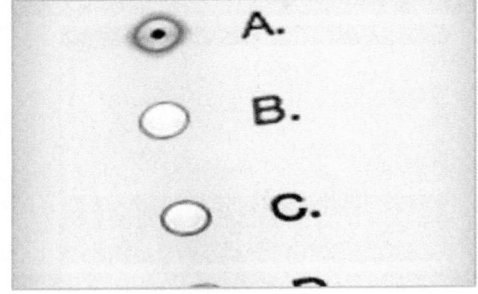

Assign the online Lesson Quiz for this lesson if you haven't already done so. Students will be offered automatic remediation or enrichment based on their score.

In *African Americans and the War*, you learned about the events that led up to the Emancipation Proclamation and the impact it had. You also learned about the different ways African Americans participated in the war.

Post these questions to the class on the Discussion Board:

Generate Explanations Why did the Emancipation Proclamation apply only to enslaved people in the Confederacy not currently under occupation and not to those in Union states?

Summarize the actions African Americans took to support the Union in the Civil War.

Topic Inquiry
Have students continue their investigations for the Topic Inquiry.

Everyday Life During the War

Supporting English Language Learners

Use with the reading, **Daily Life in the South**.

Learning
Explain that students will use what they learned in the previous text to compare daily life in the North and in the South during the Civil War.

Beginning Display a list of five to ten facts about daily life either in the North or in the South. Invite students to help you sort them into a two-column chart. Then discuss similarities and differences between the columns.

Intermediate Display a list of facts about daily life in the North. Read each fact together, and invite students to discuss how daily life in the South was like or unlike the North in regard to that fact.

Advanced Invite pairs of students to complete a Venn diagram that compares and contrasts daily life in the North and in the South. Then have them discuss which region had a harder life and why.

Advanced High Ask students to write a paragraph explaining whether inhabitants of the North or the South had a more difficult daily life, and encourage them to use supporting facts and inferences to defend their position. Provide time for partners to share and discuss their paragraphs.

Use with the reading, **A Soldier's Life**.

Listening
Explain that the verb *to lack* means "not to have." Point out its use in the last sentence of the text's fourth-to-last paragraph.

Beginning Make affirmative and negative statements that include the verb *lack*, such as: Soldiers lacked clean drinking water. They did not lack weapons. Ask students to restate the sentences without using *lack* to demonstrate understanding.

Intermediate Say: Soldiers lacked clean drinking water. What else did they lack? Invite students to answer your question using a complete sentence and the verb *lack*. Repeat with a negative statement and question.

Advanced Explain that *lack* can be a noun as well as a verb, as demonstrated in the text's third-to-last paragraph. Say: Not having a clean, healthy environment is a lack of sanitation. What is malnutrition? What is captivity? Have pairs of students define these words using the noun *lack* (e.g., lack of food, lack of freedom).

Advanced High Explain that *lack* can be a noun as well as a verb, as demonstrated in the text's third-to-last paragraph. Invite pairs of students to use *lack* as a noun and a verb as they discuss the hardships of Civil War soldiers.

▣ Differentiate Instruction

Use the Differentiated Instruction notes throughout the lesson plan to support the varied skill sets, levels of readiness, and interests in the mixed-ability classroom.

Challenge These notes include suggestions for expanding the activity for advanced students.

On-Level These notes include suggestions for modifying the activity to address different interests or learning styles.

Extra Support These notes include ideas for providing more scaffolding or reading spuport.

Special Needs These notes provide ideas for adapting instruction to support the needs of various special needs students.

■ NOTES

Everyday Life During the War

Objectives

Objective 1: Analyze how the war changed the economy and society in the North and the South.

Objective 2: Discuss how northern and southern soldiers experienced the war.

Objective 3: Explain the impact of the war on women.

LESSON 5 ORGANIZER		PACING: APPROX. 1 PERIOD, .5 BLOCKS			
				RESOURCES	
		OBJECTIVES	**PACING**	**Online**	**Print**
Connect					
	DIGITAL START UP ACTIVITY **Predicting the Effects of the War**		5 min.	●	
Investigate					
	DIGITAL TEXT 1 **Daily Life in the North**	Objective 1	10 min.	●	●
	DIGITAL TEXT 2 **Daily Life in the South**		10 min.	●	●
	DIGITAL TEXT 3 **A Soldier's Life**	Objective 2	10 min.	●	●
	INTERACTIVE GALLERY **New Ways of Waging War**		10 min.	●	
	DIGITAL TEXT 4 **Women's Roles in Wartime**	Objective 3	10 min.	●	●
	INTERACTIVE ILLUSTRATION **Hardships on the Home Front**		10 min.	●	
Synthesize					
	DIGITAL ACTIVITY **Evaluating Your Predictions**		5 min.	●	
Demonstrate					
	DIGITAL QUIZ **Lesson Quiz and Discussion Board**		10 min.	●	

PEARSON **realize**™
www.PearsonRealize.com

Go online to access additional resources including:
Primary Sources • Biographies • Supreme Court cases •
21st Century Skill Tutorials • Maps • Graphic Organizers.

CONNECT

INVESTIGATE

DIGITAL START UP ACTIVITY
Predicting the Effects of the War

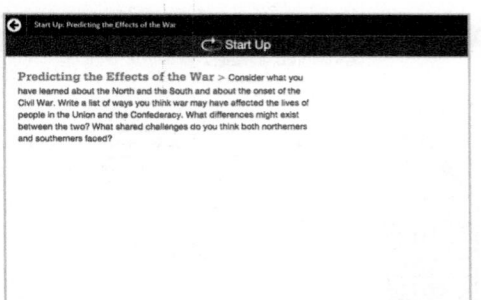

DIGITAL TEXT 1
Daily Life in the North

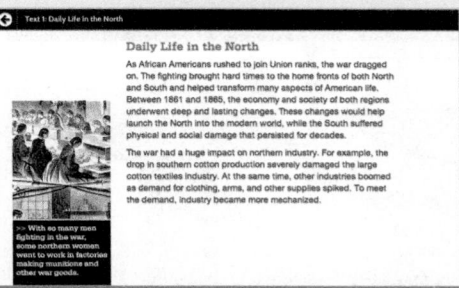

DIGITAL TEXT 2
Daily Life in the South

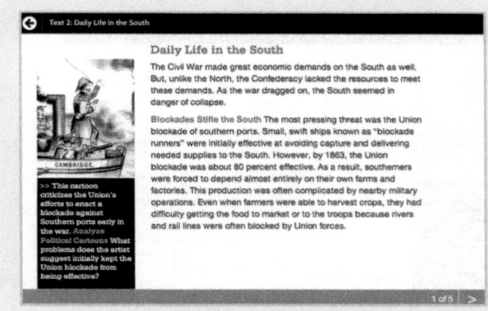

Project the Start Up Activity Have students record their predictions as they enter the classroom. Then ask them to share and discuss their ideas with partners.

Discuss What differences might exist between the two? *(Possible response: Southerners likely faced more hardships with lack of goods and food, whereas the North had so much industry that its economy did better. Also, more fighting took place in the South, near the homes of southerners, than in the North.)*

Tell students that this lesson examines the effects of the Civil War on daily life in both the North and the South. It also tells about what life was like for soldiers and women during the war.

Aa Vocabulary Development: Use the Interactive Reading Notepad to preview the Key Terms and Academic Vocabulary in this lesson with students.

⥮ FLIP IT!

Assign the Flipped Video for this lesson.

■ STUDENT EDITION PRINT
PAGES: 261–266

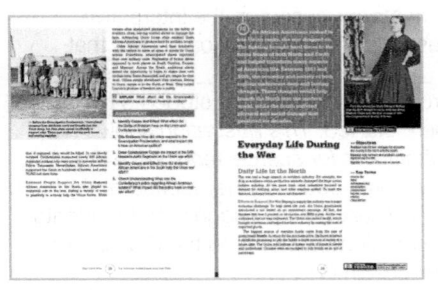

Objective 1: Analyze how the war changed the economy and society in the North and the South.

Quick Instruction

Analyze Information Display the infographic titled *Financing the Civil War* and discuss the information presented. Point out that the war was costly for both North and South. Ask: How did the cost of war strain the economies of both the North and South? *(The costs strained the economy of the North by requiring citizens to pitch in and pay taxes on their hard-earned income. The strain on the South was worse because it did not have the industrial production in place to support a war effort or a trusted government to issue bonds and enforce tax collection.)*

Support a Point of View with Evidence

Why did President Lincoln feel he was justified in suspending the right of habeas corpus during the war? *(Many people opposed to the war and demanding an end to the fighting were outspoken in their beliefs, even as most still supported the Union. However, President Lincoln believed any public opposition would subvert the war effort and undermine faith in the Union. He authorized anyone considered disloyal to the Union to be arrested and held without charge.)*

ELL Use the ELL activity described in the ELL chart.

Further Instruction

Express Problems Clearly Why did workers protest with draft riots in the North? *(Because men could pay to get out of the draft, common laborers bore the brunt of the responsibility of fighting. They rioted in protest of conscription because they believed they should be treated equally to wealthy men.)*

Determine Relevance Why was the Union Navy integral to the war effort? *(The Union Navy was able to blockade ports, blocking Southern access to needed supplies and necessities. Because the South had no navy to begin, it was unable to do much about the blockades.)*

Everyday Life During the War

DIGITAL TEXT 3

A Soldier's Life

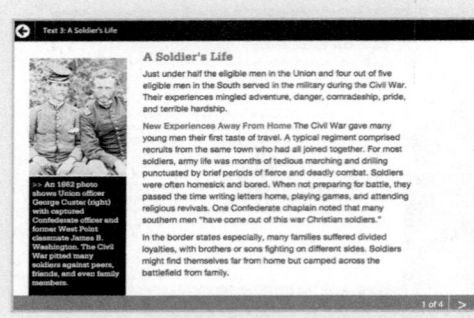

INTERACTIVE GALLERY

New Ways of Waging War

DIGITAL TEXT 4

Women's Roles in Wartime

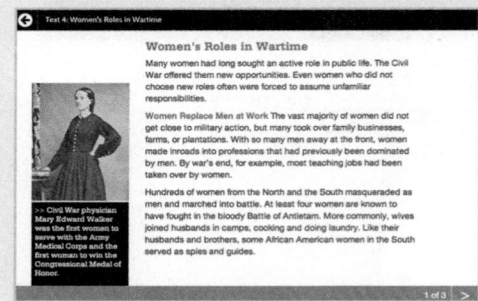

Objective 2: Discuss how northern and southern soldiers experienced the war.

Quick Instruction

Interactive Gallery: New Ways of Waging War Project the Interactive Gallery and navigate through the images. Prompt students to make connections between the innovations and the soldiers' experience of war.

Categorize Have students categorize the images. For example, they might divide the images into those that caused damage and those that prevented damage. Or they might categorize them into weaponry and support. Invite students to share their categories with the class.

📷 ACTIVE CLASSROOM

Use the Rank It strategy to further investigate the importance of the innovations featured in the Interactive Gallery. Display a list of the innovations and ask students to rank them according to which had the biggest impact on the way the war was fought. Have students record their rankings and the justifications for them. Then, pair students and have them share rankings and justifications. Finally, poll the class to see if there is agreement on the ranking.

🅳 Differentiate: Extra Support Display and describe each image for students, clarifying the content and its importance. For example, point out the hot air balloon in the distance and discuss how this technology would allow armies to gather information about the landscape and the enemy position with relatively little danger.

ELL Use the ELL activity described in the ELL chart.

Further Instruction

Generate Explanations Why did so many soldiers die as a result of causes not directly related to battle? *(Little was known about infection, sanitation, or clean drinking water at the time, so many soldiers died of disease as a result of bad water or poor sanitation. Antibiotic drugs to prevent infection had yet to be discovered, so many others died from minor wounds that became infected. Finally, those captured and held in camps often died of starvation.)*

Objective 3: Explain the impact of the war on women.

Quick Instruction

Interactive Illustration: Hardships on the Home Front Project the Interactive Illustration and navigate through the images. Prompt students to discuss the shortages and the way in which those shortages were addressed. Point out that women were usually the ones left on the home front. With so many men away fighting, women were left with the task of filling their jobs, taking care of the home, and dealing with the shortages caused by war. Navigate the illustration, clicking on the hot spots and discussing the shortages people experienced and the ways they addressed these shortages.

Summarize What were two significant causes that accounted for the shortages? *(The blockades left the South without access to imports of such goods. The lack of money limited people from buying the things they needed. The destruction of farmland limited the amount of food people could grow.)*

📷 ACTIVE CLASSROOM

Conduct a My Metaphor activity. Give students the following frame to create a metaphor based on the interactive illustration. This illustration shows that _____ was/were like _____ because _____. Provide an example for students to get them started: *This illustration shows that substitutes for scarce items were like wax sculptures because they looked good but lacked substance.* Suggest that students post their metaphors on the Classroom Discussion Board.

SYNTHESIZE

DEMONSTRATE

INTERACTIVE ILLUSTRATION
Hardships on the Home Front

Further Instruction

Infer How did women's rights benefit from the war? *(Women were allowed to take on traditionally male careers, some of which they took over in the long term, such as teaching. They proved that they were capable of performing challenging work. They even received recognition for their contributions on the battlefield.)*

Distinguish How did women's roles on the battlefield differ from men's? *(In general, women were in the camps to work as nurses, cooks, and cleaners. Instead of taking up arms, they tended the wounded and cared for the troops, although some did experience combat.)*

DIGITAL ACTIVITY
Evaluating Your Predictions

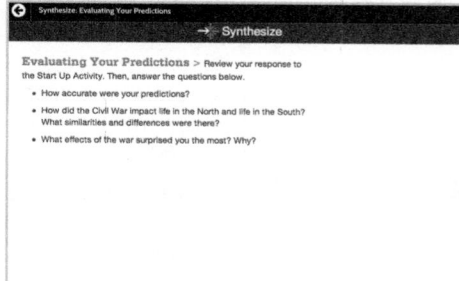

Allow students time to review their answers to the Start Up activity and consider what they have learned during this lesson before they respond to the questions.

Discuss Poll the class to see if there is agreement on events students found most surprising. Invite volunteers to share the reasoning behind their choices.

DIGITAL QUIZ
Lesson Quiz and Discussion Board

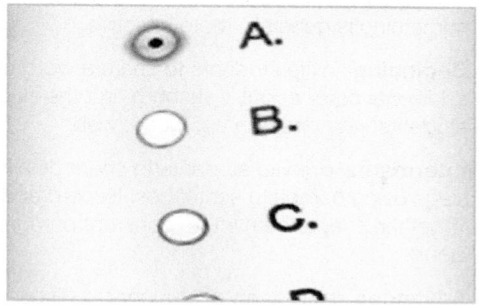

Assign the online Lesson Quiz for this lesson if you haven't already done so. Students will be offered automatic remediation or enrichment based on their score.

In *Everyday Life During the War*, you learned about how the war impacted daily life in the North and South. You learned what life was like for soldiers and women during the war.

Post these questions to the class on the Discussion Board:

Compare and Contrast How did the changes caused by the war affect the North? The South?

Summarize What was life like for soldiers on the battlefield? For women at home?

Topic Inquiry
Have students continue their investigations for the Topic Inquiry.

Topic 7   239   Sectional Divisions and Civil War

Key Civil War Battles

Supporting English Language Learners

Use with the reading, **The Siege at Vicksburg**.

Speaking
Explain something to students in a familiar context, first without details and again with important details. Discuss why using details to explain something is generally more effective.

Beginning Invite students to share a word or phrase that provides additional detail about Vicksburg and the siege. Record and display students' responses in a concept web.

Intermediate Invite students to share details about Vicksburg and the siege using complete sentences. Record and display their responses. Together, shape them into a coherent paragraph and have students read it aloud.

Advanced Invite pairs of students to discuss the five most important details about Vicksburg and the siege. Then have them shape the details into a coherent paragraph (along with a topic sentence).

Advanced High Invite pairs of students to discuss Vicksburg and the siege in detail. Have them take turns adding details about the siege (using complete sentences). Encourage pairs to include at least ten details, or sentences, in all.

Use with the reading, **Confederate Advances Are Met at Gettysburg**.

Reading
Review the difference between active and passive voice. To clarify the definitions, offer familiar examples of both (e.g., She read the book; The book was read).

Beginning Display simple sentences about the text that use the passive voice but have each auxiliary verb blocked out. Invite students to read each sentence and supply the correct verb form. Review conjugation as needed.

Intermediate Display the text's title, ask students to identify the voice as active or passive, and help them to revise it for an active voice. Ask: What are met at Gettysburg? Who meets them? How do you know?

Advanced Invite pairs of students to locate the passive voice in the text's last paragraph and revise the sentence to be in the active voice. Ask pairs to discuss the following questions: How do you know who recognizes the speech today? Why do you think the sentence was written in the passive voice?

Advanced High Invite students to write a paragraph about Gettysburg that uses both active and passive voices. Then have partners read each other's paragraphs, circling the active voice and underlining the passive voice.

▣ Differentiate Instruction

Use the Differentiated Instruction notes throughout the lesson plan to support the varied skill sets, levels of readiness, and interests in the mixed-ability classroom.

Challenge These notes include suggestions for expanding the activity for advanced students.

On-Level These notes include suggestions for modifying the activity to address different interests or learning styles.

Extra Support These notes include ideas for providing more scaffolding or reading spuport.

Special Needs These notes provide ideas for adapting instruction to support the needs of various special needs students.

■ NOTES

Objectives

Objective 1: Explain what the Union gained by capturing Vicksburg.

Objective 2: Describe the importance of the Battle of Gettysburg.

Objective 3: Analyze how the Union pressed its military advantage after 1863.

LESSON 6 ORGANIZER		PACING: APPROX. 1 PERIOD, .5 BLOCKS			
		OBJECTIVES	PACING	RESOURCES Online	Print
Connect					
DIGITAL START UP ACTIVITY **Civil War Battles**			5 min.	●	
Investigate					
DIGITAL TEXT 1 **The Siege at Vicksburg**		Objective 1	10 min.	●	●
DIGITAL TEXT 2 **Confederate Advances Are Met at Gettysburg**		Objective 2	10 min.	●	●
3-D MODEL **The Battle at Gettysburg**			10 min.	●	
DIGITAL TEXT 3 **The Union's Total War**			10 min.	●	●
INTERACTIVE MAP **Turning Points of the Civil War**		Objective 3	10 min.	●	
INTERACTIVE GALLERY **Sherman's March to the Sea**			10 min.	●	
Synthesize					
DIGITAL ACTIVITY **Significant Military Events**			5 min.	●	
Demonstrate					
DIGITAL QUIZ **Lesson Quiz and Discussion Board**			10 min.	●	

Topic 7 Lesson 6

Key Civil War Battles

CONNECT

DIGITAL START UP ACTIVITY
Civil War Battles

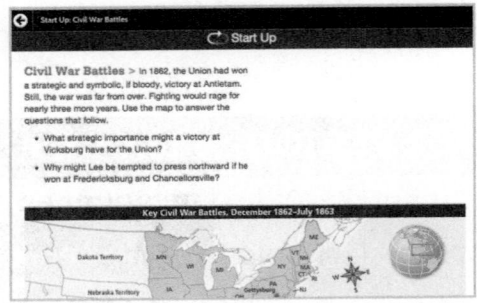

Project the Start Up Activity Have students study the map and answer the questions as they enter the classroom. Then ask them to share and discuss their ideas with partners.

Discuss Why might Lee be tempted to press northward if he won at Fredericksburg and Chancellorsville? *(Because they were so close to slaveholding border states, he might have considered pressing northward to rally support for the Confederacy while taking control of Union land.)*

Tell students that this lesson examines key battles in the Civil War.

Aa Vocabulary Development: Use the Interactive Reading Notepad to preview the Key Terms and Academic Vocabulary in this lesson with students.

⌦ FLIP IT!
Assign the Flipped Video for this lesson.

■ STUDENT EDITION PRINT PAGES: 267–273

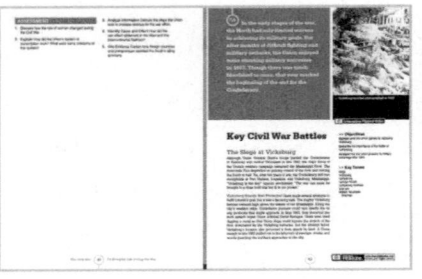

INVESTIGATE

DIGITAL TEXT 1
The Siege at Vicksburg

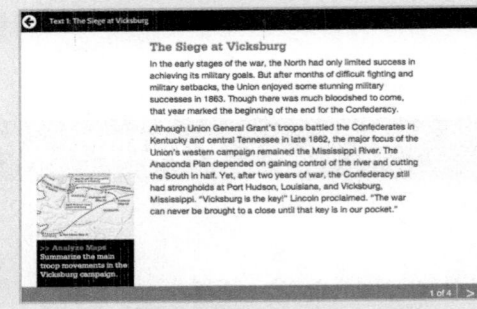

Objective 1: Explain what the Union gained by capturing Vicksburg.

Quick Instruction

Analyze Maps Display the map titled *Campaign for Vicksburg, 1863.* Discuss why the fortress at Vicksburg was so difficult to conquer. Note the position of the fortress in relation to the water and the surrounding terrain. Ask: Why did Lincoln believe Vicksburg was a strategic location necessary to ensure a Union victory? *(Taking control of Vicksburg would allow the Union to move forward with the Anaconda plan, which would enable the Union to control the Mississippi River and restrict supply lines.)*

ELL Use the ELL activity described in the ELL chart.

Further Instruction

Display the map titled *Campaign for Vicksburg, 1863* to help students put the strategic importance of Vicksburg into context. Prompt them to see the role physical geography played in Grant's strategy.

Sequence Explain how General Grant finally captured Vicksburg, sequencing the events that led up to the capture. *(In the spring of 1863, he marched his troops south of Vicksburg and ordered a diversion attack in Central Mississippi at the same time. Then, he took around 20,000 men to capture Jackson, the state capital. After that, the troops moved west toward Vicksburg and cut off railroad access. Finally, he put Vicksburg under siege until the Confederates surrendered.)*

Predict Consequences What impact do you think the capture of Vicksburg will have? *(It will give the Union the upper hand in the war, because the Confederate supply lines to and from the western states and territories will be limited given Union control of the Mississippi.)*

DIGITAL TEXT 2

Confederate Advances Are Met at Gettysburg

3-D MODEL

The Battle at Gettysburg

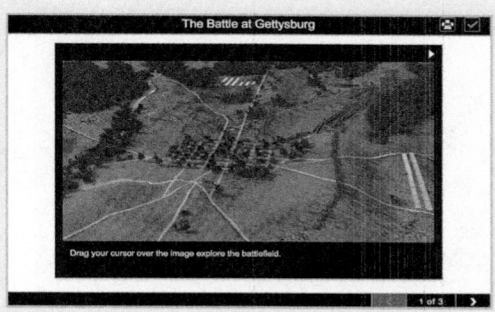

DIGITAL TEXT 3

The Union's Total War

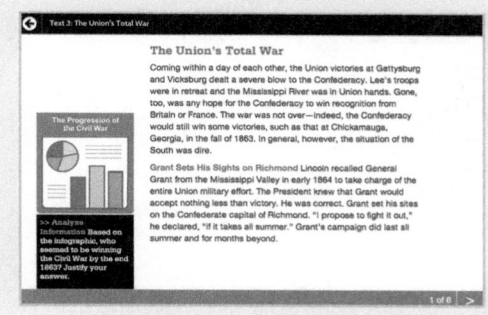

Objective 2: Describe the importance of the Battle of Gettysburg.

Quick Instruction

3-D Model: The Battle at Gettysburg
Project the 3-D Model and navigate through it with students. Discuss how the different fights played out over the terrain and the time frame. Ask: Why was it important for the Union army to reinforce its position on higher ground? *(Higher ground generally offers more defensible positions.)*

👥 ACTIVE CLASSROOM

Conduct a See-Think-Wonder activity. Pair students and have them navigate the model together. Have students take turns responding to these questions: What do you see? What does that make you think? What are you wondering about now that you have seen this? Have pairs share their insights with the rest of the class.

D Differentiate: **Extra Support** Display the map titled *The Battle of Gettysburg, 1863* alongside the 3-D Model. Help students better understand the sequence of events and results of skirmishes by making connections between the two assets.

ELL Use the ELL activity described in the ELL chart.

Further Instruction

Determine Relevance Why was the Battle at Gettysburg such an important event in the war? *(It was an offensive Confederate attack on northern soil, which showed the confidence the Confederacy had gained. It occurred at a time when the Union had suffered many defeats in the East and morale was particularly low.)* Why was it critical for Union forces to win that battle? *(Because it was fought on northern soil, it was vital for the Union to win to preserve the land, the cities, and their supplies. Also, if Lee's forces won a big battle in the North, it would motivate the South and demoralized the North.)*

Determine Author's Purpose Assign Primary Sources: Abraham Lincoln, Gettysburg Address. After students read the speech, ask: What were Lincoln's two main purposes for delivering this speech? *(to commemorate the dead and to urge support for the democratic ideals upon which the country was founded)*

Objective 3: Analyze how the Union pressed its military advantage after 1863.

Quick Instruction

Interactive Map: Turning Points of the Civil War Project the Interactive Map and navigate through each layer with students. Review the details of the battles students' have already learned about and point out that after Gettysburg, the Union adopted a policy of total war that sought to debilitate the Southern infrastructure and economy and further limit the supply lines of Confederate troops. Ask: Why might a strategy of total war be controversial? *(Purposefully damaging Southern infrastructure would also cause civilians to suffer.)*

👥 ACTIVE CLASSROOM

Conduct a Take a Stand activity. Ask students to take a stand on the following question: Was the Union justified in waging total war? Divide the class based on their answers and have each group move to separate areas of the room. Allow time for groups to discuss reasons for their answers. Then, have a representative from each side present and defend the group's point of view.

Interactive Gallery: Sherman's March to the Sea Project the Interactive Gallery and navigate through the images with students. Prompt students to connect the images with the Union's policy of total war.

Key Civil War Battles

INTERACTIVE MAP

Turning Points of the Civil War

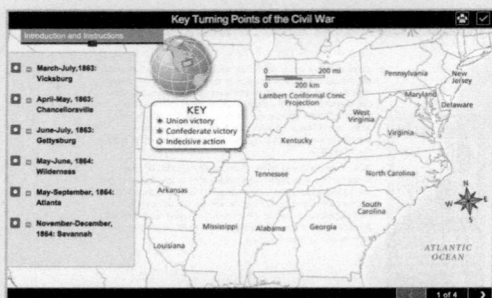

INTERACTIVE GALLERY

Sherman's March to the Sea

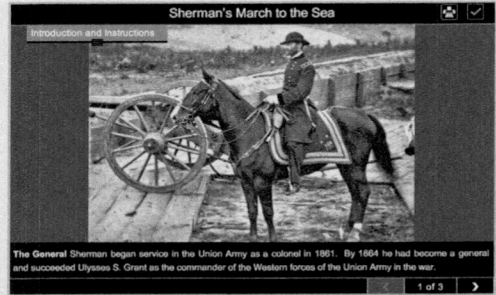

👥 ACTIVE CLASSROOM

Conduct a See-Think-Wonder activity. Pair students with a partner and ask them to answer the following questions together as the class navigates through the images in the Interactive Gallery: What do you see? What does that make you think? What are you wondering about now that you've seen this? Ask volunteers to share their insights with the class.

Further Instruction

Generate Explanations What did the Union hope to achieve by engaging in a total war strategy as they moved deeper into the South? *(Union commanders understood that the Confederates were under-resourced and lacking necessary supplies. The Union therefore hoped to deny further resources to Confederate troops, turning the conflict into a war of attrition.)*

Hypothesize How would things have turned out differently had McClellan won the election in 1864? *(Given McClellan's campaign promises to find grounds for compromise, the war may have ended sooner with some sort of negotiated peace between the two sides.)*

 **SYNTHESIZE**

DIGITAL ACTIVITY
Significant Military Events

 DEMONSTRATE

DIGITAL QUIZ
Lesson Quiz and Discussion Board

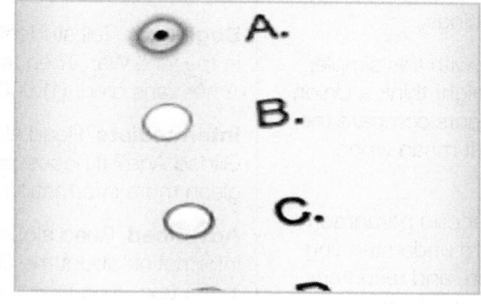

Review 21st Century Skill Tutorial: Sequence. Then, allow students time to construct their timelines and evaluate the impact of events.

Discuss Poll the class to see if there is agreement on the turning point of the war. Invite students to share their reasoning for the events they chose.

Assign the online Lesson Quiz for this lesson if you haven't already done so. Students will be offered automatic remediation or enrichment based on their score.

In *Key Civil War Battles*, you learned about the siege at Vicksburg, the Battle of Gettysburg, and the waging of total war in the South.

Post these questions to the class on the Discussion Board:

Compare and Contrast How did the events on the battlefields in the West differ from those in the East?

Express Ideas Clearly Why was Lee's attack on Gettysburg so daring? Was it foolish? Defend your answer.

Topic Inquiry
Have students continue their investigations for the Topic Inquiry.

Topic 7 Lesson 7

Impact of the Civil War

Supporting English Language Learners

Use with the reading, **Explaining the North's Victory**.

Learning
Explain that when students encounter unfamiliar words in a text, it can be helpful to focus first on the words they do know. They can then use that accessible language to determine the new words' meanings.

Beginning Display the first sentence of the text, along with this simpler sentence meaning the same thing: Looking back, we might think a Union victory was a sure thing, but that is not true. Have students compare the sentences in order to answer this question: What does it mean when something "is not the case"?

Intermediate Display the first sentence of the text's second paragraph and ask a series of questions that guide students toward understanding the word *marshal*, such as: Were technology, population, and resources good or bad things? What might the North want to do with them?

Advanced Invite pairs of students to locate the words *hindsight, marshal,* and *prowess* in the text. Have them analyze the language surrounding these words in order to determine their meanings.

Advanced High Ask students to locate three unfamiliar words in the text and analyze the language surrounding them in order to determine their meanings. Have partners share their words and analyses with each other.

Use with the reading, **The Costs of War**.

Listening
Explain that you are going to read aloud part of the text and ask students questions related to it.

Beginning Tell students to listen for the number of American casualties in the Civil War. Then read aloud the text's first paragraph. Ask: How many Americans died: (1) 600,000, (2) 6,000, or (3) hundreds of thousands?

Intermediate Read aloud the text's third paragraph. Ask: What was the Gilded Age? If necessary, reread the paragraph in order for students to glean more information before answering.

Advanced Read aloud the text's third paragraph, adding further information about the Gilded Age and the post-war economy not included in the text. Ask: Was the post-war economy strong in the North? What details did you hear that support your answer?

Advanced High Using details not found in the text, tell students about the Land Grant College Act (also known as the Morrill Act). Include information on how it was expanded, as well as its legacy today. Ask: What has been the impact of the Land Grant College Act on this country's past and present?

▣ Differentiate Instruction

Use the Differentiated Instruction notes throughout the lesson plan to support the varied skill sets, levels of readiness, and interests in the mixed-ability classroom.

Challenge These notes include suggestions for expanding the activity for advanced students.

On-Level These notes include suggestions for modifying the activity to address different interests or learning styles.

Extra Support These notes include ideas for providing more scaffolding or reading spuport.

Special Needs These notes provide ideas for adapting instruction to support the needs of various special needs students.

▮ NOTES

Objectives

Objective 1: Analyze the final events of the Civil War.

Objective 2: Explain why the North won the war.

Objective 3: Assess the impact of the Civil War on the North and South.

LESSON 7 ORGANIZER			PACING: APPROX. 1 PERIOD, .5 BLOCKS		
		OBJECTIVES	PACING	Online	Print
Connect					
DIGITAL START UP ACTIVITY **A Solemn Surrender**			5 min.	●	
Investigate					
DIGITAL TEXT 1 **The War's End**		Objective 1	10 min.	●	●
INTERACTIVE GALLERY **Lincoln's Assassination**			10 min.	●	
DIGITAL TEXT 2 **Explaining the North's Victory**		Objective 2	10 min.	●	●
DIGITAL TEXT 3 **The Costs of War**		Objective 3	10 min.	●	●
INTERACTIVE CHART **Costs of the War**			10 min.	●	
Synthesize					
DIGITAL ACTIVITY **Debating Reasons for the War's Outcome**			5 min.	●	
Demonstrate					
DIGITAL QUIZ **Lesson Quiz and Discussion Board**			10 min.	●	

Impact of the Civil War

■ CONNECT

DIGITAL START UP ACTIVITY
A Solemn Surrender

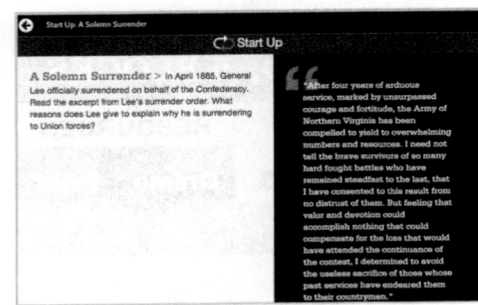

Project the Start Up Activity Have students read the quotation and answer the question as they enter the classroom. Then ask them to share and discuss their ideas with partners.

Discuss What reasons does Lee give to explain why he is surrendering to Union forces? *(He explains that there is no use to keep fighting because, despite the valor and devotion of his troops, the only possible outcome is defeat. There are no resources left.)*

Tell students that this lesson examines the final battles of the war, the reasons for the Union victory, and the financial and social impact of the Civil War.

Aa Vocabulary Development: Use the Interactive Reading Notepad to preview the Key Terms and Academic Vocabulary in this Lesson with students.

↰↳ FLIP IT!

Assign the Flipped Video for this lesson.

■ STUDENT EDITION PRINT PAGES: 274–278

■ INVESTIGATE

DIGITAL TEXT 1
The War's End

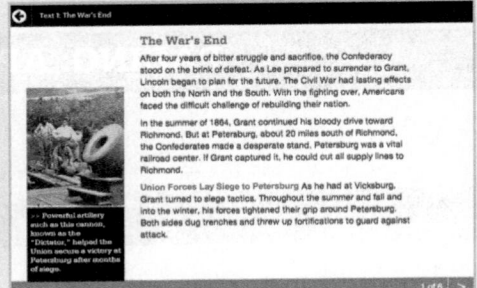

INTERACTIVE GALLERY
Lincoln's Assassination

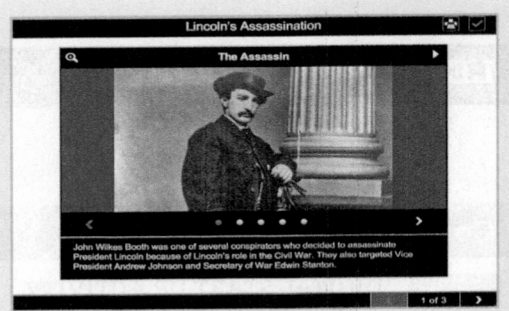

Objective 1: Analyze the final events of the Civil War.

Quick Instruction

Tell students that when Grant laid siege to Petersburg, the Confederates hung on as long as possible to protect Richmond, but it was eventually lost. Confederate forces under Lee's command were soon trapped near Appomattox Court House, Virginia, where Lee surrendered. Over the following weeks, several other Confederate generals formally surrendered as well, bringing the Civil War to a close.

Interactive Gallery: Lincoln's Assassination Project the Interactive Gallery and navigate through the images with students. Point out that despite Lee's surrender on April 9, John Wilkes Booth continued with the plan to assassinate the President whom he blamed for the crushing defeat of the South. What did Booth hope to accomplish by killing the President? *(He wanted to create political upheaval in the North and rid the country of a president he thought was a tyrant.)*

Identify Central Issues What effect did proposals to adopt the Thirteenth Amendment have on negotiations in February 1865 to end the Civil War? *(The Thirteenth Amendment proposed to ban slavery throughout the United States, and the Confederate delegation made it clear they would not negotiate a diplomatic surrender if the amendment was passed and ratified.)*

◀◼ ACTIVE CLASSROOM

Conduct an If Photos Could Talk activity. Have students choose three people from the images and answer the following questions about each: What do you think he or she would say if they could talk? What's your evidence? Invite students to share their responses with the class.

Further Instruction

Connect Lincoln hoped Americans would "[w]ith malice toward none, do all which may achieve and cherish a just and lasting peace." How does this sentiment connect to his original reasons for undertaking the war? *(He fought the war in order to preserve the Union, so this sentiment reflected his hope that political unity would be maintained after the war's conclusion.)*

Draw Conclusions Why did African Americans in Texas celebrate Juneteenth? *(The Southwest region of the country finally learned of the Confederate surrender on June 19, more than two months after Lee surrendered at Appomattox.)*

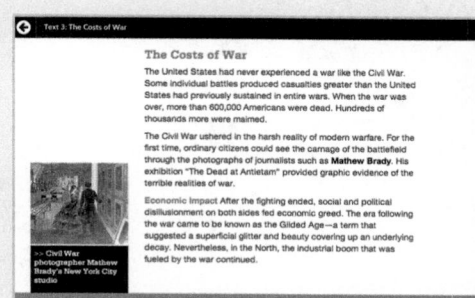

DIGITAL TEXT 2

Explaining the North's Victory

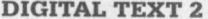
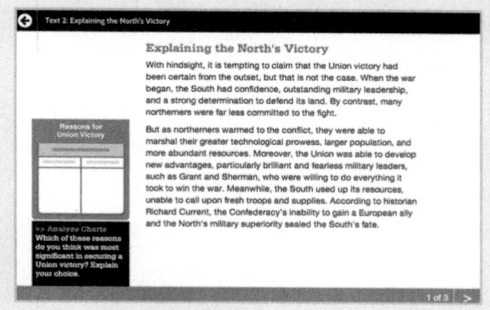

DIGITAL TEXT 3

The Costs of War

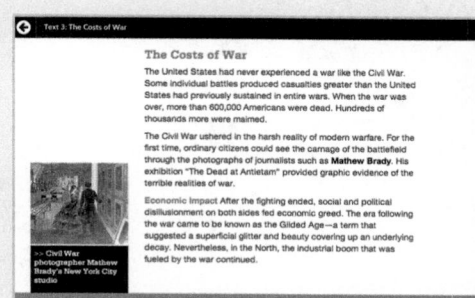

INTERACTIVE CHART

Costs of the War

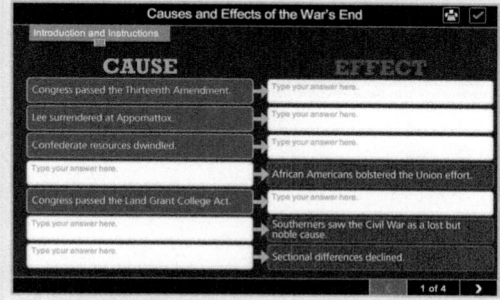

Objective 2: Explain why the North won the war.

Quick Instruction

The Union's military began the war with the support of significant industrial production, a large population, and steady supply lines. These resources proved significant in the war's outcome.

Hypothesize How would circumstances have differed for the South had it won a European ally? *(If the South had garnered some support from Britain or France, the war likely would have lasted longer because the Confederate military would have been better supplied to continue the war.)*

ELL Use the ELL activity described in the ELL chart.

Further Instruction

Support Ideas with Examples Identify three things Lincoln did that support the idea that he was an extraordinary leader. *(Possible response: His choice in military leaders, his Emancipation Proclamation, and his determination to preserve the Union all point to his extraordinary nature.)*

Objective 3: Assess the impact of the Civil War on the North and South.

Quick Instruction

Tell students that both the North and the South paid a high price for the war. However, the North, with its advanced technology and industry, recovered much more quickly than did the South, which lay in ruin as a result of Sherman's march and much of the fighting having occurred there.

Interactive Chart: Costs of the War Display the Interactive Chart and prompt students to pair causes and effects by asking questions. For example, ask: What became law as a result of the Thirteenth Amendment? *(Slavery became illegal.)* When did many African Americans more fully support the Union cause? *(after Lincoln issued the Emancipation Proclamation)*

📷 ACTIVE CLASSROOM

Conduct a Quick Write activity. Give students a short period to choose one of the effects in the Interactive Chart and share what they know about it by writing for thirty seconds. Ask volunteers to share their thoughts in small groups or with the class as a whole to refine what they have written.

D **Differentiate: Extra Support** To help students articulate cause-and-effect relationships, explain that they can use key words or phrases such as *because, as a result of,* and *therefore.* Provide sentence frames to prompt students to connect the causes and effect in the chart: _____ *because* Congress passed the Thirteenth Amendment. African Americans bolstered Union efforts *as a result of* _____. Confederate resources dwindled; *therefore,* _____.

ELL Use the ELL activity described in the ELL chart.

Further Instruction

Compare and Contrast economic development in the North and South following the conclusion of the Civil War. *(Protective tariffs and minimal fighting on northern soil during the war maintained northern industries, and the North's industrial war production easily shifted to consumer-based manufacturing following the war. Without a strong industrial base and little functional infrastructure, the southern economy continued to rely primarily on agriculture. These factors partially accounted for a significant economic gap between the two regions.)*

Hypothesize How might the Land Grant College Act prove to be an investment in the northern economy? *(The Land Grant College Act provided funds for the establishment of universities. A more educated workforce would in turn be better able to adapt to an evolving industrial economy.)*

Impact of the Civil War

■ SYNTHESIZE

■ DEMONSTRATE

DIGITAL ACTIVITY
Debating Reasons for the War's Outcome

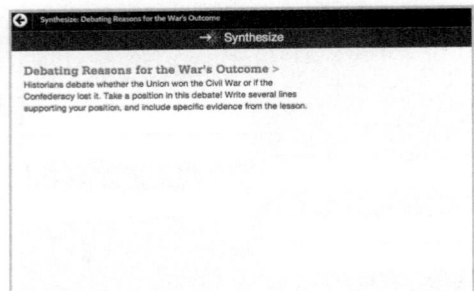

DIGITAL QUIZ
Lesson Quiz and Discussion Board

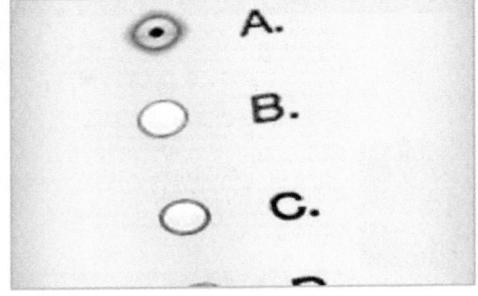

Clarify for students the terms of the debate. In other words, did the actions of the Union or the actions of the Confederacy cause the outcome of the war? Allow time for students to record their responses.

Discuss Group students based on the side they chose. Then, debate as a class whether the Union won or the Confederacy lost. Be sure students support their opinions with evidence from the lesson.

Assign the online Lesson Quiz for this lesson if you haven't already done so. Students will be offered automatic remediation or enrichment based on their score.

In *Impact of the Civil War*, you learned about the final battles of the war, Lincoln's assassination, and the reasons for the North's victory. You also examined the impact of the war on the North, the South, and the country as a whole.

Post these questions to the class on the Discussion Board:

Identify Cause and Effect What factors contributed to the South's slow economic and social recovery?

Identify Bias Why did some northerners blame the South's slow recovery on southerners?

Topic Inquiry
Have students continue their investigations for the Topic Inquiry.

Topic 7

PEARSON realize. www.PearsonRealize.com
Access your Digital Lesson

The Civil War

■ SYNTHESIZE

DIGITAL ACTIVITY
Reflect on the Essential Question and Topic

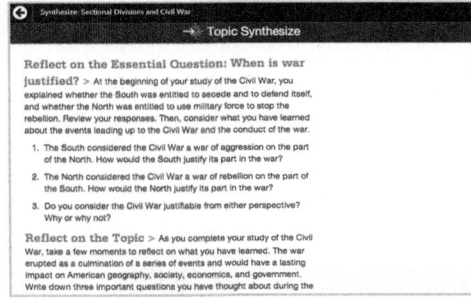

Ask students to reconsider the Essential Question for the Topic: When is war justified? Remind students of the possibilities they considered at the start of the Topic. For example, Abraham Lincoln argued that any state's attempt to secede would be seen as an act of insurrection, which justified going to war.

After students have responded to the questions, ask volunteers to share their writing with the class. Encourage discussion and debate as students share their reflections. Invite students to post their answers on the Class Discussion Board.

Next, ask students to reflect on the Topic as a whole and to answer the questions posed. Remind students to provide explanations and valid reasoning to support their opinions. Invite students to post their answers on the Class Discussion Board.

Topic Inquiry
Have students complete Step 3 of the Topic Inquiry.

■ DEMONSTRATE

DIGITAL TOPIC REVIEW AND ASSESSMENT
The Civil War

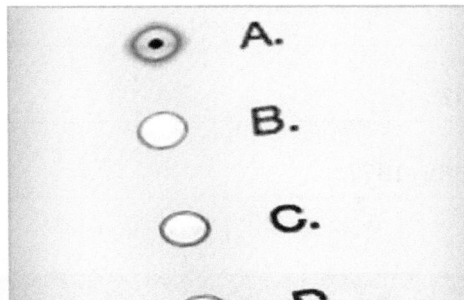

Students can prepare for the Topic Test by answering the questions in the Topic Review and Assessment online or the Assessment questions in the Print Student text. They can also prepare by reviewing their answers to the Interactive Reading Notepad questions or reviewing their notes in the Reading and Notetaking Study Guide.

DIGITAL TOPIC TEST
The Civil War

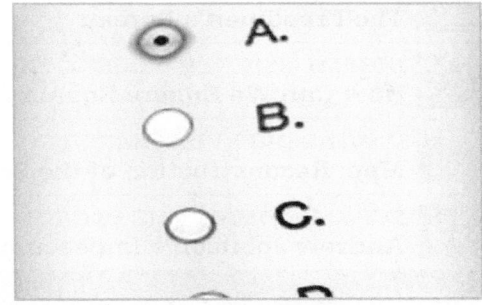

TOPIC TEST
Assign the Topic Test to assess students' understanding of topic content.

BENCHMARK TESTS
Assign these benchmark tests as you complete the relevant topics to monitor student progress toward mastering the course content and as preparation for the End-of-Course Test.

Benchmark Test 1: Topics 1–3
Benchmark Test 2: Topics 4–6
Benchmark Test 3: Topics 7–9
Benchmark Test 4: Topics 10–12
Benchmark Test 5: Topics 13–15
Benchmark Test 6: Topics 16–18
Benchmark Test 7: Topics 19–20

Topic  8

Reconstruction

TOPIC 8 ORGANIZER	PACING: APPROX. 6 PERIODS, 3 BLOCKS
	PACING
Connect	1 period
MY STORY VIDEO **The Freedmen's Bureau**	10 min.
DIGITAL ESSENTIAL QUESTION ACTIVITY **How Can We Ensure Equality for All?**	10 min.
DIGITAL OVERVIEW ACTIVITY **Map: Reconstruction of the South, 1865–1877**	10 min.
TOPIC INQUIRY: CIVIC DISCUSSION **Andrew Johnson's Impeachment**	20 min.
Investigate	1–3 periods
TOPIC INQUIRY: CIVIC DISCUSSION **Andrew Johnson's Impeachment**	Ongoing
LESSON 1 Plans for Reconstruction Clash	30–40 min.
LESSON 2 Reconstruction Changes the South	30–40 min.
LESSON 3 Reconstruction's Impact	30–40 min.
Synthesize	1 period
DIGITAL ACTIVITY **Reflect on the Essential Question and Topic**	10 min.
TOPIC INQUIRY: CIVIC DISCUSSION **Andrew Johnson's Impeachment**	20 min.
Demonstrate	1–2 periods
DIGITAL ACTIVITY **Reflect on the Essential Question and Topic**	10 min.
TOPIC INQUIRY: CIVIC DISCUSSION **Andrew Johnson's Impeachment**	20 min.

TOPIC INQUIRY: CIVIC DISCUSSION

Andrew Johnson's Impeachment

In this Topic Inquiry, students work in teams to examine different perspectives on this issue by analyzing several sources, arguing both sides of a Yes/No question, then developing and discussing their own point of view on the question: **Was the impeachment of Andrew Johnson justified?**

STEP 1: CONNECT
Develop Questions and Plan the Investigation

Launch the Civic Discussion

Divide the class into groups of four students. Students can access the materials they'll need in the online course or you can distribute copies to each student. Read the main question and introduction with the students.

Have students complete Step 1 by reading the Discussion Launch and filling in Step 1 of the Information Organizer. The Discussion Launch provides YES and NO arguments on the main question. Students should extract and paraphrase the arguments from the reading in Step 1 of their Information Organizers.

Next, students share within their groups the arguments and evidence they found to support the YES and NO positions. The group needs to agree on the major YES and NO points and each student should note those points in their Information Organizer.

Resources
- Student Instructions
- Information Organizer
- Discussion Launch

⏻ PROFESSIONAL DEVELOPMENT

Civic Discussion
Be sure to view the Civic Discussion Professional Development resources in the online course.

STEP 2: INVESTIGATE
Apply Disciplinary Concepts and Tools

Examine Sources and Perspectives

Students will examine sources with the goal of extracting information and perspectives on the main question. They analyze each source and describe the author's perspective on the main question and key evidence the author provides to support that viewpoint in Information Organizer Step 2.

Ask students to keep in mind:

- **Author/Creator:** Who created the source? An individual? Group? Government agency?
- **Audience:** For whom was the source created?
- **Date/Place:** Is there any information that reveals where and when the source was created?
- **Purpose:** Why was the source created? Discuss with students the importance of this question in identifying bias.
- **Relevance:** How does the source support one argument or another?

Suggestion: Reading the source documents and filling in Step 2 of the Information Organizer could be assigned as homework.

Resources
- Student Instructions
- Information Organizer
- Source documents

 TOPIC INQUIRY: CIVIC DISCUSSION

Andrew Johnson's Impeachment *(continued)*

STEP 3: SYNTHESIZE
Use Evidence to Formulate Conclusions

Formulate Compelling Arguments with Evidence
Now students will apply perspectives and evidence they extracted from the sources to think more deeply about the main question by first arguing one side of the issue, then the other. In this way students become more prepared to formulate an evidence-based conclusion on their own.

Within each student group, assign half of the students to take the position of YES on the main question and the others to take the position of NO. Students will work with their partners to identify the strongest arguments and evidence to support their assigned YES or NO position.

Present Yes/No Positions
Within each group, those assigned the YES position share arguments and evidence first. As the YES students speak, those assigned NO should listen carefully, take notes to fill in the rest of the Compelling Arguments Chart (Step 3 in Information Organizer) and ask clarifying questions.

When the YES side is finished, students assigned the NO position present while those assigned YES should listen, take notes, and ask clarifying questions. Examples of clarifyin questions are:

- I think you just said [x]. Am I understanding you correctly?
- Can you tell me more about [x]?
- Can you repeat [x]? I am not sure I understand, yet.

Suggestion: You may want to set a 5 minute time limit for each side to present. Provide a two-minute warning so that students make their most compelling arguments within the time frame.

Switch Sides
The students will switch sides to argue the opposite point of view. To prepare to present the other position, partners who first argued YES will use the notes they took during the NO side's presentation, plus add any additional arguments and evidence from the reading and sources. The same for students who first argued the NO position.

STEP 4: DEMONSTRATE
Communicate Conclusions and Take Informed Action

Individual Points of View
Now the students will have the opportunity to discuss the main question from their own points of view. To help students prepare for this discussion, have them reflect on the YES/NO discussions they have participated in thus far and fill in Step 4 of their Information Organizers.

After all of the students have shared their points of view, each group should list points of agreement, filling the last portion of Step 4 on their Information Organizers.

Reflect on the Discussion
Ask students to reflect on the civic discussion thinking about:

- The value of having to argue both the YES and NO positions.
- If their individual views changed over the course of the discussion and why.
- What they learned from participating in the discussion.

Resources
- Student Instructions
- Information Organizer

INTRODUCTION

Reconstruction

After the Civil War, the country debated how to best rebuild and reunite. Congress pushed ahead and instituted sweeping political, economic, and social changes in the former Confederate states. During this era of Reconstruction, African Americans gained political and economic rights. They were still, however, denied full equality, especially in the South. After Reconstruction ended, southern states worked to reassert the status quo in the South so that the rights of freed African Americans and other minorities were severely restricted in the late 1800s. Influential African American leaders, however, refused to accept the status of second-class citizens and continued to fight for full equality.

◼ CONNECT

MY STORY VIDEO
The Freedmen's Bureau

Watch a video about the work of the Freedmen's Bureau.

Check Understanding Why was the Freedmen's Bureau established? *(to help freed people, as well as white refugees, with basic needs after the Civil War; also to set up many schools and colleges for African Americans)*

Make Generalizations For what reasons might white southerners have opposed the work of the Freedmen's Bureau? *(Students may point out that white southerners, having just been defeated by the North in the Civil War, may have resented the help being given to formerly enslaved African Americans. The racial prejudice that was common at the time no doubt played a role as well.)*

DIGITAL ESSENTIAL QUESTION ACTIVITY
How Can We Ensure Equality for All?

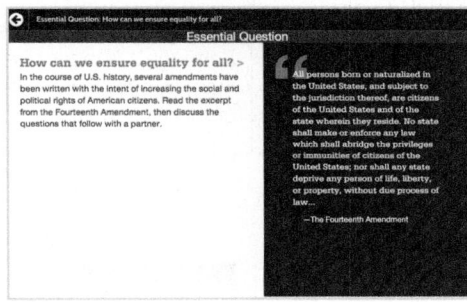

Ask students to think about the Essential Question for this topic: How can we ensure equality for all? The sectional conflicts around which the Civil War was fought divided the United States. What role should the federal government play to make sure all citizens have equal opportunities and rights?

If students have not already done so, ask them to respond to the questions in the Essential Question activity. Then go over students' responses as a class.

Generate Explanations In your opinion, should local and state governments have the ability to override federal or constitutional law? Explain.

Make Predictions What strategies do you think Americans will use to address their positions about the passage of the Fourteenth Amendment?

DIGITAL OVERVIEW ACTIVITY
Map: Reconstruction of the South, 1865–1877

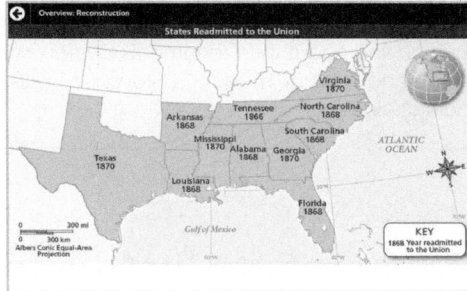

Display the map showing the southern states affected by Reconstruction. During this topic students will learn about how citizens and leaders in these states reacted to the federal government's Reconstruction policies. The map will provide a visual framework to help students better understand the sectional tension created by Reconstruction policies.

Infer Based on the years by which many states were readmitted to the Union, what can you infer about the effectiveness of Reconstruction? *(Some states were not readmitted until 5 years after the Civil War ended. This suggests that the reunification process and Reconstruction policies did not go smoothly.)*

Topic Inquiry
Launch the Topic Inquiry with students after introducing the topic.

Plans for Reconstruction Clash

Supporting English Language Learners

Use with the reading, **Competing Reconstruction Plans**.

Speaking
Review the text as needed, and encourage students to refer to the text as they try to answer the informational questions you ask.

Beginning Ask students informational questions requiring responses of a word or phrase, such as: Who proposed the Ten Percent Plan? When was the Wade-Davis Bill passed by Congress? Who wanted African Americans to have the right to vote?

Intermediate Ask students informational questions that require a longer answer, such as: To what does "ten percent" refer in Lincoln's plan? What was Lincoln's general position toward white southerners? Encourage students to build on one another's responses.

Advanced Ask students questions that require them to synthesize information from more than one place in the text, such as: How did the plans of Lincoln and the Radical Republicans address African American rights differently? Encourage students to build on one another's responses.

Advanced High Ask students questions that require them to locate extra information through research, such as: What three interesting facts can you find about the Freedmen's Bureau? What are some details about the life and work of Thaddeus Stevens? Invite students to share their findings aloud.

Use with the reading, **Congress Passes a Plan for Reconstruction**.

Reading
With students, brainstorm reasons for taking notes on a text (e.g., grasping a text's structure, memorizing content, increasing comprehension).

Beginning Provide students with a partially filled-in outline for the section titled *The Fifteenth Amendment*. Then reread the section together, pausing when necessary so students can complete corresponding parts of the outline. Ask: Is the outline missing any key information? If so, what?

Intermediate With students, reread the section titled *The Fifteenth Amendment*. After each sentence, pause and ask students what (if anything) is important enough to take notes on. Together, create an outline of the text and then review it for content and consistency.

Advanced Have pairs of students take notes on the section titled *Johnson's Impeachment*. Ask pairs to share their work and answer these questions: How did you decide which facts were important enough for your notes? How did you organize your notes to make them readable later on?

Advanced High Invite students to take notes on the section titled *Johnson's Impeachment*. Assign each a different method, such as a Roman numeral outline, a concept map, or a bulleted list. Then have students compare and discuss their notes.

▣ Differentiate Instruction

Use the Differentiated Instruction notes throughout the lesson plan to support the varied skill sets, levels of readiness, and interests in the mixed-ability classroom.

Challenge These notes include suggestions for expanding the activity for advanced students.

On-Level These notes include suggestions for modifying the activity to address different interests or learning styles.

Extra Support These notes include ideas for providing more scaffolding or reading spuport.

Special Needs These notes provide ideas for adapting instruction to support the needs of various special needs students.

▮ NOTES